D0070671

The Manufacturing Challenge

VNR COMPETITIVE MANUFACTURING SERIES

Quality Control/Reliability

PRACTICAL EXPERIMENT DESIGN, 2E by William J. Diamond
VALUE ANALYSIS IN DESIGN by Theodore C. Fowler
A PRIMER ON THE TAGUCHI METHOD by Ranjit Roy
RELIABILITY AND MAINTAINABILITY MANAGEMENT by Balbir S. Dhillon and
Hans Reiche
APPLIED RELIABILITY by Paul A. Tobias and David C. Trindad
GUIDE TO RELIABILITY ENGINEERING: Data, Analysis, Applications,
Implementation and Management by R. Sundararajan
ENGINEERING APPLICATIONS OF RELIABILITY ANALYSIS by Shu-Ho Dai and
Ming-O Wang

Product and Process Design

INDUSTRIAL ROBOT HANDBOOK: Case Histories of Robot Use in 70 Industries by
Richard K. Miller
ROBOTIC TECHNOLOGY: Principles and Practice by Werner G. Holzbock
MACHINE VISION by Nello Zeuch and Richard K. Miller
DESIGN OF AUTOMATIC MACHINERY by Kendrick W. Lentz, Jr.
TRANSDUCERS FOR AUTOMATION by Michael Hordeski
MICROPROCESSORS IN INDUSTRY by Michael Hordeski
DISTRIBUTED CONTROL SYSTEMS by Michael P. Lucas
BULK MATERIALS HANDLING HANDBOOK by Jacob Fruchtbaum
MICROCOMPUTER SOFTWARE FOR MECHANICAL ENGINEERING by
Howard Falk

Management

DEVELOPING PRODUCTS IN HALF THE TIME by Preston G. Smith and
Donald G. Reinertsen
MANUFACTURING IN THE NINETIES: How to Become a Mean, Lean, World-Class
Competitor by Harold J. Steudel and Paul Desruelle
THE MANUFACTURING CHALLENGE: From Concept to Production by
S. E. Stephanou and Fred Spiegl
WORKING TOWARDS JUST-IN-TIME by Anthony Dear
GROUP TECHNOLOGY: Foundation for Competitive Manufacturing by
Charles S. Snead
COMPETITIVE MANUFACTURING by Stanley Miller
STRATEGIC PLANNING FOR THE INDUSTRIAL ENGINEERING FUNCTION by
Jack Byrd and L. Ted Moore
PRODUCT LIABILITY HANDBOOK: Prevention, Risk, Consequence and Forensics
of Product Failure edited by Sam Brown
TOTAL MATERIALS MANAGEMENT: The Frontier for Cost-Cutting in the 1990s by
Eugene L. Magad and John Amos

THE MANUFACTURING CHALLENGE

From Concept to Production

S.E. Stephanou, M.S., Ph.D.
Professor Emeritus, Systems Management
University of Southern California

F. Spiegl, M.S., P.E.
Director, Manufacturing Technology and Management Programs
Northrop University

COMPETITIVE
Manufacturing
S E R I E S

VAN NOSTRAND REINHOLD
———————————— New York

Xavier University Library
New Orleans, La. 70125

670
S827m
1992

Copyright © 1992 by Van Nostrand Reinhold

Library of Congress Catalog Card Number 91-19990
ISBN 0-442-00408-7

All rights reserved. No part of this work covered by the copyright hereon may be reproduced or used in any form or by any means—graphic, electronic, or mechnical, including photocopying, recording, taping, or information storage and retrieval systems—without written permission of the publisher.

Manufactured in the United States of America

Published by Van Nostrand Reinhold
115 Fifth Avenue
New York, New York 10003

Chapman and Hall
2-6 Boundary Row
London, SE 1 8HN, England

Thomas Nelson Australia
102 Dodds Street
South Melbourne 3205
Victoria, Australia

Nelson Canada
1120 Birchmount Road
Scarborough, Ontario M1K 5G4, Canada

16 15 14 13 12 11 10 9 8 7 6 5 4 3 2 1

Library of Congress Cataloging-in-Publication Data

Stephanou, S.E.
   The manufacturing challenge : from concept to production / S.E. Stephanou, F. Spiegl.
     p.   cm. — (VNR competitive manufacturing series)
   Includes index.
   ISBN 0-442-00408-7
   1. Production management. 2. Production planning.   I. Spiegl, F.
II. Title. III. Series: Competitive manufacturing series.
TS155.S775   1991
670—dc20   91-19990
                                  CIP

Xavier University Library
New Orleans, La. 70125

To our families.

Contents

Preface

This text is written at a time when national and international economic competition is at an all-time high, particularly for the manufacturing segment of our economy because it is there that competition is most pressing. Although in the past we have led the way in innovation, new technology, and new product development and production, we are now being challenged successfully and in some cases surpassed by other developed countries such as Germany and Japan and those in the Pacific rim. This development is reflected in our serious trade imbalance. It is not that we are not still highly innovative, technologically advanced, and on the frontier of most important product areas, but other factors appear to be placing us at a serious disadvantage. Of these factors the most critical seem to be the quality and cost of our products, which in turn are dependent on our manufacturing effectiveness. A key part of manufacturing effectiveness is the maintenance of quality without an inordinate outlay of capital. Another key factor is the time and money consumed in bringing a product on line from concept to production and use. These are the basic aspects of manufacturing that constitute the challenge presently facing the American manufacturing community; methods and techniques for successfully responding to this challenge are the focus of this text.

An ancillary objective, but in some respects of no less importance, is filling a gap in the management literature that has prevailed for many years. For reasons that are not clearly evident, the symbiotic relationship between manufacturing and reserach and development (R&D) has not been recognized or has been generally ignored by the academic community as well as industrial management. Few writings feature this relationship, let alone courses that train and integrate the disciplinary lines of R&D management and manufacturing. Graduate programs in business (MBA) and other management programs, except in special options in industrial management, rarely include this aspect of manufacturing. Only in the last few years have courses in the management of technology been offered as an area of specialty in MBA programs, and then only in a relatively few universities.[1]

This book is written as a text as well as a practical management guide by authors who have been personally involved in the subject matter discussed and, because of first-hand experience, have the combined viewpoints of industry, government, and academia. It contains time-saving and cogent information for managers and practitioners alike, with questions for discussion at the end of each chapter. It is particularly geared to senior-level and graduate students who have had little or no experience with R&D and manufacturing process management.

The book is unique in describing traditional and proven management techniques and relating them to the development of successful technological innovations that are so vital in today's rapidly changing and competitive real world. It stresses the theme that intimately interwoven with bringing a concept to successful production and use is the ability of management to integrate the efforts of the research, development, manufacturing, and marketing segments of the company and obtain the full support of all the people involved. It also points out changes in management style and procedures that today's market conditions demand if companies are to compete successfully. The inclusion of new technology into product and process development, culminating in successful manufacturing processes and new products, has been and continues to be a difficult hurdle for many organizations.

To illustrate management principles and practices, paradigms are presented that we have derived as a result of a combined 55 years of hands-on experience as engineers, managers, and executives in research, engineering, and manufacturing facilities of major U.S. corporations and research organizations. The real-life examples described in the text have been further enhanced by the inclusion of material derived from teaching graduate-level technology and manufacturing management courses during the last 15 years as well as extensive study of the literature. Associates in industry, students, and fellow faculty members in the Systems Management Center of the University of Southern California and Northrop University have contributed to the development of the subject matter through discussion and research studies.

We are indebted to Malcolm Romano and John H. Kusmiss, patent counsels, for their review of the chapter on patents, trade secrets, and copyrights and also Paul Braendli, president of the European Patent Office, for his review of the section on international patents. Their suggestions and updating were most helpful.

We also wish to express our appreciation to Professor Robert M. Krone of the University of Southern California and Robert L. Winstead, manager TQM, Space

---

[1]Massachusetts Institute of Technology (MIT) and the University of Southern California are examples.

Applications Corporation, for their valuable criticism of and suggestion for the chapter on total quality management, and to Dr. J. Kowalick of Aerojet-General Corporation for his review of the section on Taguchi methods. The reading of the text and constructive suggestions made by Professor James P. Todd, dean of the College of Engineering and Technology, Northrop University, were most helpful and sincerely appreciated. Also we extend sincere thanks to John and Andrea Britigan for the artwork and graphs and to John Russey IV for drawing the cartoons, all of which have enhanced the text.

S. E. Stephanou
F. Spiegl

The Manufacturing Challenge

1

Overview of Technology and the Manufacturing Environment

1.1 Introduction
1.2 Brief History of Science, Technology, and Manufacturing
1.3 The Present R&D Environment
1.4 The Present Manufacturing Environment

1.1 INTRODUCTION

A major factor in the competitive national and international environment facing American industry today is the manufacturing segment of operation. There is an urgent need for management to realize and appreciate optimum techniques as well as deficiencies in our way of conducting the research and development (R&D) process so that it effectively integrates with manufacturing as well as with marketing and sales. Manufacturing engineers themselves will have to modify their present role and interests to coincide with the requirements of the 1990s and beyond. As stated by D. K. Kosta and A. T. Kearney (1989);

> The 21st century is only a short time away and manufacturing engineers are not ready. They must wake up to change their orientation toward work, what role they should play, and their attitude. Working with and through people is the key to their future success.

To exacerbate further the situation for the United States, Japan, Germany, and other developed countries are successfully threatening our economic prosperity by the quality, innovative nature, and attractive price of their products vis-à-vis

1

ours. Intimately related to this condition is our inability to bring new concepts rapidly to production and successful manufacture and use.

This book applies the systems approach to the problem of bringing a concept expeditiously through the various phases of R&D to successful production. It does so by discussing each phase of the R&D process in chronological order, emphasizing the importance of the human factor, which in the final analysis is the most important ingredient in the structure and operation of any organization. The various phases or parts of the process are treated independently as chapters to allow for review and a focus on details, but all of these phases must be integrated in time and corporate effort. Integration means that personnel and groups that are or can be involved in the various phases are brought in early when a new product or process is identified as being worthy of development (concurrent engineering). Integration also means identifying and solving problems that often develop between the various groups (and personnel) involved in the concept-to-production process. These and other problems are discussed in the chapters that follow, along with the all-important problem of achieving high quality (total quality management) and the motivation of scientists, engineers, and manufacturing personnel.

Later chapters enumerate and discuss the major contributions of Deming, Juran, Taguchi, and others to the improvement of manufacturing management as well as methods of implementing these improvements and techniques. The significant roles of computer-aided design (CAD), computer-aided engineering (CAE), computer-aided manufacturing (CAM), computer-integrated manufacturing (CIM), and just-in-time manufacturing (JIT) are described with respect to how they affect the concept-to-production process. Finally, the future of technology and manufacturing in the 1990s and twenty-first century is discussed, a future that can hold high promise of prosperity for our country or the unthinkable alternative of relegation to the role of a second-rate power.

Before proceeding it is instructive to review briefly the history of science, technology, and manufacturing since the time of early humans (Section 1.2). Such a review, although admittedly brief, provides an insight to the process and trends that have motivated and shaped technology and manufacturing efforts over the years and the changes in emphasis that have occurred. As has been said time and time again, although not in these exact words, those that ignore the past will most likely repeat its failures as well as most, but not necessarily all, its successes.

1.2 BRIEF HISTORY OF SCIENCE, TECHNOLOGY, AND MANUFACTURING

The history of technology and manufacturing parallels the development of human knowledge and the ability to live better. In early history there were large gains to be made in health and longevity, ease of existence, safety, and other basics of life. Today technological improvements are frequently of a less basic nature but, nevertheless, continue to be impressive in their effect on the overall quality of life.

Primitive Man and the Prehistoric Era

In early times, primitive people gained knowledge through trial and error, observation, generalization from repetition of events, and accident. Even to this day important scientific discoveries occur as a result of a chance event or experiment that was directed at some other goals, a byproduct recognized by an observant experimenter. One of the most celebrated of these incidents is the discovery of radioactivity by A. H. Becquerel in 1896. He noted that a set of photographic plates he was planning to use were already darkened before exposure. Upon investigating, he found that they had been located on a work bench near some uranium ore (pitchblende). Testing of the uranium ore revealed that it was emitting radiation, and soon after the process of radioactive decay was discovered.

The power to reason, the ability to communicate (language), and the development and use of tools enhanced people's ability to hunt and defend themselves so that they survived and flourished. Events that could not be explained by personal experience were attributed to magical or supernatural powers. Human impact on the environment and on nature was minimal and relatively insignificant in prehistoric days. One of the first great impacts on nature resulted from the discovery of how to make and use fire. This knowledge had, and still has, far-reaching environmental effects. There was no regard for the environment because food, shelter, and safety were primary needs. With the discovery of tools of wood, stone, and bone, people soon began to farm and also to raise animals for food (animal husbandry). The discovery of the wheel was indeed a technological breakthrough.

Primitive man, many thousands of years before Christ, fabricated tools and eating utensils as well as spears and shields, probably individually and certainly by hand. Later (Bronze Age and subsequently) materials superior to animal skins, stone, and wood were identified. At that time, the development of weapons, pots, and utensils probably became more of a group project with a chief artisan (e.g., a blacksmith) and helpers. Then, as now, it was important to satisfy the customer—then the very life of the producer could be at stake. This could be considered the first semblance of a manufacturing process. As more and more spears, shields, pots, and related items were developed, special skills and production techniques improved, until by the time of the ancient Assyrians and Babylonians, considerable sophistication had developed in the production of these essential items. Even in those early days defense needs, as with our present Department of Defense (DOD), provided a stimulus for technology and manufacturing improvement.

The Bronze Age

During the Bronze Age (approximately 3000 B.C.–1000 B.C.), metallurgy came into being, wind power was harnessed for sailboats, the potter's wheel was developed, and bricks came into use. These endeavors marked the crude beginning and application of what is now called technology. The Minoan civilization (3000 B.C.–1000 B.C.) on the island of Crete, as exemplified by its palaces, ornate artistry, and intricate jewelry, exhibited outstanding examples of pre-Christian craftsmanship and technology.

The Egyptian Era

Architecture and civil engineering were among the contributions of the prime period of Egyptian civilization (1000 B.C.–100 B.C.); construction of the pyramids and the great cities of the Nile and the ports on the Mediterranean is an example of the remarkable engineering know-how of that era. Hieroglyphics were the first organized writings and can be considered the start of communication systems, although prehistoric humans did chisel scenes and characters on rocks and in caves. Commonly used items such as utensils, pots, swords, and shields were mass-produced. These first factories consisted of slaves supervised by skilled craftspeople, usually under the overall direction of, or management by, a merchant.

It has been speculated, and with justification, that during the thousand years before Christ the manufacturing technology that allowed the replacement of relatively soft bronze weaponry by iron and steel was the reason for victory in several important wars, for example, the wars between the Greeks and the Persians. Approximately 2,500 years later it can be rightfully claimed that the success of the six-week Persian Gulf war of 1991 between the U.N. coalition forces (led by the United States) and Iraq was the result of superior technology as well as effective planning and execution.

The Greek Era

The great thinkers of the Greek era (500 B.C.–100 B.C.) set forth the doctrines of democratic government, and men such as Plato, Aristotle, and Archimedes developed formalized procedures for mathematics, including geometry. Knowledge in philosophy and the abstract sciences advanced markedly, although improvements in technology were not as spectacular; one exception was building technology, which flourished in the form of majestic temples and amphitheaters such as the Acropolis and the adjoining buildings. This era was a tremendous positive force in human history, and there were advances in many fields. For the first time human values were openly discussed and emphasized; something other than food, shelter, and safety assumed importance in people's existence. People realized they had the freedom to think in their own way and be involved in the choice of their own form of government. Alexander the Great's conquest of much of the ancient world was one of the first attempts to bring diverse nations together into a political system. However, the fact that laboratory experimentation was shunned was a serious failing of this era. Learned men spent much time discussing a particular problem or natural phenomenon when often a simple experiment could have provided a solution. In ancient Greece, technology and the beginnings of manufacturing were evidenced primarily by individual artisans and groups of skilled craftsmen working in craft shops.

The Roman Era

Management was a dominant theme of the Roman era (80 B.C.–AD. 400). Military and political expertise was developed, and the Roman Empire was organized into an efficient military and political system. Civil engineering techniques initiated by the Assyrians, Babylonians, Egyptians, and Greeks were further advanced by the Romans, resulting in impressive buildings, aqueducts, bridges, and even sewer systems, some of which are still standing. The Roman Empire tended to make a world system of peoples and increased dependence of various parts of the empire on goods from other parts.

The Middle Ages

The Middle Ages (400–1450) was characterized by stagnation in the development of science and technology and by an increase in domination of the Church. People who disagreed with the rulings of the Church on matters relating to natural phenomena, as well as religion, were persecuted; it was a generally held belief that all essential knowledge had been discovered. Roger Bacon was one of the first to attack the system of reasoning by quoting authority or selecting a conclusion and then choosing the facts and principles to support it. Leonardo da Vinci stressed reaching conclusions through direct observation. During this period of limited scientific discovery and advancement, the printing press was developed and water mills were first used for the production of power. This latter development had immediate application to manufacturing-type processes such as the processing of wheat to produce flour and other applications.

The Renaissance and the Rebirth of Science

During the Renaissance (1450–1600) art, sculpture, and fine craftsmanship flourished. This period marked the emergence of humanity from its preoccupation with food and war to endeavors that appealed to the esthetic sense. The seventeenth and eighteenth centuries saw the rebirth of science in the rise of the experimental method and the numerous contributions of the great scientists of the age. Galileo's experimental work in physics, the development by Newton of his famous laws, and Boyle's work on physical chemistry added new dimensions to scientific knowledge, which were to have an impact on all future generations. Scientists as a whole worked on their own time and at their own expense, so that science in that era was the hobby of a few wealthy men, sometimes supported by a benevolent monarch. The artisans and skilled craftsmen continued to flourish as individuals and also as groups producing quantities of needed items in workshop-type environments.

The Industrial Revolution
The Industrial Revolution, which began about 1760 in England, gave added impetus to the development of science; the steam engine was invented, and mass production as we know it was applied to the manufacture of clothing, shoes, and other consumer items as well as military weapons. An outgrowth was the use of large, automated craft shops (factories), which in turn were a result of the new principles of science and engineering applied to manufacturing. In this era, an order-of-magnitude increase in consumption of the earth's natural resources and degradation of the environment took place. One of the effects of the Industrial Revolution was to bring people and nations of the world much closer together than it had ever been before because of the need for raw materials to satisfy manufacturing requirements for worldwide markets. Economic interdependency has continued to increase up to the present and has accelerated technological growth.

The emergence of science as a profession came about as a result of the development of university laboratories during the nineteenth century; the well-known universities fostered the birth and growth of scientific societies. The scientific method, which is used today as a basis for modern research and development, was developed by Charles Darwin as a theory to relate data (see Section 2.2).

The Twentieth Century
The twentieth century has seen the widespread use of the scientific method and the general inclusion of scientists and engineers in industrial organizations. Industrial research laboratories have flourished and technology has accelerated as a result of two major world wars. Although wars are generally considered to be a negative activity, they often bring about major technological accomplishments that have important peacetime applications. Commercial aircraft, atomic energy, computers, and radar are examples of technologies that were initiated or further developed as a result of war- related efforts. More recently, the development of lasers and their subsequent applications to numerous communication, medical, and other systems is a further example of technology benefits resulting from defense efforts.

The Systems Era and the Information Explosion
The "systems era" began approximately at the time the Manhattan Project was initiated and continues today. This era has seen the development of nuclear reactors; computers; advanced aircraft and missiles; and improved communica-

tion, space, and a host of other complex systems. Note that these system developments have been very much an outgrowth of, and received considerable impetus from, government-sponsored work and needs. Private industry has paralleled this development as suppliers and consumers of large and small systems.

The importance of the manufacturing phase of product development in the world today cannot be overemphasized. The effectiveness of manufacturing processes have in a major way influenced the economic, social, and political course of events worldwide. The availability of an abundance of consumer goods has become an expectation for common people in most developed countries. Improved communication technology, particularly through the use of satellites and now fiber optics, has made clear and instantaneous transmittal of information a reality. The Persian Gulf war, terrorist attacks, and revolutions such as those that occurred in China and eastern Europe have become news events, with the world as the audience.

The Computer Revolution and Manufacturing
The advent of the computer as well as the concurrent advances in the development and production of relatively low-cost electronic devices have strongly influenced industrial capacity worldwide. The full impact of electronically generated design (CAD) that can be linked to computer-aided manufacturing (CAM) has yet to be realized. This capability, along with many other support services that can be integrated with computers such as manufacturing requirements planning (MRP), can ultimately create a computer-integrated manufacturing (CIM) system. Many of these systems also utilize automated material-handling systems through robotics. Thus the need for specialized mannual labor is gradually being reduced and supplemented with the demand for more technical and well-coordinated personnel. Automation can provide for a much closer control of processes, thus improving quality at a lower overall cost. (Techniques for applying such tools will be discussed in Chapters 12 through 14.) It would not be realistic to leave a discussion of the history of technology and manufacturing without mentioning the increasing need to manage negative effects, such as the safety of workers and the protection of the environment and the consumer from dangerous processes and products.

1.3   THE PRESENT R&D ENVIRONMENT

Until the last decade or so, the primary objective of technical developments, with the exception of government-sponsored research and development, has been economic, with little or no consideration of environmental, ecological, sociological, or other factors. Although new products and systems had to comply with a certain degree of safety and lack of undesirable public effects, standards were minimal, the degree of compliance was frequently overlooked, and there were often no set rules or requirements. As a result of serious pollution of our rivers, inland waterways, lakes, seashores, and air, and ceaseless degradation and depletion of our natural resources (mineral deposits, wildlife, forests, and so on), the public and government have become acutely aware of the consequences of failing to evaluate technical developments for environmental and societal impacts. The dilemma of the Three-Mile Island nuclear accident and the tragedy at Chernobyl are cases in point.[1] Thus there has arisen a movement, primarily sponsored by government agencies, to guide and control the manufacturing and/or introduction of new products, systems, or operations into the public sector. That is, new technological developments (and also manufacturing facilities) are evaluated for environmental, ecological, sociological, energy consumption, and other impacts.

To further this concept, one of its foremost proponents, Emilio Q. Daddario, former member of Congress from Connecticut, introduced a bill to establish a technology assessment board, which would provide a method for identifying, assessing, publicizing, and dealing with the implications and effects of applied research and technology. To date, the implementation of the technology assessment movement has been primarily carried out by local, state, and federal agencies in the form of setting up and enforcing requirements for environmental and other types of impact statements. In the private sector, technology assessment is accomplished with the goal of the maximum economic gain allowable within the environmental, political, and societal constraints that are in force.

There are strong feelings by many individuals and organized groups (e.g., the Sierra Club) that technological advances in many cases attack our natural environment and that some established technologies and manufacturing operations must be modified or discontinued because of their environmental impact. Existing nuclear power plants have been shut down because of public distrust concerning their safe operation. The building of new plants has stopped because of safety considerations and the problem of disposing of nuclear waste. It is interesting to note that France, whose energy supply is now over 70 percent nuclear-based, has no record of serious nuclear accidents or nuclear waste disposal problems. The closing down of many mining and metallurgical operations in our country in the face of world competition is a further example. Such closings have also been due to the low labor and operating costs, and resultant low world market prices, in developing countries that have little or no concern for the environment or safety.

The golden age of science and technology is considered by many to have

---

[1] It is interesting to note that in the Three-Mile Island accident, not a single life was lost and no claims of illness due to radiation have been substantiated.

passed.[2] The space effort, which culminated in the landing of men on the moon and awed the world, is viewed by many Americans as an unnecessary waste of taxpayers' money. Fortunately, subsequent technology breakthroughs such as those in computers, communication systems, robotics, laser application, and medicine and health, as well as the development of all types of equipment for home, office, and factory use, have improved this image. Political pressure exerted by environmentalist, consumer, and other organized groups is already influencing government spending on technology and R&D. Further influence is being exercised by the combined effect of inflation and increasing costs and recent political, social, and economic trends.

Although R&D expenditures (federal and industrial) have risen rapidly over the years, from $10 to $15 billion in the 1950s to approximately ten times that amount (about $120 to $130 billion) in the late 1980s, in terms of real dollars they have not increased that much. As a percent of gross national product, R&D expenditures have decreased from a maximum value of 3.0 percent in the 1960s to less than 2.5 percent in the 1980s (Garnato 1980; and *Orange County Register* 1988). Industry-funded R&D as a percentage of U.S. gross domestic product is appreciably less than that in Germany and Japan (Figure 1-2). Fortunately, the need for new products and improved manufacturing capability provides continued and increasing stimulus for technical activities, particularly in the private sector. With respect to world competition, however, "The United States is no longer the dominant technological innovator in the world. It now faces challenges to its technological power from both the West and the East" (Bugelman and Maidique 1988).

1.4   THE PRESENT MANUFACTURING ENVIRONMENT

The present manufacturing environment can also be characterized by the presence of intense national and international competition and a number of factors or trends that tend to emphasize the improvement of manufacturing techniques and operations. These trends, as stated by S. E. Stephanou and M. M. Obradovitch (1985), include the following:

- High rates of technological innovation both nationally and internationally.
- Progressively shorter product-life cycles (market life) along with shorter time-spans from discovery to commercial use.

---

[2]The brilliant military success of U.S.-led coalition forces in the Persian Gulf has been attributed in part to superior technological weaponry (Figure 1-1), which can lead to increased R&D spending by the DOD, with subsequent technical spillover into the industrial sector.

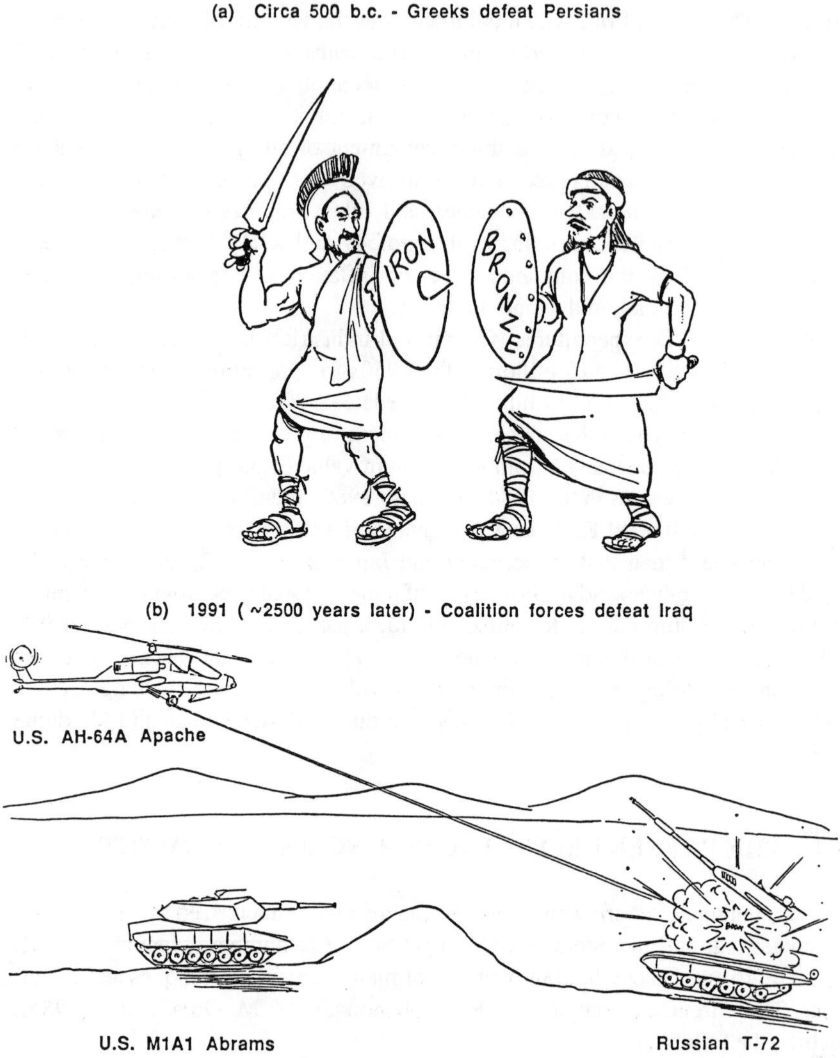
(a) Circa 500 b.c. - Greeks defeat Persians
IRON
BRONZE
(b) 1991 (~2500 years later) - Coalition forces defeat Iraq
U.S. AH-64A Apache
U.S. M1A1 Abrams
Russian T-72

Figure 1-1. Superior Technology Triumphs.

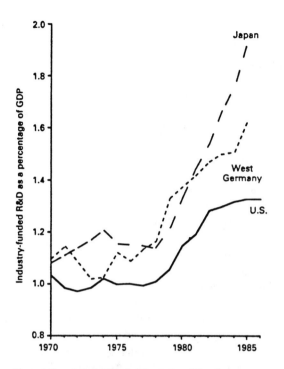

Figure 1-2.   Industry-Funded Research and Development.
Source: M. L. Dertouzos, M. L., R. K. Lester and R. M. Solow,
Made in America (New York: HarperCollins, 1989) p. 58.
Published with permission of MIT Press, the original publisher.

- Cost-price pressures resulting from profit squeeze, competitive pressures, and the complexity and expense of new technology.
- Smaller production lots and discontinuous runs.
- Increasing demand for a higher proportion of technical specialists and professionals in all phases of product development.
- Increased quality of products and manufacturing effectiveness.

In reaction to these trends toward improved cost, quality, time to develop, and overall manufacturing effectiveness, there has been a continuous flow of new schemes and policies, which top management has embraced and attempted to implement with varying degrees of success. These new methods of improving operational effectiveness have been characterized by buzzwords and accompanying acronyms and terminology that have come forth over the years in all phases of technology and manufacturing. Such topics have included

- Fly before you buy

- Zero defects (ZD)
- Value analysis (VA)
- Sensitivity training
- Quality circles (QC)
- Management by objectives (MBO)

More recently some popular topics have been

- Concurrent engineering
- World-class manufacturing
- Team building
- Participative management
- Total quality management (TQM)
- Just-in-time (JIT)
- Search for excellence
- Crisis management
- Situational management

Each of these procedures or ways of doing business has merit and is worthy of pursuit. However, in some cases they are no more than reinvention of the wheel or just plain common sense. For example, managers of small companies and businesses have known since time began that they should be "close to the customer," that is, know and be responsive to customer needs. Yet books have come forth in the last decade propounding this and other time-tested philosophies (e.g., Peters and Waterman 1982). Surely the spear and shield- makers of ancient Greek and Roman times must have been aware of the importance of pleasing their clients, as were the sandal and pot makers. Top management has in many cases been quick to respond to these catch phrases and concepts and has proceeded to implement them in the apparent firm belief that each policy or philosophy will greatly benefit manufacturing and related operations or even bring to an end their management woes and manufacturing deficiencies. However, none of these concepts, old or new, or others that will most certainly follow can *singly* end the basic problems that face American manufacturing operations today. These problems include the following:

1. Transfer of technology from R&D to production
   - Difficulties in communicating R&D findings to manufacturing personnel, so that the implementation of a new process is not carried out expeditiously or properly—partly the result of the failure of manufacturing personnel to understand the technology involved (Burgelman and Maidique 1988)

- Resistance of the manufacturing team to changes in the existing production operations—exemplified by the "not-invented-here" attitude taken by manufacturing personnel when R&D-proposed changes are introduced for inclusion into production operations
- Failure of R&D personnel to recognize the problems of mass production and manufacturing, particularly where many intricate subsystems and components are being produced and integrated into complex systems
- Problems of scaling up product output to the prototype/pilot plant level and beyond within acceptable cost limits and design changes, frequently compromising the performance of a product, so that it is less effective than the original product designed by the engineer designed.
- How the organization is configured and copes with the problems of transferring new products from R&D to manufacturing, which can often facilitated by "people transfer"—a team transfer, with R&D personnel participating in operations or operations personnel participating in the R&D process; a mixed transfer team from both functional areas; or a production development group.

2. Competing with nations that have distinct advantages
   - Lower wage scales[3]
   - Less stringent or no safety or health requirements for workers
   - Lower cost of capital
   - Government subsidization of the R&D process and even the provision of the necessary capital for setting up or modifying manufacturing facilities (e.g., the MITI[4] activities in Japan)
   - More favorable tax treatment of capital gains
   - Higher productivity, partly due to the apparent loss of the work ethic among a large number of American workers
   - More emphasis and greater student enrollments in engineering and science programs[5]

3. Adversial relationship between labor and management
   - Sometimes excessive demands of unions for increased wages, time off, and health and other benefits regardless of the financial plight of the company
   - Management's insensitivity to labor, labor relations, and the needs of

---

[3]Many competing nations have less powerful unions or no unions at all.

[4]Ministry of International Trade and Industry.

[5]According to a 1990 report by the Association of American Universities, there will be a shortage of 7,500 doctoral graduates in the natural sciences and engineering each year by the early part of the next century.

their workers, e.g., automobile companies giving large bonuses and pay increases to company executives when the company is experiencing heavy financial losses and unions are striking

- Interests and objectives of the workers seldom agreeing with those of top management—reflected in less than maximum productivity by the workers as well as a relatively high rate of personnel turnover, especially at the higher skill and professional levels
- Multilayered organizational structure between the bottom and highest levels of the company (often eight or more), resulting in poor or distorted communication and lack of understanding between top management and labor
- Cross-functional training and assignments underutilized by management and unions for different reasons

4. The difficulty of raising productivity
   - The "me-me" attitude of the present so-called "yuppie" generation of professional workers and managers who want and expect the maximum salary; interesting work; and very little, if any, commitment to the organization
   - Management itself, according to Judson's findings (In a survey of 195 corporate representatives of 36 industries, 60 percent of the 236 senior managers polled felt that the problem of low productivity was generally the fault of management [Judson 1982]. For example, there is a definite lack of commitment of American management to retain personnel during slow and transition periods.)

5. The low level of education of our present manufacturing work force
   - A source of dismay for most industries, forcing them to institute programs (at company expense) for remedial reading, writing, and arithmetic so that production operations can be carried out with some degree of efficiency (Even at the lowest levels of plant and factory operations, clear and effective communications and documentation are essential. The level of scientific education in the United States has been going down while the demand for computing and technical skills has been rising.)

6. The adoption of automation and CAD/CAM
   - Inclusion of computer-based techniques into technology development and manufacturing processes, causing major changes (not always for the better) in the manufacturing community (Improvements in manufacturing process efficiency necessitate substantial costs and process modification and control difficulties.)

7. Capital investments
   - Unwillingness of the industrial and business sector in the United States

to make capital investments (Figure 1-3), a problem closely associated with the need for U.S. management to focus more on long-term rather than short-term gains, including more expenditures on R&D and up-to-date manufacturing equipment and facilities

In addition to these factors there appears to be an overemphasis in our business and industrial environment on the need for quick profits rather than long-term investment that will bring future lasting rewards. This is a malady that fosters the promotion of what is called "the fast-burner" type of executive, relatively common in American industry. Such an executive is often a "con man" type, with a "public relations" (PR) personality, who cuts costs by such measures as decreasing the performance and quality of the product, not replacing capital equipment that is reaching the limit of its productivity, not incorporating changes in the manufacturing process or materials that are needed but are initially capital-consuming, not introducing new technology that ultimately will lead to a better product and a more efficient manufacturing process, decreasing the amount of testing, and so on. These executives usually move on (usually upward) and are long gone by the time the "fruits" of their efforts have been fully realized and the company starts experiencing the negative consequences of their short-term goal to show immediate profit and/or cost reduction.

The Japanese view is the antithesis of this philosophy; executives carry out long-range plans for manufacturing advanced state-of-the-art items and process

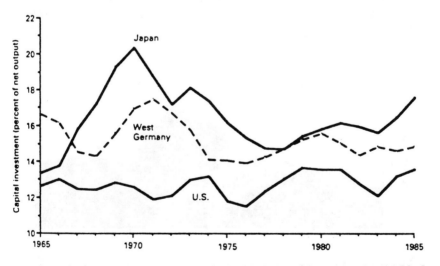

Figure 1-3.   Business-sector capital investment in the U.S., Japan and Germany.   Source: M.   L. Dertouzos, M. L., R. K. Lester and R. M. Solow, *Made in America* (New York: HarperCollins, 1989) p. 57. Published with permission of MIT Press, the original publisher.

improvements and are willing even to lose money while such new processes are under development. This attitude can be attributed to a major extent to the fact that they can receive substantial financial support from Japanese banks (as dictated by the government). An example of U.S. lag in key areas of manufacturing and sales is the increase in the share of imported machine tools in the U.S. market from 4 percent in the mid-1960s to nearly 50 percent in 1986 (Figure 1-4).

Finally, the effect of leveraged buyouts (LBOs) must be mentioned as a trend that has to have a negative effect on expenditures for R&D and manufacturing process improvements (Greenwald 1989). These buyouts cause indebtedness, whose servicing draws on resources and funds that otherwise could have been available for plant improvements and new product and process developments. Although the government has become aware of the potential hazards to our economy resulting from LBOs, nothing has been presented in the form of legislation to mitigate the possible negative effects.

Despite these factors, the United States still remains a viable industrial leader among developed nations and has great potential for future growth and successful competitiveness in world markets. Reasons for this include:

1. An unfulfilled capacity for industrial growth based on updating manufacturing equipment and operation and quality control techniques.
2. A culture that traditionally promotes individual initiative and innovation. The Horatio Alger philosophy still exists, although the implementation is more difficult and usually requires more than one individual.
3. The laissez faire attitude of government, which allows the private sector to

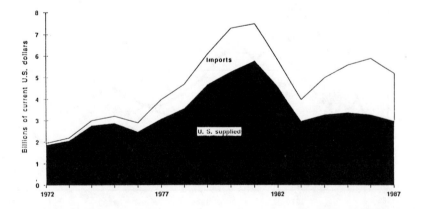

Figure 1-4.   Total U.S. Machine-Tool Sales.   Source: M. L. Dertouzos, M. L., R. K. Lester and R. M. Solow, *Made in America* (New York: HarperCollins, 1989) p. 235. Reprinted with permission of MIT Press, the original publisher.

proceed with new product plans and manufacturing developments with few or no impediments from government. This has always been a factor, especially when Republican administrations have been in power. This noninterference policy of government, except in matters of health and safety, has had a positive influence, but on the negative side, there has been no monetary support in product areas where support has been needed. An example of this type of support is the Japanese MITI sponsorship of the development, manufacture, and improvement of new electronic and computer products, which has made a difference in worldwide competition for the sale of such products (e.g., Sony).

4. A "free" society, where all ethnic groups have been or are being integrated into a single nation and all cultures and groups are given full privileges of citizenship and opportunities to contribute. This is not the case in all developed countries; for example, in Germany the attainment of citizenship by foreign nationals is extremely difficult, if not impossible. The same is true of Japan and other countries. Such policies deter the inclusion of talented and innovative people into leadership roles in industry and science and hence is a distinct disadvantage compared to the American way.

5. A major investment of capital facilities that when properly updated and utilized can easily make the United States once more the leading industrial nation of the world.

6. Sponsorship of R&D and specialized industrial production of weapon, defense, and space systems by government agencies (primarily DOD and NASA), has providing a continuous source of new technology, a sizable portion of which has spilled over and been used effectively by the civilian sector. The large expenditures of the so-called military-industrial complex has resulted and will continue to result in major technology improvements and occasional breakthroughs. All developed countries do not have technical efforts subsidized to this extent.

The chapters that follow will discuss proven ways, with these factors in mind, that we can increase our competitiveness and regain our industrial leadership and production advantage.

QUESTIONS AND TOPICS FOR DISCUSSION

1.1   Show how the growth of systems has historically paralleled the growth of technology.

1.2   What are possible reasons for the anomaly of ancient Minoan and

Egyptian technological development, which in some areas was as advanced or more advanced than technology today?

1.3   How have technological developments been accelerated by wars? Give examples and explain.

1.4   Construct a graph showing the approximate degree of technological development throughout history from prehistoric times to the present. Indicate on the graph the occurrence of some key technological events.

1.5   Approximately when did the systems era start? List sample systems and show how they have paralleled computer development.

1.6   Name four areas of technology development in which environmental concerns have significant impact and describe that impact.

1.7   What is the background of the "military-industrial complex" and what has been its effect on technological development?

1.8   Enumerate four key problems in U.S. society today, estimate the percentage of technical content or technological dependence of each and describe the technologies involved.

1.9   How is American management responsible, at least in part, for the increasing noncommitment of workers to company progress and interests? Or restating the question, why is the so-called "company man" of two decades ago less visible and less common in today's industrial environment?

References

Bugelman, Robert A., and Maidique, Modesto A. 1988. *Strategic Management of Technology and Innovation*. Homewood, IL: Irwin.

Garnato, George. 1980. "Estimates of R&D Expenditures." Paper read at third annual R&D Conference sponsored by the AIAA, TMSA, and TTS, Boston.

Greenwald, John. 1989, August 14. LBO: Let's bail out. *Time*, p. 50.

Judson, A. S. September–October. 1982, Awkward truth about productivity. *Harvard Business Review*. p. 93.

Kosta, D. K., and Kearney, A. T. March 20-23. 1989, "Countdown to the Future: The Manufacturing Engineer in the 21st Century." Paper presented at the WESTEC '89 Conference of the Society of Manufacturing Engineering, Los Angeles.

Orange County Register. 1988, September 14.

Peters, Thomas J., and Waterman, Robert A., Jr. 1982. *In Search of Excellence*. New York: Harper & Row.

Stephanou, Stephen E., and Obradovitch, Michael M. 1985. *Project Management, Systems Development and Productivity*. Bend, OR: Daniel Spencer.

2

General Concepts
and Definitions

2.1 MANAGEMENT OF TECHNOLOGY
AND CONVENTIONAL MANAGEMENT

The growth of research and the application of technology during the last 30 to 40 years has been truly phenomenal when considered from the aspects of financial outlay and utilization of personnel and facilities. Excluding expenditures for technology applications, the total R&D budget for the United States can be expected to exceed $150 billion in the early 1990s. This is a sizable increase from the few billion dollars budgeted in the 1950s. Other nations around the world have shown similar growth in their R&D and technology-related expenditures, particularly the developed countries.

Where initially a company may have had one or two engineers or even the proprietor looking at ways of improving the products and processes of the company, now there are often hundreds or even thousands of engineers and scientists employed by a large company to perform these same functions—not to mention the personnel of government laboratories and research institutes.

Special Requirements of Technical Personnel

As this growth has continued, there has been insufficient effort toward the development and nurturing of talented individuals and effective teams doing this special type of creative work. In many industrial plants, technical personnel have operated under the same general company policies concerning hours worked, time off, and other procedural details as shop or plant production-line workers. Some companies have even required researchers and engineers to punch time cards. In view of the additional years of training and education that professional scientists or engineers have spent preparing for their positions and because of their value to the company in generating new products and improved processes, as well as their potential for bringing about substantial savings in the operation of the company, they require different management treatment than others with less training and education.

It has been stated repeatedly that R&D effectiveness is not a matter of how much money is spent but how well the R&D is managed. In other words, major expenditures in new technology development do not necessarily ensure that new products and processes will be forthcoming. How creative scientists and engineers are, either singly or in team efforts, will determine the success of the expenditure and is highly dependent on how well they are managed. Since personnel is the major ingredient of technology development, the management of the personnel giving birth to the new technology is critical. (*Technical personnel* in the context of this book refers to scientists and engineers who have had several years of college-level training in their field and usually have a B.S. or advanced degrees.)

For maximum productivity, managers of technology, be it product or process improvement, must take into account the fact that the level of education of their personnel is in its totality significantly higher than that of the usual type of personnel in other businesses. Technical organizations usually include a number of individuals with doctoral or master degrees as well as numerous college-level personnel. Such highly specialized workers have a fund of factual knowledge to draw on and are keyed to a high level of logic in matters of science and engineering. They are often outspoken and sometimes nonconforming to strict company regimentation.

It has been said that industrial organizations tend to be almost as autocratic as the military. In industry, the schedule is important, sometimes all important, as is cost consciousness and strict adherence to company procedures. Under these rather constraining conditions, the new research scientist and engineer is not as satisfied and understanding a worker as those, who have not been trained in the free-wheeling, free-thinking, and relatively independent environment of a university or college, particularly in graduate school. This situation is somewhat different from the social culture and behavior reflected in Japanese universities, which teach that conformity to group (company) practices and needs are expected and must be adhered to religiously. From the standpoint of individual contributions and creativity, our way has been superior, but from the standpoint of group or team contribution, the Japanese system appears at this time to be more productive.

Differences Between Managing Technology and Managing Other Activities

Besides the differences in the nature of the personnel, there are other significant differences in the managing of technology as contrasted with other management activities. Large investments are involved, from which tangible results are difficult to gauge. The success of the technical effort must often be measured in terms of process and product improvements; increased prestige to the company; continued awareness of the state of the art in important product-line areas; training of personnel for sales, administration, and other positions; and problem solving for customers and related activities—all of which in their entirety are of considerable importance to the functioning of the company but are not always easy to measure in dollars.

Examination of the annual reports of major companies over a ten-year period reveals that sales have increased as much as 25 times or more, primarily because of the utilization of new technology as well as a population increase. Those companies that have gained the most have done so because of better management of their technology programs. Other studies have shown that 50 percent of all R&D projects fail because of nontechnical rather than technical reasons (Stephanou 1981).

Problems in Managing Technology

Major problems in technology management are as follows:

- Communication—Lack of understanding of the importance of technology by upper management and the difficulty of successful information transfer
- Motivation—Instilling a desire to perform and a sense of urgency in carrying out key R&D projects; keeping morale and output at a high level
- Planning—Inadequate strategic as well as day-to-day planning; maintaining a viable program for product or process development
- Integration—Successful input and cooperation of all involved individuals and units in the development and fulfillment of a new concept, including R&D, manufacturing, marketing, and sales
- Funding—Lack of enough funds to fund all the promising projects, let alone explore a given subject area fully
- Government—Coping with changes in government requirements and regulations
- Supervision—Promoting engineers, because of their expertise in a particular technical area, to supervisory positions; often without the necessary management training and, even worse, the inherent desire to be managers except for

the extra compensation involved (In many such cases, the company has gained a poor manager and lost a good engineer. The selection of engineers who will be good managers is a difficult task.)

These problems will be discussed further in later chapters.

Another important factor peculiar to the technology environment is the constant need for innovation (Chapter 3). Technological innovation as defined by J. A. Morton (1971) is "the process of perception or generation of relevant science and its transformation into new and improved products, processes and services for which people are willing to pay."

Responsibilities of Technology Managers

With today's highly competitive conditions, management must provide a creative and motivating environment to catalyze a constant flow of ideas for new product, process, and operational improvements. Technology managers should be optimistic people, have empathy for the research worker, and ideally have the charisma of leadership and the quality of creativity themselves to stimulate enthusiastic effort from their personnel. The requirement for constant innovation on a year-in, year-out basis can become onerous and the results eventually sterile if one is attempting to exploit the same technical area. There must be adequate scope for ingenuity over a broad range of technical possibilities. It is a responsibility of technology managers to see that work assignments remain interesting and challenging and yet are directed toward the meaningful goals of the company. This is a responsibility in addition to the standard functions of planning, organizing, staffing, communicating, directing, monitoring, and controlling.

Managers must have the capability of knowing when to stop a project and when to start new ones and how to placate the technical personnel who resent change of direction when market conditions or a technical impasse dictates a work stoppage in a certain technical area. Starting and stopping projects is a characteristic of technical work that is not typical of other types of businesses. The dynamic nature of R&D and the constant improvement of the state of the art require a dedication of personnel that is indeed demanding of time and energy. It is most difficult with the present information explosion to keep up and remain knowledgeable in one's own specialty, let alone a general area of technical knowledge.

The importance of good human relations with technical personnel, as with all types of personnel, cannot be overemphasized. In fact, the management of technology can be examined from two aspects: the behavioral or the functional and operational. Both aspects are equally important and must be considered if success is to be achieved in bringing a concept through the difficult steps necessary for successful production and sales.

2.2 DEFINITIONS, CONCEPTS, AND TERMINOLOGY

Technology

Technology is defined in the *Random House Dictionary* in four different ways:

1. The branch of knowledge that deals with the creation and use of technical means and their interrelation with life, society, and the environment, drawing upon such subjects as industrial arts, engineering, applied science, and pure science
2. the terminology of an art, science, etc., technical nomenclature
3. a technological process, invention, method, and the like
4. the sum of ways in which social groups provide themselves with the material objects of their civilization.

In the context of this book definition 3 will predominate in reference to technology, but in some instances definition 1 is applicable and is implied.

Basic Research

Research may be basic or applied and usually precedes the design and development of a product, system, or process. Basic research can be defined as original investigation directed toward the development of scientific knowledge with no commercial application in mind. It is carried out primarily at universities, but some basic research is done at research institutes and government laboratories. Although there was a time when companies performed basic research related to their product lines, this type of activity has dwindled to a small segment of the research effort and will probably disappear altogether. Despite the fact that basic research is performed without commercial application in mind, it frequently leads to new products, processes, and improvements. There are many examples of advances or technical breakthroughs that have occurred during basic research and have been utilized to produce important products and processes. Radioactivity and atomic energy, lasers, and new chemical compounds produced in the laboratory and later found to have medical or other valuable applications are examples. Basic research is sometimes referred to as fundamental, pure, blue-sky, or ivory-tower research. These terms have a connotation of idealism that is in fact true since success in the marketplace and the derivation of profit is not the driving force.

Applied Research

Applied research, in contrast to basic research, is completely commercial in its objectives. It can be defined as investigations directed toward the discovery of new scientific knowledge that has specific applications to products, processes, or needs. It is also often referred to as engineering, developmental, industrial, or product research. Examples of applied research are the applications of nuclear fusion to electric power generation; the use of lasers in communication systems; and the search for cures for the common cold, cancer, and AIDS. Some authors define still another type of research, *developmental research*, or commonly, *development*, which is the creation of methods and tools to produce a product or a new manufacturing process. The term *research* is also used in other applications, such as market research, library research, and so on, but in the context of R&D, the term refers to science and technology.

Design and Analysis

In the development of a system, new process, or operation, design usually follows applied research, so that the following sequence occurs (there is potential iteration between all the steps):

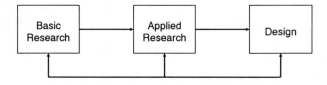

Figure 2-1.   Sequence of Activities Leading to Design.

In present R&D and manufacturing activities the concept of *concurrent engineering* has been gaining acceptance and is being gradually introduced. In practicing this concept, the objective is to carry out applied research, design, development, evaluation, and even preparation for manufacturing simultaneously as soon as a new product shows promise of success. Concurrent engineering will be discussed further in later chapters (Section 12.1).

Engineering (or system) design can be defined as "the activity wherein various techniques and scientific principles are employed to make decisions regarding the selection of materials and the placement of these materials to form a system or device which satisfies a set of specified and implied requirements" (Middendorf 1969). This does not mean to imply that feedback and iteration between these sequential steps are not carried out. Feedback and iteration resulting from communication among the personnel involved in the various phases is a necessary requirement for successful design and development of the product or process.

More simply, design can be described as the process of applying available techniques and scientific principles for the purpose of defining a device, a process, or a system in sufficient detail to permit its physical realization. Design usually involves making a dimensionalized diagram or sketch of the concept or idea.

Conventionally, designs are eventually depicted as blueprints; they are sometimes set up as physical or computer models, if the system consists of hardware, or are in the form of a flow diagram or a computer program, if it is an operation or a process. Where hardware design is the objective, steps in the system design process can be depicted as shown in Figure 2-2. The process is iterative; therefore, there can be frequent changes and modifications between the preliminary and final design.

Design is vital to the development of systems no matter what the type; it represents the advanced planning that will completely designate or define the system in minute detail. It can include systems or product analysis, in that the application of all available scientific and engineering techniques is necessary to arrive at the most feasible solution to the need or requirement. System analysis would precede design since the results of analysis are necessary to arrive at an optimum design. The analysis could include calculations, modeling, simulation,

1. **Development of a concept or several concepts to fit the need.**
   a. This can be derived from experience and previous knowledge or from the literature including the patent literature.
   b. It can involve invention and may be patentable.
   c. The literature should be checked to see if there are systems that already satisfy the requirement or can be modified slightly to satisfy the requirement.

2. **System analysis or activity analysis.** Defines input/output relations and constraints.

3. **Set up preliminary design** and preliminary specifications for a particular concept or for several concepts. These will be "broad-brush" and will be a first cut at what is required in the way of configuration, general dimensions, and materials.

4. **Consider the feasibility of the proposed design(s).** Considerable money can be saved if the effort is terminated here due to technical or economic nonfeasibility.

5. **Evaluate alternative designs and select design.**
   a. Develop criteria for comparing various designs.
   b. Select the most promising designs.

6. **Model the selected design concept.**
   a. The model may be a math or physical model.
   b. Use the model to determine relationships between component and subsystem performance and effects on the total system.
   c. The model can vary dimensions and materials.
   d. The model can vary components and subsystems.

7. **Optimize the design.** Based on results and relationships developed in 6; determine the optimum materials, components, and configurations.

8. **Implement the design.**
   a. Prepare final design specifications.
   b. Fabricate experimental prototype (may be a mockup) and ask: Is it suitable? Does everything fit together?

Figure 2-2.   The System Design Process.

definition of input/output relations, and so on. The advent of computer-aided design (CAD) has revolutionized the design and analysis process in that instant changes and improvements can be made on the component or system by the designer. This process is accomplished by first programming and then displaying a model of the proposed design on the display screen and providing for instant modification by the operator to determine optimum dimensions, configuration, and performance. The reduction of time and the increase in effectiveness attained in this interactive process as compared with the previous methods of design improvement is truly phenomenal.

The term *designer*, as used in engineering companies, has been applied to various levels in the organizational hierarchy, from draftsperson to the top design engineer of the company. The chief design engineer for major automobile companies, for example, is often a vice president of the company.

Development

Development follows design and can be defined as the engineering activity required to advance the design of a product or process to the point where it meets specific functional and economic requirements and can be turned over to manufacturing units. For hardware systems, development usually starts immediately after, or even before, the design is finalized and can end at different points in the system development and use cycle. If it is a product or system, development can include setting up a pilot production line, developing tooling, solving manufacturing problems, and eventually building the manufacturing facility. During the development stage an experimental prototype is often built, tested, and evaluated. There can also be manufacturing prototypes as the first units are produced at the manufacturing facility.

Development has also been defined as "the systematic use of scientific knowledge directed toward the production of useful materials, devices, systems, or methods, including designs and development of prototypes and processes" (National Science Foundation 1983). In this broader context it can include applied research. As in most fields, semantic problems in the terminology of engineering and technology are quite common and frequently ambiguous and confusing (Stephanou 1972).

Test and Evaluation

Test and evaluation, or T&E, as it is often abbreviated, is a necessary activity in the system or product development process. In industry it is customarily included as part of the R&D process and not designated as a separate activity. It is an important and necessary phase in any product or process improvement but receives different degrees of emphasis depending on the particular circumstance. In government procurements, particularly for the Department of Defense, T&E is a critical activity for a number of reasons. First and perhaps most important, military products and systems must be as effective and as fail-proof as possible because the nation's safety and security are at stake, as well as that of the armed forces personnel using the equipment. Second, because of the public nature of military systems, they are subject to constant public and congressional scrutiny, which invariably focuses on cost as well as performance. Third, DOD and other government systems are frequently highly complex and expensive (sometimes the government is the only organization that can afford to build the system), and as a result overexpenditures and failure to meet performance goals can assume major proportions.

Testing and evaluation involves testing models and experimental, preproduction, and manufacturing prototypes; in the case of DOD, there are extensive qualification tests of the final product by the particular armed service. In industrial product development, the customer often performs the final T&E necessary to evaluate the product fully. This represents a saving to the manufacturing company, a portion of which can be reflected in a lower price of the item to the customer. Understandably, T&E is expensive, and when many thousands of items are produced, only limited testing of a statistically suitable sampling is economically feasible.

Manufacturing

The generally accepted definition of commercial manufacturing as given in the *Random House Dictionary* is "The making of goods or ware by manual labor or by machinery, especially on a large scale." S. D. El Wakil (1989), in *Processes and Decisions for Manufacturing*, defines manufacturing as "the transformation of raw materials into useful products through the use of the easiest and least expensive methods." This definition assumes that the easiest and least expensive method is known and that the desire and the capital are available for implementing it. Also it must be mentioned that not only must the product be manufactured by the easiest and least expensive method but also it must have the desired quality in performance and reliability.

Since manufacturing can involve a variety of processes and techniques with an infinite number of variations, cost-effective manufacturing processes that can produce a quality product may require as much or more innovation as the initial product created in the laboratory and are much more expensive to develop and implement.

The Scientific Method

In most successful scientific and technical work the philosophy of operation is based on the classical scientific method developed by the giants of science in the eighteenth and nineteenth centuries. (Chapter 1 gives a brief history of the development of science and technology from early times to the present.) The classical scientific method is based on the observation of a physical phenomenon; the formulation of a hypothesis to explain the phenomenon; the testing of the hypothesis by experiment; and finally, the modification of the hypothesis to fit the observation or, if the hypothesis was erroneous, the formulation of another hypothesis and repetition of the process. In the growth of the physical sciences and engineering this logical procedure was of primary importance in the establishment of basic laws and principles. With the advent of industrial research, the scientific method has been extended and modified to solve all kinds of problems and has become the basis for what is called the systems approach to problem solving (see Section 2.5).

State of the Art
State of the art (SOA) is currently used in present-day technology to refer to the present state of development or capability of a product, component, subsystem, system, process, or technology. If an item can be readily purchased or is readily available—that is, can be quickly manufactured or fabricated—it is said to be "off the shelf" or SOA. The connotation is that there is no technical or R&D work needed to develop the product; it has already been developed. Off-the-shelf hardware refers to components that represent the SOA. Current products and systems are usually built from SOA components. In industry there is a constant effort to improve the SOA to make products more effective, reliable, and economical to produce so that a commercial advantage can be gained. Companies must constantly be "pushing the SOA" to remain current and to gain a technical advantage over the competition (offensive research). Maintaining at least a currency in the SOA is an essential activity that a company must fund to remain viable in today's dynamic technical environment (defensive research).

In military applications the need to push the SOA is even more pressing since the security of the nation and to a certain extent our economic health depends on an ability to protect ourselves with the most cost-effective defensive and offensive systems. Failure to advance the SOA in weaponry can lead to a defensive weakness that can provide political and other advantages to our enemies. Although the Communist threat appears to have disappeared, at least for the present, there can always be new enemies, and the need for military capability is ever present; witness the Persian Gulf war. For the present, increased economic competition is the challenge or enemy of the United States, more so than physical security. One can say we are in an economic war both at home and abroad.

2.3   THE R&D PROCESS AND THE SYSTEM LIFE CYCLE

The totality of the R&D process, whose constituent parts have been described in the previous section, can be represented by the block diagram shown in Figure 2-3.

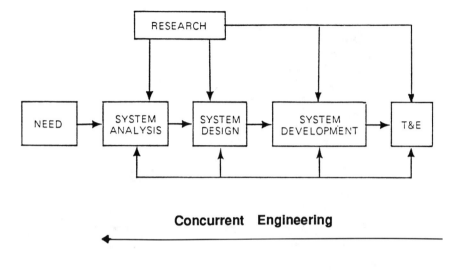

Concurrent   Engineering

←———————————————————————————————————

- Research supports all phases of the process.
- Concurrent engineering starts as soon as the new product or process improvement appears viable.
- Sales and marketing monitor progress and make plans accordingly.

Figure 2-3.   The R&D Process (Iterative)

If the development is successful—that is, the product is producible and economically attractive—and funds are available for the production facility, manufacturing the product can commence. Note that development is a step in the R&D process. In practice, however, the term *system development* is frequently used to describe the total R&D process and, in such usage, is synonymous with R&D. There is, therefore, an ambiguity of terminology in that *system development* can refer to either the system development step in the R&D process or the whole R&D process.

The R&D Process

The R&D process is initiated by identifying a need, either real or imaginary. This need can be recognized by a customer, salesperson, technical person, or some other perceptive individual within or without the company. (Need and need analysis are discussed in Section 10.2.) Sometimes a key scientific breakthrough, such as the discovery of lasers, may trigger applied research to investigate the use of the new technical phenomenon. In the case of lasers, several practical applications were found soon after the phenomenon was revealed. Following identification of the need, analysis of the problem or system is necessary. This analysis can be in the form of a preliminary or feasibility study (Section 10.3) if a major project is foreseen, or it may be a small analytical effort with possibly computer modeling

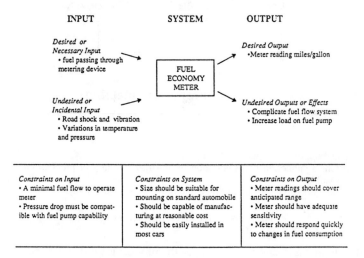

Purpose: To determine the boundary conditions of the system even though its exact form
is not known. This will aid in formulating the concept and design of the system.

Requirements: Must define inputs, outputs, and constraints for the system.

Example:

Effective Need: to be able to read continuously, while the car is in operation, the
performance of an automobile with respect to fuel economy.
(a) Could adjust speed to optimize fuel.
(b) Could determine when motor tuning is needed or something
is wrong with engine operation.

| INPUT | SYSTEM | OUTPUT |

*Desired or
Necessary Input*
• fuel passing through
metering device

FUEL
ECONOMY
METER

Desired Output
•Meter reading miles/gallon

*Undesired or
Incidental Input*
• Road shock and vibration
• Variations in temperature
and pressure

Undesired Outputs or Effects
• Complicate fuel flow system
• Increase load on fuel pump

Constraints on Input	*Constraints on System*	*Constraints on Output*
• A minimal fuel flow to operate meter • Pressure drop must be compatible with fuel pump capability	• Size should be suitable for mounting on standard automobile • Should be capable of manufacturing at reasonable cost • Should be easily installed in most cars	• Meter readings should cover anticipated range • Meter should have adequate sensitivity • Meter should respond quickly to changes in fuel consumption

Figure 2-4.   Input/Output Analysis.   Source: Morris Asimow, *Introduction to Design,* © 1962 pp.
54–55. Adapted by permission of Prentice Hall, Englewood Cliffs, New Jersey.

or simulation to determine the parameters and variables. In making such a preliminary study, the use of input/output analysis, sometimes referred to as activity analysis, is useful. An example of the use of input/output analysis is shown in Figure 2-4. Research, basic and applied, can feed information into all steps of the R&D process but primarily into analysis and design.

Product or system design must include the development of concepts to meet the need. This conceptual plan is appreciably clarified as a result of the system analysis, which shows what the product or system must accomplish and under what conditions, the technical problems that must be solved, and possible solutions. It may be necessary to initiate applied or directed research to solve these critical technical problems; modeling and simulation may be necessary either in a physical mode or by use of a computer. Fabrication of an experimental model followed by testing can lead to the final product or system design.

The system development step can involve further refinement of the product prior to manufacture, the building and operation of a pilot plant, the solution of manufacturing problems, and the development of manufacturing techniques. In government procurement the T&E step usually terminates the R&D process.

The System Life Cycle

The system development process is part of the total system life cycle, depicted in Figure 2-5. If the R&D process has proven that the system or product is capable of being built or produced, the economics and need are favorable, and the performance of the product is satisfactory, manufacturing can proceed and the system can be marketed, sold, and used. After the life cycle of the product is fulfilled, obsolescence will occur and improvements to the product will become evident. Such improvements will probably be implemented, or it may be necessary at some time to abandon the product completely and develop a new system. Often new requirements arise, and it is no longer feasible to modify and update the old system. Then the system is retired or skeletonized by salvage, if it is a hardware system. If it is a nonhardware system, such as a chemical product or an item sold to the public or industry on a mass scale, production is stopped. Upon development of new requirements that the old system cannot possibly fulfill, the need for a new system becomes evident and the cycle starts all over again.

The development and improvement of the common typewriter is an example of the system life cycle in that it has undergone continual changes and modifications over the years until now it is completely electric, is electronic, or has been superceded by a microcomputer using a word-processing program. Another example is the B-52 bomber: Although it was designed in the early 1950s and was operational in the late 1950s, it has continually been improved and modified to

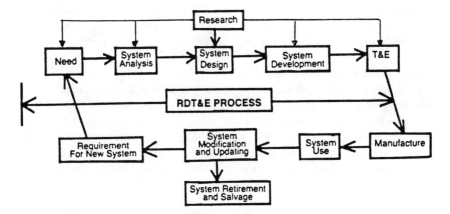

Figure 2-5.   The System Lifecycle (Iterative).

provide additional capability and include up-to-date technology until finally, after more than 15 years, the development of a new system, the B-1 bomber, was initiated to replace it.[1] Later the B-1 was replaced by improved versions, and finally it was considered outdated and deleted in congressional budget cutting.

In the computer industry, the R&D process and the system life cycle is much shorter, with new, more versatile computers being produced almost annually to replace "obsolete" models presently in use. An even more striking example of the rapidity of the system cycle is the development and marketing of software programs; such programs may have product lifetimes of as little as a year or less. Similar short product cycles are operative in most dynamic industries and high-technology operations.

2.4   SYSTEMS CONCEPTS AND RELATED TERMS

In research and manufacturing development, a number of terms, concepts, areas of knowledge, and disciplines are intimately interrelated. Included, and of major importance, is the hierarchy of terms related to systems and systems theory, such as *systems management, project management, systems engineering, systems integration,* and so forth. In the past some of these terms have been used ambiguously and in an overlapping manner, although in reality they have distinguishably different meanings and connotations. Their common meanings and relationship to technology are discussed here. Project management is discussed in Chapter 11.

Before proceeding to the description of various systems terms and their interrelationships, it is necessary to review briefly the growth of the systems concept and its applicability to R&D and manufacturing processes as well as to management in general. An outgrowth of the scientific method (already described) systems thinking and the use of the systems approach allow for the attack and solution of complex problems by considering all aspects, including interfaces, and proceeding to solve these problems by using a multidiscipline or team approach.

History and Origin of Systems Theory

The emergence of the systems way of thinking and the systems approach has an interesting and somewhat diffuse beginning. Some give credit to Frederick W. Taylor as the first to introduce the scientific approach to management late in the nineteenth century (Chartrand 1971; Locke 1982). Others appropriately relate the systems approach to general systems theory and give credit to Ludwig von Bertalanffy (1951) and Kenneth Boulding (1956) as the first proponents. Most

---

[1]Despite efforts to replace the B-52, considerable numbers of these workhorse aircraft remain viable and were used with great success in the recent Persian Gulf war.

authors agree that the operational research teams formed just before and during World War II to develop military technology and solve war-related problems were the first major proponents of the systems approach. An important characteristic of these teams was their interdisciplinary nature. They played an important role in the winning of World War II and the subsequent continuance of war-initiated technology such as radar, computer, communication, and aircraft developments. A significant outgrowth of this success was the setting up of "think tanks" such as the Rand Corporation to study complex problems related to national defense. Rand has since expanded its horizons to the study of other complex public and societal problems, as have other government-subsidized think tanks, for example; Mitre and Aerospace Corporation.

Industry paralleled government efforts in operations research-type activities. Companies such as Westinghouse, Du Pont, General Motors, and General Electric, to name a few, began adopting scientific management techniques in the early decades of the twentieth century, and during and after World War II they had in place formidable management staffs that included interdisciplinary teams. Since World War II the systems approach to management has been used by essentially every major industry and government agency. The spectacular space flight to the moon, the worldwide communication systems employing satellite links, the complex systems used by banks and business, and many other successful developments can be traced to the application of the systems approach.

On the academic side the treatise of R. A. Johnson, F. E. Kast, and J. E. Rozenzweig (1963), *The Theory and Management of Systems*, marked a milestone in the development of the systems concept. It had as its purpose the description of a new approach to management, namely, the concept of managing by system. C. W. Churchman (1968), in his classic, *The Systems Approach*, further promoted the systems concept by examining what the systems approach means and its validity. The use of systems theory and the systems approach has expanded to applications in almost every field, including education, social science, agriculture, government, health, and medicine, as well as management (Stephanou 1982).

Systems

Systems can be considered to be an aggregate of elements (subsystems and components) that function together in response to inputs to achieve certain outputs. Systems usually involve more than one discipline or area of knowledge or technology and are relatively complex. There are innumerable types of systems, depending on the basis for classification, for example, hardware, software, procedural, political, and social systems. An organization can be considered to be a system, and the division of groups and subgroups the subsystems. People can be considered to be the components of the subsystems. Components make up subsystems, which in turn make up systems. A digital computer can have subsystems or components consisting of input devices, such as card or tape reading devices; data-processing units and output devices, such as printers; and display devices—which together make up the data system.

The Systems Approach
The term *systems approach* can be described as the approach to the solution of complex problems or the development of complex systems that ties together the pertinent disciplines in a logical manner in order to build or manufacture products, develop an operational procedure, and bring together subsystems in an orderly and efficient manner to accomplish some predetermined goal. More generally, it can be considered to be a method for solving a problem or developing a procedure or system. It looks at a problem in its entirety and uses all the available science and technology to solve it. The concept of total quality management (TQM) uses the system approach to introduce and maintain quality in a product or service. As already mentioned, the systems approach to problem solving has been applied generally in almost all fields of endeavor.

Systems Management
The term *systems management* involves the application of the systems approach to the design, development, manufacture, and operation of systems or to the solution of complex problems. Systems management can be concerned with one or more of these areas, either singly or in combination. For example, it can refer to the management of the hardware development phase and can subsequently include the installation and operation of the system. In this context it is a more encompassing term than R&D since it can be concerned not only with the development of the system but also with its manufacture and use. Systems management can also be concerned with, and have as a responsibility, marketing; selling; and ancillary detailed areas such as packaging, merchandizing, distributing, warehousing, and so on. In this broad context it goes beyond project management and operations research.

Systems Engineering
The practice of systems engineering is involved in any development of hardware or manufacturing system that occurs in the R&D process. It can be very simply defined as the combination of various engineering disciplines required to carry out the R&D process, including the systems analysis and the systems design and development steps. Although a number of texts include the term *systems engineering* in their title, there seems to be a disparity in what it really means (Stephanou 1972). Each appears to cover different areas of application of technology and reflects the particular experience and exposure of the author to the subject; the thread of similarity is the recurring procedures used to create, design, develop, and make operational complex systems and processes.

Systems Integration

The term *systems integration* refers primarily to bringing together components into subsystems to form systems. It often involves coordination of diverse technical efforts and hardware developments that can culminate in testing of the total system. An example of systems integration would be bringing together the components of a special-purpose computer, such as input, output, processing, and memory units, into a compatible physical volume, properly packaged or encased and working harmoniously to operate as designed. The term is closely related to systems engineering but emphasizes bringing the components together rather than their design and development. It is particularly concerned with the identification and correction of any interaction problems between components or subsystems and the optimization of the components to give maximum performance of the total system. In bringing a concept to successful fruition, first, on a laboratory scale, then as a manufacturing process, and finally as a successful product, integration of the various functions (systems) involved is necessary, namely, the research, engineering, manufacturing, and marketing and sales organizations.

Operations Research

Carrying out operations research (OR) is closely interwoven with systems and technology management. As with the other terms discussed, many definitions are given by various authors. One of the classic texts on OR (Miller and Starr 1960) defines it in this manner:

> OR, in the most general sense, can be characterized as the application of scientific methods, techniques, and tools to problems involving the operation of systems so as to provide those in control of the operation with optimum solutions to the problems.

What should be added is that OR utilizes the scientific method and the systems approach to solve management problems. As redefined in another classic text (Thierauf and Grosse 1970);

> OR utilizes the planned approach (scientific method) and the interdisciplinary team in order to represent complex functional relationships as mathematical models for the purpose of providing a quantitative basis for decision making and uncovering new problems for quantitative analysis.

The value of the latter objective, that of uncovering new problems for quantitative analysis, is debatable since it implies finding more work for the operations research analyst.

2.5   THE SYSTEMS APPROACH TO THE MANAGEMENT OF TECHNOLOGY

The systems approach as applied to management can be considered a technique for solving a problem or developing a procedure or system. It represents an extension of the scientific method to business and management problems. It is the approach to the solution of complex problems or development of complex systems that ties together the pertinent discipline in a logical manner to accomplish some predetermined goal. It has the following important characteristics:

1. It looks at a problem in its entirety.
2. Key factors or subsystems associated with the problem are identified and their interactions recognized; that is, it examines the "environment" of the problem.
3. It takes into account the important interactions between components in a subsystem and subsystems with one another (systems integration).
4. It uses to the maximum extent possible all available knowledge, science, and technology needed to solve the problem.

To apply the systems approach, various authors have developed their own sequence of steps and/or guidelines. We have found the following sequence to have a wide range of applicability:

1. *Identify and define the problem.*
   This step may involve the development of a new system or the correction, improvement, or replacement of a present system. In defining the problem or system, the pertinent scenario or background in which it occurs must be considered.
2. *Define objectives and goals to be obtained.*
   Why is a solution of the problem or the development of a new, modified system needed?
3. *Set forth the constraints and/or assumptions that will be used (bound the system).*
4. *Develop possible solutions (alternatives).*
   This step may be done by using mathematical relations and a computer or it can be done qualitatively without the use of a computer. It requires some creativity and analytical skills.
5. *Decide on criteria for evaluating the alternatives.*
   What is really important and to what degree?

6. *Evaluate the alternatives.*

Use this selected criteria to determine the best alternative. Take into account interacting areas. This step can also be computerized or can be done qualitatively.

7. *Implement your solution.*

It is desirable first to test your solution or system in the form of a model or trial operation (simulation) before fully implementing it.

8. *Note results of the implementation and modify problem solution as needed (feedback).*

It is fully recognized that there is no simple recipe that can be prescribed for attacking and solving all problems, no matter what the approach. The preceding sequence is suggestive of a form of logic in technical problem solution and management problem solving that has had considerable success. As already mentioned, it is an extension of the scientific method described earlier in this chapter.

To restate these steps as they apply to the management of technology and the development of new products and manufacturing processes, the systems approach or systems method involves identifying the desired system, determining what the subsystems are and how they interact, setting objectives, defining the details of the environment in which the system must operate, modeling and designing the system, testing it, and finally implementing it. Iteration usually occurs between steps repeatedly during the process. Subsequent to the implementation process there can be feedback to improve the system. During the process, methods or criteria must be developed for measuring or evaluating the effectiveness of the system.

If one considers the management of technology to be the system, the subsystems are the various functions of management, which include planning, organizing, staffing, monitoring and controlling, managing scientists and engineers, interacting with other involved segments of the organization, and finally evaluating results. These results provide feedback for correcting the management process and thus ending the systems approach sequence of steps, although there can and should be further iterations. To these steps can be added the transfer of the technology or concept to a successful manufacturing process and use of the product, process, or system. Although these subjects are treated separately in individual chapters for clarity of discussion and emphasis of principles, their symbiotic relationships and the synergistic effects that can occur in their interaction must be emphasized. The effectiveness of how well these various functions of management are integrated to provide a timely manufacturing process and a "quality" product is directly related to the success of the concept-to-production process.

QUESTIONS AND TOPICS FOR DISCUSSION

2.1   In what ways could technical personnel be treated differently in a company than manufacturing, plant, and other company personnel? What would be the pros and cons for such special treatment, considering the problem from a total company personnel viewpoint?

2.2   Would flexible work schedules for scientists and engineers be a reasonable solution to the management problem of workers who cannot keep strict working hours? Discuss the pros and cons of such a solution.

2.3   Studies have shown that 50 percent of all R&D projects fail for nontechnical rather than technical reasons. What are possible explanations for this failure?

2.4   How does management of technology differ from conventional management? Discuss at least three differences.

2.5   Why is basic research being performed more and more by universities and less and less by private industry, despite the fact that a number of profitable products and systems have originated from basic research?

2.6   What is meant by system analysis?

2.7   Why is knowledge of the appropriate technical jargon important in a management position in which there are one or more interactions with technical groups or personnel?

2.8   Why do industrial products have so little T&E as compared with DOD products and systems?

2.9   How is the scientific method related to the systems approach? Be specific.

2.10   Develop an input/output analysis for a contemplated drug-control program for a local municipal area. Show how you would use the results of your analysis to design the program.

References

Boulding, Kenneth. 1956, April. General systems theory: The skeleton of science. *Management Science*, pp. 197–208.

Chartrand, R. L. 1971. *Systems Technology Applied to Social and Community Problems*, p. 1. New York: Spartan Books.

Churchman, C. W. 1968. *The Systems Approach*. New York: Dell.

Johnson, R. A., Kast, F. E., and Rozenzweig, J. E. 1963. *The Theory and Management of Systems*, p. 4. New York: McGraw-Hill.

Locke, Edwin A. 1982, January. The ideas of Frederick W. Taylor: An evaluation. *The Academy of Management Review*, pp. 7–23.

Middendorf, W. H. 1969. *Engineering Design*. p. 2. Boston: Allyn & Bacon.

Miller, D. W., and Starr, M. K. 1960. *Executive Decisions and Operations*, p. 104. Englewood Cliffs, NJ: Prentice Hall.

Morton, J. A. 1971. *Organizing for Innovation*, p. 4. New York: McGraw-Hill.

National Science Foundation. 1983. September. Review of data on research and development. *NSF Bulletin* 41.

Stephanou, S. E. 1972. *Semantic Problems in Systems Engineering*. International Symposium on Systems Engineering, Vol. 2, p. 338. West Lafayette, IN: Purdue University.

Stephanou, S. E. 1981. *Management: Technology, Innovation and Engineering*, pp. 19–21. Bend, OR: Daniel Spencer.

Stephanou, S. E. 1982. *The Systems Approach to Societal Problems*, pp. 229–. Bend, OR: Daniel Spencer.

Thierauf R. J., and Grosse, R. A. 1970. *Decision Making Through Operations Research*, p. 14. New York: Wiley.

von Bertalanffy, Ludwig. 1951, December. General systems theory: A new approach to unity of science. *Human Biology*, pp. 303–361.

Wakil, S. D. El. 1989. *Processes and Decisions for Manufacturing*. Englewood Cliffs, NJ: Prentice Hall.

3

Planning for Innovation and Improvement

3.1 THE NEED FOR TECHNOLOGY AND MANUFACTURING PLANNING

Most major companies are required to maintain ongoing technical and engineering programs, including technical service to customers, in order to remain viable; many of the products that are on the market today were nonexistent ten years ago. Long- as well as short-range product and process improvements and new products must be continually brought forth to maintain the company's competitive position in the marketplace. Existing product lines must be given strong technical support to provide customer satisfaction and ensure future sales. Continuing technical effort in the general product areas of the company must be carried out so that state-of-the-art knowledge is at least maintained and, more important, advanced, to generate improved products before or concurrently with the competition.[1] Process problems must be solved and manufacturing processes improved in cost and efficiency so that products can be made more economically and with higher quality.

A company that does not participate in technology and product improvement programs of some kind may find itself bypassed and eventually out of business as the flow of improvements and new products continues incessantly from competing firms who are actively engaged in technology. With this obvious need for technical activity, there is a concomitant requirement for well-conceived programs, and adequate short- and long-range planning is essential. Since technically based programs must compete for the financial resources of the company with many alternative strategies for the generation of revenue, they must be well founded and have a reasonable chance of success.

3.2   SETTING GOALS AND OBJECTIVES

A well-managed organization with an established group of product or service lines will normally have developed short- and long-term objectives for product goals and improvements that the organization would like to achieve in the future. Short-term objectives commonly encompass a one- to three-year period, whereas long-term objectives are directed toward a longer period, say, three to ten years (Figure 3–1). There could be a further classification of intermediate goals and objectives, which could arbitrarily be set for a three- to five-year period. These goals and objectives are frequently set forth in company management plans and have had the blessing of higher management and the board of directors. Company objectives are dynamic in that they are subject to modification every year, depending on what has occurred during the previous year, the technical developments in the industry as a whole, the success of the previous year's technology programs, and market conditions. Both defensive and offensive research programs must be planned and the distribution of resources between these two types of research determined. Such distribution would depend on the resources available and the level of support needed for existing product lines.

The various divisions, departments, groups, and subgroups of the company also establish objectives within their areas of responsibility that support the principle company objectives and product areas. These supportive objectives are often determined by the manager's own thinking, as well as the input from technical, marketing, and sales personnel. The result is a hierarchy of objectives, which is similar to the organizational structure pyramid, with each organizational level

---

[1]This policy corresponds to actively pursuing both defensive and offensive research.

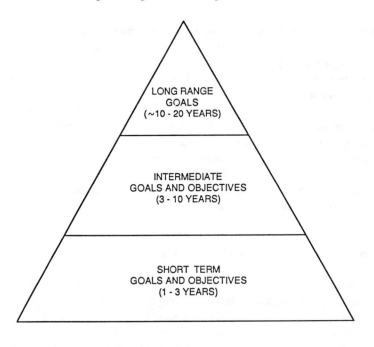

• Time spans are arbitrary and approximate.
• Each level is supportive of the level above.

Figure 3.1   Planning Pyramid

expanding and supporting specific objectives of the next higher level. These objectives can be documented by setting forth divisional, departmental, and other organizational group charters. The position guides for managers reflect company objectives and can also serve as group charters.

3.3   LONG-RANGE OR STRATEGIC PLANNING

The importance of the involvement and guidance of top management in determining the long-range goals of the technical effort cannot be overemphasized. Without long-range goals and planning involving top management, research programs can drift along the lines of interest of the participating scientists and engineers, fall into set patterns of service determined by sales and marketing personnel (in answer to customer needs), or focus on the pet projects of influential managers. None of these alternatives would necessarily reflect the true desires of the top management of the company. The very nature of research dictates that long-term planning must be done before research is initiated. Programs that are cut off after two, three, or more years of operation because they do not conform to company needs and requirements are a serious economic loss and reflect the lack of appropriate planning. This, of course, does not preclude the termination of programs that no longer are viable because of a market condition resulting from a changed social, economic, or political environment.

Questions That Should Be Addressed

Long-range or strategic planning by top management should include consideration of such questions as the following:

1. What kind of products do we wish to make in the future? The same or different product lines? If changes are desired, there should be some indication of which general direction they should take.[2]
2. Is our research operation a showplace for important customers and stockholders or is it a productive organization that plays a key role in company survival? Ideally it should be both.
3. Should there be a central research laboratory, should each product area have its own support laboratory, or should there be both? The decision depends on the size of the company, the nature of the business; and the geographical location of the various units, suppliers, and customers.
4. Are the research and engineering laboratories going to provide the basis for future company growth or is growth going to occur through acquisition or merger? This decision could affect the amount of resources put into research and engineering laboratories. If rapid growth is desired, it is usually more expedient to acquire other companies or effect a merger. If growth is desired through internal development, other operating, functional parts of the company must be coordinated and disciplined to capitalize on new technology.
5. How much of the funding, personnel, and facilities of the R&D laboratories should be provided for supporting customer needs on present product lines and how much for new products and improved processes? This figure can vary from year to year, but some policy guidelines should be set.
6. How much, if any, work from government agencies should be solicited? A tendency in the past has been for many companies, especially smaller

---

[2]Closely associated with this, topic is the broader question of what kind of company we wish to be in the future, the same or something different. Here it is important to take a system view. What type of system are we involved in and should we expand, contract, or remain the same? Also, and perhaps most important, what kind of company do we want to be? For example, an oil company could ask this question: "Do we want to be an oil company or an energy company?" This decision would have far-reaching effects on strategic planning.

companies, to play it by ear. This strategy can be satisfactory for short periods of time and for a limited number of government contracts. In the long run, however, a policy of how such work is to be handled, administratively and functionally, must be developed so that the mainline technology operations of the company are not constantly disrupted.

7. What ratio of defensive to offensive research should the company undertake? Also, how much, if any, basic research can the company afford? Defensive research maintains the technical capability and state-of-the-art knowledge of a company in its product-line areas so that the competition cannot achieve a major coup in an improvement or new product without some effective response from the company. Offensive research reaches out to develop new or improved products in an aggressive, well-financed manner. Defensive research may be, and often is, financed in a minimal manner, barely to maintain capability, so that if a technical breakthrough is achieved by a more aggressive competitor, the catch-up effort is not excessively great or overwhelming in time and/or money.

Documentation of the results of discussions of these questions, providing meaningful conclusions and consensus are arrived at, can be a valuable guide to research managers in initiating and conducting programs and projects. Long-range planning could include short-range plans but would deal with them in a general way and only in relationship to the long-term goals and objectives. Technological forecasting can provide valuable input to the process of determining long-range product goals (see Section 4.6).

The Role of Top Management

Unfortunately, involvement in technology planning is an area that has been generally neglected by top management. Some executives rationalize that technological breakthroughs cannot be scheduled or that the technical effort should consist of staying abreast of new developments; others have the philosophy of waiting to see what the competitors develop that shows promise and then jumping in to surpass or circumvent them. Still others maintain that since they are not familiar with technical details, they can make policy judgments only on plans developed at lower levels. Success is attained by those companies that plan for innovation rather than follow it. If management fails in its responsibility to plan, the planning effort will by default pass to lower levels, where company interests and goals are not as well known or adhered to.

Strategic Planning Versus Strategic Intent

The process of strategic planning varies from company to company. Hamel and Prahalad (1989) make notable distinction between strategic planning and strategic intent. Strategic *intent* involves the development of an overriding corporate goal, which is broad in scope and constant in time. It represents winning (hopefully) commitment to a course of action or product achievement with a long planning horizon (10 to 30 years) and a target worthy of personal effort and commitment. An example of such a strategic intent would be the goal of a major U.S. motor company to decrease the quality defects in its cars to a specific low value by the year 2000 or for the sales division of a company to achieve a 60 percent market share of a major product within a certain time. In contrast, strategic *planning* looks at the ways to accomplish such goals within the constraints of resources that will be available over the time frame involved.

Improving the Strategic Planning Process
It is essential in the strategic planning that

1. All the players should be involved, including top executives, middle-level managers, line managers, and key sales personnel.
2. Strategic plans should be developed over a period of time and modified as the need arises, depending on the internal and external environment of the company. The process of strategy formulation is both evolutionary and always subject to change. The final plan should spell out the consequences for each functional area of the business and should represent a consensus.
3. Considering today's volatile and fast-changing environment, planning should be continuous but within reason. It should be reviewed at least annually.

For high-technology companies, and to a major extent for all companies, technological innovation should be a vital concern to all levels of management and the corporate climate should communicate this concern. Technical innovation should be an essential part of corporate planning, particularly in high-technology companies, where corporate plans are synonymous with innovative plans. For example, successfully innovative companies such as Texas Instruments (TI) have a distinctively aggressive strategy in planning, as expressed by one of the company's senior managers:

> We are convinced that useful products and services as well as long-term profitability are the result of innovation. Further, we feel that profitability above the bare compensation for use of assets can come only from a superior rate of innovation and can no longer exist when innovation is routine. This is why our long-range planning system is fundamentally a system for managing innovation. (Martin 1984)

In its development of silicon semiconductor technology, first with integrated circuits and later with advanced products utilizing these devices, TI institutional-ized, introduced, and implemented a long-range planning system called Objec-tives, Strategies and Tactics (OST). This system became a way of life at TI in that it achieved success through well-conceived strategies and well-executed tactics in support of them (Martin 1984). Its objective was to promote a consciousness of the importance of innovation in all its managers and prevent the onset of "bureausis," which inevitably sets in as organizations become increasingly more successful, larger, and more convoluted or complex. The key for TI was placing as much emphasis as possible on the administration skills required to manage innovation and stimulating ideas and proposals that could be expressed as corporate objectives and strategies for the future.

It is worth repeating that management at all levels should be constantly aware of the importance of innovation and include the prospect of new concepts and their step-by-step development, evaluation, and implementation in their strategic plan-ning. Innovation awareness and pursuit can also be done informally, with the lead taken by top management and transmitted to the lower levels in the form of acknowledgements and rewards for innovative accomplishments; or it can be carried out formally, with appointment of special groups or standing committees for presentation, review, and decision regarding innovations. The fostering of innovation and related subjects will be discussed further in Chapter 4.

3.4   RESEARCH AND DEVELOPMENT STRATEGIES

A company's plan to proceed in the development of a particular product or product line is dependent on the business strategy it has devised for exploiting a scientific development or technical breakthrough. The technological portion of the overall plan must converge in time and be compatible with the manufacturing and market-ing plans for the new product, along with the financial and business considerations.

Planning strategies for new products and/or processes could involve the following:

1. New product or process—new plant
2. New product or process—general purpose plant
3. Planned product series—special plant
4. Same product—new plant.

The specific plan that is used will vary with the business opportunity and the state of the art of the particular product or process being developed.

Other aspects of research strategy that a company must consider are the proportion of research activity that should be devoted to defensive and offensive types of research, how much for existing product improvement, how much for new product development, and the mix of funding for various product areas. The proportion of funding in these categories would depend on the resources available, the level of support needed for existing product lines and manufacturing process improvements, and the actions of the competition. Decisions on these matters also depend on the thinking and goals of upper management and are specific to the particular company. A category of defensive research that is increasing in the percentage of total research relates to product and process safety and liability. As the number of lawsuits against companies mounts, the amount of research in this area increases.

In considering future product lines, marketing and management must evaluate the type of market the developed product may encounter. Research leading to a cure for a disease like AIDS and the development of methods of producing such a drug would clearly encounter a "pull" market. On the other hand, the development of the SONY Walkman and the compact disc for music and television signals were originally in a "push" market; in other words, funds had to be allocated to create a market for these new items. All too many innovators and inventors have found that the world is not necessarily waiting for their better mousetrap. People first have to be convinced that this is a better way of eliminating mice and, furthermore, that this indeed is what they want to buy. Therein lies the importance of close cooperation of R&D with sales and marketing personnel.

3.5 SHORT-RANGE PLANNING

Short-range planning (one to three years) can be a separate exercise for management or it can be included in long-range planning. It can be most conveniently discussed and documented along with the long-range plan since the immediate direction, policy, and thrust of the R&D effort would be guided by and dependent on annual planning and budgeting. Obviously, short-range planning must be integrated with, and is a vital part of, long-range planning. The determination of how much money is going to be spent on technology each year represents an extensive and critical exercise in planning. The final decision should represent a compromise between what top management feels it can and wishes to spend and what the technology managers and personnel request and need.

From the Top Down
The process of budget determination is usually carried out in two directions, from the top down and from the bottom up. Since the power of the purse is in the hands of top management, let us first look at a typical process that occurs annually at that management level and at some of the attendant considerations in budget determi-

TABLE 3-1.   R&D Spending

Firm	% Sales	% Profits	Firm	% Sales	% Profits	Firm	% Sales	% Profits
AT & T	2.1	16.0	Ford	3.4	92.1	Motorola	6.0	106.6
Arco	0.5	8.0	GE	2.6	42.4	NCR	5.3	71.3
Beckman	7.9	121.5	GM	2.6	46.6	Polaroid	6.3	73.0
Bendix	1.4	39.1	GTE	1.5	20.3	RCA	2.1	50.5
Boeing	5.1	85.5	Goodyear	2.0	67.1	Rockwell	1.1	29.0
Burroughs	5.9	56.3	HP	8.9	100.7	Sperry-Rand	5.3	110.5
DEC	8.1	81.4	Honeywell	5.3	103.1	TI	4.4	79.1
Dow	3.4	40.2	IBM	6.0	40.3	TRW	1.4	30.7
DuPont	3.6	47.9	ITT	2.4	56.1	Union Carbide	2.0	39.5
Eastman-Kodak	5.5	43.1	McD'L Douglas	4.1	104.8	United Tech.	7.0	187.9
Exxon	0.5	10.5	Merck	8.1	52.5	Westinghouse	2.3	48.8
Fairchild	9.4	202.3	3M	4.4	36.2	Xerox	5.3	66.9

Note that profits are defined as the differences between sales or revenues and costs (including depreciation + taxes + interest). Source: Martin, M.J.C. 1984. *Managing Technological Innovation and Entrepreneurship.* Reston, VA.: Reston, p. 24

nation. First and most important, the principal officer of the company and the officer's staff or some other top decision-making group must decide on the total money that will be allocated to research for the year. The previous year's budget is usually used as a guide and a starting point. Depending on the profits of the company during the previous year, R&D success in new product and process improvement, market conditions, and competing needs for funds in other areas of company endeavor, the initial budget figure may be the same, more, or less than that of the previous year.

Companies in the United States vary in their allocation of funds from zero to about 10 percent of the previous year's sales,[3] although some highly technically oriented companies may spend slightly higher percentages (Table 3.1). Electronic, computer, communication, aerospace, chemical, and pharmaceutical companies, because of the highly technical nature of their products and the constant need for innovation to remain competitive, plow back a considerable portion of profits into R&D. In contrast, many companies, usually the smaller companies, spend very little or nothing on product development and process improvement. Some companies try to maintain R&D expenditures over the years as a constant percentage of sales. However, this policy may be in error since it is not necessarily responsive to special needs of the technology organization or economic and market conditions that are pending but not yet reflected in the previous year's sales. Other companies take a defensive stance and allocate their research budgets according to what expenditures are being made by the competition, as determined by annual reports.

---

[3]Instead of last year's sales, an average over a number of recent years may be used.

Availability of personnel and facilities, as well as plans for growth (or contraction), may also affect the final R&D budget.

A further subdivision of the budget by top management can include the allocation of percentages of various types of research. A number of allocations are possible, for example;

- New ideas and product areas (basic   20-30%
  or fundamental)
- Improvement and expansion of ex-   40-50%
  isting product lines
- Manufacturing process im-   25-35%
  provements

Following determination of the resources that are to be dedicated to R&D, the research or engineering vice president or director can allocate budgets to the various divisions or groups within the organization. In so doing, the director must reflect the goals and objectives set forth by top management in their short- and long-range planning. These amounts are then further allocated to the various departments or subgroups. Each division and subgroup is allocated a certain budget based on such factors as

1. Desired R&D emphasis by top management—perhaps certain product lines or a new field
2. Sales volume and customer service requirements associated with that division or group
3. The financial needs of the division or group as presented by the division, departmental, and group leaders
4. Previous performance of the particular R&D segment

In a similar manner the funds allocated by division or department heads to their subgroups reflect these factors. The seasoned research director or engineering head usually holds back an arbitrary percentage (10 percent is common) of the total amount to be allocated for what is sometimes called the "director's reserve." This figure can provide budget safety, so that programs that overrun can be financed and new promising technical developments that arise during the year can be pursued and exploited. In an era of fast-moving technology and rapid advancement of the state of the art, it behooves a company to have funds readily available to finance and capitalize on any technical breakthrough that may occur. Pursuit of an advantage of a company's product over that of the competition as a result of a technical breakthrough can bring substantial rewards to the fortunate company that makes the technical advance.

From the Bottom Up

The research or engineering director or vice president can request from the middle management or input from the scientists and engineers about what projects should be initiated, continued, or stopped. Previous direction and guidance given by upper management in verbal communications, memos, and short- and long-range plans must be heeded in selecting work to be done in the ensuing year.

First-line supervision and senior personnel must review the previous year's projects and determine which should be dropped and which should be continued. Questions about whether projects are to be continued and how they should be modified must be answered. These are extremely important questions and can have considerable impact on the personnel involved. It is therefore advantageous to have input from the concerned technical personnel as well as readings from upper management and marketing and sales personnel. Informal or formal meetings can provide relevant information for making these decisions. If the technical personnel are consulted and their input utilized, they may respond and perform better when the work is actually carried out. This fundamental principle of the participative management school as applied to technical personnel can be very effective in achieving high performance. Although discussions with and input from the technical personnel are necessary, the final decisions must be made where the responsibility lies—namely, by the research manager or director.

Final Program Formulation

The question of what new projects or programs should be initiated is as important as which projects should be dropped or modified. In addition to the directives of upper management, there will be suggestions from technical personnel themselves as well as from marketing, sales, and other sources of new ideas (see Chapter 4). Again it must be stated that any ideas proposed should be discussed with marketing and sales personnel to make certain that the particular product or service is needed and would be marketable. The new ideas, projects, and programs indicated by top management will have the highest priority in the lineup of new work to be undertaken. Next would be the suggestions from the other sources mentioned. In addition to the opinions of marketing and sales personnel, there must be a sounding out of upper management's reactions to costly new ventures other than the ones that upper management has proposed. There also must be an evaluation by the technical manager or senior personnel about the technical feasibility of the proposed work and resulting product and an economic analysis by the new product group or some comparable evaluation group (see Chapter 6).

The potential new products, systems, and process improvements usually far exceed the financial capability and desire of the company to fund; therefore, choices must be made. Projects should match available personnel as much as possible, but there may be a need for new personnel where technical expertise in a particular area is lacking. Facility requirements should be identified so that the plant or facility engineering group can properly allocate funds for needed new facilities.

In this budget and program formulation process there is review of the proposed work at all management levels in the technical organization, starting with the first level of supervision and progressing up to the research or engineering director or vice president. Feedback and modification are common, as overlapping areas are integrated to avoid unnecessary duplication and undesired work is eliminated. Middle management and even top management may reduce, increase, or redistribute work and corresponding budgets in the review process. There may be several iterations of the budget and the attendant documentation before the final definition of work and budget for the various R&D segments is arrived at. The engineering or research director or vice president integrates all departmental and groups' requests in one final budget figure that is submitted to top management for final approval. Usually this figure will be exactly equal to or close to the amount initially designated by top management, but it may vary, depending on the persuasive powers of the research and/or engineering director, the financial conditions of the company, and the perceptions of the executive officer of the company or division.

3.6   ZERO-BASE BUDGETING

Zero-base budgeting (ZBB), as it is known today, was developed by Peter A. Pyhrr at the Texas Instruments Company in 1969. It was later used by former President Carter when he was governor of Georgia for the preparation of the fiscal 1973 Georgia state budget and more recently in budget preparation for some, but not all, government agencies. The technique has applicability in planning company operations and technology expenditures, particularly when available R&D funds are in a declining mode.

The basic steps involved are these:

1. Develop work or decision packages.
2. Evaluate and rank all these packages by cost-benefit analysis.
3. Allocate resources accordingly.

In ZBB the manager is required to justify his or her entire budget request in detail. Each year the process starts with a zero base; that is, no past activities or expenditures are taken for granted. Each project or activity is identified and described so that it can be ranked and either approved or disapproved. The package should contain the following:

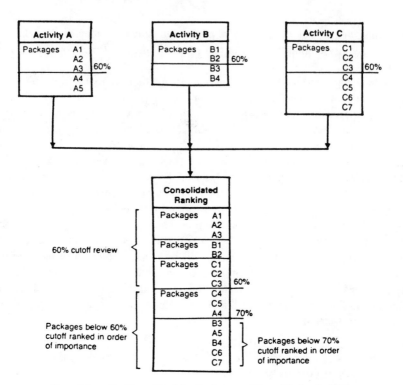

Figure 3-2.   Ranking of Decision Packages and Consolidation for ZBB.

- Purpose of the work
- Consequences of not performing the activity
- Measures of performance
- Alternate courses of action
- Costs and benefits

Ranking the projects or decision packages in decreasing benefit order gives upper management a guide to how limited resources can be allocated. Figure 3-2 is an example of how various activities in an organization could be evaluated and funded by their workload priorities with the ZBB approach. In this case a 60 percent cutoff of expenditures is used as the "consolidation" line.

This constitutes a very brief introduction to ZBB. Further details on its use and implementation can be found in the literature.[4] It is discussed here because of its

---

[4]See, for example, Pyhrr (1977) and Sherlekar and Dean (1980).

continued use by some federal agencies in determining how R&D expenditures will be made and its potential for technology planning and budgeting. It has the distinct advantage of evaluating and emphasizing each year the priorities in the spending of available funds, particularly when such funds are on the decline.

3.7   DOCUMENTATION OF THE R&D PLAN

In the iterative process that is used to arrive at the final budget figure, documentation is developed to give justification for, and a record of, the budget requests from the various groups and subgroups. The request for this documentation is initiated by upper management, and the work is passed down the line to the first level of supervision, who in turn ask for input from scientists and engineers, who will actually do the work. The following type of input can supply the needed information for a particular project:

- Objectives
- Technical approach
- Tasks and subtasks (work breakdown structure)
- Task bar charts and milestones (Figure 3-3)
- Costs
- Graphs of estimated costs versus time (Figure 3-4)

Objectives, Technical Approach, and Tasks

The objectives point out the goals for the work that year and how they relate to company product goals. The technical approach section spells out the critical technical issues and their proposed solutions, will determine the success or failure of the program or project. Tasks and subtasks represent a brief, well-structured description of what is planned and,it is hoped, what will be accomplished. In technical work, what is planned initially and what is actually done do not always coincide; this is an inherent characteristic of technical development that is very difficult for nonscientific executive personnel to understand. Work that is planned will not necessarily be done; technical advances and breakthroughs cannot be scheduled. Accountants and financial officers in particular find it difficult to understand this fact of R&D life. Their thinking is, "If you said you were going to do a certain task or job, then why didn't you do it, particularly if you have spent the money?"

Task Bar Charts and Milestones

Task bar charts are a valuable planning tool in that they show intervals of time during which work on the various tasks and subtasks will proceed. Personnel

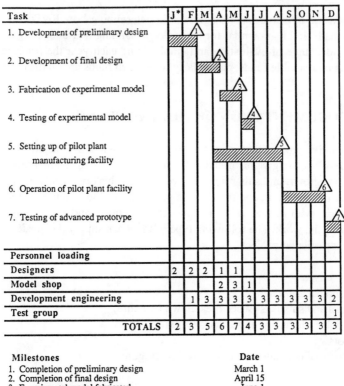

Task	J*	F	M	A	M	J	J	A	S	O	N	D
1. Development of preliminary design												
2. Development of final design												
3. Fabrication of experimental model												
4. Testing of experimental model												
5. Setting up of pilot plant manufacturing facility												
6. Operation of pilot plant facility												
7. Testing of advanced prototype												
Personnel loading												
Designers	2	2	2	1	1							
Model shop				2	3	1						
Development engineering		1	3	3	3	3	3	3	3	3	3	2
Test group												1
TOTALS	2	3	5	6	7	4	3	3	3	3	3	3

Milestones	Date
1. Completion of preliminary design	March 1
2. Completion of final design	April 15
3. Experimental model fabricated	June 1
4. Testing of experimental model completed	July 1
5. Pilot plant completed	Sept. 1
6. Pilot plant operated successfully for 3 months	Dec. 1
7. Testing of advanced prototypes	Jan. 1

*Instead of names of months, numbers can be used to indicate months after start

Figure 3-3.   Task Bar Chart for Planning a Program or Project.

requirements can also be shown on the charts. By estimating the time for the work to be done, the manager can better plan and visualize what allocation of labor will be required and the most logical sequencing of the technical effort. It is important to have the technical personnel make up their own task bar charts. This job gives them a sense of involvement in the planning exercise and influences them to hold to the schedule in every possible way. Also, the technical personnel will provide more realistic estimates of times since they are usually more familiar than the manager with the actual details of what is necessary to carry out the technical work.

One important advantage of the task bar technique is that it can help set

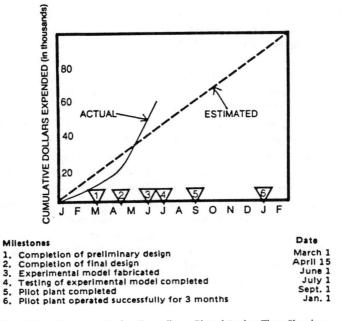

Milestones   **Date**

1. Completion of preliminary design   March 1
2. Completion of final design   April 15
3. Experimental model fabricated   June 1
4. Testing of experimental model completed   July 1
5. Pilot plant completed   Sept. 1
6. Pilot plant operated successfully for 3 months   Jan. 1

Figure 3-4.   Program or Project Expenditures Plotted Against Time, Showing Milestones.

milestones or key events in the program or project (Figure 3-4). Milestone dates usually mark the completion of an important technical effort such as

- Completion of a design
- Completion of a key component, subsystem, or system
- Completion of fabrication of a model
- Completion of testing

Milestones are also used to signal the initiation of an effort, but this usage seems to be less acceptable; it is usually possible to initiate an effort, but completing the job is much more difficult and important. The milestone date represents an estimated date at which a given segment of work will be completed. Unfortunately, in many instances this is taken as a firm date by nonsympathetic or nonunderstanding upper management or contracting agency, and failure to meet it is considered a failure in performance; more often than not, the failure to meet milestone dates is the result of a technical impasse, an overly optimistic estimate, an unexpected reduction of available funds, or other factors over which the technology manager has no control. The ability to meet a given milestone in a technical program is directly dependent on the nature of the technical task. A difficult technical task with a high level of uncertainty will require a flexible milestone date. Technical breakthroughs cannot be scheduled in advance.

Milestone dates in contracted R&D, such as projects being carried out for an outside company or government agency, may be estimated by the systems or project manager or they may be dictated by the contracting organization. In the latter case, delivery dates of hardware or completion of services such as testing may be involved.

In monitoring programs and projects during the year, task bar charts and milestone dates can be important guideposts to the status of the work. Occurrence of key events before the scheduled milestone dates indicates better than expected technical progress, and conversely, milestone dates that are not met can indicate technical or other difficulties. A graph (Figure 3-4) of estimated accumulated expenditures versus time, showing milestones, can be a valuable tool for monitoring program and project progress in technical performance and cost. Actual cumulative expenditures versus time can be plotted as the project progresses and compared with the estimated values. Chapter 10 describes this tool as well as work-flow methods of planning and monitoring technical effort, such as program evaluation and review technique (PERT) and critical path method (CPM).

Program and Project Costs

The cost category spelled out by the senior scientist or principal engineer in charge of the work includes direct expense items:

- Technical personnel
- Special equipment and facilities
- Materials
- Computer and programmer costs
- Consultants
- Travel
- Support from other groups

All these and other expenses must be paid for from the budget allotted to the particular program or project. Indirect expenses, such as secretarial costs, utilities, and salaries of middle and upper management, are usually not charged to the technical effort but may be considered overhead costs necessary for the operation of the R&D organization. This allocation is handled by the accounting or financial control departments of companies in different ways. For projects contracted with government agencies such as DOD, the overhead rate of the company is an important factor in the original pricing and procurement.

In defining costs it is important to evaluate the cost of each task and subtask in the program or project. For example;

Task 1. Development of Preliminary Design
      a. Perform literature and patent search $1,200
      b. Evaluate previous design by computer analysis   600
      c. Draw up preliminary new design   500
      d. Program and evaluate preliminary design   200
                      Total for Task 1 $2,500

Defining costs during the planning stage allows for easier elimination of tasks or subtasks if there is a budget cut since the work that might be eliminated is spelled out in both a technical and a financial way. Each project or program is assigned a code number so that charges to it can be quickly identified for input into computer programs. These computer programs are used to provide cost data for financial control while the technical program is carried out.

There can also be code numbers for sick leave, travel, or company business so that projects are not charged for nonproject expenditures. The preparation of work flowcharts such as PERT and CPM can also be used, as well as graphs (as in Figure 3-4) showing anticipated expenditure versus time.

Here again, as in the case of director's reserve, it is desirable to set forth a slight overage of funds (10 percent if possible) to allow for unplanned expenditures and increasing costs. It is not always possible to obtain such a cushion, but it is extremely realistic if one considers that the greater the technical risk in the project or program, the more unreliable the cost prediction will be. Final adjustments upward are usually required for high-risk programs, as are schedule adjustments that prolong the program.

Finalization of the R&D Plan

The input from the working-level personnel is "massaged" by the first level of supervision—that is, reviewed with some culling of unnecessary tasks or subtasks, expansion of product areas to be emphasized, and even elimination of some projects entirely. The individual projects and programs are combined into a departmental R&D program and submitted to the next management level, where the various departmental programs are integrated into a divisional or company R&D plan. A sample format for a departmental R&D annual program plan is shown in Table 3-2. There are critiquing and feedback of both the work content and the allocated funds at each next higher level of management until the plan is finally approved by top management. As the plan moves to higher levels of management, the considerations and judgments are more of a general and budgetary nature and are less concerned with details of the technical work.

Following finalization of the plan, including the budget, by lower and middle management and acceptance by upper management, engineering work orders or work authorizations are issued. The name given these work authorizations varies

TABLE 3-2. Annual R&D Program Plan—Materials Department

Job Code No.	Product	Critical Technical Issues	Tasks and Subtasks	Project Leader	Funds	Labor	Materials	Other	Facilities
401	Auto storage battery	1. At low temperatures battery performance decreases due to thickening of electrolyte. 2. Sloshing and leakage of electrolyte causes crustations on terminals, which decreases current flow and sometimes causes stoppage of current.	1. Investigate low-temperature performance of battery using several new electrolyte compositions. 2. Investigate temperatures for reducing formation of crustations on terminals. (a) Investigate leakproof breaker devices. (b) Determine effect of coating on maintaining terminal performance.	I.M. Eager	$54.5 K	(a) $30 K research engineer (b) $15 K technician ------ $45 K Total	(a) 100 lbs. of Cpd. X at $4/lb. $400 (b) 100 lbs. of Cpd. Y at $3/lb. $300 (c) Miscellaneous materials $800 ------ $1,500 Total	$8 K. purchase of special test equipment	Electrical testing laboratory
402	High-temperature furnaces	1. Thermal and mechanical properties of new high-temperature materials. 2. Fabrication techniques for promising new materials.	1. Test candidate materials at high temperature. 2. Investigate correlation of thermal properties with method of fabrication and chemical composition. 3. Fabricate promising materials into components of a furnace structure and test at furnace temperature.	J. Smith	$70 K	(a) $25 K research engineer (b) $10.5 K technician ------ $35.5 K Total	New materials $21.5 K (see EWO)	Travel $1.5 K Subcontract Consultation $1.5 K ------ $13.0 K Total	High temperature laboratory
403	Improved transistor								
404 etc.									

with the company, but in essence they are brief statements of the necessary technical and financial requirements of the particular program or project (see Figure 3-5). This standard form serves as a "blank check" authorizing the principal investigator or project head to accumulate expenses in accordance with the funding allocated. Note the graph of estimated cumulative expenditures plotted against time, with milestones shown at the end of the work order. This system allows for the close monitoring of both the financial and technical performance of the R&D effort during the year. As expenses are incurred, cumulative actual expenses can be plotted and compared with estimated values and whether or not technical milestones were achieved. Careful examination and appraisal of such graphs can provide an excellent monitoring and control tool for technology managers.

3.8   MANUFACTURING PLANNING

The inclusion of manufacturing planning is an important part of planning for innovative processes. This need has been accentuated by increased international competitiveness, and the issue has become not just greater profitability but survival. According to Preece (1989);

Manufacturing strategy must include the implementation of new manufacturing technology in its planning, selection and implementation process. Such strategic planning can result in a number of benefits including products of superior quality, shorter manufacturing times, reduced inventories, more product proliferation, reduction of investments in plant and equipment, etc. Such technology-oriented strategy along with computer and integrated manufacturing (CIM) can bring major benefits to the organization.

The Need for Integrated Manufacturing Planning
The virtual disappearance of the U.S. manufacturing base for consumer electronics and automatic cameras is an example of the failure of adequate planning for innovation. Also, the ability of foreign competition to build quality through robust design and production has made a serious dent in the market share of previously predominant U.S. car makers. The number of viable remaining U.S. passenger car manufacturers has been reduced from many a generation ago to three: General Motors, Ford, and Chrysler. The ability of Japanese automobile manufacturers to move new car models from concept into production in less than two years has presented a serious challenge to U.S. automobile makers, who typically required more than twice as long to introduce a new model into the market. The formal process of telescoping the development and production cycle into a more time-efficient effort has been called *concurrent* or *simultaneous engineering* (Section 12.1). One of the key aspects of this iterative process is to address the manufactur-

Group	Engineering Hours	
Advanced structures	811	hours
Materials	1,000	
Test	300	
Illustrations	100	
Manufacturing	210	
Total Hours	**2,421**	**hours**
Total Engineering Labor	**$35,500**	

Other Costs	Dollars
Materials	$21,500
Travel	1,500
Subcontract	10,000
Consultant	1,500
Total other costs	**$34,500**

Title: High Temperature Materials
Reference: Program 618 — High-Temperature Furnace Development
EWO No. 618-592
Product Line: High-Temperature Furnaces
Project Leader: J. Smith, Ext. 4095
Research Manager: G. Jones, Ext. 3508
Date: 12-15-79
Total Budget: $70,000
Work to be completed by: 12-31-80

All charges to this EWO must be authorized by the Project leader.

1.0 Objectives
1.1 To investigate the thermal and mechanical properties of advanced high-temperature materials.
1.2 To relate the thermal and mechanical properties of these new materials to their method of fabrication and chemical composition.
1.3 To design and test samples of these materials fabricated into components of a furnace structure.

2.0 Technical Approach
2.1 Subject new materials to increasingly high temperatures ranging up to 1500 degrees F for various lengths of time and test mechanical properties after exposure. Note dimensional changes.
2.2 Investigate correlation of thermal properties with method of fabrication and chemical composition.
2.3 Fabricate most promising materials into components of a furnace structure and test at furnace temperatures.

3.0 Facilities and capital equipment
Existing facilities at high-temperature laboratory are adequate.

4.0 Milestones
4.1 Test all materials before thermal treatment   March 15
4.2 Expose materials to thermal treatment   June 10
4.3 Test materials after thermal treatment   August 10
4.4 Fabricate promising materials   October 1
4.5 Test new components   December 30

5.0 Estimated Expenditures vs. Time

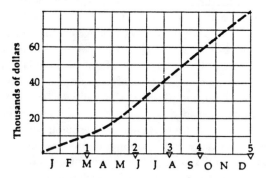

Figure 3-5.   Engineering Work Order.

ing problems as early as possible in the development cycle to ensure feasible, timely, economic, and effective solutions (Figure 3-6).

It is significant in making international comparisons that manufacturing employment has declined in the United States in the post-World War II years from 35 percent to about 20 percent of the total work force. However, the number of people employed in government service has risen from 11 percent in 1946 to about 22 percent in 1986 and, for the first time in U.S. history, exceeds the number of people employed in manufacturing (Figure 3-7). Although the reasons for this phenomenon are complex, ranging from the demise of on-shore manufacturing to the demand for more services by working households, the need for more effective manufacturing planning has been recognized. Unfortunately that awareness came in the form of a shock to many U.S. companies, which were content to pursue the traditional engineering/development/prototype/production approach, only to find themselves unable to compete with the more integrated and efficient approach of the Japanese. The irony is that Japanese management took the teachings of such American tutors as Deming, Juran, and Drucker much more seriously in the post-World War II period than their U.S. counterparts. They vigorously implemented the lessons of integrated planning for manufacturing to make quality products that meet consumer demands. It is therefore instructive to examine closely the important fundamentals of effective manufacturing planning and the closely associated control systems that implement and ensure the planning process.

Manufacturing Planning and Control Systems

Manufacturing planning is the activity that specifically describes how parts and the product are to be manufactured, including required materials, processes, tooling, equipment, sequence of operations, required verification, inspection, and testing.

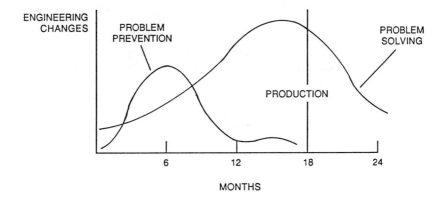

Figure 3-6.   Concurrent Engineering.

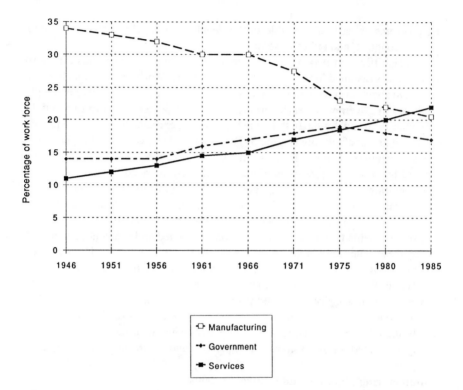

Figure 3-7.   Percentage of Work Force Employed in Manufacturing, Services, and Government.
Source: Economic Report of the President, 1985.

Manufacturing planning and control (MPC) systems deal with all aspects of the activities, from acquisition of raw materials to delivery of completed products. The control systems are also designed to support the integration of various functions, from strategic planning, budgeting, and cost control to customer service. Successful management of an MPC system requires planning the appropriate timing for the purchase of parts and the most economic distribution of purchased and manufactured parts. It also requires scheduling the needed levels of resources in concert with the company's capacity and output objectives. However, this need entails more than planning; it requires effective control and coordination of all related functions. Detailed implementation in strict conformance to the plans is critical to the MPC process, yet MPC management must also be treated in an evolutionary context.

Progress in production is usually measured in units produced, whereas monetary values may be used at the gross product level (Figure 3-4). The organization should never be satisfied with existing levels of achievement since improvements are always possible and should be implemented systematically. Improvements that yield the greatest potential benefits, such as better responsiveness to customer requests, reduced lead times for new product introductions, and higher quality levels, should be strategically selected by management with specifically assigned responsibilities for implementation.

An effective MPC system has by itself been a top priority system that manufacturing companies believe they have to implement to be competitive. Current interests focus heavily on linking various computer-activated systems into what is called computer-integrated manufacturing (CIM) (Figure 3-8). The resulting islands of automation may vary with the type of company and its products. Invariably, effective manufacturing planning and control will be a critical centerpiece of such efforts. Contrary to some popular conceptions, the use of more rapid and sophisticated equipment is not the solution to fundamental planning and control problems; it will only more rapidly bring to the surface material shortages, tooling, equipment, or manufacturing problems. In other words, unless a company is willing to invest in the necessary resources and disciplines to have an effective MPC system, further investments in CIM and attempts to institute just-in-time (JIT) manufacturing may be futile expenditures.

One important advantage of MPC systems is that they can reduce organizational slack. Savings can be measured in terms of improved output, reduced overtime, shrunk inventory investment, more rapid inventory turnover, lowered distribution costs, improved customer service, and ultimately more economic operations. One of the more direct benefits is meaningful controls, particularly if they did not previously exist. It is hardly feasible to manage a manufacturing system without being able to have measurable controls. Although the mere message that results are being measured is desirable, much more direct motivational schemes are required.[5]

The ultimate success of almost all control systems is based on the dedication and commitment of the people that operate them. Consequently, the term *empowering people* is frequently used in discussions of total quality management, to indicate that workers on all levels should have the authority to influence constructively any aspect of the system that they see to be out of control. Management of companies involved in manufacturing processes should focus on solving "control" problems, even if the solution is beyond the capability of the person who identified them. Care has to be taken no to punish the bearer of bad news. No wonder that "Eliminate Fear" is one of Deming's recommended management principles. Frequently workers assume that their inability to perform a task flawlessly may be

---

[5]In the classic Westinghouse experiments, workers responded favorably with increased output, despite worsening physical conditions, when they became aware that attention was focused on them.

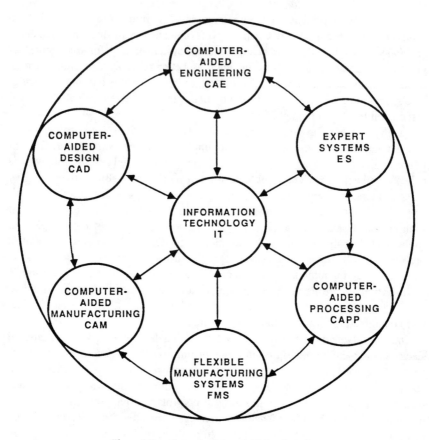

Figure 3-8   Computer-Integrated Manufacturing.

their fault, but often a machine tool may be so worn out that it cannot possibly hold to required tolerances. Such shortcomings are really management problems.

3.9   CAPACITY PLANNING

Capacity planning is the activity whose primary goal is to ensure sufficient processing capability within an organization to accomplish the required production within the desired time. If sufficient capacity cannot be made available either inside or outside the firm, management may than have to adjust the material plan based on the available capacity, assuming that satisfactory arrangements can be made with the customer. However, this decision may result in a loss of market share. For example, the inability of a major U.S. aircraft manufacturer to deliver commercial aircraft at projected delivery schedules resulted in a switch of a significant order to the consortium that produces the European Air Bus.

Producing under the capacity of the organization can be an equally serious problem for management since facilities, equipment, and people represent major cost factors and their underutilization can cause quite significant losses. The specific planning methods used to determine the capacity of a machine or a plant can be quite complex and dependent on the particular industry, plant, process, and equipment. A number of labor-intensive and semiautomated techniques are described in the literature (see, e.g., Vollman, Berry, and Whybark 1988) for carrying out the manufacturing and control process. Such systems track such factors as material availability, usage, work in progress, percent completion, rejection rates, production time, and machine loading.

The application of such techniques has been substantially extended by computerized systems. For example, personal computers (PCs) are now available for planning and implementing production, with power almost equalling that of mainframe computer systems. Additionally, modestly priced PCs can be linked together and tied into existing mainframes, which greatly enhances the flexibility, capacity, and capability of these systems. These techniques can also be very sophisticated, and all parts bar-coded and tracked by devices, similar to those at many checkout counters, that are connected to computerized tracking systems. These systems can translate the received information into many different areas, like individual product readiness and individual worker productivity. The real management challenge is of uniform loading of the capabilities to ensure maximization of costs and profits. The examination of some common optimization problems and their potential solutions is helpful in understanding the fundamental concepts involved. To minimize the total variable cost when manufacturing various quantities of parts, the lot size that will minimize the total variable cost can be calculated (Figure 3-9).

Just as airlines will try to optimize capacity through methods ranging from advanced bookings of round trips to standby seats at reduced rates, manufacturing concerns will discount large orders or accept miscellaneous job-shop work at lower than usual rates to maintain a reasonably uniform production level.

The time factor also relates to capacity planning in that raw materials can deteriorate in storage and delivery times can vary. Outdated materials are encountered in the manufacture of plastic, composites, and adhesives, in which on-dating, economic buys, and delivery schedules have to be continually balanced. The cost of waiting for materials, if fairly rapid deliveries are a possible solution, also has to be minimized. Methodical consumption records with related computer-based predictions can alleviate such problems. By utilizing effective materials controls and quality with deliveries just in time for the transformation process, desired savings can be achieved. This approach has been termed just-in-time (JIT) manu-

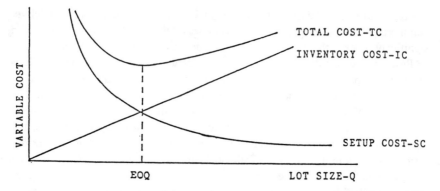

Figure 3-9.   Variable Cost Versus Quantity. EOQ is lot size which minimizes the total variable cost. Source: C. S. Snead, *Group Technology* (New York: Van Nostrand Reinhold, 1989) p. 156.

facturing. However, it sounds much easier than it actually is and deserves special consideration (see Section 12.5). Although control techniques are inevitably different for different industries, some common ground rules can be utilized in devising and implementing methods to optimize capacities and costs:

- Capacity plans must be prepared concurrently with material plans if the material plans are to be realized.
- Specific capacity planning techniques must be selected to suit the actual organizational circumstances and detail necessary to make effective management decisions.
- The more detail desired in the capacity planning system, the more data and data base maintenance will be required.
- Not only must capacity be planned but also its use must be methodically monitored and controlled (Figure 3-10).
- Capacity planning and controlling can be applied to key resources in the transformation processes encountered in manufacturing and delivery of services.

3.10   COMMON PITFALLS IN THE PLANNING PROCESS

1. The short-range view and concern of top management with the immediate profit and loss picture, preventing adequate funding and consideration of the longer-range requirements; goes hand in hand with sacrificing long-term economic gains and product viability for short-term gains
2. Lack of management understanding of important aspects of the technology involved in the business, particularly new technology; closely associated

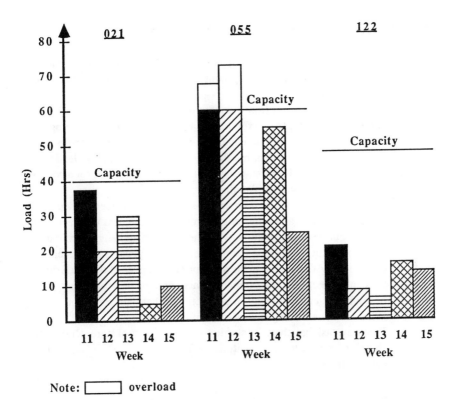

Note: ▭ overload

Figure 3-10.   Work Center Load Profiles.   Source: J. R. Meredith, *The Management of Operations* Copyright © 1980 by and reprinted by permission of John Wiley and Sons, Inc.

with tunnel vision—not seeing beyond the traditional boundaries of the business

3. Overemphasis and involvement of top management in political, accounting, legal, and other administrative aspects of company operations at the expense of close attention to product development, process improvements, and manufacturing operations

4. Failure to take even small risks and the "wait-and-see" attitude that invariably places the company in a catch-up mode relative to more versatile and mobile competition

5. Incompletely formulated plans that have not been well conceived because of lack of adequate communication between those who do the work and those who direct or are responsible for the work

6. Lack of follow-up in the form of actions and a meaningful control process throughout the product cycle

QUESTIONS AND TOPICS FOR DISCUSSION

3.1   How can a small company that cannot afford an R&D program maintain its product sales and keep up with competition that is funding its own R&D program?

3.2   How can planning for improving a product line be carried out? Outline some necessary steps or exercises in a product improvement program.

3.3   It has frequently been stated that long-range planning is given lip-service by company management but that actually most companies lead a year-to-year existence. If this statement is true, what is the risk for a company that does no long-range planning?

3.4   The chief executive of a company instructs the engineering department to perform short- and long-range planning for the next ten-year period. The executive does not know what the research and engineering groups want to do but will decide if something they suggest is not beneficial to the company. Comment on the appropriate response of the R&E division to such a directive from top management and the possible consequences of top management's position of reaction rather than proaction.

3.5   What are the advantages of documenting plans?

3.6   Prepare a task bar chart for starting a university bookstore. Draw a chart showing anticipated expenditures and milestones. (Estimate costs and activity times.)

3.7   What are the advantages of preparing engineering work orders before initiating a major technical effort?

3.8   Show diagramatically how there can be a hierarchy of plans and objectives that parallels the company organization.

3.9   A utility company that has never had a technical development group decides that it is necessary to initiate one because of increasing local, state, and government regulations; public reaction to environmental effects; and the need for new energy sources. Outline a set of plans for developing such a group and implementing its operation.

3.10   What are some of the key aspects of manufacturing planning?

3.11   What relationship should manufacturing planning have to manufacturing planning control?

3.12   How should capacity planning be integrated with manufacturing planning?

References

Hamel, Gary, and Prahalad, C. K. 1989; May/June. Strategic intent. *Harvard Business Review*, pp. 63–76.

Martin, Michael J. C. 1984. *Managing Technological Innovation Entrepreneurship*, pp. 49–50, 307. Reston, VA: Reston.

Preece, D. A. 1989. *Managing the Adoption of New Technology*, p. 82 London: Routledge.

Pyhrr, Peter A. 1977, January/February. The zero-base approach to government budgeting. *Public Administration Review.*

Sherlekar, V. S., and Dean, B. V. 1980, August. An evaluation of the initial year of zero-base budgeting in the federal government. *Management Science*, pp. 750–772.

Vollman, Thomas E., Berry, William L., and Whybark, D. Clay. 1988. *Manufacturing Planning and Control Systems*. Homewood, IL: Irwin.

4

Sources of Ideas for New Products and Processes

4.1 FOSTERING A CREATIVE ENVIRONMENT

Ideas for new and improved products and processes can come from a variety of sources both from within and outside of the company. Regardless of where the idea comes from, in today's competitive environment there must be an awareness on the part of managers at all levels of the importance of innovation and its potential advantages. Moreover, they must be instilled with the desire and motivation to identify innovation opportunities and pursue them to full evaluation, either personally or through appropriate organizational channels. This in turn means that they must appreciate the importance of innovation to their future as well as that of the organization. The company with a culture that nourishes such a spirit of innovation in its managers cannot help but improve its competitive position. That type of company culture has been proven again and again to make the important difference between success and stagnation and failure for many companies. For example, what ever happened to the companies that made Friden and Marchant calculators or the leading company in slide rule production (Keufel & Esser)?

Managers themselves can be inventors, but more likely they are not; however, they should be trained to appreciate the importance of innovation and given the responsibility of promoting it. This task can be accomplished in several different ways. In the method used by Texas Instruments, managers are given not only operational responsibility but also responsibility for identifying and putting forward new proposals and ideas, from whatever source (Haggerty 1979). At Texas Instruments about 50 key individuals were allowed to fund up to $25,000 for the preliminary investigation of new ideas. Beyond this figure additional approvals were required. Training managers in techniques for recognizing and promoting innovations is an important part of such a program.

Rewards and Recognition

Another important factor is the recognition by top management of the importance of innovation (more than lip-service) and the award of tangible rewards to personnel that make meaningful contributions.[1] In the past, inventors working for large companies received $1 for developing and filing a patent application that was accepted and published by the Patent Office. We, the authors of this text, have received twelve such dollars. The companies involved received an enormously greater monetary benefit. Today, companies are more liberal, and amounts as much as a $1,000 or more are given as rewards; in some cases, a small fraction of the profits or savings that accrue from the innovation is given to the inventor(s).

In some organizations, the head of the laboratory or the CEO privately or publicly acknowledges the contributions of an individual for a cost-cutting suggestion or invention. This and similar acknowledgments, monetary and otherwise, develop a reward system that encourages and enhances the innovation process. In one incident during a tour of a major Army research laboratory, the general who was in the touring party asked one of the junior scientists about a new development that the young man had initiated and was presently involved in. The young man's face lit up, and it was clearly evident that he was impressed with the fact that the general spoke to him by name and was familiar with his work. This is the type of recognition that helps build morale and motivation; in the long run, it can have a favorable impact on the growth and success of the company.

---

[1]Tangible rewards can be money, goods, services or percentage of profits and/or savings. Such rewards are much more meaningful then a "warm" handshake from the chief executive officer (CEO) accompanied by a certificate or plaque acknowledging the contribution.

4.2   TECHNICAL PERSONNEL

Ideas for new products and product and process improvements can come from many sources, but primarily they stem from research personnel, with marketing and salespeople a close second. It is understandable that a product or system of relatively high technical content would be most likely to be improved by scientific and engineering personnel who were heavily involved in its creation and development. Although technical personnel are an excellent source of ideas, care must be taken by the research manager to scrutinize the ideas carefully to make sure that technical challenge to the researcher is not the prime attraction rather than utility and marketability. Thus, in the development of new products and process improvements, it is necessary for marketing personnel to be consulted at various stages in the product development process, particularly in the initial stages, since at that time the greatest cost benefit can be obtained. The gain in cost benefit would be the money saved by not embarking on excessive development of a product that would not be successful in the marketplace. Manufacturing personnel must also be consulted because a salable new product that is expensive and/or difficult to manufacture may not be a worthwhile prospect.

4.3   MARKETING AND SALES PERSONNEL

Marketing and sales personnel are particularly good sources of ideas because of their daily contacts with customers and their knowledge of market conditions. Special needs for new products and improvements on existing products are often brought to the attention of the company sales representatives by the customer who is using the product and is directly affected by its shortcomings. In addition, marketing and sales personnel often come up with ideas of their own which can be worthwhile starting points for new products or product improvements. Their attendance and involvement in local, national and international sales meetings, market expositions, and product shows as well as their familiarity with the trade literature expose them to a variety of related products and activities of competing organizations. This exposure can, for the bright, enterprising salesperson, generate a host of new ideas and possibilities.

The thinking and suggestions of sales and marketing personnel should be solicited by the research manager through personal discussion with knowledgeable company salespeople and through group or individual meetings of the salespeople with key research personnel. This communication exchange is often achieved by having a formal meeting, in which the personnel heading up the various research efforts give presentations on their area of work. Salespeople and marketing personnel are invited and encouraged to comment, criticize, make suggestions, and otherwise contribute to the meeting. Such meetings can be very productive. It is advantageous to concentrate on a particular product area; personnel in the various technical groups working in that area are asked to make formal presentations, usually of 20 to 40 minutes duration, with time allowed for discussion after each presentation.

4.4   NEW PRODUCT DEVELOPMENT GROUPS

Many companies have groups whose sole function or one of their functions is to collect, generate, and evaluate ideas for new or improved products or process improvements. The name of such a group may be New Product Development Group, Technical and Economics Study Group, Advanced Systems and Technology Group, and so on. Regardless of the title, the function is primarily to serve as a clearinghouse for new ideas. The personnel may perform need analysis, feasibility studies, and economic analyses to determine how profitable a new or improved product or manufacturing process will be at various estimated levels of production. Detailed descriptions of some of these techniques are given in Chapter 6.

In addition to making the economic evaluations of the profit potential, development time, required capital investment, needed facilities, and other important criteria necessary for making the final selection decision, the new product development group often serves as a coordinator between sales and R&D. It can arrange for meetings of representatives from these two organizations and other involved departments of the company. Following such meetings, and upon conclusion of their analyses, the new product development group can make recommendations to higher management.

If there is no product development or technical and economic studies group, this function must be carried out by R&D in some other manner. It could be coordinated and spearheaded by the particular research manager involved or by a special ad hoc group or a standing committee set up specifically. Since the review and evaluation of new ideas is usually an annual exercise or performed even more frequently, it is convenient to have a group set up that performs this and related functions on a continuing basis.

Being knowledgeable and familiar with new product developments reported in the trade literature and at trade meetings and fairs as well as what is being worked on within the company, the personnel of a new product group often come up with their own ideas and suggestions for products.

4.5   IDEAS FROM CUSTOMERS AND THE PUBLIC

New ideas from the customers are always welcome because the customer, being the user of the product, has first-hand information about its efficiency, reliability, and general performance. Product improvements and new products suggested by the customer directly or through salespeople should be carefully screened and analyzed. Although customers may recognize a need, they may not know what is technically or economically feasible.

Ideas from the public must be treated with caution. If, for example, a letter is sent to the company suggesting an idea for a new product, it should be treated very carefully because of patents and the possibility of subsequent legal complications. In every instance when such a letter is received, the legal department or legal consultant of the company should be notified (M. C. Crawford 1975). If the suggested idea has no merit, all papers, drawings, letters, and other evidence of the invention should be returned with an accompanying letter thanking the individual for contacting the company and telling him or her that the company is not interested in pursuing the idea at this time. If the idea suggested does have merit, the company can invite the individual to meet company representatives to discuss the possibility of developing it. At such a meeting the idea can be more fully evaluated, and if it still seems to have potential, the necessary legal papers can be signed by the two parties. It is advisable to have a lawyer present, preferably one who is also a patent attorney.

If a patent application has not yet been applied for, and the company is really interested in the idea, the necessary information for filing should be obtained and the company should file as the assignee; or the company can ask the inventor to initiate a patent application and then negotiate with him or her further. In any case, the papers and other information submitted by the outside inventor should be handled very carefully and kept from technical personnel who could utilize the proposal. Misuse of this confidential information could lead to a subsequent lawsuit against the company by the outside inventor, claiming that the idea had been stolen. There have been numerous cases in the courts in which inventors disclosing ideas to companies have sued for many thousands of dollars, with ancillary large legal expenses for the company. See Chapter 5 for further information on patents.

4.6   TECHNOLOGICAL FORECASTING

As the need for continued technical improvements persists, companies are looking for methods of accurately predicting new product areas and process improvements that should be investigated to ensure the viability of the company. Several methods or techniques have been developed for making such estimates or predictions; these have been categorized under the general heading of technological forecasting. Forecasting can be directed toward short- or long-range planning. Although needs can be predicted as far as 20 or more years ahead, the further ahead the prediction is, the less accurate it is.

The techniques for technological forecasting have been classified in many ways by specialists in the field:[2] individual or "genius" forecasting, polls and panels, Delphi, trend extrapolation, regression analysis, correlation analysis, and so on. For the nonspecialist the various techniques can be simply categorized into two main classifications: subjective and objective.

Subjective techniques of technological forecasting are (1.) library search, (2.) scenario writing, (3.) brainstorming,[3] (4.) Delphi technique.[4] In these techniques the forecasting depends on individuals who have been selected because of their expertise or experience in a particular technical field. Ideally, these persons would be specialists in the field of interest; often they are staff scientists, engineers, or company consultants reporting to higher levels of management. They may be executive officers of the company in charge of specific product areas, although such executives are usually more versed in the operational and management aspects of the business rather than the technical aspects. When specialists are used, they have had outstanding track records in the initiation and development of new products—they tend to be both inventive and visionary. The forecasting may be done by a single individual or a group of individuals working together as a committee.

Objective techniques include trend extrapolation and trend correlation analysis and are usually carried out by specialists particularly versed in these techniques. Further description and examples both subjective and objective techniques follow.

Library Search

In this type of forecast, published articles and books on future trends are examined to see where company product areas and interests might be compatible. Public opinion polls, company reports such as market research reports, and customer surveys are examined for clues to possible new product areas. The library search

---

[2]See for example; J. R. Bright, and M. E. F. Scholman, *A Guide to Practical Technological Forecasting* (Englewood Cliffs, NJ: Prentice Hall, 1973); Henry E. Riggs, *Managing High Technology Companies* New York: Van Nostrand Reinhold, 1981), p. 25; J. E.Ullman, and B. H. Christensen, *Handbook of Engineering Management* (New York: Wiley, 1986), pp. 54–57.

[3]Although brainstorming can and is used in technological fore- casting, it is more customarily used to attack more immediate problems and activities. It is discussed in detail in Section 4.7.

[4]Delphi technique is also a common method of technological forecasting, but since it is a form of "brainpower tapping" it, too, is discussed in Section 4.7.

may be used along with any of the other techniques with the exception of brainstorming, but it can also be used singly as a basis for forecasting.

Scenario Writing

The scenario writer predicts future events with respect to product areas in a logical, chronological sequence, taking into account social and government trends as well as technological considerations. Scenario writers must be gifted and prophetic in that they must take into account nontechnical factors that may override technological considerations. As future developments are predicted and set forth, the possible role of the company's present and possible new product lines in the future environment is evaluated. With government regulation and control of manufactured products becoming more prevalent, government policies, which often reflect public opinion, can influence the future of existing company product lines. In addition, national and worldwide political events can also exert an important influence.

For example, the continued dependence on foreign oil imports (particularly from the Persian Gulf) and the depletion of oil resources has caused the U.S. government not to let up on its pressure on automobile manufacturers to develop cars with improved fuel economy. This foreign dependence on oil has also forced automobile manufacturers to continue R&D on non-gasoline-fueled vehicles. In addition, increased public and government awareness of air pollution has caused auto manufacturers to spend sizable sums on pollutant-control devices and oil companies to investigate nonfossil fuels. The increasing concern for passenger safety and decreasing repair costs are further examples of public trends in thinking that already have, and will continue to have, an appreciable impact on the R&D expenditures of automobile companies.

The desire for nonpolluting fuels will require considerable research and engineering by power-producing companies, with heavy emphasis on environmental concerns. Public reaction to the possibility of accident or sabotage and pollution of all kinds must be taken into account in long-range planning. With a realistic backdrop of an estimated range of future events, a company can better plan its course of action with respect to new and continued product areas. No less important in scenario writing is the depletion of natural resources and the prediction of upcoming technological breakthroughs and their effects. There is guesswork in this technique since admittedly it is subject to socioeconomic and political factors that are not predictable. Nevertheless, it can serve to initiate a pattern of R&D effort that can be changed or adjusted as events dictate. Furthermore, any forecasting technique selected would be subject to the same unpredictable events.

Extrapolation and Trend Analysis

Trend analysis depends only to a limited extent on the experience and prophetic talents of the individual(s) making the forecast. Instead, it requires knowledge of relatively simple arithmetic and graphic techniques. If the information available lends itself to mathematical analyses, programming the data on a computer can enhance the prediction. The events of the past can thus be used to predict the future. In Figure 4-1, for example, an extrapolation of past sales figures is used to predict future sales for a manufacturer of tennis balls. With this information the manufacturer can estimate future plant production. The company may want to initiate or emphasize technology that is oriented toward improving the quality of the tennis balls, perhaps making them more visible, more long-lasting and durable, and even cheaper, and thus increase its share of the total market. Such extrapolation assumes no changes in the factors that affect the continuance of people playing tennis.

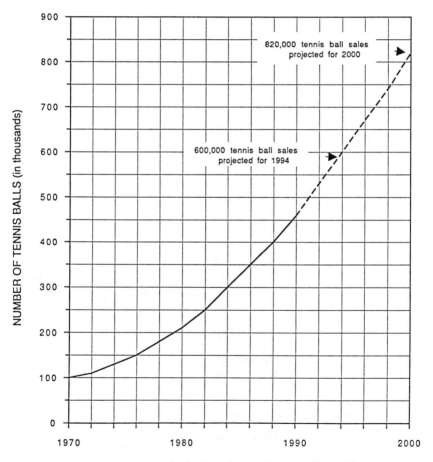

Figure 4-1.   Use of Simple Extrapolation to Determine Future Sales.

In another example (Figure 4-2) an envelope curve could be used to predict the computational capability of future high-speed computers. Still another example would be the use of an S-shaped growth curve to predict the growth in sales of a product, after some initial sales figures versus time were plotted (Figure 4-3). The constants for the exponential equation could be calculated from the growth curve of a similar product.

These extrapolations and trend analysis techniques assume that state-of-the-art technology advancements will continue at their previous historical rate and that other existing conditions such as socioeconomic and political factors will not change. This has not always been the case. Major technical breakthroughs can occur and cause discontinuities in the extrapolated curve and a stepwise, unpredicted increase. Similarly, government regulation, resource depletion, or a

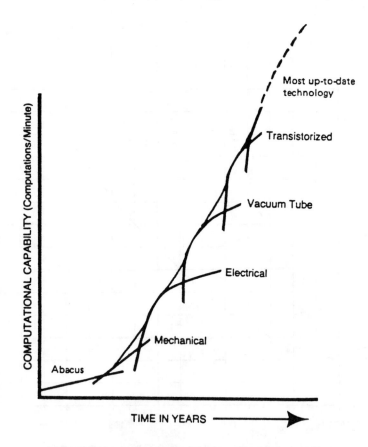

Figure 4-2.   Trendfitting for Predicting Computational Capability.

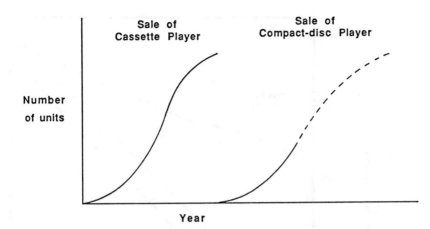

Figure 4-3.   Use of S-Type Growth Curve for Extrapolation.

political event such as war can cause a sharp decrease. In the dynamic world of today, environmental effects, political events, government decisions, international affairs, the state of the economy including the degree of unemployment, and the status of the money market can all have an effect on the sales of certain products and can upset conclusions based on extrapolations of previous performance. The development of smaller, more fuel-efficient cars is an example of government regulation affecting technical developments. Similarly, political and government decisions, as well as environmental and economic factors, are affecting the rate of development and use of many chemical products (e.g., aerosol sprays and DDT).

Although extrapolation and trend analysis techniques can be useful in predicting new product goals and the ancillary technology, there are pitfalls. A spectacular example of the failure of naive extrapolation is shown in Figure 4-4. Here extrapolation of federal R&D expenditures and the gross national product (GNP) from 1947-1968 into the future shows that the two would be exactly equal at about the year 2000. This obviously is an erroneous prediction and cannot be used as a guide for R&D planning; it would constitute a misuse of the extrapolation technique.

Despite the pitfalls of extrapolation methods, the advantages outweigh the disadvantages. These methods can be used effectively for predicting technology trends and the need for product improvement and development, providing their limitations are recognized.

4.7   TECHNIQUES FOR TAPPING BRAINPOWER

Numerous techniques have been successfully used for tapping brainpower,; for example, brainstorming, Delphi method, quality circles, and suggestion boxes.

3 1303 00179 6706

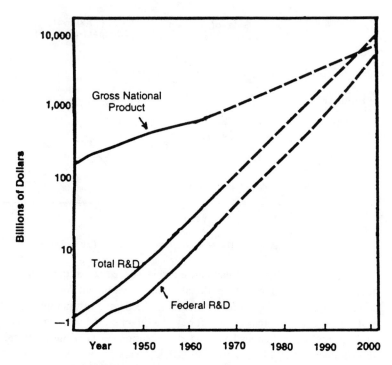

Figure 4-4.   GNP and R&D: Failure of Naive Extrapolation.   Source: Adapted from D. Allison, "The Civilian Technology Lag," *International Science and Technology*, December 1963, p. 48 Based on NSF and business statistics in *Statistical Abstracts*.

Brainstorming

This subjective technique brings together knowledgeable people or preferably experts in a certain subject area and promotes an interchange of ideas. Companies employ this technique to obtain guidance in planning new directions and product areas or for solving a complex problem. The members of the panel may all be employed by the company or they may also be consultants drawn from outside the company. The coordinator or moderator of the meeting enunciates certain ground rules initially so that the expenditure of time (and money) is limited to the greatest extent possible since the personnel involved are usually highly paid. One important ground rule is that all ideas are welcome, no matter how "wild" they may seen, and no ideas are ridiculed. Another rule is that everybody is given an opportunity to express his or her ideas, and the more ideas the better. The intent is to provide an atmosphere of free discussion with no inhibition of ideas.

Under such circumstances a synergistic effect can occur, in which one person builds on the idea of another, and the net result is that the totality of the ideas presented is greater than the sum of each individual's ideas when presented separately. The group leader or moderator must make certain that a dominant individual or several such individuals do not monopolize the discussion, thereby not allowing time or opportunity for less aggressive members of the panel to participate. The moderator must not allow the discussion to be sidetracked in consideration of irrelevant material, which dissipates the time, energy, and concentration of the participants. It is advisable to have members of the panel at more or less the same organizational level—the presence and vociferations of higher-level management personnel can intimidate those with less authority and defeat the purpose of the brainstorming session.

Advantages of the technique can be summarized as follows:

- Many new ideas can be generated in a relatively short time.
- There is no inhibition of ideas—everyone is encouraged and has the opportunity to contribute.
- A synergistic effect enhances the discussion and can lead to promising suggestions.
- It is often possible to obtain a consensus on a particular product area or problem.

Constraints on the technique are the following:

- A dominant, vociferous, or overly aggressive individual may monopolize and stifle the discussion and the generation of ideas by the group.
- The members of the panel should be in the same peer group so that a member of higher management cannot impose ideas on the group, limiting attendance and participation.
- Irrelevant material may be brought up that wastes the time, energy, and concentration of the participants.
- Group pressure (a "bandwagon" effect) may suppress good ideas. It is usually instigated by a desire of the group to get the matter and the meeting over with.
- Disagreements and even personality clashes may disrupt the idea-generating process and prevent consensus.
- An effective moderator or coordinator is required.

All in all, the advantages of the brainstorming technique more than outweigh the disadvantages.

Following the brainstorming session the group leader, preferably with a select committee, can examine the ideas and suggestions made and select the most reasonable and promising. These are then written up and presented to upper management as new product possibilities, process improvements, or problem solutions.

Crawford Slip Method

An interesting and convenient variation of the brainstorming technique is the Crawford Slip Method (C. C. Crawford 1985). It carries out the brainstorming process in a manner that allows a number of questions on a specific topic to be answered in relatively rapid order with effective documentation. The members of the brainstorming session record brief responses to key questions on small slips of paper or cards. The response time is limited, usually less than ten minutes per question, and the slips or cards are collected by the coordinator or group leader. The principal advantage of this technique appears to be a rapid, organized, and disciplined manner of conducting brainstorming sessions with a high probability of obtaining a large number of documented responses within a short time. According to Krone (1988):

> The method normally gathers a group's know-how, views, and recommendations INDEPENDENTLY, ANONYMOUSLY, and RAPIDLY. You can expect about 400 ideas on problems and solutions to those problems from a group of 20 people in a 30 minute session. Quality will be good as well as quantity because the anonymity feature removes most of the fear people have in exposing their ideas orally in a group and the parallel brain-processing format precludes the inefficiencies of sequential oral discussions. This is a qualitative systems analysis tool and has almost as many variations as possible applications.

Delphi Technique

The Delphi technique, named after the legendary oracle, has received considerable attention in recent years. It was developed by Norman Dalkey and Olaf Helmer for military estimation problems at the Rand Corporation in the early 1950s and lay dormant until the early 1960s, when Helmer (1966) revitalized the method by applying it to a major technological forecasting study. It is similar to brainstorming, except that the panel of experts do not have to be together at a meeting place, but instead can work separately at their own locations and are coordinated by a moderator or coordinator.

The effort is usually initiated by top management's desire to know what product or process improvement areas the company should emphasize in the future with respect to R&D funds and company activities in general. A staff consultant, vice president, or some other knowledgeable person is selected to head the effort. This individual, either alone or with the assistance of a staff, selects a panel of experts who have had a good track record in making similar predictions in the past. This requirement is not easily met, and the coordinator must usually settle for the best people available. The experts may be employed by the company as executives, specialists, or staff consultants, or they may be outside consultants. The coordinator and staff then prepare a set of questions whose answers can provide the information that top management is seeking. This is a critical step; how well it is accomplished is the basis for the success or failure of this particular forecasting technique. A copy of the set of questions is sent to each of the selected panel experts, who is requested to answer the questions and return the completed questionnaire within a certain period of time.

Upon receipt of the answers to the first questionnaire, the coordinator and staff analyze the results to determine the median value and the intraquartile range (IQR) for the responses to each question. The IQR is the interval containing the middle 50 percent of the responses; 25 percent of the answers fall on one side and 25 percent fall on the other side of the median value. Since the method is particularly suited to the estimation of probable dates for a particular event, treatment of the data in this manner is convenient and advantageous.

Following analysis and summation of the data from the first questionnaire, the second questionnaire is sent out asking the same questions, but this time the median value and the IQR range obtained from the answers in the first questionnaire are shown next to each question. The experts are asked to reconsider the questions in view of the results reported. If their second responses are outside the IQR, they are asked to provide reasons for their answers. The answers to the second questionnaire are received by the coordinator and staff and again analyzed to determine the median and the IQR. Arguments for, say, an earlier or a later date are recorded next to the particular question, and the third questionnaire is sent out.

The third questionnaire asks that the experts answer the same questions taking into account the arguments for the later and earlier dates. If they have a rebuttal to the arguments given by those outside the IQR, they can present them. Again the opportunity is given for answers to be changed and reasons stated. Upon return of the third questionnaire the analysis is repeated, the median and IQR ranges once more adjusted, and the questionnaire sent out once more, this time with both the arguments for and against being outside the IQR documented next to the appropriate questions. This usually consitutes the final round of questions and offers the experts the opportunity to see the opinions of the other experts and make their final decisions.

The results are summarized by the coordinator and staff and presented to the management personnel who requested the study. If the Delphi analysis has been successful, there will be guidance for future goals and the rate of R&D expenditures that should be initiated to achieve them. At the Corning Glass Works the Delphi technique has been successfully used in a number of instances to estimate demand for new products (Stephanou 1981).

Advantages of the Delphi technique can be summarized as follows:

- It allows the use of experts who are not locally available.
- There are none of the disadvantages of brainstorming, such as the effect of

dominant personality, group pressure, the bandwagon effect, or loss of time because of discussion of irrelevant material.

- Each panel member has the time to deliberate and carefully think out answers.
- Information available to some experts is made available to all so that there is valuable exchange of information.
- The results can be quantified.

Disadvantages are the following:

- It is not suitable to all types of product opportunity predictions. It seems to be particularly adaptable to the timing of R&D effort, although it can be modified to determine other facets of R&D.
- It is very much dependent on the ability of the coordinator, working alone or with a staff, to develop a meaningful set of questions that will adequately reveal the new product, marketing, and process opportunities in which the company is interested.
- Group pressure is not eliminated completely since there is a tendency even for experts to go along with the group that is within the intraquartile range.
- The method does not allow for person-to-person and person-to-group interaction, so there is no opportunity for open discussion and the building on another's ideas and thoughts, as with brainstorming.

This technique for condensing ideas from a number of sources has had considerable success, but it is somewhat limited in the type of problems it can conveniently treat.

Quality Circles

The technique of quality circles, which includes brainstorming, is described in Section 13.6. As a method of generating ideas it has value because it involves personnel actually working with the manufacturing processes.

Other Techniques

There are, of course, many other techniques for obtaining ideas: suggestion systems, polling, questionnaires, creativity seminars, interactive groups, idea-association sessions, and so on (Krone 1988).

An excellent example of how a suggestion program can be successful in obtaining contributions from employees is the Productivity Improvement Program (PIP), which has been in force at the Southern California Edison Company. This program has given substantial financial awards to employees over an 11-year period for suggestions that have cut operational costs, increased efficiency, or improved the quality of service. Such suggestions have included the design and development of new tools for transmission line repairs, new electrical metering devices and switches, and improved techniques for cable installations. Awards have ranged from $2,400 to $12,000, depending on the cost saving, safety feature, or other effectiveness measure (*Edison News* 1990).

4.8   GOVERNMENT SOURCES

Government publications obtainable from the U.S. Government Printing Office and from individual government agencies can sometimes provide ideas for new products or processes. Examples of such agencies and publications are the following:

- U.S. government research reports
- Publications of the National Science Foundation
- Publications of the National Academy of Science
- National Bureau of Standards journal and reports
- NASA reports and documents (Office of Technology Utilization)
- Unclassified ASTIA[5] documents
- Office of Technical Service

In addition, the government has a number of patents, acquired as a result of sponsoring technology and R&D work, that are available for use by the general public. These patents are itemized in a government publication entitled *Patent Abstracts of Government-Owned Inventions for License*, which can be obtained from the U.S. Government Printing Office, Washington, DC. However, the various agencies differ in their policy concerning how such patents are made available to industry and the public. NASA, (1979), for example, grants waivers of patent rights to contractors and individuals: "The grant of waivers give a petitioner for patent waiver exclusive rights to commercialize an invention for the ultimate use by the general public while reserving to government free use of the invention." Other agencies, such as DOD, are more restrictive.

Information of specific product and technology areas can be obtained by contacting the Federal Laboratory Consortium for Technology Transfer (FLC). Initiated by DOD in 1971, it has grown to 180 laboratories representing 11 federal agencies. Its objective is to transmit technology developed in government laboratories to industry and state and local governments. An important publication of this

---

[5]Armed Services Technical Information Agency.

organization is "Resource Directory," available from the National Science Foundation, Washington, DC.

If a company is interested in performing technical work or developing a new system for a government agency, the *Commerce Business Daily*, issued by the Department of Commerce, can be a fruitful source. This publication lists brief descriptions of all government procurement invitations, contract awards, R&D, and technical work, as well as subcontracting possibilities and foreign business opportunities when work for a U.S. government agency is involved.

The *Official Gazette of the United States Patent Office* can also be a source of new ideas since it classifies and describes over 5 million patents dating back almost 200 years. Although this is an overwhelming quantity of material, classification and computerized retrieval techniques allow for ready information in any particular product area.

4.9   OTHER SOURCES

Some companies, especially those with offices in foreign countries, keep a constant watch for new products that might be suitable for manufacture in the United States or elsewhere. There would be patent rights to respect, royalties to pay, and licensing agreements to be made with the particular foreign country. This is not impossible, however, and many products exhibited in trade fairs in Europe and other countries find their way eventually into the American market through agreements between foreign and American companies. A company president or other company executive may see the product advertised or exhibited in a foreign country and contact the producing company. The American companies may further develop the product, if it is still in the infant stage, before marketing it.

Many American companies fund university laboratories or research institutes to carry out research in the areas of their product interest. These research programs often lead to new products or improved processes for the company. However, universities like to have research work published, and the right to publish is usually spelled out in the contractual agreement with the funding company. Since secrecy on new product development cannot be maintained under such circumstances, the nature of the new development can shortly become known to the competition. Some universities may agree to the inclusion of a secrecy clause, which would be honored if the research leads to new products, but this would be against the generally accepted practice of publishing research results in the technical archive journals.

The agreement about patent rights should also be spelled out in contractual agreements with outside organizations performing funded research. It is to the advantage of the company to include in the contract a clause giving the company exclusive and license-free use of any patent that develops as a result of the funded research. In the case of contracting with a research institute, the publication problem is eliminated because most research institutes are more interested in obtaining the economic benefit from doing the work than in publishing it. Most of their technical personnel already have degrees, and the institute has goals that have higher priority than publishing technical and scientific papers.

Constant perusal of the current technical and trade literature in the product and manufacturing fields of interest can often lead to new ideas for products or processes for the company.[6] This research could be carried out by librarians, by the technical personnel of the research and engineering laboratory, and by sales and marketing personnel.

Questions and Topics for Discussion

4.1 It is predicted that most successful product ideas will result from technology pull (market-driven forces), rather than from technology push (technology-drive forces). Explain what this statement means and why it is probably true.

4.2 Many new product areas stem from the supervisory and managerial levels of companies. How can this be explained?

4.3 Enumerate the duties of a new products development group in the form of a group charter.

4.4 Outline a program that a company could use to explore systematically government publications for new product and technology spinoff ideas.

4.5 What cautions and procedures must be taken if an unsolicited idea that has considerable promise is received by the company in the mail?

4.6 The Delphi technique for technological forecasting is negatively evaluated by some critics. Under what conditions could the Delphi technique be valuable? Not valuable?

4.7 It has been stated that defensive research will constitute a larger proportion of future technology effort than ever before. Explain what is meant by this statement and comment on its validity.

4.8 Enumerate and discuss some of the pros and cons of extrapolation and trend analysis techniques for technological forecasting.

4.9 In what situations can brainstorming be most effective in assisting the decision maker?

---

[6]Archive journals for the fields of engineering, chemistry, physics, and so on could also be included in the literature review. They would supply more basic scientific studies but could provide ideas for new concepts and possible applications.

References

Cetron, M. G., and Monahan, T. I. 1968. An evaluation and appraisal to technological forecasting. *Technological Forecasting for Industry and Government: Methods and Application*, ed. J. R. Bright, pp. 144–179. Englewood Cliffs, NJ: Prentice Hall.

Crawford, C. C. 1985, Spring. Crawford Slip Method (CSM). *Air Force Journal of Logistics*, pp. 28–30.

Crawford, Merle C. 1975, January. Unsolicited product idea—Handle with care. *Research Management* 18(1), 19.

Edison News. 1990, May. 46 employees honored at PIP/QSRA luncheon, p. 6.

Graham, Russell. 1984, February 2. "Quality Circles in the Professional Environment." Talk given at the meeting of the Project Management Institute, Los Angeles.

Haggerty, Patrick E. 1979. "The Corporation and the Individual." Address in a series of lectures, The American University: Community and Individual, University of Texas, Dallas.

Helmer, Olaf. 1966. *Social Technology.* New York: Basic Books.

Krone, Robert M. 1988, October 19–21. "Brainpower Productivity." Paper presented at the annual regional conference of the Society for Public Administration (ASPA), Oakland, CA.

Stephanou, S. E. 1981. *Management: Technology, Innovation and Engineering*, p. 65. Bend, OR: Daniel Spencer.

5

Patents, Trade Secrets, and Copyrights

5.1   IMPORTANCE OF PATENTS IN TECHNOLOGY MANAGEMENT

As a result of the innovative nature of R&D work, situations involving potential patents often arise. To protect the company's interest, the technology manager should be able to recognize these situations and know the appropriate, legally accepted procedures to follow. Patents can be a source of considerable revenue to the company, either directly, in the form of royalties from licensed patents, or indirectly, in the form of sales of products that others cannot produce because the company holds the patent rights. Patents are a type of property (i.e., intellectual property) inasmuch as they can be sold, licensed, or traded, as well as kept and improved upon. The development and issuance of patents provide a measure of protection from the unfair use by competitors of the company's investment of time and money in basic and applied R&D activities. Large companies involved in technology usually have one or more patent lawyers in their legal department or on staff; smaller companies that cannot afford full-time legal assistance will have an outside patent lawyer handle their patent work (often on a retainer contract).

There is a school of thought that considers patents to be an unreliable barrier to encroachment by the competition. Riggs (1983) argues,

> First, most patents can be legally circumvented or avoided if the market opportunity is sufficiently attractive to potential competitors. Second, patents are expensive, particularly filing them in foreign countries (a necessary step for any important patent). Third, a distressingly high percentage of patents is held to be invalid (typically because of the existence of "prior art") when tested in court. Fourth, defending a patent position either offensively or defensively is expensive. Frequently, the smaller high-technology company has no practical alternative but to license its patents to larger competitors or take licenses from large companies under patents that it feels are of questionable strength.

This argument may apply to high-technology companies, in which product life cycles and improvements are short-lived (six months to two years, for example), but for the average company with products that serve a never-ending, essential need, the protection afforded by patents is absolutely necessary. Consider the fact that the number of patents issued increased from 1,600 a week in 1988 to 2,100 in 1989. According to Herbert Warmsley, executive director of Intellectual Property Owners, a Washington association that represents inventors, this increase has caused the largest backlog in the issuance of patents in 20 years (*New York Times* 1989).

Large and small companies and organizations that employ engineers or scientists and do development work almost invariably require a newly employed technical worker to sign an employment agreement that includes a patent application assignment clause. In signing this agreement, the employees essentially agree to assign any patent application for work they invent that is within the scope of their employment. Thus they waive all ownership rights to the use and disposition of any patent that they are the inventor of during and even subsequent to their period of employment. An example of such an agreement is shown in Figure 5-1. This particular agreement is fairly generous; many companies do not pay royalty income but give the inventor a monetary reward when the patent is issued. It is interesting to note that the right of companies to require patent agreements as a prerequisite to employment has been under criticism for some time and has been the subject of proposed legislation in defense of engineers and scientists. An

INSTITUTE PATENT POLICY: Certain of the inventions made by employees in the line of duty or with the use of Institute facilities will be patented in order to protect the Institute and the public. These patents will be assigned to the Institute or its nominee, and all costs involved in obtaining patents borne by the assignee.

The Institute Patent Agreement is included here for your information and all employees are required to sign it upon employment.

Inventors will receive a proportion of royalty income accruing from patent properties in accordance with the established and announced patent policy in force at the date of signing of the Institute Patent Agreement.

Inventions and discoveries made by an employee on his own time and without the aid of Institute facilities are the sole property of the inventor.

PATENT AGREEMENT

WHEREAS, the XYZ Research Institute, a California corporation (herein referred to as "the Institute"), has certain responsibilities to see that inventions made at the Institute be administered for the best interests of the public and of the Institute; and in accordance with its contractual agreements with sponsors of research at the Institute;

THEREFORE, by this agreement, executed by me and accepted by the Institute, I hereby promise and agree as follows:

I will notify the Institute promptly of any discovery, innovation or invention (hereinafter all designated "invention") which might possibly be patentable and which is made in the course of my duties at the Institute, or with the use of Institute facilities. At the request of the Institute or its nominee, I will assign to the Institute or its nominee all patent rights I may have to any such invention in the United States and foreign countries. I will supply all information and execute all papers necessary for the purpose of prosecuting patent applications on such inventions. Expenses for such applications shall be borne entirely by the Institute or its nominee. I understand that the Institute reserves the right to abandon the prosecution of any patent applications.

Furthermore, I will disclose promptly and fully to the Institute all matters, whether patentable or not, that I may solely, or jointly with others, develop wholly or partly in the course of any work in which I may engage covered by any contract between the Institute and others (including the United States government). If called upon, I will execute all documents and supply all information which the Institute or its nominee deems necessary or desirable in order to perform its patent obligations under any such contract.

It is understood as a part of this agreement that if the Institute receives revenue from patents on inventions assigned to it by me pursuant to this agreement, I shall share in these funds according to the established and announced patent policy of the Institute in force at the date of this agreement.

This agreement is made in consideration of my employment by the Institute, in consideration of the continuance of my employment and of future employment, and for other valuable consideration.

It is further understood that this agreement is part of terms of my employment, and any contract of employment heretofore or hereafter entered into between me and the Institute shall be deemed to include this agreement except to the extent that an express provision of such contract of employment is inconsistent therewith.

It is further understood that performance on my part of the terms of this agreement is one of the purposes for which I am employed and that such performance will be taken into consideration and relied upon by the Institute in making decisions as to the assignment of work to me.

It is further understood that the Institute may and will rely upon the foregoing agreement in making contracts with others in which the Institute may undertake obligations with respect to discoveries made by its employees.

Dated: . . . . ,19 . . . . .

Name (Print). . . . .

Signature. . . . .

ACCEPTED: XYZ Institute

By. . . . .

Figure 5-1.   Example of a Patent Agreement.

In consideration of my employment by the ABC Co. or by any of its subsidiaries, affiliates, or successor entities (hereinafter referred to as the "Company"), I agree as follows:

1. During the period of my employment I shall discharge such duties as may be assigned to me by the Company and shall exercise my inventive faculties for and on behalf of the Company to the best of my ability and shall not engage in any other employment or any other activity that conflicts with or impairs my obligations as an employee of the Company.

2. I understand that the Company engages in engineering, design, research, development and consultation and that the Company does accumulate, and from its customers does receive, confidential information which is not published or otherwise in the public domain. I shall at all times during the period of my employment and at all times thereafter hold in confidence for the use and benefit of the Company all such confidential information acquired by me from either the Company or its customers relating to the Company's or its customers' products, processes or business, including, but not limited to, its or their instructions, departmental procedures, circular letters, inter-organization forms, notes, records, curves, drafts, tracings, calculations, techniques, formulae, drawings, apparatus, and all other data in any way concerning the business of the Company or its customers. During and subsequent to my employment by the Company I shall not disclose or use (except in the course of my employment by the Company and pursuant to the rules of the Company) any such information described in this paragraph.

3. On termination of my employment with the Company I shall return to the Company all originals, copies or duplicates of any and all papers, documents, models, samples or other matters relating to the business of the Company and I shall not retain a copy, draft, duplicate, representation, or extract thereof.

4. I shall not disclose to the Company or its customers, or permit the Company or its customers to use, any confidential information or material belonging to others.

5. All inventions, discoveries, developments and improvements (whether patentable or not) made or conceived by me, solely or jointly with others, during my employment with the Company, which pertain to the products, processes or business of the Company, or which result from or are suggested by or otherwise arise out of my work, are the sole property of the Company. I shall keep complete records of such inventions, discoveries, developments and improvements and shall promptly and fully disclose and assign them to the Company.

6. At the Company's expense, I shall execute such assignments, patent applications and other documents and do such other things as may be deemed necessary or proper by the Company to enable the Company to perfect its title and obtain patents on such inventions, discoveries, developments and improvements during the period of my employment and for one year thereafter.

7. Attached is a list and brief description of all inventions, discoveries, developments and improvements made or conceived by me prior to my employment with the Company on which no patent application has yet been filed. Should any question arise as to whether an invention, discovery, development or improvement was made or conceived during my employment by the Company, all such items not on this list shall be presumed to belong to the Company.

8. This agreement shall be governed by the law of the State of California.

Dated. . . . . .Employee . . . .

Witness. . . . .

Figure 5-2.   Employee Agreement—Invention and Data.

agreement that includes patents and precludes disclosure of company and customer data is shown in Figure 5-2.

Because of the possible major monetary and competitive value of patents, it is imperative that new product and process development managers maintain a sharp lookout for patentable items; they should also see that notebooks are properly kept and that patent disclosures and applications are made available to the company's legal staff in a timely and expeditious manner.[1]

---

[1]Patent disputes totaling many millions and even billions of dollars have involved major competitors such as Polaroid and Kodak, Motorola and Hitachi, and Smith International and Hughes Tool.

5.2   THE U.S. PATENT SYSTEM

Patents are legal documents that describe and then claim the parameters of the invention. They represent a legal agreement between the government and the inventor or his or her assignee. Invention involves the creation of something that did not exist before. The invention may be a completely new method or apparatus, or it may be a combination of old methods or components that give rise to a new use, performance, or effect.

The steps in the development and lifetime of a patent are the following:

1. Idea
2. Patent search
3. Preparation for filing
   a. Reduction to practice
   b. Patent disclosure
4. Application
5. Granting of patent by U.S. Patent Office
6. Expiration 17 years after grant

A knowledge of the important essentials of each of these steps by the R&D manager is necessary so that no key elements are omitted and the company's interests are protected.

Patents are available in the United States as well as in most foreign countries; the U.S. patent system will be the system discussed in this section (international patents are discussed in Section 5.12). The original intent of the U.S. Patent Law, passed in 1790, was to protect inventors from the usurping by others of their independent and original efforts. It gives them inventor the monopolistic rights of manufacture and sale of the patented product for a limited time (17 years) and thus encourages innovation and progress. They may grant these rights to someone else (assignee). The patent statue requires the inventors to disclose the details of their invention in the specification of the patent; at the end of 17 years, the patent expires and thereafter the invention is freely available for production and use by others. Through the years the intent of the law has remained the same, although there have been many revisions and additions. Recently there have been reappraisals of our patent laws by Congress, which may result in some further changes (see Section 5.13).

Since 1790 there have been over 5 million patents issued by the U.S. Patent Office. Presently over 100,000 patents are issued each year. It has been pointed out by knowledgeable observers that a high percentage, perhaps over 90 percent, of these patents are of no commercial value. Regardless of this and other objections, the approximately 10 percent of useful patents issued constitute a sizable number that can have considerable economic value. The patents for the Polaroid Land Camera is an excellent example of a patent that has provided protection and continued profit for many years. As a result of its strong patent on this type of camera, the Polaroid Corporation increased its sales by a factor of about 14 in the 1950s and realized further substantial sales increases in the 1960s. More recently Kodak marketed a competitive instant camera but lost heavily in an infringement lawsuit brought by Polaroid.

There are two general categories of patents, utility patents and design patents.[2] Examples of utility patents are mechanical and electrical devices, methods of manufacture, processes, and chemical compositions. Examples of design patents are wallpaper patterns, chinaware, and car ornaments. Design patents are less important than utility patents and will not be discussed in any detail. They provide protection for a period of 14 years. Utility patents are enforceable for 17 years and cannot be renewed; they make up the major portion of current U.S. patents. Under certain conditions patents may be extended, for example, if marketing is delayed because of clinical testing requirements by the Food and Drug Administration or if the patent has military significance and is kept secret by the DOD.

5.3   REQUIREMENTS FOR PATENTABILITY

A number of conditions or criteria have been prescribed by the U.S. Patent Office as necessary so that an invention may be qualified as sufficiently inventive to warrant the issuance of a patent:

1. The invention must contain something new; that is, there must be a degree of novelty over the state of the art in the field of the invention. The novel aspect can be exhibited by a single element or system or by a new combination of old elements. Immediately after the passage of the Patent Law in 1790 and for some time later, a "flash of genius" had to be discernible in the patent application. This clause was later eliminated by Congress because of the obvious difficulty of deciding whether such an inspiration really did occur and when.

2. The applicant must be the first inventor, that is, the first to conceive and reduce the invention to practice. The patent application must be filed within one year prior to the first public disclosure or offer for sale of the subject matter. Such disclosures include oral and written presentations at symposia,

---

[2]One other category is a plant patent, which involves the invention or discovery of an asexually produced variety of plant. This type of patent is relatively rare and will not be discussed here.

conferences and sales meetings, and critical publications such as under-graduate and graduate theses available from university libraries. If a patent application has already been filed with the Patent Office, an "interference" may be declared. An interference arises when two inventors claim the same invention or, more precisely, have a major portion of identical claims or subject matter. In this case the inventor who is first to conceive and diligently reduces the invention to practice is granted the patent.

3. The patent must be useful. This requirement can be satisfied, for example, by a toy, in which the utility lies in the satisfaction of a need for entertainment. The question of what is useful can be controversial, but for companies this is an academic question since a company would not want to apply for a patent on an item that had little possibility of being used. For the item to be salable it would have to be useful in some way.

4. The invention must not be obvious to one skilled in the art to which the invention pertains.[3] The determination of what is and what is not obvious is often a difficult task and can be controversial. If the concept is already known by others skilled in the art, is presently being used, or has been referred to in the publicly available literature, no patent can be issued.

5. The patent application must be filed no later than one year after it has been patented in another country.

The substitution of a new material or part in an existing system is not considered patentable unless it produces some new or unexpected result. Merely changing the size and not the operation of a device also does not in and of itself constitute novelty. A newly discovered scientific principle or law of nature cannot be patented, nor can a new mathematical formula or algorithm. Computer programs are usually copyrighted although there can be a possibility of a patent if the program is used in conjunction with hardware. A few years ago the Supreme Court decreed that new products or processes that employ computer software in a special way are eligible for patent protection (*Inside R&D* 1981). Sometimes it is preferable to treat a unique computer program as a trade secret (see Section 5.9) rather than disclose it in a copyright.

In court decisions what *cannot* be patented has been well defined; therefore, when patentability is in question it may be necessary to apply for the patent in order to obtain a final determination. Because of the cost of patent prosecution it would be done only in cases in which the promise of economic gain was worthy of the

---

[3]Questions of obviousness generally arise when the patent examiner combines several references in contending that a skilled artisan would view these references and conclude that the invention as claimed may be obviously obtained from such a combination.

expenditure necessary for obtaining the patent. The essence of patentability is that the invention is new, novel, and useful.

Although an idea or concept cannot be patented without "reduction to practice," confirmation of reduction to practice is not required by the Patent Office. Reduction to practice would mean building and testing a model, for example. Filing an application has been considered by the Patent Office to constitute a type of constructive reduction to practice. However, if interference occurs and there is subsequent litigation, the case can be considerably weakened if there has been no real reduction to practice.

5.4   KEEPING RECORDS

An important procedure in conducting research and technology is to document properly all technical work that can lead to patents. The work must be described in a bound, stitched notebook (not looseleaf) by the engineer or scientist doing it. A ledger-type record book with numbered pages is suitable for this purpose; writing should be in indelible ink. The description of the work does not have to be exhaustive in detail but it should accurately and briefly describe the experiment, test, or procedure that will be involved in the patent. In most research laboratories research notebooks are issued to each scientist or engineer, who is instructed to keep daily records of the experimental and other laboratory work. In addition, the person's supervisor should read and sign the notebook at periodic intervals—not necessarily every day. Usually a stamp is prepared that reads

> **Read and understood by (name of reviewer). Date** . Every page of the notebook is so stamped. The supervisor signs in the blank space and dates his or her signature. The corroborating signature could be provided by a peer working in the same laboratory and familiar with the work, but it is better done by the immediate supervisor so that he or she can be more knowledgeable of the work being done and also recognize patent possibilities.

Drawings and diagrams should be used wherever possible to explain how equipment or components were configured and to verify the conception and diligent reduction to practice. The details of important tests, including the apparatus used, the conduct of the test, and the results, are particularly important because they can provide proof of reduction to practice, often a key factor in patent litigation. Frequently records kept in this manner will never be used, but in the event there is patent litigation, the appropriate evidence is at hand to refute the challenge and provide basis for a defense.

Keeping notebooks becomes, therefore, a matter of insurance for the company as well as providing a record of research for subsequent referral. Such records are also valuable to the research employee for writing progress reports and memos. If the employee leaves the company or is transferred, a new employee can have access to the details of what has been done and carry on the work with minimum interruption and loss of continuity.

5.5   THE PATENT SEARCH

The patent search is usually done by a patent lawyer or by a specially trained patent searcher, although it could be done by an engineer. The trained specialist who is 100 percent devoted to this type of work is the most proficient and effective person to perform the exhaustive search that is necessary. The principal source of patent information is the U.S. Patent Office Search Room Files. The patents in the search room are cataloged in a computer data base and are accessible to the public by the use of computer terminals in the Patent Office.[4]

Design patents are designated by D before their number; the number is determined by the chronological sequence of patents that have been issued. There are only a relatively small number of design patents compared to the much larger number of utility patents. This latter type is divided into over 300 groupings or classes. The classes are further subdivided into more than 64,000 subclasses.

With the large number of classes and subclasses, it can be a formidable task to make a patent search. However, computerized and microfiche techniques have substantially simplified the process. One can obtain guidance by asking the Patent Office what classes and subclasses would contain patents pertinent to a particular subject area. The *Official Gazette*s of the U.S. Patent Office are available at major cities in the United States, primarily at public and large university libraries. The *Official Gazette* is a weekly publication listing patents that have been issued for that week. Each listing contains the identification of the patent and a figure showing the invention and Claim 1 of the patent. The enumerated claims describe briefly the subject matter of the invention, reciting the distinctive features that make it different from what is old or previously used. A complete listing of locations can be obtained by writing to the Department of Commerce, U.S. Patent Office, Washington, DC. The patent search centers each have an index to classification as well as yearly indexes of patents, both of which are published by the Patent Office.

Sometimes large companies will maintain a patent file on subject matter of

---

[4]Private on-line computer services also provide patent search capability, and a skilled searcher can complete a search quickly and inexpensively.

interest to the company. The *Official Gazette* and other publications of the Patent Office are used to keep the file current. This file can be of considerable assistance to the scientist or engineer who is anxious to move ahead on a new idea and does not want to, or cannot, wait for the more formal and lengthy search involved in working with the patent or legal department of the company. If the idea is preempted by an existing patent, found as a result of the patent search, abandoning the idea at this early date in the R&D program can save considerable expense. If new ideas are the object of the patent search, it may be that several expired or existing patents can provide clues to new concepts that should be considered. In using concepts or offshoots of concepts from existing patents, care must be exercised not to infringe the claims of the existing patents (Section 5.8).

5.6   THE DISCLOSURE

The disclosure of invention, or patent disclosure, is a form that is filled out by the inventor to establish the essential details of the invention and a record date that can stand up in court or be used in any litigation concerning the patent. The purpose of this form is twofold. First, it can summarize and supplement notebook data, which may be spread over many pages. Second, it establishes and documents the date of conception and the date of the first reduction to practice with corroborating witnesses. It is signed by the inventor and at least one witness. The date of conception is the date when the inventor first thought of the idea. For legal authenticity this date must be verified or established by a notebook entry or a patent disclosure, both of which would have to indicate communication of the details of the invention to one or more individuals. These individuals would be capable of understanding the technical aspects of the invention and would so attest in the disclosure. The first reduction to practice is a key event in the patent process since it establishes that the concept is operational and therefore has credibility. It is sometimes referred to as the *proof of principle*. Depending on what the invention is, the reduction to practice may involve testing, fabrication, and operation of a prototype or the first preparation and analysis, for example, of a chemical compound.

As with the date of conception, the date of the first reduction to practice can be crucial in any litigation that may result from the patent. If the construction of a working model is too expensive or complicated, a detailed description of how such a model could be constructed is acceptable to the Patent Office. This requirement is accomplished by the filing of a patent application and is referred to as a *constructive reduction to practice*. It is a good idea to present drawings of any apparatus or equipment that are important in the patent.

The disclosure-of-invention document is kept by the patent or legal department of the company in its files so that it will be available if the patent is contested by any company, organization, or individual. A well-documented disclosure form is of inestimable value in such litigation. It also can be useful in preparing and filing the actual patent application. In the past firms have mailed such documents to themselves in the form of registered letters to establish firmly the dates of conception and reduction to practice.

5.7   THE APPLICATION

Following the preparation of the disclosure of the invention and completion of further work, a patent specification is prepared to provide support for the claims of the application. The general format and specific headings are dictated by the U.S. Patent Office in specific instructions regarding the preparation of patent applications. The information given at the beginning of an issued patent includes the U.S. Patent Office number, the name of the invention, the name and location of the inventor, the assignee (if any), the date the patent was issued, the date it was filed with the Patent Office, the number of claims, and the classification number.

Four Sections

Four essential sections of a patent are the introduction, which gives background information and explains what the patent is and why it is important or useful; the specification, which is a very detailed description of the invention written with reference to the drawings; the claims; and the drawings. Recent patents also include an abstract, which precedes the introductory section. The drawings precede the specification, and the claims are presented last. In the claims section, which is actually the most important section, the advances or novel features of the invention are spelled out first in broad terms and then more specifically. The purpose for broad claims is that they define the bounds of the invention in a broad sense, which can cover a wide range of equivalents even though they were not specifically described in the specification. They can include embodiments, configurations, compositions, and so on that may not have actually been examined but can, nevertheless, be extrapolated from the language of the broad claims. Broad claims give more protection but run the risk of being declared invalid because a wider range of prior art may be used to challenge novelty and unobviousness of the claims. The more narrow and restricted claims, which stem from the broad claims, are easier to enforce since they contain specific information that limits them to the specific embodiment the inventor considers the "best mode" of the invention. However, narrow claims are easier to design around.

Patent Office Procedures

Upon receipt of the patent application by the Patent Office, the application is given a filing date and a serial number (the serial number assigned is not the patent number of the final patent that will be issued). One of the many examiners in the Patent Office, who is knowledgeable in the field of the invention, reviews the application and examines prior art and references, including patents that pertain to the subject matter of the invention. If the examiner finds that certain claims are obviated by claims in already existing patents or by information already published in the technical literature, he or she will reject those claims based on prior art—or even all the claims. It is necessary for the inventor to be resolute in the conviction that something really new is involved, and it is also necessary for the legal department of the company to provide strong support so that there can be a rebuttal to any rejection of claims.

The Patent Office allows the inventor or an authorized agent six months to respond to the objections raised by the examiner. The burden of proof is on the inventor to show why the objections raised and prior art cited do not, in fact, invalidate the inventor's claim. To develop convincing rebuttal arguments, it is necessary for the inventor and the legal staff of the company to examine carefully the patents and other references cited. These are available from the Patent Office and the literature. Upon answering the objections, the examiner may or may not allow some or all of the claims that were objected to previously. Rebuttals and counterrebuttals may continue for a year or longer, but ultimately the Patent Office will make a decision concerning the disposition of the application. Sometimes two or three years can elapse before a patent is finally issued. During the interim period the company can mark the product "pat. pending." This mark can dissuade prospective manufacturers from proceeding with a similar product and attempting to patent and market it.

Joint Inventorship

The problem of joint inventorship can lead to difficulties for the R&D manager. If the patent is ever brought to court, it can be invalidated if it can be shown that one of the inventors was not a true inventor or that one of the true inventors was not named. The names that appear on the patent must represent personnel who exercised original thinking and inventiveness in attainment of the novelty of the patent. This requirement usually excludes personnel who set up and ran tests or machinists and others who fabricated the equipment needed. The assignment of a problem by a supervisor and its subsequent solution by a technical worker does not automatically make the supervisor a joint inventor of any patent that develops from the work. However, a creative supervisor may contribute some key ideas that prove to be the solution to the problem. In this case the supervisor could very well be entitled to joint or even sole inventorship.

This discussion brings up perhaps the most sensitive and difficult problem in determining joint inventorship—the problem that arises when one person has the idea and the other reduces it to practice. Strictly speaking, the person having the idea is the true and only inventor. However, if the reduction to practice involves some inventiveness or novel features, there can be controversy about whether the person who brought about the reduction to practice is entitled to joint inventorship, particularly if the contribution was so crucial that the original idea would never have reached fruition without this person's ingenuity and novel ideas. This can be a very controversial issue and a difficult problem for the manager to arbitrate.

5.8   INTERFERENCE AND INFRINGEMENT

Interference

If two patent applications are filed in the Patent Office by two different inventors that claim the same subject matter, an *interference* is declared. The interference proceedings, which are used to determine priority of invention, are carried out under the cognizance of the Patent Office and can be quite complex and expensive. Most interference actions involve companies since most individuals seldom have the financial resources to pay for the expensive legal action required. Such action can include testimony from expert witnesses, depositions from personnel witnessing tests, and peers and supervisors who signed notebooks and disclosures. The first party to file an application has the advantage and is called the senior party; the burden of proof falls on the second party, called the junior party. Questions that must be resolved in an interference suit are these:

1. Who had the first date of conception?
2. Who had the first date of reduction to practice?

If the junior party can prove that he or she conceived the idea first and can show diligence in reducing it to practice and applying for the patent, this party may be declared to have priority of invention and eventually have a patent issued in his or her name. Good documentary evidence is therefore required, including properly executed and witnessed notebooks, patent disclosures, and corroborating testimony from witnesses.

Infringement

Infringement is the manufacture, sale, or use of an item, process, or composition of matter already covered by the claims of an existing patent held by another party. Infringement may occur inadvertently by a company because its patent department overlooked a pertinent patent, or it may be done intentionally. If it is done intentionally, it would be for the express purpose of testing the validity of the patent or gambling that no litigation would be initiated. In some cases an issued patent is not on a sound basis, and a court investigation and action could easily invalidate it. If the company holding the patent was aware of its tenuous nature it might not contest the infringement. The government does not initiate infringement action; it is the responsibility of the patent holder or the assignee.

Designing Around a Patent

Companies can get around patents in a number of different ways other than directly challenging it by infringement. Infringement can turn out to be quite costly and is not recommended except when the patent is on shaky ground; that is, the claims are weak and not well substantiated, either in content or true novelty. One common method is for a company's engineers or scientists to develop a comparable device, product, or process that produces the same effect but is neither identical nor equivalent to the item claimed in the patent. For example, the "water bumper" that saw limited use on automobiles for cushioning impacts and crashes is patented but can be replaced by bumpers that ride on pistons capable of absorbing shocks or by other devices and designs that absorb shocks. The automobile companies have preferred to develop their own techniques for reducing this hazard rather than pay royalties or licensing fees. Sometimes portions but not all of several claims of a patent will be used as a basis for a new device. The idea is to design around a patent and develop a comparable product that performs the required tasks but does not infringe on the original patent. As a last resort, companies can negotiate with the company holding the desired patent and pay royalties or licensing fees until they have had an opportunity to develop a product of their own. Sometimes it is cheaper in the long run to license the new device or technology.

5.9   TRADE SECRETS

Many companies rely on trade secrets to protect their technical processes and products. By keeping certain types of information secret, the company can often maintain an advantage over existing or would-be competition. For reasons of cost and immediate as well as long-range protection, the company may elect not to patent the process, or know-how. *Know-how* refers to special procedures a company uses in making a product or conducting an operation that are not patented but are necessary and valuable in obtaining the desired end product. The composition of electroplating baths and the sequence or procedures used for electroplating are examples, as are the ingredients and preparation techniques for Coca-Cola syrup and wine-making procedures. Companies sometimes prefer to keep a manufacturing process secret rather than attempt to patent it and allow it to become known, especially if it is questionable whether the process or procedure is really patentable.

Trade secrets have legal status and are protected by common law. For example, if an employee who has signed an employment agreement leaves a company and is employed by a competitive company, he or she cannot disclose valuable know-how or trade secrets to the new employer that were revealed in confidence by the previous employer. Numerous lawsuits have resulted from the transfer of valuable trade secrets to competitors by ex-employees. In some states the illegal disclosure of trade secrets is classified as fraud, and employees can be fined or even jailed for such activities (*Pulp and Paper* 1975). Customer lists, supplier identities, equipment, and plant layouts cannot be patented because of their nature, yet they can be important in the conduct of a business and therefore are protected as trade secrets. As a result, there has been and continues to be industrial spying. With the present high mobility, a tendency toward job-hopping, and a decreased commitment of employees to the companies that employ them, disclosure of trade secrets is a serious problem for management. Signing an initial agreement (see Figure 5.2) diminishes but does not eliminate the problems. Ultimately there is the matter of the court's interpretation.

In recent years trade secrets have assumed an important role in the field of "legally protectable ideas." Industry has shown a tendency to rely less on patents; instead, it prefers to depend whenever possible on the trade secret concept, relying on common law for protection. The reason for this change is primarily based on the stiffening of the standard of inventiveness as interpreted by courts and the long delays between the filing of a patent application and the subsequent grant of a patent. The owner of a trade secret may disclose it in confidence to another by means of an express or implied contract under which the other agrees to limit use of the secret.

5.10 PATENTS AND TRADE SECRETS IN GOVERNMENT CONTRACTING

Since government agencies sponsor a large amount of R&D, their patent policies have a major effect on the patent rights of companies with whom they do business. There are two dramatically opposite positions in patent ownership: The government agency obtains the title, or the contractor retains the title. Unfortunately, all government agencies do not operate under a uniform patent policy. The Department of Defense requires royalty-free use and can withhold publication of the patent for as long as security conditions require; companies are usually allowed to retain commercial rights. Other agencies take title to the invention and ownership as if they were companies (e.g., NASA). If carrying out the contract involves the invention and first reduction to practice of a new concept, the government agency obtains title and royalty-free use of the invention.

This policy has been a source of considerable disagreement and negotiation between companies and government agencies. For example, consider patents developed by a subcontractor working for the prime contractor in which the patents are an extension or part of work that the subcontractor has been financing from its own company funds. Such problems have brought about extensive litigation and many court cases. Because of these and other possible complications some companies will try to do as much preliminary work on a new concept (using company funds) as is necessary to establish a patent position before using the new concept in the execution of a government contract. Then they can rightfully claim that the invention was conceived and reduced to practice before the contract was granted.

The DOD practice of withholding publication of patents that have security implications can be troublesome for companies since the invention may become obsolete by the time issuance of the patent is allowed. The DOD may not allow foreign patents to be applied for or the product sold to a foreign government without agency approval. In the past, the State Department has withheld the sale of certain high-technology products (such as special-purpose computers) to Russia and certain other countries; however, this situation appears to be changing.

The question of know-how and trade secrets is a legal matter that must be addressed in contractual relations with government agencies or other companies. It is in this area of trade secrets that the government has had considerable difficulty with industry regarding government rights to those original ideas that may have originated under government contracts. And it is in this area that the buyer and contract administrator will frequently become uncomfortably involved. Some government agencies allow the purchase of trade secrets from contractors in return for reasonable compensation. Companies do not normally like to disclose know-how, even for a price, but it is sometimes necessary so that the company can bid on government contracts. The company may be asked to turn over manufacturing drawings and procedures, detailed design specifications and drawings of equipment, and the like. When so doing, the company may leave out key bits of information not immediately discernible to the uninitiated but necessary for the particular system development.

An additional problem of government contracts and patents is the view taken by Public Citizen, Inc., a nonprofit organization headed by Ralph Nader, that granting patents by a government agency to a private company is unconstitutional (Johnson 1974). It can be logically argued that private companies should not be allowed to profit from products or processes developed from the expenditure of public funds. The counterargument is that if the technology is not going to be further developed or used, it is justifiable to give it to a company that will proceed with its development and use by the public, and the public will then benefit.

5.11 COPYRIGHTS

The importance of copyrights for the engineering, manufacturing, or R&D manager stems from the fact that in many cases important technical documents are frequently developed in the course of carrying out technical work. Original drawings or designs of a scientific or technical character would be candidates for copyright, as would diagrams, models, blueprints, plans, and software programs. Similarly, operating procedures (fixed in a tangible medium of expression) for certain types of machinery, mechanisms, processes, and so forth could be copyrighted. Copyrighting can preclude use by competitors of the identical documents, blueprints, designs, and so on.

Ornamental designs that could be protected by a design patent may also be copyrighted; the originator of the design must decide between them. Design patents offer protection for 14 years, whereas the copyright extends for a much longer period (the lifetime of the originator plus 50 years).

In the past there have been two types of copyright for unpublished work (Library of Congress 1981):

Common Law Literary Property. This type of protection against unauthorized use of an unpublished work is a matter of state law and arises automatically when the work is created. It requires no action on the part of the Copyright Office. It may last as long as the work is unpublished, but it ends when the work is published or when statutory copyright is secured by registration.

Statutory Copyright. This is the protection afforded by the federal law upon compliance with certain requirements (see below). The following types of works are typical of those that can be registered for statutory copyright: books, articles, musical compositions, dramas, works of art, drawings and sculptural works of a scientific or technical character, photographs, motion pictures, and works prepared for oral delivery.

These two types of copyright have been replaced by a single, unified national system of statutory copyright that protects all works from the moment of their creation.[5] One can obtain common law protection by writing

© John Doe 1991

on the original and all copies. To obtain a copyright registration an application must be filed with the Copyright Office of the Library of Congress. The filing

---

[5]Creation occurs when the work is "fixed" in a tangible medium of expression such as writing or printing.

process consists of filling out a relatively simple application and mailing the form along with two copies of the work to the Library of Congress.

As already mentioned, computer software programs are subject to copyright and may even be included in a patent when used in conjunction with hardware in special applications and when they are essential ingredients in a hardware or manufacturing process. Whether such a patent qualifies for issuance is usually decided on an individual basis.

It is important to note that the copyright is permanently lost unless all published copies have the appropriate copyright notice. When a work is published (printed and distributed) without such notice, it falls into the public domain and becomes public property.

Before leaving the subject of copyrights, it should be noted that copyright does not offer protection for ideas; it protects only the form of the expression of the idea. The idea may be used by anyone. The copyright protects the writer or originator from someone else reproducing a part or all of the work and selling it for profit. Thus a copyright has little value in protecting technical innovations except in the case of software programs.

5.12   INTERNATIONAL PATENTS

To obtain patent protection for new products, processes, and so on in foreign countries, one of two procedural paths can be taken:

1. One can apply for a patent from the particular countries where the person or organization (assignee) seeks protection, that is, countries where the patent will be used.
2. One can apply for a patent from the European Patent Office, which is located in Munich and cooperates closely with national offices in several European countries.[6] This organization, created by the European Patent Convention (EPC), determines patentability and grants European patents for each of the represented nations.

Present members of the EPC are Germany, Denmark, Austria, Belgium, the United Kingdom, Switzerland, Sweden, Spain, France, Liechtenstein, Luxembourg, Italy, Greece, and the Netherlands. The patent application is examined by an Examining Division of the European Patent Office, made up of three examiners who are experts in the field concerned and are joined if necessary by a lawyer. They verify

---

[6]Address of the European Patent Office (EPO) is Erhardtstrasse 27, D-8000 Munchen 2, Germany. The EPO also has branches in The Hague, Berlin, and Vienna.

whether the three criteria for patentability—novelty, inventive step (nonobvious-
ness), and industrial application—and other substantive or formal requirements
have been met and maintain a constant dialogue with the applicant or his or her
representative (*European Patent Office Bulletin* 1989).

The requirements for patentability and the patent examinations and processing
are essentially the same as for U.S. patents except that there is no possibility of
interference; the first to apply is the person(s) who has the patent rights. There is
no consideration of who conceived the idea first, who reduced the idea to practice
first, and so on. This important difference between the U.S. and the European
patent system is a controversial issue. Another difference is that within nine months
from the date on which a patent is granted, any third party can file notice of
opposition if it believes that the patent should not have been granted. Opposition
proceedings, which are the responsibility of the Opposition Division in Munich,
can result in one of three different rulings:

- Revoke the patent.
- Decide to maintain it but in amended form.
- Reject the opposition's claim that the patent should not have been granted.

The decision is valid for all the contracting states designated in the patent, but
there is a right of appeal that can bring about reconsideration of the patentability
issue.

Publications of the EPO include the following:

- *The Official Journal* appears monthly and contains legal information on the
  organization, the office, and the application of the European Patent Convention (EPC) and Board of Appeal case law.
- *The European Patent Bulletin* is published weekly and is the key document
  for procedural data on published applications and granted patents and contains
  information entered in the Register of European Patents.
- *Monographs* on various technical fields can be obtained from Pergamon
  Press, Headington Hill Hall, Oxford OX3 OBW, England.

The EPO in 1989 processed over 60,000 patents, and the number continues to
increase from year to year. With the advent of the European Community in 1992
there will be, according to an agreement initially made in Luxembourg in 1975 and
later supplemented in 1985, a Community patent. This patent will be granted by
the EPO and will apply in all Common Market countries that are parties to the
Luxembourg Convention.

With respect to previously so-called Eastern Bloc and non-Western countries,
there are no publicized agreements at this time on the observance of patent rights

and copyrights. With the easing of East–West tensions and the liberalization of Communist countries, such agreements may be forthcoming. In the past, certain countries in the Pacific Rim and Communist countries in particular have paid no attention to patent rights or copyright privileges. For example, there are continued offerings of popular software programs and books in Hong Kong and other Pacific Rim cities at prices that are a fraction of those in America. These are usually copies of the originals or copies of copies. Similarly, there are copies (usually less expensive) of many other Western products that are sold without observance of patent rights, copyrights, or trademarks.

5.13   PATENT REFORMS AND CHANGES

Since its inception in 1790, and particularly during the last decade, the U.S. patent system has come under severe criticism. Such criticisms have been centered on several key issues:

1. The large percentage of patents that have been found to be invalid when tested in court (ranging from 50 to 70 percent)
2. The fear by antitrust forces in the government that the "monopoly" aspect of patents is being taken advantage of by companies, to the detriment of the public
3. The large number of patents (estimated to be over 50 percent) presently being granted to foreign applicants
4. The arbitrary limit of 17 years, which is too long a period for the monopolistic condition to persist
5. The large number of patents that go into litigation

In response to these and other criticisms various bills have been introduced in Congress to modify the patent law. For example, S.2255 attempted to modify the monopolistic aspect and provide more stringent requirements for both the inventor and the corporation. It called for the corporation (to whom the patent is assigned) as well as the inventor to disclose the best mode for carrying out the invention. Companies have argued that this disclosure could involve trade secrets, and furthermore the inventor and officers of the company might not agree on the best mode. The bill also challenged validity, according to its advocates—but this is debatable. Although the bill had its good points, critics contend that it would jeopardize this country's leadership in technology. They also stated that the attempt to transform the patent law into an antitrust vehicle would make it more difficult, time-consuming, and costly to obtain patent protection. Individual inventors and small business people would suffer most from the expensive and protracted litigation that could result. It could encourage greater reliance on trade secrets and add to the cost of using the patent system, to the overall detriment of the public.

There have been other proposed changes on patents, some of which have been voted into law by Congress in the last decade. Among these is a law that allows colleges and smaller companies to retain patent rights to inventions that are developed under government-funded research projects.

QUESTIONS AND TOPICS FOR DISCUSSION

5.1   What are the essential points about patents that a technology manager must keep in mind in supervising technical personnel?

5.2   What are the key elements of the preemployment agreement?

5.3   What are some of the precautions a company can take to protect its trade secrets and know-how?

5.4   What are the principle criteria that must be evaluated and found favorable before a company decides to file a patent application?

5.5   What are some of the possible actions that must be considered if a company is faced with the problem of a new product (appropriately patented) on the market that essentially will make its main product line obsolete?

5.6   What are some of the conditions under which a company might deliberately infringe on an existing patent?

5.7   The patent system has been under serious attack for a number of years. Reasons for this attack include extended monopoly by one company and collusion among companies to produce a monopoly. Comment on this allegation.

5.8   In the last two decades there have been numerous lawsuits over patent rights between aerospace companies and government agencies. These controversies stem from patents arising as a result of technical work performed by the contractor for the government agency. What are possible solutions to this continuing problem?

5.9   Some government agencies such as NASA waive patent rights to contractors to allow them to exploit commercially technology developed with public funds. Discuss the pros and cons of such a policy.

5.10   What are the cost trade-offs and other considerations that must be made by a small to medium-sized company about whether or not to (a) hire a full-time patent attorney, (b) keep a patent attorney on a retainer basis, or (c) go to a patent attorney on an as-needed basis without a retainer?

References

European Patent Office Bulletin. 1989. EPO 89-001E.

Inside R&D. 1981. March 11. p. 1.

Johnson, K. 1974, March 18. Defense patent rights policy challenged. *Aviation Week and Space Technology*, p. 59.

Library of Congress. 1981. Circular R1. Copyright Basics. pp. 4-5.

NASA Activities. February 1979. Waiver of Patent Rights. p. 41.

New York Times. 1989, August 27. p. 10.

Pulp and Paper. 1975, April. Legal aspects of management, pp. 102-104.

Riggs, Henry E. 1983. *Managing High-Technology Companies.* New York: Van Nostrand Reinhold.

6

Selecting Projects for New Products and Processes

6.1 INTRODUCTION

As a result of new product planning (Chapter 4) there will usually be more ideas for new projects, new products, and manufacturing process improvements than the company can possibly finance. Decisions must be made about which new possibilities should be pursued; which current programs should be expanded; and which should be maintained at the same level, curtailed, or eliminated. These difficult decisions must be made by middle and upper management, in consort with input from the scientists and engineers performing the technical work as well as marketing personnel in the case of new products. Where manufacturing improvements or new processes are involved, there has to be close coordination with the cognizant operational personnel about feasibility, timing, cost, and so on. Even if the needs for defensive research, customer good will, satisfaction of government regulations, and satisfied R&D workers are considered, the final decision must be based on how profitable the technology venture will be. Therefore there must be a preliminary evaluation of the economic impact to determine whether the expenditure is financially attractive.

Past and Present Practices

Years ago the selection of what technical areas to pursue was often made by one individual—the executive officer of the company, the engineering or research director, or the manager—and this is still true for many small companies today. In large companies such decisions are made by special groups or committees after extensive study and deliberation. Technical as well as economic feasibility must be considered. As indicated, not only are technical personnel consulted but also representatives from marketing, manufacturing, and financial groups.

If the technical effort is an ongoing activity that involves improvement of a long-standing, successful product line, the only decisions to be made are what improvements to seek and how to modify existing areas of effort, if at all. In this instance, the question is not one of starting or stopping a program but rather evaluating, modifying, and redirecting. An example would be a paint improvement program being carried out by a major paint company. The investigation of new pigments, new vehicles for suspending the pigments, and the resulting characteristics of paint made up from these new materials would probably be a constant area of effort for such a company. New materials and compositions as well as new manufacturing techniques are continually appearing in the literature or being developed within the company.

The more difficult decisions about technology efforts often concern starting and stopping major programs and projects. The disruptions that occur in such instances can be troublesome because of the personnel, equipment, facilities, and other resources involved.

Who Is Involved?

In the case of new ventures, all aspects should be considered before approving expenditures: technical feasibility, economic considerations including marketability, company compatibility, environmental impact, government regulations and policies, safety and liability aspects, and finally use. The evaluations for new products, manufacturing processes, or projects are carried out by different groups in different companies. Sometimes the research engineer suggesting the product will make the sales potential estimate with guidance and data from marketing and sales personnel. More often the calculations and estimate of economic potential will be made by a group especially versed in this type of calculation. The groups have different names in different companies, such as New Product Development Group, Technical and Economic Studies Group, and so on. Personnel are more business- and engineering-oriented than science- or technology-oriented and have been trained formally or by experience for such evaluations.

Overall Methods

In the literature as well as in actual practice a variety of methods is used for evaluating new projects leading to new or improved products and manufacturing processes. For project selection, Cleland and Kocaoglu (1981) have made the following classification of methods that have been developed in order of increasing sophistication:

- Rank-ordering method
    Simple rank ordering
    Q-sorting
    Weighted ordering
    Successive comparisons
- Scoring models
    Simple scoring models
    Probabilistic scoring models
- Utility models
    Simple utility models
    Probabilistic utility models

These methods, many of which have been developed by academics, can be quite mathematical and require special programming or software packages for computerization. In the real life of the industrial world the simpler and less arithmetically involved methods are more frequently used. Amos and Sarchet (1981) suggest simple ranking charts based on evaluations of the following aspects:

- Financial
- Production and engineering
- Research and development
- Marketing and production

Of these factors probably the evaluation of market potential for new products is probably the most critical and often the most difficult to make. The ability to make decisions about new or improved manufacturing processes is a more straightforward and tangible process, particularly since it pertains to equipment, facilities, personnel availability, technical skills, and other factors that are internal to the company and relatively well known.

In the discussions that follow, the evaluation of technical feasibility, economic potential, company compatibility, and other relevant factors in the project selection process will be considered. The matter of marketability of new products will be alluded to but not expanded in detail since it is a speciality field in itself about which volumes have been written; it falls beyond the scope of this book. Other relevant factors that must be taken into account include safety, environmental impact, and compliance with government (state and federal) regulations. The selection techniques discussed will include only those that are most commonly used in actual practice.

6.2   TECHNICAL FEASIBILITY

In the evaluation of the technical feasibility of projects for new products, manufacturing processes and improvements, the critical technical issues must be identified and evaluated. Questions that must be answered include these:

- Is the technical advancement required possible with a reasonable extension of the present state of the art (SOA)?
- Assuming it is possible to achieve the SOA improvement, how long will it take and how much will it cost?

The second question is intimately related to economic considerations (Section 6.3). If the technical effort requires the creation and design of a hardware component or system, will it be physically possible to build such an item? Can the specifications and requirements be achieved? These are difficult questions to answer, and the answers that are arrived at are not always clear-cut and decisive. Nevertheless, the evaluations must be made to help decide whether or not the effort should be funded.

Critical Technical Issues
The technical personnel that will be doing the actual work should be consulted about the difficulty and complexity of the technical problems. The development of an electrical power system that utilizes nuclear fusion is a research effort that has great technical challenge. Whether it can be achieved or not depends on complex technical problems (critical technical issues) that have yet to be resolved. Because of the extent of the problems and the cost and time required for their attempted solution, only the government has had the resources to fund such an effort. Although various companies have in-house programs in various facets of this system development, the major technical effort and funding continues to come from government agencies. This becomes a problem of economic as well as technical feasibility and is typical of the symbiotic relationship between the two factors.

Modeling

In determining the technical feasibility of a proposed system, product, or process improvement, it is often necessary and usually cost-effective to build a model or perform a few preliminary experiments. The characteristics of the project or system examined in such tests or experiments are carefully selected to obtain an insight into the solution of the critical technical issues. It is hoped that the preliminary results will be definitive, but this is not always the case, and often further experimentation is required. Even then a compromise must be made or a calculated risk taken.

This type of effort is performed with minimal equipment and material to keep costs as low as possible. For a hardware system development, a few tests, "mock-ups," "breadboards," or "brassboards" can save the company considerable expense and time. The savings that can be realized in the early stages of new product development and the accumulation of costs as research proceeds to development and commercial exploitation are indicated in Figure 6-1. The R&D process itself

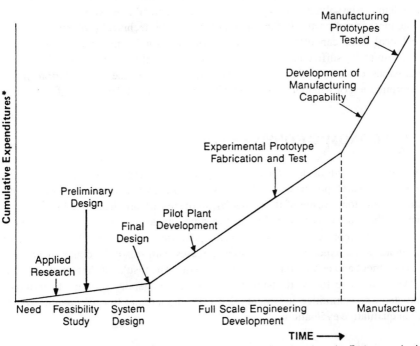

* Depending upon the particular product, this could be a logarithmic scale. Early steps in the development process are at least one order of magnitude less in cost than subsequent steps.

Figure 6-1.   Cummulative Expenditures in the Development of a New Product.

could be considered an overall feasibility program or test of feasibility because it precedes manufacture and commercial exploitation and can be stopped at any stage when it appears that the development will not be technically or economically feasible. It may be that the tooling required is not available or that the specifications to be met are not possible for a manufactured product.

Physical Realizability (Producibility)

In developments that involve engineering design, physical realizability can be a problem. For example, it may be desirable to expand the size of a product but it may not be physically realizable or operational. A historical, vivid example was the extension of wooden transport aircraft to the maximum possible size by Howard Hughes in building the *Spruce Goose*. This is an example of a concept pushed beyond its physical practicability. Changes in structures and materials technology have since proven that this was not a worthwhile channel of product improvement.

Although technical feasibility has been considered separately here, it is closely associated with economic feasibility. There is an old cliché that any technical problem can be solved if enough money can be "thrown" at it. Although not strictly true, there is some truth in the statement. A difficult technical problem or critical technical issue can often be solved if adequate funds and time are available. Unfortunately, sufficient time and money are usually not available. There are numerous cases in which "time to develop" has been the key criterion in the determination of whether to proceed with a technological development.

6.3   ECONOMIC CONSIDERATIONS

A number of simple arithmetic techniques can be used to evaluate costs for possible research projects, and almost every company has its own way of making such evaluations. Some of these, but by no means all, are described briefly here. The methods are not completely accurate since "guesstimates" are often involved, but they do represent an effort toward quantification and can be made more accurate as the experience of the user increases with steady feedback of product development and commercial exploitation costs. The results of these methods can serve as a guide to the decision maker and are generally superior to intuitive unilateral or committee judgments that make no attempt toward quantitative or even qualitative evaluations.

Determination of Potential Profit

In addition to the costs of a product development effort itself, the costs associated with manufacturing and marketing a new commercial product must be estimated to determine whether a sufficient profit will be possible to justify the R&D expense and other financial outlays. Similar cost estimations must be made for a proposed improved manufacturing process.

The following are typical costs that must be considered:

- Salaries and wages of scientists, engineers, and other technical personnel
- Special test equipment, facilities, and materials
- Costs of pilot plant and manufacturing facilities, including machines and tooling
- Labor and other costs for plant operation
- General and administrative expense (G&A) for middle- and upper-management salaries, salaries of secretaries, office supplies, utilities, and the like
- Depreciation costs
- Marketing and sales costs

The total cost is essentially a life-cycle cost in that it takes into account not only these items but also support functions (logistics) and system phase-out.

The rise and fall of major costs with time during a product's development and life cycle are depicted in Figure 6-2. Note that in this example income from sales does not occur until two to three years after the initiation of the product development effort, and the break-even point occurs after six years. The break-even point is here defined as the time when all the investment has been recovered. The lifetime of this particular product appears to be about six years. Costs must be normalized to some standard year to take into account inflation; also the loss or payment of interest as a result of the use of money during the development period should be included as a cost. This cost will vary depending on the length of time of the product development and the prevailing interest rates.

Upon determination of all the costs associated with the candidate project, the total sales anticipated for the product during the life cycle must be estimated; then the profit can be calculated and compared for various possible products and projects. Those projects that can lead to the greatest potential profit can be considered to be prime candidates for funding if technical feasibility, company compatibility, and other requirements can be met.

Although this technique may seem approximate and subject to many possible errors because of unforeseen market developments and technical problems, it can be quite meaningful in obtaining relative merit values for comparable technical efforts. The engineers and financial personnel performing such evaluations have usually had considerable experience in this type of determination and have access to files of data that have been calculated previously for other similar projects. Errors in estimating techniques for development, manufacturing, and marketing

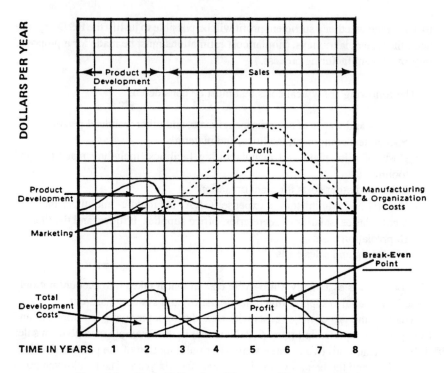

Figure 6-2.   Product Lifecycle and Recovery of Development Costs.

costs are corrected as new products are developed and marketed, so that there is an increasingly sound basis for future estimates of similar products. With such a background of experience and data, relative predictions can become definitive and meaningful.

However, this method of determining profit criteria for evaluating projects does not consider the time required to develop the product, a factor that can be extremely critical. It also does not take into account the probability of R&D success or the probability of commercial success, both of which are key elements in the innovation process.

Gain-to-Risk Ratio
In the gain-to-risk ratio approach, the gain (profit) to be derived from the technical venture is divided by the money invested in the project. The profit is determined as described above, and the money invested in the project is the money invested in the technical effort alone, although it could also include the estimated manufacturing, marketing, and other costs. The merit factor for comparison of

various candidate projects is P/C rather than P. The costs would have to take into account the interest lost because of the use of the money over a finite period of time and the effect of inflation. The candidate projects can be evaluated and compared with respect to the gain-risk ratios calculated. The company may arbitrarily establish a limit of 2.5 as being acceptable for further consideration of an R&D project.

This method is relatively simple and straightforward but suffers from the same disadvantages as the determination-of-profit method. It does not consider the probability of technical and commercial success, nor does it take into account development time.

Carl Pacifico Formula

The formula developed by Carl Pacifico for chemical products overcomes the objection to the previous two methods of not taking into account the probability of technical and commercial success (Stephanou 1981):

$$\text{Project rating} = \frac{R_t\, R_c\, (P_n - C\,)VL}{\text{total costs}}$$

where
R_t = probability of technical success (0.1 to 1.0)
R_c = probability of commercial success (0.1 to 1.0)
P_n = price of product ($/lb)
C = manufacturing plus selling costs ($/lb)
V = sales volume (lb/yr)
L = commercial life (years)
Total costs = the sum of research, engineering, plant cost, marketing, working capital, and other ancillary costs

The formula can be readily adapted to a per-unit rather than a per-pound basis. With this formula, a project rating of 1.0 is considered the break-even point and is obviously not acceptable. A rating of 2.0+ indicates that the project is worthy of consideration and should be compared with other candidate projects having a rating of over 2.0. Disadvantages of this formula are that it does not distinguish between long-range and short-range projects or between low-risk/low-profit and high-risk/high-profit combinations.

Sidney Sobelman Formula

A formula developed by Sidney Sobelman takes into account both the development time and the commercial lifetime of a candidate product (Stephanou 1981):

$$Z = pT - ct$$

where Z = product value or comparison factor
       p = average net profit per year
       T = estimated life of the product or process
       c = average development cost per year
       t = years of development

The loss of interest because of development time can be corrected by applying the following formula to each cost item:

$$C^*_i = C_i(1 + r)^t$$

where C^*_i = future cost calculated to present time for each cost element
       C_i = actual cost before correction for interest loss
       r = prevailing average interest rate over the time period involved
       t = number of years elapsing from the time effort was initiated

For all the cost items the formula becomes

$$\text{Total costs} = \sum_{i=1}^{n} C^*_i = \sum_{i=1}^{n} C_i (1 + r)^t$$

The Sobelman formula then takes the form:

$$Z = PT - \sum_{i-1}^{n} C^*_i$$

This method takes into account development time but neglects the probability of commercial success. Many companies will not undertake a project if it has less than a certain probability of commercial success and a reasonable payback time (see Section 6.4).

Other Techniques

The above are typical techniques that can be used for the economic evaluation of candidate research projects but they are by no means the only techniques. Every large company has its peculiar ritual and procedure that it carries out every year to select the technical efforts that seem best suited to its future needs and offer the greatest economic gain. Often development time as well as anticipated profit are the key factors.

6.4   PAYBACK TIME

Some companies examine the estimated expenditure and sales curves (Figure 6-2) for the estimated life cycle of the product and use the break-even point as a criterion for whether to go ahead on a project. If the break-even point occurs too far in the future, the candidate project is scrapped. The exact length of time that is tolerated for the break-even point to occur depends on company policy and thinking at the time of the decision. Here, as in the Sobelman technique, the cash flow (income minus expenditures) must be considered as well as the time value of money based on the current and anticipated interest rates. By taking into account the depreciation of equipment, the time it will take before the company will earn its money back can be determined. Thus companies can rank projects according to payment time and also cash flow (Amos and Sarchet 1981). The results of surveys of Fortune 500 companies and others indicate payback times of three to four years and anticipated probability of technical success of at least 70 percent (Stephanou 1981). For high- technology and special product companies (e.g., computer software), the payback time can be considerably shorter.

A relatively simple screening procedure that some companies use is to consider the gross sales or the net profit that the candidate R&D effort can yield. If it is below some arbitrary amount, the project is not pursued. For example, a large company could use an arbitrary figure of $10 million as the estimated gross annual sales or savings that was necessary before a candidate project would even be considered.

6.5   CHECKLISTS

In this discussion we have considered one principal factor at a time, such as technical feasibility, profit potential, or payback time. However, in the final analysis, management must consider the project from an overall standpoint, taking into account all the factors already mentioned plus possible additional factors. There are a number of techniques for accomplishing this analysis, varying in complexity from simple arithmetic to sophisticated computer models. One of the most commonly used is the checklist approach, which combines technical and economic aspects with marketing, manufacturing, and whatever other factors the company considers important (see Figure 6-3). This is a relatively simple example. In some companies this evaluation can include many pages of questions about technical development, use of company funds, marketing, and salability. Answering such a questionnaire can be a research job in itself; it is usually carried out

Proposal number _____   Title _____

Name of Evaluator _____

Technical Factors:	Favorable	No Opinion	Unfavorable
Long term objective(s)	✓		
Interim objectives	✓		
Technical approach	✓		
Availability of technology within Company			✓
Availability of technology outside Company	✓		
Availability of scientific skills			✓
Adequacy of facilities			✓
Adequacy of support manpower			✓
Tie-in with existing projects			✓
Anticipated output of current approach	✓		
Innovation or novelty of output	✓		
Estimated chance of technical success	✓		
Patent situation	✓		
Production capabilities	✓		
Totals	**9**	**0**	**5**
Economic Factors:			
Competitive environment	✓		
Market potential	✓		
Market stability	✓		
Marketing advantages of project output		✓	
Promotional requirements		✓	
Capital expenditure requirements	✓		
Research investment payout time	✓		
Totals	**5**	**2**	**0**
Timing Factors:			
Time to accomplish interim objective(s)	✓		
Time relative to supporting marketing objectives	✓		
Totals	**2**	**0**	**0**

Figure 6-3.   R&D Project Evaluation Worksheet.

product development that is already past the initial stages of research and has a high degree of acceptability. Specialists and/or generalists in each of the pertinent areas can be involved in such a checklist evaluation. Xerox over the years has used a corporate committee made up of R&D engineering, finance, and marketing representatives to evaluate checklists for candidate R&D projects (Martin 1984).

6.6 RATING MATRIX

This technique in its simplest form identifies key criteria for evaluating the various candidate projects and assigns ratings for each. A sample set is shown in Table 6-1. The simplest technique is to rate each project in terms of each criteria on a scale, say, 1 to 5, where 5 would be the highest score and 1 the lowest. The project with the highest total score would be selected. A more accurate method, which takes into account the relative importance of the criteria, is shown in Table 6.1. In this case there is an arbitrary maximum value for each criterion. This number value reflects the importance of the particular criterion. The number value can be broken down into constituent components based on certain characteristics, for example;

Development	Time Points
1 year	4
2 years	3
3 years	2
More than 4 years	1
Cost to Develop	
Less than $100,000	10
$100,000–$300,000	8
$300,000–$500,000	6
$500,000–$800,000	3
More than $800,000	1

A number of qualified personnel can be given blank matrices or a committee can be assigned to the evaluation. The totals can be readily determined for the various projects and the most promising projects selected, based on the chosen criteria. Further selection and thinning out can be carried out by upper management based on the corporate strategic plan, state of the economy, competitive products, capital available, and so on.

6.7 THE DECISION TREE

In special situations, when the decision to develop the product is subject to chance events that can seriously affect the desirability of proceeding with development, setting up a decision tree can be helpful (Lapin 1985).[1] Such events could result

---

[1]There are several formats and ways of using decision trees. The format presented here is particularly suited to product development and R&D decisions.

TABLE 6-1.　Decision Matrix for Evaluating Candidate Projects

Key Criteria [a]	Maximum Value	Project A	Project B [b]	Project C	Project D
1. Cost to develop	10	3	8	6	1
2. Development time	4	1	3	4	2
3. Technical feasibility	10	4	7	5	6
4. Customer acceptance	20	10	15	8	7
5. Manufacturing facilities	6	4	5	3	4
6. Technological assessment	5	3	4	1	2
Totals	55	25	42	27	22

(a) A maximum value for a key criterion indicates the optimum or most desirable situation.

(b) Project B, with a total of 42, is the most attractive project to pursue based on these criteria and weighting factors.

from competitors' activity, technical changes, market conditions, or government regulation. The course of action is planned in advance, taking into account that the final outcome will depend on certain actions and chance events.

This technique can be best explained by examples. Figure 6-4 is a purposely simplified example to show the general concept. Each circle represents a decision point or event. Probabilities, stated at decision points or events, are based on previous experience. If there has been no previous experience and there is no basis for a probability estimate, the probability for each possible branch is taken as the reciprocal of the number of alternatives. Overall probabilities for each branch can be calculated by multiplying together all the probabilities of the branch segments.

A more complex situation is shown in Figure 6-5. With the information developed in this example it can be seen that if the company decides to proceed with the development, there is a 40 percent probability that the company will go into production of the improved product, a 24 percent probability that it will buy from the competition, and a 36 percent chance that it will have to cancel plans to add the improved product to its line. Cash flow estimates can be made from the decision tree if appropriate assumptions and estimates are made. The cash flow would be multiplied by the overall probability for each branch, and the resulting product value would give an indication of the desirability of each branch.

6.8　COMPANY COMPATIBILITY

Although this question might appear to be one that would seldom arise, it comes up relatively often. A number of factors related to company practices and opera-

Situation: You have requested funds for replacing an old system that is gradually becoming outdated.

Question: What is the probability of events that will occur with respect to this system replacement?

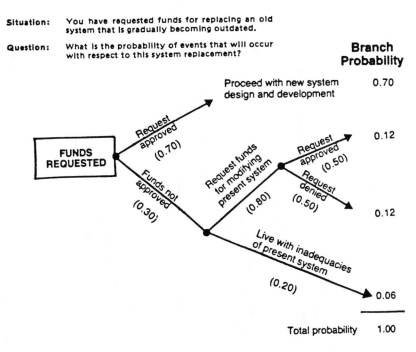

Branch Probability

Proceed with new system design and development   0.70

FUNDS REQUESTED

Request approved (0.70)

Funds not approved (0.30)

Request funds for modifying present system (0.80)

Request approved (0.50)   0.12

Request denied (0.50)   0.12

Live with inadequacies of present system (0.20)   0.06

Total probability   1.00

Summary: Probability that you will obtain a new or modified system is 82% while the probability that you will have to live with the old system is 18%.

Figure 6-4.   Simplified Decision Tree.

tions must be considered in making the decision to proceed with a new product or process development; for example;

1. Is the company's top management really interested in this new product or development so that they will support it fully?
2. Are facilities and manufacturing equipment available within the company for manufacturing the item at the desired production rate? Will special equipment be needed?
3. Does the company have personnel with the required skills for the technical effort and will they be available for this development? Will personnel have to be hired?
4. How will the sales effort be handled? Can the existing sales organization handle the new product or will a new department or group have to be set up?
5. How will the entry of the new product affect the sales of present company products?

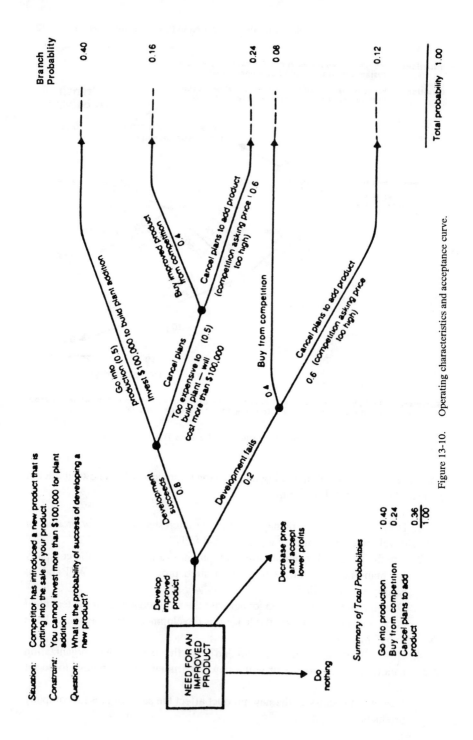

Figure 13-10.   Operating characteristics and acceptance curve.

126

The answers to these and related questions can be answered by consultation of technical personnel with management, plant engineering and production, marketing, and sales personnel.

A striking example of what can happen when candidate products are not acceptable to a company is the situation in which engineers, scientists, or officers of a company have resigned to start their own business, making a product in which the company had indicated no interest. Although there have been many failures in such bold ventures, there also have been outstanding successes. Many times the company officials did not feel there was enough profit in the new product to warrant use of the company's facilities and resources. A small company could be satisfied with fewer sales and less profit. Perhaps the new product would compete with the product line of a good customer and alienate that company so that it would no longer buy the company's products.

There are many other reasons why top management might turn down the development of a new product. Often the requirement for facilities that are not available to the company may be a valid reason for not embarking on a new technical venture. Perhaps the manufacturing equipment is excessively expensive or not available. The financial outlay must be considered as well as the feasibility of whether such manufacturing equipment could even be made. In regard to the availability of the required technical skills, it may be that the company does not want or is not able to make the financial commitment required to hire the personnel needed for entering the new product area. Perhaps the technical personnel required are already in the company but are needed for existing product lines and new product effort. The need for an adequate sales force to handle the marketing of the new product is another consideration. The necessity of a new sales department can be a negative factor. The ideal situation is one in which the existing sales force can handle the product initiation into the market and future sales.

If the new product to be developed satisfies a similar or identical customer need that is presently being satisfied wholly or partially by an existing company product, the gain in sales of the new product may be offset by the loss in sales of the existing product. An example of such a situation can occur when an automobile company introduces a new line of cars. Many customers who might have bought the existing line could and probably would buy the new line.

6.9   OTHER FACTORS

In recent times factors other than economics, technical feasibility, marketability, and company compatibility have come into play in determining whether a given research project should be undertaken. In previous generations such factors were not taken into account at all or, if they were, only in a minimal fashion. A listing of such factors has to include environmental effects, consumption of critical resources such as energy, safety considerations, and effects on the community where the manufacturing is to be done. If a new laundry detergent is going to contaminate the water supply of the community, its effectiveness as a more powerful cleansing and washing agent becomes secondary in importance. If the new product is going to pollute the air or decrease the ozone layer of the upper atmosphere, these undesirable characteristics must be taken into account in the evaluation.

Although companies are now making such considerations when deciding on new products and processes, factors like environmental effects, safety, and product liability have been made more urgent by pressures from government agencies, consumer groups, and the public. Concern about the impact of new technology has led to "technology assessment," an activity that considers the broad societal and public effects of an innovation before it is introduced. This term was first introduced and popularized by former Congressperson Emil Daddario a number of years ago, its main purpose being to control the speed and manner in which a new technology or innovation was introduced so that serious side effects would not result. To date the principal effort in this field has been by federal government and independent research centers such as research institutes. As mentioned, companies have already taken cognizance of this factor in evaluating new products or projects. The public image of a company as represented by the safety and environmental impact of its products can be an important factor in its gross sales and profits. The rapid growth of the number and magnitude of lawsuits against private corporations is causing hard evaluation of new ventures with respect to public liability.

6.10 COMPUTERIZED TECHNIQUES

A considerable effort has been expended in the development of project selection models in the past, primarily by academics. As long ago as 1964, Baker and Pound found over 80 different formal models (mostly arithmetic) in the literature for making project selections (Martin 1984). More recently, industry as well as academia have developed a variety of computerized models based on risk analysis; statistical decision analysis; and linear, dynamic, and integer programming. Such complex programs offer the prospect of optimizing R&D expenditures and allocation of resources, but whether they really do so and also take into account all product development and marketing aspects is questionable. Attractive and fashionable as such models have appeared to be initially, they have not gained the general acceptance hoped for by their authors. A number of reasons have been offered for their lack of acceptance. One is that many practitioners are instinctively wary of sophisticated techniques they do not fully understand, and they do not really believe the results of the computerized evaluation and selection process.

6.11   MORTALITY OF NEW PRODUCT DEVELOPMENT

The selection of new product areas and process improvements is probably one of the most important decision-making exercises of R&D management. With only a limited quantity of funds available, it is critical that they be expended on programs and projects that have the highest possible probability of success. Failure to achieve a reasonable number of successes year after year can cause a serious loss in credibility of the R&D organization and the contributing groups, as well as a loss of hard-to-come-by venture capital. Various studies have shown that only a small percentage of research ideas eventually become commercially successful products. One successful new product or process out of 40 ideas is not uncommon.

With these kinds of odds it is obvious that new product development is a gamble with very high stakes and an uncertain payoff. However, when there is a payoff, it can lead to substantial profits. Today's company is forced to perform R&D or at least expend a minimal effort toward product improvement; otherwise it is doomed to oblivion, as were the harness makers and the buggy whip manufacturers who failed to change their product lines when horseless carriages came into being. In large, technology-oriented industries such as the chemical industry, a particular product division may have as many as 50 to 100 separate research projects and engineering studies in progress. It is not anticipated that they all will be successful. If only a few are successful, say 2 or 3 out of 100, to the extent that major facilities have to be built or plant changes have to be made, this number is usually adequate to meet the company's need for expansion. Most companies have only a limited amount of funds available for expansion, not to mention limitations in trained personnel and in administrative and other support capability.

During the evolution of a new product six stages can occur:

- Search for new ideas
- Screening (product selection)
- Applied research
- Development
- Testing
- Marketing and commercialization

There is a considerable reduction of ideas in the early stages of product evolution.

This is as it should be because the longer a potentially successful product is carried through the product development process, the greater the financial loss to the company (Figure 6-1). It behooves a company to expend special effort to ensure that projects are not initiated or carried through development that have less than 50 percent probability of success. Many companies require at least 70 percent. Furthermore, as products move through the development process, it is necessary to monitor market and economic conditions constantly to make sure that something has not occurred that would make the new product obsolete or not desired by the customer. Therein lies another important reason for good liaison among technical, marketing, and sales personnel.

QUESTIONS AND TOPICS FOR DISCUSSION

6.1   How could computerized project selection techniques in the project selection process be used, taking into account their possible failings?

6.2   What are some essential factors that must be considered before a company makes the decision to seek government contracts for technical work?

6.3   What is advanced state of the art as contrasted with state of the art? Explain.

6.4   What are some of the possible difficulties encountered in estimating the potential profitability of a new product?

6.5   Discuss the major factors that must be considered in deciding which new products to develop.

6.6   What would be a possible explanation for the fact that companies vary in the payback time expected from technology developed by as much as a factor of 2?

6.7   What are disadvantages of the "laundry-list" approach for evaluating new products or projects (see Figure 6.3)?

6.8   Use the evaluation matrix approach (weighted) in selecting a new car. Assume that you have narrowed your choice to three models. Indicate how you would arrive at various values for a particular criterion.

6.9   Draw a decision tree for one of the following: (a) your future career, (b) a real or hypothetical problem in an organization, or (c) selecting a new product.

References
Amos, M., and Sarchet, B. R. 1981. *Management for Engineers*, pp. 101-9. Englewood Cliffs, NJ: Prentice Hall.

Baker, N. P., and Pound, W. H. 1964, December. R&D project selection: Where we stand. *IEEE Transactions on Engineering Management* 11(4), 124–34.

Cleland, D. I., and Kocaoglu, D. F. 1981. *Engineering Management*, pp. 339–56. New York: McGraw-Hill.

Lapin, L. L. 1985. *Quantitative Methods for Business Decisions*, pp. 114–22. San Diego: Harcourt Brace Jovanovich.

Martin, M. J. C. 1984. *Managing Technological Innovation and Entrepreneurship*, pp. 180–94. Reston, VA: Reston.

Stephanou, S. E. 1981. *Management: Technology, Innovation and Engineering*, pp. 92–109. Bend, OR: Daniel Spencer.

7

Organizing the Technical Effort

7.1 THE LINE ORGANIZATION

An organization has been described as a system of structured authority relations and is usually manifested in an organizational chart, in job descriptions, in group charters, and in documentation of executive and supervisory responsibilities. Individuals are differentiated with respect to their authority, status, and role. The formal line, or tiered, organization provides guidelines for controlling and coordinating technical as well as other activities; otherwise duplication, gross inefficiency, and even chaos can result. In a less formalized organization, technology workers could expend their time and the company's resources down some path in which the company has little or no interest. The desires and objectives of the research workers do not necessarily coincide with those of the company.

132

In today's industrial and organizational climate, there is little of the practice of previous eras, when the "lone wolf" researcher, working perhaps with a technician or helper, came up with innovative, money-making products or process improvements. Instead the team approach is prevalent. This approach is needed because present-day research involves a wide variety of disciplines and skills for successful solution of complex technological problems that cut across many fields of science and engineering. For example, the development of a geothermal power system requires physicists, chemists, geologists, mechanical engineers, chemical engineers, electrical engineers, construction specialists, and those with still other skills and areas of knowledge. It is highly unlikely that one person could have all the expertise needed for such a development. Thus the growth of the multidiscipline approach has become necessary for attacking complex product development and system problems. With the proper organization of technical groups, duplication among various projects can be minimized; the necessary talents can be brough to bear on the various problems; and the efficient use of personnel, materials, and facilities can be maximized.

Among the key requirements of a technical organization are the following:

1. It should be responsive to the present and future needs of the company as continually redefined through ongoing system analysis.
2. There should be designated an increasing degree of authority as one proceeds up the organizational structure.
3. Duplication of technical effort among various technical groups should be minimized.
4. The organization and mode of operation should allow for problems to be solved at the lowest possible level.
5. The organization should provide support personnel and services so that the needs of the research scientists and engineers are taken care of, including an adequate library, a well-equipped storeroom for supplies and materials, proper equipment and laboratory facilities, appropriate technician help, and administrative assistants or accounting personnel.

Organizational Charts

The skeletal chart showing the chain of authority from the top of the organizational pyramid to the lower echelon of supervision is referred to as the line organization (Figure 7-1). Organization charts that show the relationships among various groups in the company and the hierarchy of authority in each group have been used since the Industrial Revolution and probably before then. Without being documented, but by actions of power, the hierarchy of authority has been operative among people ever since they started working together in groups rather than as individuals. Through the years it has been found to be the best way to organize and

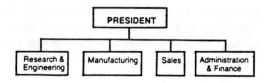

Figure 7-1.   Organization for a Small Company

control a number of personnel doing work toward a common goal. Line functions refer to those functions that concern the day-to-day operation of the company. These can be contrasted with staff functions, which refer to company operations and interests that are of general importance for the company but are not directly related to, and necessary for, day-to-day operation. Kast and Rosenzweig (1974) describe the line organization as being vested with the primary source of authority and performing the major function of the organization while the staff supports and advises the line.

Number of Levels
The number of levels in the line organization of a company varies with the size and complexity of the company's operations. A guiding principle is that the number of levels between the executive officer and the first-line supervision should be kept at a minimum. If there are too many levels of management, communication up and down the line becomes distorted and personnel at the bottom and top levels are seriously insulated from one another. Too many managers, commensurate with too many management levels, can cause unnecessary expense. In technical organizations an average number of levels between the scientist or engineer and the engineering or research director seems to be about three to five. This range can allow for adequate information flow and the minimum number of supervisory levels and hence management expense. The General Electric Company has for many years maintained a minimum of layering in its organization; it claims six levels between the working engineer and the company president (Obradovitch and Stephanou 1990).

Span of Supervision
The size of the group supervised varies with the level of the group in the line organization and the complexity of the work. The number of people that the manager or supervisor is responsible for is referred to as the span of management. Scientists and engineers with degrees usually require less supervision than personnel without degrees, such as technicians, laborers, and so forth. However, scientists and engineers do require considerable administrative support so that their time and effort is not spent and interrupted performing duties and tasks that are not directly

related to their technical effort. For routine work with many repetitive tasks, such as in a testing laboratory, a supervisor may be in charge of as many as 15 to 20 technicians. For less routine work, requiring highly skilled technical personnel, a span of 5 to 6 is common.

Technicians are here defined as laboratory helpers to the scientists and engineers with degrees and usually do not have degrees themselves, although they may have had a few years of college training. Their prestige, status, and pay scale are usually lower than those of the professional scientist or engineer. Companies or organizations conducting extensive technology operations group their technical personnel in a number of different ways. Some common groupings are described in the following sections.

7.2   DISCIPLINE- OR TECHNOLOGY-ORIENTED GROUPINGS

In the technology- or discipline-oriented grouping the technical personnel are grouped according to their specialties (Figure 7-2). They serve as in-house consultants for operational groups in the company for the solution of product and processing problems as well as problems from customers, that is, problems that have to do with the products sold by the company. If other parts of the company are carrying out special projects, the technical problems can be farmed out to the R&D or engineering group. Sometimes such work requires merely a brief consultation with the knowledgeable technical experts, or it may require full-time effort on the part of the specialist for an extended period of time. The technical personnel in such an organization often carry out their own company-funded projects, which often require their full and uninterrupted attention. In such cases every attempt should be made not to divert these personnel from their main objectives; when necessary they can be available for consultations to a limited extent.

Advantages of this type of grouping are that the personnel are more comfortable surrounded by peers who have the same professional background and general interests as themselves. It allows for discussions of technical issues, cross- fertilization of ideas, and a suitable environment for remaining current in a particular

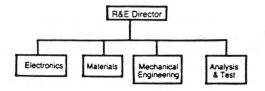

Figure 7-2.   Discipline-Oriented Technical Organization.

field or specialty. A technical problem that is offering one person considerable difficulty may be discussed with a fellow worker; at a meeting, alternative solutions may be suggested that the individual working alone would not have come up with.

A possible disadvantage is that the technical specialty groups tend to become insulated from other groups and may become "islands," where there is inadequate contact with product sales groups that are close to market conditions and customer needs. Perhaps a more serious disadvantage (one that we have seen frequently) is that really competent scientists and engineers will be in continued demand by specific product and manufacturing groups and will not be able to give proper attention to other company problems as they arise. A senior scientist may become so involved in solving a particular product or plant problem that a request from another part of the plant or another customer will have to remain unanswered for an inordinate amount of time. As more requests come in than can be accommodated by the personnel available, priorities may have to be set up, pressure exerted through appropriate organizational channels, or additional personnel hired. In project- and product-oriented groupings of technical personnel, discussed below, this problem is eliminated.

7.3   FUNCTIONALLY ORIENTED GROUPINGS

The organization of technical personnel within an R&D or engineering organization can often be functional. The term *functional* can be interpreted to mean that each group has a specific function to perform in carrying out the technology organization goals, and the technology manager must integrate these efforts in a cost-effective manner to produce the desired result. The project organizations of Figure 7-3 are such an arrangement. This type of grouping can be used in carrying out projects or in product and process development. However, all product and project groupings do not have to be functionally oriented, although this has proven to be an effective form for work identification and accomplishment. Figure 7-1 is an example of a functional-type organization for a whole company.

The differentiation between a functional and discipline type of organization structure can be hazy—for example, when the discipline-oriented groups are really carrying out particular and necessary functions. The subgroupings of the research and engineering division of Figure 7-4 (hybrid grouping) illustrate this point. Large product or project organizations may contain both functional- and discipline-oriented groupings (see Figure 7-5). Functional groupings have similar advantages and disadvantages as technology- or discipline-oriented groupings.

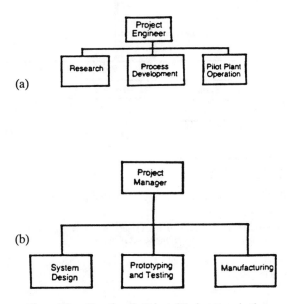

(a)

(b)

Figure 7-3.   Functionally Oriented Project Organizations.

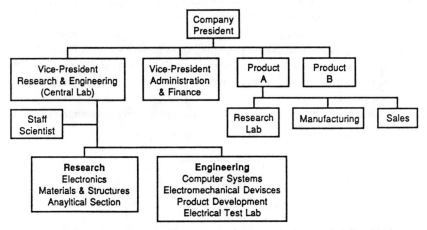

Notes: (a) The research and engineering portions of the organization are discipline- and functionally oriented.

(b) The level next to the chief executive officer contains both product and functional groups.

(c) The product divisions have a functional structure.

Figure 7-4.   Company Organization Showing Hybrid Grouping of Technical Personnel.

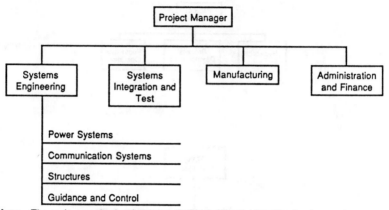

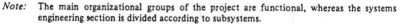

Note: The main organizational groups of the project are functional, whereas the systems engineering section is divided according to subsystems.

Figure 7-5.   Project Organization for a Satellite System Showing both Functional and System-Oriented Groupings (Pure Project).

7.4   PRODUCT-ORIENTED GROUPINGS

Technical personnel can be grouped to support specific product lines of the company. Such groups are essentially the same as the project-oriented groupings (see below), with one major exception. In the product groupings there is a continuum of activity; that is, technical development in a given product area is a continuing, ongoing effort, not a "one-shot" type of activity as is the case with projects. A typical product-oriented organization is shown in Figure 7-6. The technical personnel are 100 percent involved with the product area and are a permanent part of the product organization. This system has the advantages of stability for the scientist or engineer and also the opportunity to become extremely

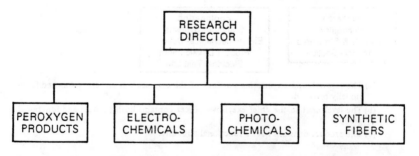

Figure 7-6.   Product-Oriented Grouping of Technical Personnel.

knowledgeable in the specific product area. From the company's standpoint, the technical people in these product groups become valuable assets because of their expertise and knowledge of the particular product. On balance sheets companies will sometimes list as an asset a dollar value for their technical personnel based on what it would cost to replace and train them.

There is the potential disadvantage that personnel working in product laboratories for many years may become stagnant and "grooved" in their thinking, so that as the years progress they contribute less in the way of innovation. However, the opposite can also occur: The individual keeps coming up with new ideas and refinements so that he or she never ceases to be a valuable contributor to the company. How the research scientist or engineer matures with age is very much a function of his or her personal qualities, the challenges of the position, and the working environment.

Product groups also work on the development and improvement of manufacturing and production processes, as well as the improvement of existing products and the solution of industrial customer problems with company products.

7.5 HYBRID GROUPINGS

Most large companies involved in extensive technology development group their technical personnel in a hybrid form, which is a combination of two or more of the preceding groupings (see Figure 7-4). In this way a large company can benefit from the advantages of the various arrangements (and suffer the disadvantages). Special and long-range programs that cut across product lines can be initiated and carried out by the central research and engineering laboratory, and the specific problem areas of the products or projects can be investigated by the divisional or product laboratories. Often problems that cannot be solved by the product or project teams will be referred back to the central laboratory for additional study. The central research or engineering laboratory often has more sophisticated and extensive equipment for basic studies than do the product group laboratories. Companies that deal in complex systems and products with high technical content often organize and maintain specialized groups for initiating and developing new systems and products. These groups have been referred to as advanced systems or product development groups (see Chapters 4 and 6).

7.6 PURE PROJECT ORGANIZATION

The purest form of project organization allows the project or systems manager 100 percent access to, and control of, all technical personnel needed for the project's fulfillment. Figure 7-7 shows a grouping for a company that is completely project-oriented; possible internal organization for the projects is shown in Figure 7-3. The technical specialists needed are hired or transferred to the project and devote all their time to its needs. There is no dilution of their effort on other projects, programs, or products. Other advantages are that there is usually high morale in such a grouping and rewards can be high.

However, if the project or similar projects are not continued, the quantity of work required from the technical employees can diminish and even disappear completely, in which case transfer or dismissal may be necessary. This is a serious defect or risk of the pure project system from the standpoint of the technical worker, but if the company is dynamic and successful, there are always new projects starting up to take up the slack when projects end. Another disadvantage in is that similar concurrent projects may require the same type of technical expertise; therefore there can be duplication of personnel as projects are phased in and out. Still another disadvantage, from the technical specialists' standpoint, is that they may be isolated from their technical peers and not stimulated and kept current to the same extent they would be if they were in a technology-oriented grouping.

Nevertheless, many scientists and engineers are perfectly content in a project environment, and if the project is successful, they advance to important positions in an organization because of the project's success. This is an advantage that is not present to the same extent in the discipline-oriented organization. There are individuals who like project-type existence because of the continual challenge of new problems and new areas and the exposure to a variety of other disciplines and techniques—it can be a broadening experience.

This pure form of project grouping is advantageous when the technical effort is sufficiently funded and important to warrant physical separation as a task force. The project manager can report to the department manager, or the department manager may be designated by the engineering or research director as the project manager. If the project is large enough, the project manager may report directly to the engineering director, to a division vice president, or even to the president of the

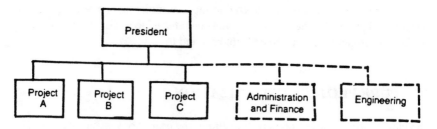

Figure 7-7.   Organization of a Project-Oriented Company.

company (Figure 7-8). When many subsystems and components are needed to develop the system and there is considerable subcontracting, a hybrid type of organization is advantageous.

Figure 7-5 shows such a project organization, with principal emphasis on primary tasks or functions, such as engineering, testing, and manufacturing, and subgroupings reflecting particular subsystems or subdivisions of the main function. In the systems engineering division of Figure 7-5, for example, each system group is responsible for the complete development, from design to completion, of its particular system. This task can include preparing requests for proposals, evaluating proposals, and monitoring subcontractors producing components of the system. At the same time the system group must often perform the same general functions for components being manufactured for the project within the company. The systems integration and test group shown in Figure 7-5 assembles the various subsystems to make up the system and then tests the total system. Following systems integration and testing, the system can be prototyped and manufactured.

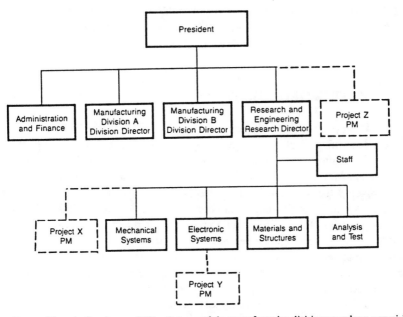

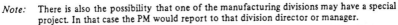

Note: There is also the possibility that one of the manufacturing divisions may have a special project. In that case the PM would report to that division director or manager.

Figure 7-8.   Organization Chart Showing Possible Reporting Relationships for a Technical Project Manager.

Variations of the Project Organization

Variations of the project technique allow the personnel to remain in their functional group location and report directly to the project manager. This system may be necessary if the facilities needed for carrying out the project are at the functional- or discipline-oriented group's location. Then the personnel may be working full or part time on the project. In this type of operation the project manager reports to the president, general manager, or other managerial head.

They act as an assistant to the line function executive and analyze data, recommend, expedite, and coordinate. He or she works with the functional operating groups performing the work of the project but has no direct control of these groups. This mode of operation has the advantage of not creating any new groupings since it utilizes the existing functional organization; the disadvantage is that the project manager does not have complete control and other work of the functional groups is diluted.

In such arrangements there can be one or more project managers, and technical personnel can work on several projects. In deciding which project organizational mode should be utilized, the money available for the various projects, the importance of the projects to the company, the nature of the projects, and the personnel available must be considered. These variations are really degradations of the pure project-type organization and generally fall into the category of matrix organizations. Their important feature is that they allow for the carrying out of projects within the boundaries of the functional organization.

7.7   MATRIX ORGANIZATION

When a company has a number of projects, none of which is sufficiently funded to justify the setting up of pure projects, a matrix-type organization can be set up, as shown in Figure 7-9. Personnel may remain in their functional groups or loaned out on an as-needed basis to various projects. When the particular technical work is completed, the personnel return to their home group or are transferred to another project. All the project managers can be administratively placed under the research and engineering (R&E) director or a project office director, who can report to the R&E director or to a higher level. Such an arrangement can be quite cost-effective since personnel work only on the project as long as their effort is needed and then go on to other projects or tasks set by their functional supervisor. Such tasks are usually continuing in-house programs supporting certain technical subject areas important to the product lines of the company.

The project manager coordinates, monitors, and reports on the work done by the personnel in the various functional groups. The functional manager can play a minor or major role in guiding the work, depending on the nature of the project and the organizational climate of the company. If the company operations are primarily

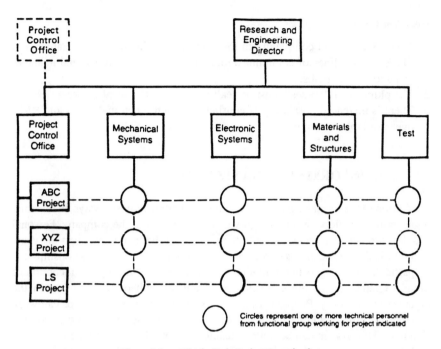

Figure 7-9.   Matrix-Type Project Organization.

projectized—that is, projects funded by outside companies or the government are
the main source of income—the project manager (P.M.) will probably have the
overriding voice in decision making (strong matrix organization). If the company
is primarily product- or process-oriented and projects are secondary activities and
not the main source of revenue, the functional manager will probably be the
controlling manager (weak matrix organization).

There are, of course, advantages and disadvantages to the use of a matrix
organization for R&D projects (Obradovitch and Stephanou 1990):

Advantages

1. Personnel are used only as long as they are needed.
2. Technical expertise of all the functional groups can be fully utilized.
3. Company resources such as facilities, equipment, and personnel can be shared
   according to need, which improves cost effectiveness.
4. Technical personnel retain their expertise by remaining in contact with their
   peers in their specialty area.
5. Personnel have somewhere to go and something to do after projects are
   completed.

Disadvantages

1. There is increased complexity in the operation of the technical organization. There are two lines of communication, one involving the functional manager and another the P.M.s.
2. The plurality of "bosses" must be dealt with by the technical workers.
3. There is increased possibility of conflicts between functional heads and P.M.s over available resources.

7.8   THE INFORMAL ORGANIZATION

In addition to the formal organization, which is charted, almost always an informal organization develops during the growth and operation of the company. Personal ties develop between technical and other personnel that persist through the years as individuals age and change positions in the organization. Such relationships can be particularly strong if the individuals worked together during the inception or initial organization of the company or during difficult or trying times in the organization's history. People with these types of personal relationships can work together informally and accomplish much without going through organizational channels. This system can be quite valuable when work needs to be done rapidly without going through the red tape and paper work required by company procedures. It can also have negative effects when the chain of command is circumvented or arrangements made by friends in different segments of the organization. Obradovitch and Stephanou (1990) state,

> At best, the informal organization can represent a group of truly "company-men" who have been successful at various levels in the organization and work for the best interests of the company. They also can have a hierarchy of authority (not documented but nevertheless present and operative). They represent the "memory" of the company and are true representatives of its culture.

Today's technology manager should learn to recognize the informal ties that exist in the organization, try to use them to his or her benefit, and be aware of their potential pitfalls.

7.9   STAFF FUNCTIONS

In carrying out complex technology there is a need for expertise in many areas. Often the company cannot afford, nor does it have a need for, a group of full-time employees knowledgeable in a particular technology or technical area. The presence of one individual who is particularly expert in the specific field of interest may be sufficient. Such an individual is usually a senior member of the technical staff, either an experienced researcher for the company with a proven track record or perhaps someone brought in from the outside. This expert can serve as an in-house consultant and can be hired permanently by the company to provide guidance and direction in an area of expertise. His or her position in the organization is usually at a relatively high level, such as reporting directly to the engineering or research director. The expert is not involved in the day- to-day operations of the company; that is, he or she is not in the direct chain of command as shown by the organization chart in Figure 7-4.

This type of position is referred to as staff. It is comparable to the position in which many companies place their legal counsels and lawyers. Staff employees may have a group of people working for them; their authority and assignments are given to them by the company officer they report to. Often the assignments entail special projects or programs that cut across organizational lines. The research director may not want to disturb the in-line organization and functions and therefore assigns this "special agent" to accumulate and analyze the information needed from the various groups to assist the director in making an important decision. Staff scientists, staff engineers, and staff consultants can play important roles in the overall planning and operations of a technical organization.

7.10   COMMITTEES AND TASK FORCES

Committees are appointed to provide an informed decision or recommendation to higher management on one or more matters of considerable importance to the company. The participants are usually selected on the basis of their knowledge of key areas of the problem since a number of work areas or technical disciplines that cross organizational lines can be involved. The appointment of a committee is an effective way to evaluate, plan, or make a decision on a matter about which the responsible executive may not be sufficiently knowledgeable or have the time to investigate; the problem under consideration is of such a complex nature that no one individual could possibly have all the information or expertise needed to make the decision or recommendation. A committee may be temporary (ad hoc) or permanent (standing committee), depending on the nature of the problem.

The advantages of using a committee include obtaining informed and applicable input to the problem from knowledgeable sources and the potential of arriving at a consensus rather than one individual's decision. In addition committee members become better acquainted with one another and their respective work areas. Possible disadvantages are that the time of relatively expensive personnel will be consumed, that possibly no agreement will be reached, that personnel clashes may develop, that a dominant personality may try to enforce his or her views on the other committee members, and that much time can be wasted in needless and spurious debate. Nevertheless, the manager should seriously consider the use of committees when the conditions mentioned above prevail. The potential advantages outweigh the disadvantages.

A few rules that make a committee more effective are the following:

1. Draw up and distribute an agenda to the invitees a few days before the meeting.
2. The committee should not be too large—ten people are more than enough. The more people there are, the less likelihood of reaching an agreement on issues.
3. The committee meeting time and duration should be specified initially so that unnecessary expenditure of time is minimized.
4. There should be closure on as many items as possible for what action is needed, who is responsible, and due dates for response.
5. Participants should be at comparable organizational levels, although the leader may not be.
6. Minutes of the meeting should be recorded and distributed. Conclusions arrived at and actions to be taken should be spelled out clearly.

Task forces resemble committees in most ways except that the people designated to make up the task force are also expected to perform the work. Committee members in many cases are not the personnel who ultimately perform the work. Because the task force must complete the mission within a specified period of time, there is an urgency related to the work that may not be present in the work of a committee.

7.11   GROUP CHARTERS AND JOB DESCRIPTIONS

To minimize duplication of effort it is necessary for the exact areas of responsibility of specific groups and key personnel to be spelled out in a formal document that can be referred to when questions arise about who should be doing a particular job. This often takes the form of a documented guide for the manager of the group. It should set forth the basic functions of the manager, who he or she reports to, responsibilities and authority, and internal and external or relationships that should be maintained. It is usually signed by the manager and the company official to whom he or she reports. An example of such a position guide is shown in Figure 7-10. Scientists and engineers are also frequently given position guides so that they, too, are told what their responsibilities, duties, and relationships are in the

---

Title: Manager, Engine Research Department, Research and Engineering Division

---

Reports To: Research and Engineering Division

Basic Functions:

Directs the total operation of the Engine Research Group of the Research and Engineering Division including the modification and improvement of present automobile engines. The operation encompasses combustion studies, thermodynamics and heat transfer, engine structures, materials and testing, and all the engine-related technical disciplines.

Responsibility and Authority:

1. Fulfill the requirements incumbent upon all research and engineering supervision.
2. Manage the overall planning and execution of all the engine technology programs in a manner that will assure compliance with the overall department and division goals.
3. Provide technical support to other departments, customers, and management as needed in the area of engine technology.

Relationships:

1. Collaborate with other department heads in the division to ensure that they receive adequate scientific and engineering support for meeting their objectives and the objectives of the division.
2. Ensure liaison, cooperation, and good working relationships with other company activities in order to attain company goals.

Supervisors:

Chief: Thermodynamics and Heat Transfer Section
Chief: Engine Mechanics Section
Chief: Engine Test Section

Signed:

John Smith, Manager   James Jones, Director
Engine Research Department   Research and Engineering

Figure 7-10.   Position Guide for an R&D Manager.

company (Figure 7-11). With clear-cut definitions of such factors, there is less likelihood of duplication or conflict. Attempts by overly aggressive managers to take on the work of other groups can be identified and curtailed. Individuals know what is expected of them and in what areas they should concentrate their efforts.

Needless to say, the effectiveness of group charters and job descriptions depends on how well they are written and whether they are observed and monitored. Too loose a charter or job description can be confusing. The responsibilities and assignments should be in accord with the authority indicated by the organization chart; responsibility for a work area without appropriate and necessary authority can undermine the group or individual performance and create serious personnel problems and group conflicts. The group or individual can become ineffective and frustrated, and the quality and quantity of work can suffer. Despite these possible disadvantages, preparing and setting forth such documents is extremely effective in improving the quality and efficiency of the R&D operation.

Title: Senior Scientist, Engine Research Department, Research and Engineering Division
Reports To: Manager, Engine Research Department
Basic Functions: 1. Maintain cognizance of current turbojet engine technology. 2. Perform tasks assigned by the manager of the Engine Research Department. 3. Serve as a consultant for other units of the company requiring knowledge and solution of problems related to turbojet engines. 4. Prepare reports and memoranda needed to indicate progress and document work on engine development. 5. Aid products group in setting operational and maintenance requirements and specifications for engines manufactured by the company.
Signed: Robert Stevens, Senior Scientist   John Smith, Manager Engine Research Department   Engine Research Department

Figure 7-11.   Position Guide for a Senior Scientist.

Linear Responsibility Charts

The linear responsibility chart has been used in the past to define the coupling of position with tasks to be performed and responsibilities (Cleland and King 1983). It offers a suitable technique for detailing in chart form the responsibility of the position or group and to what degree; it designates whether the responsibility is advisory, informational, for implementation, or some special category. Organizational titles are listed on one side of the table in decreasing organizational level, and responsibilities are listed on the other side. Responsibilities can be designated full responsibility, must be consulted, may be consulted, must be notified, and so on. An example of such a chart is shown in Table 7-1.

7.12   OPERATIONAL PHILOSOPHIES AND CHARACTERISTICS

Several operational philosophies have been utilized in technology-performing organizations as well as in other types of organizations. These reflect an increasing tendency on the part of upper management to provide a more hospitable and motivating environment for serious-minded and creative personnel who are capable and willing to make contributions to the growth and prosperity of the company and who wish to grow themselves. The two opposite poles of management philosophy have been described in a number of ways:

1. Open versus closed
2. Participative versus nonparticipative

TABLE 7-1.   Linear Responsibility Chart for Technical Support Contract

	Center Director	Marketing Manager	Proposal Manager	Contracts Manager	Accounting Manager	Project Manager	Task Leader(s)
Establish business objectives.	1	3		4			
Identifying business opportunities	2	1					
Decision to seek specific technical work.	1	3	4	4		4	
Prepare technical proposal	2	4	1				
Prepare cost proposal.	2	4	4	1	3		
Accept customer's contract	5	5	5	1	4		
Appoint project manager.	1					3	
Prepare technical plans.	2					1	4
Organize technical team	2					1	3
Supervise technical work.						2	1
Submit technical reports.	4					1	4
Submit cost invoices					2	1	3
Deliver final end products	5				5	1	4
Submit final invoice	5				2	1	3
Close the contract.	3	4		1	5		

Code:

1	actual responsibility	4	may be consulted
2	general supervision	5	must be notified
3	must be consulted		

3. Permissive versus highly disciplined
4. Theory Y versus Theory X[1]
5. Theory Z

The open, participative, permissive, or Theory Y type of management allows for more impact of the individual technical worker on the nature of the work, the operation, and even the decision-making process of the organization. This result can become undesirable if carried to an extreme. There is greater emphasis on the autonomy of individuals and less administrative control and constraint. The organization is usually more flexible and the personnel can obtain more satisfaction in their work because of their involvement in decisions affecting their work.

The nature of the closed type of management philosophy is described in Table 7-2. These characteristics of a closed-type organization and the resulting effects show the likely impact of an overly disciplined and regulated technology development or R&D organization. The comparable chart for the open type of management philosophy would be the antithesis of Table 7-2. From the standpoint of

---

[1]D. M. McGregor, *The Human Side of Enterprise*. (New York: McGraw-Hill, 1960). This is a classic and frequently quoted work in this subject area.

TABLE 7-2.   Closed Type of Management Style

Characteristics	Advantages	Disadvantages
• Close control by super- vision ("tight ship")	• Great emphasis on productivity • No deviations from prescribed and necessary activity	• Personnel tend to be subjugated • Personnel become intimidated
• Research scientists and engineers have little to say	• Efficient and businesslike	• Personnel do not contribute as much, if at all
• Authority concentrated in upper echelons	• Good implementation of management directives	• Decreases motivation and creativity

motivation and creativity, a bias toward the open organization is more effective for an R&D type of activity.

The type of formal technology organization that is best depends on the history of company growth, the nature of the company activity, the size of the company, the personality or "culture" of the company, and other factors.[2] What can be stated for certain is that any reasonable organization can be productive if the people in it are willing and motivated workers. Conversely, if the workers are not willing and motivated and the leadership competent, no organizational format will succeed. An example is the action in 1989 of McDonald Douglas to reorganize the Douglas Aircraft Division in Long Beach following many successive years of financial lossess, despite burgeoning sales of their commercial aircraft. The reorganization, as has happened so often before, particularly in aerospace companies, failed to increase productivity and cost effectiveness, and the company emerged a year later in a worse situation financially and otherwise.

QUESTIONS AND TOPICS FOR DISCUSSION

7.1   Which is more effective in a research or engineering organization, vertical or horizontal emphasis of authority? Why?

7.2   If a technology-performing organization has two-thirds of its financial support from product line (functional) activities and one-third from

---

[2]The "personality" or "culture" of a company reflects the general philosophy of the leadership. It indicates which groups are most important (finance, engineering, R&D, sales, marketing, etc.). It may dictate the relationships and interactions between workers and management and between management levels and even the style of dress that is acceptable (formal or informal).

projects, how should it be organized? Assume that the lifetime of the projects ranges from three to six months and they involve all the functional groups.

7.3   What are important differences in the management techniques of an organization that is 100 percent product oriented and one that is 100 percent project oriented?

7.4   What are the conditions that determine whether a technical organization should be functionally or discipline-oriented?

7.5   What are the advantages and disadvantages of using a staff person to act as a coordinator for carrying out a special technical effort using different functional groups? What other alternatives would a research director or manager have? What would be the basis for selecting a particular alternative?

7.6   Under what type of conditions should a research manager set up (a) an ad hoc committee, (b) a standing committee, and (c) a task force?

7.7   How can job descriptions and group charters be of value in a technology research and engineering organization?

7.8   Discuss the applicability of the Theory X and Theory Y concepts to present-day engineering and technology developments operations.

7.9   To what extent should a manager use the informal organization in a company for accomplishing his or her goals?

7.10   Develop a linear responsibility chart for a project organization.

7.11   What are the advantages and disadvantages of a matrix- type organization? How would you explain the terms *loose* matrix and *tight* matrix as two extremes of matrix-type organizations?

References

Cleland, D. I., and King, W. R. 1983. *Systems Analysis and Project Management*, pp. 303–318. New York: McGraw-Hill.

Kast, E. F., and Rosenzweig, J. E. 1974. *Organization and Management*, p. 213. New York: McGraw-Hill.

Obradovitch, M. M., and S. E. Stephanou. 1990. *Project Management, Risk and Productivity*, p. 57. Bend, OR: Daniel Spencer.

8

Staffing

8.1 SOURCES OF TECHNICAL PERSONNEL

Personnel for technology, product, and manufacturing development can be obtained from either within the company or from outside sources. Many companies maintain a constant surveillance and search for competent, talented professional people. In obtaining personnel from outside the company, the research or technology manager usually works with the personnel department, if the company is large, or a personnel officer, if the company is small.

An abbreviated, or short-form, job description is prepared for advertising for and selecting the desired type of individual. An example of a job description, also called an employment requisition, is shown in Figure 8.1. It sets forth briefly the qualifications, training, and experience required for the position and the general nature of the tasks to be performed. Job descriptions should be very carefully

152

Title of Position:	Research Engineer.
Educational Requirements:	B.S. in Chemical Engineering.
Experience:	At least two years in chemical processing, particularly pilot plant operations and process development.
Description of Duties:	1. Supervise pilot plant operations for producing new organic intermediates.
	2. Identify and recommend process improvements including conversion of existing batch method to a continuous process.
	3. Work with production engineering to design manufacturing plant.
Salary Range:	$XX,xxx to $XX,xxx per year.

Figure 8-1.   Job Requisition or Job Description.

prepared because, on the one hand, if the requirements set forth are too broad, vague, and general, an excessive number of applications will result, many of which do not fulfill the requirements of the position. On the other hand, if the job description is too narrow and restrictive, there may not be many candidates who feel qualified to apply. It is a good practice to hire technical personnel who have general capability in a particular area of technology so that they can be utilized in a variety of possible situations, rather than an overly specialized person whose applicability may be limited to only one or two specific types of problems.

Working with the Personnel or Human Resources Department

The responsibility for the mechanics of seeking personnel from outside sources is that of the company personnel department. Common procedures include advertisements in newspapers and professional magazines, visits of individuals from the personnel department to universities and colleges, and possibly the use of employment agencies. Another source is professional technical meetings. As already indicated, the personnel departments of large companies usually have a continuing program of searching out and maintaining contact with promising candidates for employment. An organized, continual search is more cost-effective for the company than a sporadic and concentrated effort on an intermittent basis. However, if the company is primarily project-oriented, hiring on an as-needed basis may be more economical if a hard core of supervisory and highly specialized personnel is maintained on a permanent basis. A select group of company employees can become extremely expert in starting, executing, and closing out projects in a cost-effective manner so that they become extremely valuable to the company.

There are additional ways that personnel from outside the organization or company can be obtained. Sometimes company personnel or customers have friends or know of competent and eligible individuals who might be interested in the positions. Sometimes department heads or managers will contact their college or university and seek assistance from professors or department heads. If a high-level manager is being sought, executive recruitment and management firms may be consulted. These firms advertise regularly in leading newspapers of major cities and also in business magazines and journals.

Obtaining Personnel for Projects
In fulfilling project requirements it is usually quicker and more convenient to obtain personnel from within the company. In such transfers it is customary for the manager to contact the supervisor of the person or type of person being sought. Formal negotiations should be made through the appropriate organizational channels rather than dealing with the desired candidate directly. It may be that the supervisor may not be able to spare anyone at that time, or the particular technical expert being sought is a valuable and nonexpendable member of the group. It is poor practice for the manager seeking personnel to contact a technical person directly and solicit a transfer without first contacting the person's supervisor. This action could antagonize the supervisor since it would ignore the supervisor's needs and could lead to wholesale raiding of the best personnel from various groups; this practice could cause excessive personnel transfer and be harmful to the company's overall operation. When the desired personnel cannot be spared from a particular group, other groups in the company can be contacted or outside sources solicited.

8.2   EVALUATION OF APPLICATIONS

Assuming that the personnel department does its job well, the manager should soon receive a number of applications for the position to be filled. These applications should be reviewed carefully and evaluated for the following characteristics:

1. Is the application filled out neatly or in a careless, slovenly manner? This is frequently an indication of the type of reports these applicants would write and even the quality of the work that they would do.
2. Are answers to questions complete and responsive or are they incomplete, minimal, or evasive?
3. Are salary requirements excessive, that is, significantly above the allowable range for the position being filled?
4. Does the applicant have the desired educational training and experience for the job?
5. Is the applicant a job hopper? This is a value judgment that the manager must make. However, an applicant who has changed jobs every one or two years over a period of several years should be considered suspect.

6. Is the applicant overqualified for the position? If overqualified, he or she may not be happy at the level that you have in mind and may seek another position shortly after being hired.

7. Is the applicant overly specialized? It is desirable to have some degree of versatility so that the applicant could be used in some other related work assignment if necessary.

8. Does the applicant indicate a geographical preference that would exclude him or her from consideration? Sometimes candidates will state an unwillingness to locate in certain areas where the company might need employees.

These considerations can serve as a basis for eliminating a number of applicants so that the manager is faced with a more workable and viable group of candidates. Depending on company practice, contacts can then be made by the personnel department for plant or facility visits, or the concerned manager may further screen the potential new employees by phoning them personally. The latter technique tends to be more cost-effective because during the course of the telephone conversation, it may be determined that the individual is not really suited, desirous of, or available for the position. This fact may somehow have been obsured or not disclosed in the application. Then the company can realize appreciable savings in transportation, lodging, and other expenses that would have been incurred if the applicant had been needlessly brought to the company for an interview.

Those applicants who still appear to be good prospects after the phone conversation are then asked to visit the plant through a letter usually written by the personnel department. Common sense dictates that the applicant should not be contacted at his or her present place of employment, which could jeopardize the individual's position. Application forms should have a space where applicants can indicate whether it is permissible to contact their present employers.

8.3   THE PLANT OR FACILITY VISIT

Professional employees such as scientists and engineers are frequently transported at company expense over large distances for the facility visit and plant interview. Since the combination of air fare, local transportation, lodging, and meals can come to an appreciable total, only a select few applicants should be invited. The hiring manager or supervisor should be fairly certain that there is a high probability the candidate will be acceptable. The expense of interview trips can be justified on the following basis:

- It allows the manager and the company to see and evaluate the candidate personally.

- It gives the applicant an opportunity to meet the prospective superior and peers and obtain a glimpse of the working environment. In addition, the applicant can see the geographical area and note the living conditions. If the applicant has a family this factor can be particularly important.

Sometimes spouses are invited for the interview trip so that they can see where the potential new home would be and thus eliminate the possibility at the outset that they will not have an opportunity to contribute to the decision of the candidate. Because of cost this invitation is usually issued only for senior or supervisory personnel.

The Interview

When the prospect appears at the company premises for the interview, it is customary for the employing manager to spend at least 40 minutes to an hour or two with the individual. Since applicants have been brought to the facility at some expense, they should not be treated curtly or briefly, nor should they be kept waiting for hours for the interviewing manager to become available. If an emergency arises, arrangements should be made to have the candidate interviewed by a suitable subordinate or substitute. Routine treatment of interviews in a manner that intimates that they are trivial or of secondary importance can cause the loss of potentially valuable personnel.

Before the interview and after full study of the application, some specific questions should be prepared. It is important that the interviewer should do more listening than talking, concentrate on specific accomplishments of the candidate, and probe job changes (reasons) and track record. The candidate should receive a thorough background check before being hired. A guide for carrying out the interview in an ethical manner is as follows:

1. Candidates should be told, without equivocation, where they would fit into the organization. This can be confirmed by showing them an organizational chart indicating the interviewer's position and theirs. It is customary and desirable for the employing supervisor to interview the applicant. In some cases this rule is not adhered to, but a secondhand interview might lead to problems later.
2. The requirements of the position—that is, what would be expected—should be set forth in crystal-clear fashion; no half-truths, inaccurate statements, and promises should be made since these could also lead to problems later, particularly if promises are made that are not kept.
3. Candidates should be asked some questions about their expertise, previous job, reasons for leaving the present job, job requirements, aspirations, and career goals. Their reasons for leaving their present employment could be

revealing. A condition that they consider undesirable may also exist in the company with which they are interviewing. If so, it should be brought to their attention. For example, if they are leaving because they want a job with promotional possibilities, the interviewer should make sure that such possibilities are, in fact, available. Applicants should also be asked whether they feel that they would be happy doing the work that was described in the initial portion of the interview and if they have any reservations concerning the type of work and assignment.

4. During the course of the applicants' responses to questions, the interviewer should note the candidates' ability to communicate, their responsiveness to questions, and their poise and self-confidence. Are they pleasant in appearance and manner? Although these characteristics are not overriding in making a decision about the suitability of an individual, taken as a whole they can have an important bearing on the evaluation.[1]

5. Candidates should be introduced to the immediate supervisor of the interviewing manager for additional input to the final decision.

6. Candidates should also be introduced to one or more of their peers, people that they would be working with, and allowed to converse with them about their work. The peers, of course, should be aware that details of proprietary information could not be disclosed in such conversations. A key senior person could take the applicants on a plant trip or tour of the laboratories or facility. This step can increase the morale of personnel since they would be involved in the hiring and decision process. It is assumed that the interviewer will consult with them about their opinions of the candidate.

7. Following or before the plant or facility tour, depending on the time schedule, applicants can be taken for lunch with another manager from a related group or a senior scientist or engineer to provide further insight and familiarity.

8. Finally, the manager can discuss the salary range and company benefits such as savings plans, stock plans, and so on. The manager should point out the growth potential of the position and the potential for salary increases. Usually no firm salary commitments are made at this time, but this can vary from company to company. The insurance, medical, retirement, and other general benefits can be explained to the candidates by the personnel department just before they leave.

9. The interview is usually culminated with a statement by the manager to the applicants that they would hear of the final decision within the next few

---

[1] Although it can be argued that a person may have unusual technical creativity and skills and yet be quite eccentric in manner and appearance, in an organization in which working with and for people is important, extreme eccentric or erratic behavior can be disruptive.

weeks. It should be explained that time is needed to obtain reference checks, medical exam results if necessary, approval of the salary offer by higher management, and the final evaluation in view of other candidates applying for the position.

8.4   THE FINAL SELECTION

With all the available data assembled, managers can now select the candidate they wish to hire. Before doing so, however, they can obtain still more information on the applicants, which can have an important bearing on the selection. Managers should first consult with their superior. If the superior was not particularly impressed or was negative, managers should be doubly certain that they really want to hire that applicant. If the individual does not work out well in the organization, a manager risks the criticism of the superior. If managers feel strongly about the candidate's potential, they can take the risk and hire that individual. Sometimes the superior may insist that the individual not be hired.

Managers should also consult the personnel (peers) who spoke to the candidate and the senior scientist or engineer who took the candidate on the plant tour to get their opinions. A phone call to one or more former supervisors can also be made to obtain their opinions of the individual and his or her performance in previous positions.[2] If the candidate is presently employed, the present supervisor should of course *not* be contacted unless the candidate has indicated on the application forms that it is permissible to do so.

In making the final selection, the manager should evaluate the following factors;

1. Does the candidate have the skills needed for carrying out the technical job?
2. Will the candidate fit into the group or be a personality problem (admittedly, not always possible to determine in advance)?
3. Is the candidate sufficiently versatile to be used in more than one job assignment? A certain degree of versatility in a technical person is desirable because of the variable nature of R&D work.
4. Will the candidate be happy in the work environment?
5. Can salary requirements be met? Are they out of line with comparable personnel already in the group?

---

[2]Because of the possibility of lawsuits, many companies refer such inquiries to their personnel departments, which give an innocuous and noncommital response with no details concerning the quality of performance—merely a statement that the person worked for the company during the indicated time

6. Is the manager satisfied with the opinions of other workers in the group who met the candidate, the opinion of the manager's superior, and the previous supervisors' statements?

8.5 SELECTION OF SUPERVISORY PERSONNEL

From Within the Organization

In obtaining supervisory personnel for technical management positions, one may have to promote a senior person, look for an adequately trained supervisor who might be available for transfer within the organization, or bring in someone from outside the organization. It is highly desirable from a management standpoint to promote from within the organization, whenever possible, for the following reasons:

1. The morale of the individual promoted is given a big boost and that of the others is maintained because they observe that one of their peers was promoted and possibly they could be too in the future. If supervisors are almost always brought in from outside the group or organization, those technical personnel seeking organizational advancement can be demoralized and antagonized. However, sometimes an outside supervisor must be brought in because the nature of the assignment calls for expertise or capability that is not present in available personnel, or the group may be so young and inexperienced that a mature, management-oriented individual is needed.

2. Individuals selected from within the organization or group are a known quantity from performance in previous assignments. Their weaknesses are also known and can be properly weighed against their attributes. Individuals hired from outside the organization emphasize their positive attributes both in their application and in their effort to make a good impression during the facility visit and interview. What are not known are their weaknesses and inadequacies. These will become apparent only after they have been in the employ of the company for a while. It is human nature to give an applicant the benefit of the doubt and not to consider potential deficiencies. This attitude works to the disadvantage of on-board personnel because when they are considered for promotion, their faults or weaknesses are generally known and can be, and often are, used against them.

3. Individuals selected from within the organization know the workings and operational procedures of the company, so that no time is lost in training them or allowing them to find out for themselves where things are and how to get things done in the new environment.

4. Individuals from within the organization are more likely to be accepted by the employees in the group they are going to supervise. If properly selected, they have already proven their worth and demonstrated leadership capability while working in a peer relationship.

From Outside the Organization

In support of bringing in new supervision from the outside, it can be argued that the new person might bring in new ideas and concepts that could improve the operation of the group. The specific situation would have to be considered to determine whether this advantage would more than compensate for the disadvantages mentioned above.

A number of professional management and executive placement firms make a business of finding positions for managerial personnel. These firms list professionals of many different backgrounds and talents including technical personnel who have come to them for employment. Advertisements of those firms can be found in large city newspapers as well as in professional, technical, and business magazines.

Key Qualities

In selecting supervisory or managerial personnel, it is advisable to look for key qualities:

1. Good communicative skills: They are articulate, listen attentively, and absorb and retain information.
2. A self-starter: They can initiate work and action on their own rather than always being guided and directed.
3. Some knowledge of the technical field. However, they do not have to be an expert in every area and facet of the applicable technology. In fact, there are advantages to being generalists—they are less likely to become intimately involved or overemphasize their particular field of specialization.
4. Energetic and dynamic: Although not a necessary condition, a person with an apparently limitless amount of energy and drive can be a tremendous asset to an R&D organization; conversely, a lethargic manager will not tend to inspire or motivate technical personnel.
5. Perceptive and responsive to the needs of people: This is a difficult attribute to assess in advance, particularly when it must be evaluated for someone who has never supervised before.

After selection it is desirable, if not mandatory, for the new supervisor to be given management training of some kind, preferably at a nearby university or training center. New managers who do not understand human relations, how to treat people, how to communicate effectively, and how to manage generally are a scourge to the people who work for them and the organization. Engineers who are promoted primarily because of their intimate knowledge of a particular product or technical area frequently fall into this undesirable category. Often they have been highly creative and are not really interested in managing (except for the increased remuneration). As a result, the organization loses a creative and productive engineer and gains a poor manager.

Acting Supervisors

Many companies utilize a trial period for breaking in a new supervisor and so indicate to the organization and the world by preceding the title by the word *acting*. One advantage of this procedure is that the individuals realize they are on trial and will make every effort to fulfill the requirements of the position so that they can be accepted as full-fledged supervisors. Another advantage is that the company is not committing itself permanently, so that if they make serious errors, they can be demoted and readily transferred back to their previous assignment or another assignment.

However, the term *acting* may also connote a temporary appointment, implying perhaps that the organization is looking for a permanent tenant for the position and that the present appointee is there only until a suitable candidate is found. With this latter interpretation supervisors may be treated with slightly less deference by both peers and the people they supervise, which can weaken their position and authority.

The specific circumstances and the nature and personality of the appointee can determine the desirability of using this term. There are times when no suitable candidate for a supervisory position is immediately available, and a temporary appointment must be made. In such instances the term *acting* is justified and understood by all parties.

8.6 TESTING AND EVALUATION OF APPLICANTS

Some companies emphasize on the results of written tests for evaluating technical applicants. This technique has been applied when there is a large number of engineering applicants for a limited number of openings as well as to individual applicants. These tests are usually technical in nature, but many also contain nontechnical questions. In addition, some companies have used psychological tests to reveal specific characteristics or qualities they are seeking in a candidate. Psychological tests should not be used alone to determine the probable competence of the applicant; rather they should be used as additional input to the total package of information. Many competent and completely adequate employees are not good test takers, and there is always the question of how applicable and accurate the test is. According to Karger and Murdick (1980),

Psychological tests are an important adjunct to personal interviews, but they should not be allowed to supplant the personal interview and personal selection techniques. The results of such tests are indicators, and it should be recognized that the indications are not always correct.

Another important factor that the company and the manager must take into account in the use of tests, particularly psychological tests, is the legal aspect, that is, the possibility of being sued by an individual on the basis of discriminatory or unfair employment practices. A number of lawsuits in recent years have resulted when applicants took psychological tests and were not hired by the company. The decisions in these cases have not established clear-cut principles or guidelines, so a manager should be aware of the potential legal hazards in psychological testing.

Despite these disadvantages, there are those who believe that the interview and other time-honored evaluation techniques are inferior to evaluation testing. The objection to the interview technique is based primarily on the fact that it can and usually tends to be subjective, that is, dependent on the likes, dislikes, and personality of the interviewing manager rather than on the true capabilities of the individual. This objection is debatable; since the manager must work with the individual being hired, his or her opinion, subjective as it may be, is an important consideration. However, the use of tests that have been validated by the correlation of test scores with success in the company is a practice difficult to argue against, if the data are statistically valid and the company's version of success is meaningful and clear-cut.

Still another testing technique is the "holistic" approach. In this method of evaluation the individual is subjected to a complex situation and his or her behavior under these circumstances is observed. Again, use of this technique is controversial, even among psychologists.

In conclusion it can be stated that the use of tests as a screening tool can be justified when a large number of applicants is to be evaluated. Their use for selecting technical employees with experience for specific technical positions is debatable and probably not necessary. The customary techniques of evaluating educational background, previous applicable experience, job aspirations and requirements of the individual, and personal appraisal by the manager and staff are still basic in making the final decision. The present trend of companies is away from testing.

8.7   SHORT-TERM HIRING

In the business endeavors of many companies involved with technology, product and manufacturing development, and projects, frequently customer needs and company activities require hiring additional technical help for a short time and on rather short notice. On such occasions the company may be forced to resort to employment agencies that have on tap specialized engineering talent for short-term assignments. These freelance engineers are interviewed and selected by the company in the same manner as other candidates, but it is understood at the outset that the length of employment is dependent on the workload, which may be predefined, and there in no implied long-term commitment.

From the standpoint of the company and the particular project or product manager, this procedure can be economically sound since fringe, retirement, and other benefits do not have to be paid. With respect to technical performance there is a slight risk since the individual hired has no long-range commitment or permanent ties with the company and hence may not be as conscientious and hard-working as a permanent employee. However, sometimes a temporary employee does so well that he or she is asked to remain with the company on a permanent basis. A temporary employee knowing of this possibility might tend to work harder and do a better job. In obtaining the services of temporary employees, the company must pay a premium, which means that their cost per unit of time is greater than comparable company personnel. Despite the increased pay rate, the overall cost is less than hiring full-time personnel and maintaining them, so the additional temporary expense can be justified.

The past practice of a few large companies of hiring hundreds of engineers and scientific workers fresh from colleges and universities, selecting within a year or two a small percentage as outstanding and suited to the company, and then dismissing the remainder is questionable ethically but may have been effective from a business standpoint. In today's environment the tendency is for young scientists or engineers to leave of their own accord after a few years with the company if their advancement and other aspirations are less than their expectations.

8.8 CONSULTANTS

The use of consultants by a technical manager is often necessary because a specific type of expertise is needed that is not available within the company or the workload of available experts in the company is so great that they cannot be utilized to fulfill the need. Sometimes the need can be fulfilled by a few visits of a consultant on a short-term basis, or the need may be recurring so that the consultant is scheduled for regular monthly or weekly visits. Many university professors and talented engineers and scientists in consulting firms are available for this type of duty. Rates vary and may or may not include per diem expenses. Consultants can be used advantageously for solving special technical problems, providing needed guidance and assistance in complex technological areas, and making unbiased appraisals of company operations. However, there is usually a penalty of time and money expended in acquainting the consultant with the true nature of the problem and the company environment. A value judgment is needed concerning the cost-benefit of such an expenditure.

8.9   STAFFING OF LARGE PROJECTS

Selection of a Project Manager
The central figure in a project is the project manager, who is autonomous in the project and should have access to all the applicable experience available in the company. It is advantageous if project managers already have experience in project management, either as a project manager or working at a level next to a project manager. They are usually generalists rather than specialists, although they may have been specialists at one time in one of the key technical areas of the project. It is advantageous for the project managers to be responsible for the project from birth to completion. They should be the same people who headed up the preliminary or feasibility study; they make the ultimate decisions on all major project problems.

In addition to the usual managerial qualities mentioned in Section 8.5, project managers must be strong in coordinating and negotiating skills since constant interaction with a variety of different groups is necessary. Such groups could include customers, government officials, subcontractors, and vendors, as well as manufacturing, marketing, and other groups and divisions within the company. An important asset is a flair for encouraging innovation and providing a creative environment. The ability to negotiate and compromise is of the utmost importance given the fact that there is a high level of competition for resources in a large company and customers, subcontractors, and vendors are all seeking maximum value, often without equal return.

Kerzner (1989) identifies ten specific skills as being necessary for a successful project manager:

- Team building
- Leadership
- Conflict resolution
- Technical expertise
- Planning

- Organization
- Entrepreneurship
- Administration
- Management support
- Resource allocation

Selection of Other Project Personnel
The acquisition of the required personnel for a project is very similar to that already discussed (Sections 8.1 through 8.4), but the time factor is usually more com-

pressed and urgent. As a result, the staffing is mostly from within the organization and there are some special requirements.

In staffing a project the selection of personnel must take into account their immediate utility to the objectives and work of the project since there is usually insufficient time and money to allow for any substantial amount of training. The technical personnel must already be well versed in their specialty and capable of immediately applying their expertise to their portion of the project effort. Such personnel may be available from the research and engineering groups of the company, from other projects that are winding down; or if the expertise is not available within the company, from the outside.

In any procedure for acquiring project personnel, it must be kept in mind that those so obtained must be disposed of at a later time when the project is in the decline or termination phase. For those skills that require less advanced training and education, the job shop can be a valuable resource. Workers with typical skills available on a short-term basis from employment agencies are draftspersons, machinists, and some types of engineers. The use of consultants can be advantageous if highly specialized expertise is needed that is not available within the company. Although consultant fees can be high, they can provide valuable know-how that can help in solving critical technical issues and result in the savings of time and money (see Section 8.8).

8.10   IDENTIFICATION OF INNOVATORS (GATEKEEPERS)

Obviously the technical personnel obtained must match the technologies important to the organization, but another aspect of the staffing issue is just as vital (Balderstan, Birnbaum, Goodman, and Stahl 1984). The often-observed fact is that only a small fraction of the total technical staff come up with 80 to 90 percent of the creative ideas developed in an R&D organization. One can then identify a creative staff that is characterized by its ability to come up with new ideas and solutions to complex problems and a relatively sterile staff that merely executes what is given to them by others.

The personnel with the new ideas are often referred to as *gatekeepers*, in that they open the gates (information channels) to new areas of exploitation. They are the ones who stay current with the literature and attend (often by invitation) national and sometimes international meetings of technical and professional organizations. They usually are in touch with other experts in their field in industry and sometimes in academia and are on the forefront of knowledge in their specialty. All technical personnel are not and should not be the same type because someone has to carry out the less exciting, day-to-day product and manufacturing improvements that are more incremental in nature. There is an important role for both the innovators and the implementers. We have observed that the relatively small, incremental improvements in products and processes that are consistently made, year after year, can after a period of many years appear to be major technological breakthroughs.

It is necessary, then, in bringing on new technical personnel to make certain that the organization is adequately staffed with innovators, or gatekeepers, because they are the ones on which the future of the company greatly depends. Gatekeepers should be recognized and rewarded in special ways, monetarily and otherwise.

8.11   STAFF IMPROVEMENT

The process of upgrading personnel in an organization is often referred to as staff improvement. It can take on several forms, such as on-the-job training, hiring new personnel, transferring personnel, or dismissing nonproductive personnel.

On-the-job training can be carried out in different ways. The selected personnel, usually those who have exhibited growth potential, are allowed to enroll in one or more special courses given by the company during or after normal working hours. These may be courses that train employees to be managers or to be knowledgeable in specific areas of company interest. Another way is to allow the promising employees to attend a class at a nearby university during normal working hours or in the evening at the company's expense. The usual requirement is that the course has some bearing on the employees' work. Many companies remunerate personnel for courses taken in pursuit of a degree that can increase their total capability and potential. Company policies vary in this regard. Sometimes companies pay the total expense, including the cost of books, and sometimes the companies pay a percentage of the cost, say, 80 percent. In either case it is a significant benefit to technical workers in that it allows them to upgrade their knowledge and become more valuable to the company.

Another method of staff improvement is to hire or transfer from other departments new, more competent personnel. This practice can upgrade the quality and quantity of work on a research program and can make up for deficiencies that have developed or are going to develop.

Still another way is to dismiss nonproductive personnel. Although this is a difficult task and is to be avoided if possible, there are occasions when technical workers have been improperly placed or have lost or are not using their full capability. In such instances it is necessary to take action so that the quality and quantity of work performed on a given program or project are not impaired. Not to take action can further aggravate the problem and is a disservice to the technical worker concerned, as well as a cost to the company. Companies will sometimes announce a *staff improvement* program, which in essence amounts to culling workers or supervisors who are not carrying their share of the workload or who are not wanted for other reasons.

QUESTIONS AND TOPICS

8.1   What are the trade-offs a small to medium-sized company must make in regard to maintaining a constant programmed search for technical personnel, including visits to universities, employment clearing houses, and the like, as opposed to making a concerted effort from time to time when personnel needs accumulate or become acute?

8.2   A company is unexpectedly the winner of a contract that requires approximately 10 percent more technical personnel than it presently has available. How should the project manager obtain the personnel needed?

8.3   What are the important considerations and evaluations that must be made before promoting a scientist or engineer to a supervisory position?

8.4   It has been said and substantiated by data that today's professional workers are more mobile and less committed than in previous generations. Frequent job hopping is not uncommon. How can the research manager minimize this potential threat to maintaining a competent and stable group of technical personnel?

8.5   Under what conditions can hiring a consultant be justified for each of the following types of service: (a) on an as-needed basis and (b) on a regularly scheduled basis?

8.6   In view of equal opportunity and affirmative action laws and requirements, what precautions must a manager take in using psychological or other tests to evaluate personnel for employment or promotion?

8.7   What are the advantages and disadvantages of using "job shops" as a temporary source of engineering personnel?

8.8   What are the key personal characteristics that should be sought in a technical supervisor?

8.9   Aerospace and defense contractors employing large number of engineers and scientists are often in a rapid hiring or layoff mode as a result of the nature of government contracting. What are possible solutions to this serious employment problem?

8.10 Discuss the problem of destaffing when a project is terminated and how you would cope with it.

8.11 Sometimes a manager will hire a friend to fill a technical vacancy, even though the friend may not be as suited for the position as some other candidate. What problems could result from this type of action?

References

Balderston, J., P. Birnbaum, R. Goodman, and M. Stahl. 1984. *Modern Management Techniques in Engineering and R&D*. New York: Van Nostrand Reinhold.

Karger, D. W., and Murdick, R. G. 1980. *Managing Engineering and Research*, p. 153. New York: Industrial Press.

Kerzner, H. 1989. *Project Management: A Systems Approach to Planning Scheduling and Controlling*, 3rd ed. New York: Van Nostrand Reinhold.

9

Monitoring, Evaluating, and Controlling

9.1 INTRODUCTION

Monitoring, evaluating, and controlling are management functions carried out chronologically after planning, organizing, and staffing. Planning, among other things, sets forth performance goals. Monitoring implies observing performance and evaluating or measuring the actual performance versus the anticipated or expected performance as developed in the plans. Monitoring can be accomplished by timely, informal conversations or formal meetings, tests, measurements, and reports. Based on the conclusions or evaluations derived from the monitoring process, action may be taken by the manager to improve performance—this is control.

Three aspects of performance must be reviewed in monitoring R&D effort: technical performance, cost, and schedule. Since technical personnel are intimately involved, monitoring and evaluating the effort must ultimately include evaluating individual as well as group performance.

To control effectively, a communications system must be developed that provides accurate information and allows for adequate time to react to problems. Such problems can center on technical impasses, personnel, facilities, funding, and a host of other difficulties that seem constantly to arise in technology development. The communications system should consist of both oral reporting and documentation. Typical management communications systems are summarized in Figure 9-1. Because of the importance of cost, some companies remove the cost control function of the technology manager and assign financial monitoring and coordinating responsibility to a financial control group. The personnel of this group provide support to the manager in the cost performance of his or her group or project and may also do the same for other groups and projects in the organization.

9.2   ORAL COMMUNICATION

Frequent contact is necessary between technology managers and the personnel leading the work effort so that the managers are kept informed of how the work is progressing. If there are problems, the managers' greater visibility and knowledge of the organization may enable them to come up with possible solutions; they know where help can be obtained within or outside of the company. Because of their position they may be able to obtain technical assistance that the scientific and engineering personnel doing the work would not have the authority to obtain. Managers can arrange for meetings with technical personnel in other groups who have faced similar problems, or they may set up a meeting with an in-house staff person or even an outside consultant.

I. ORAL

  1. Informal
- R&D managers, supervisors, and principal investigators
- R&D manager and upper management

  2. Formal
- Weekly staff meetings
- Weekly product or project meetings
- Monthly meetings between R&D managers and upper management
- Periodic product meetings with marketing, sales manufacturing and other personnel invited
- Special meetings called to meet special situations

II. DOCUMENTED

  1. Scheduled
- Weekly, biweekly or monthly reports
- Quarterly reports
- Semi-annual reports
- Annual reports
- Final reports
- Computer output showing expenditures for each product or project

  2. Unscheduled
- Memos in response to a special situation or request

Figure 9-1.   Typical R&D Management Communication Media.

Oral communication between the manager and technical personnel can be formal or informal. Informal talks can reveal much about the progress of the research if there is good rapport between the manager and the subordinate. Open discussion of progress and current problems can quickly inform the managers of the work status and allow them to evaluate and make decisions about what action is required. The frequency of informal meetings and discussions depends on the scientist or engineer and manager, their physical proximity, and the nature of the particular technical effort. Discretion should be exercised by the managers so that they do not give the impression that they are harrassing or hounding the technical employees.

Managers should also maintain contact with their superior to make certain that they are in tune with current management thinking; they should keep their superior informed of any problems that have arisen that may delay the technical effort. A common cliché of management is "Don't give me any surprises." What this cliché correctly implies is that management does not like to be told of crises at a late date when the problem has become so acute that time for action is limited or inadequate. Potential problems should be identified early in the execution of the work, and upper management should be made aware of their general solution or increasing severity and lack of feasible solution. New directives by upper management indicating a change of emphasis, need for a new program, or revision of existing goals should be transmitted rapidly to the technical personnel so that necessary action is not delayed. Rapid reaction is facilitated by frequent oral communication between research managers and their superiors. The importance of recognizing when an R&D project is off track and making the appropriate adjustments is, according to R. Szakonyi (1990), the most challenging task in managing innovation.

An important aspect of oral communication is physical distance. The studies of T. J. Allen and A. R. Fusfeld (1976) of the Sloan School of Management at MIT have shown that if the distance between R&D personnel is more than about 50 feet, the probability of their communicating at least once a week becomes very low (5 percent or less). This finding is borne out by the curve of Figure 9-2. Because distance can have a similar effect on the frequency of communication between managers and their personnel, it is important for managers to be geographically close to the personnel they manage.

Regularly Scheduled Meetings
Formal modes of oral communications can use regularly scheduled meetings or meetings that are called when the manager perceives the need. Of the two types, regularly scheduled meetings are preferred because the technical personnel can plan for them in their work schedule and also prepare for them, if preparation is needed. The spur-of-the-moment type of meeting can imply an unorganized man-

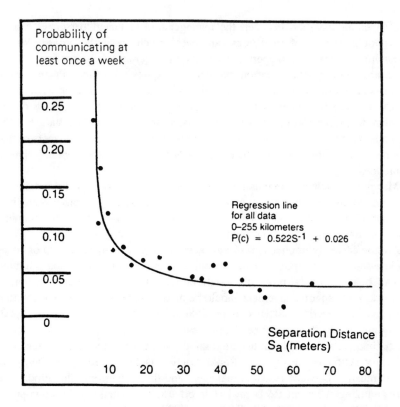

Figure 9-2.   Effect of Distance on Frequency of Communication.   Source: Thomas
J. Allen & Alan R. Fusfeld, "Design for Communication in the Research and Development
Lab," *Technology Review,* May 1976, p. 66. Copyright 1976 by Massachusetts Institute of
Technology. Reprinted with permission from Technology Review.

ager whose real concern for the work is somewhat transitory or superficial.[1] In
regularly scheduled meetings the original investigator, senior scientist, or engineer
can present a progress report to the manager alone. More often peers and subordinates in the group are invited and sometimes the head of the next managerial level
as well as personnel in other groups who are involved in the work or will have
important future interaction (e.g., manufacturing and marketing). The presentations are usually "stand-up" briefings, made more effective by a full complement
of briefing charts or visual aids.

These meetings can be informative to the attending personnel as well as being

---

[1]This is not to say that emergencies cannot arise that demand hastily called meetings, for example,
a plant breakdown, or a product failure in the field.

helpful to the speaker. Comments and questions from the audience can provide a synergistic effect, which triggers new ideas and improvements; weaknesses or omissions in the work can surface as a result of questioning. Supplementary advantages are that the individual giving the briefing becomes more expert in presenting his or her work and the work can be better understood and evaluated. However, preparing for briefings should not be allowed to take an excessively large fraction of the individual's working time. The time allotted for the review of programs or projects should be gauged to give maximum opportunity for review and yet not be too time-consuming, particularly if other technical personnel are attending. From a cost-effectiveness standpoint, a meeting can be an expensive use of high-priced technical and managerial talent.

Summary Presentations

In addition to the presentations of technical personnel based on their work, it is customary for research managers to make summary presentations to their superiors on the status of various programs and projects under their control. These briefings are usually less technical and more management-oriented, with an emphasis on cost data and overall technical accomplishment to date rather than technical detail. Some companies will hold meetings that focus on key product or system areas. Technical personnel from the various R&D groups performing work in, or related to, that product line will make presentations on the research. Representatives from marketing, sales, manufacturing, and other concerned segments of the company will attend and be allowed to make comments, criticisms, and suggestions. Such joint meetings allow for the realities of the marketplace to be brought home to research personnel since scientists and engineers often become so engrossed in their work that they lose sight of what is really important from a marketing and sales standpoint. The presence of manufacturing personnel at such meetings can identify and often preclude future production problems.

9.3   REPORTS AND DOCUMENTATION

Written reports from the technical personnel on the progress of their work are desirable for several reasons:

1. It forces them to crystallize their thinking so that it can be more precise and definitive and can be examined and critiqued by others.
2. The technical employees, in reporting on their work, can see and assess for themselves what progress they are making.
3. Such documentation serves as a record that can be referred to if something should happen to the employees, that is, if they are transferred, resign, or

become ill. Whoever else takes on the work can become current on what has been done. Undocumented work represents money lost as far as the company is concerned.

In regard to item 3, often when personnel doing important work leave a company or are transferred to another geographical location without having documented an important technical accomplishment such as a test procedure, a computer program, or an experiment, there is no way for the company to recover the desired information. In such instances it is necessary to repeat the effort and bear the unnecessary duplication of cost, assuming that other personnel can do the job again. If there has been a long dearth of documentation, it may not be feasible to repeat the effort. This can be a severe technical as well as financial loss to the company.

The frequency of reports should be tailored to the importance of the job and the number of personnel allotted to do it. Certainly a research project using one research engineer and one technician would not warrant the same frequency of reporting as a research project involving 100 or more people with important deadlines and company decisions hanging on the results. Based on need, written reports can be semiweekly, biweekly, or monthly. Quarterly or final reports should be a minimum in reporting requirements, and then only in the case of a very small technical effort. A logical format for such reports would include program objectives, program accomplishments (for reporting period), and future work planned.

9.4   FINANCIAL CONTROL

Financial Control Group

The key to effective cost control in monitoring technical effort is the day-to-day recording of expenditures made for each project or program. This record must include all direct costs chargeable to the project and should be summarized weekly, biweekly, or monthly for review by the responsible functional or project manager. Although the principal scientist or engineer can perform the bookkeeping functions of collecting and summarizing expenditures, it is more cost-effective to employ administrative assistants for this type of duty. Administrative assistants can operate within the R&D organization under a separate head of finance, who is in charge of a financial control group, which in turn can be part of an administrative group (Figure 9-3). The data for the financial reporting period can be put into a computer program, with output showing such items as these:

• How much money was spent during the reporting period for each program or project

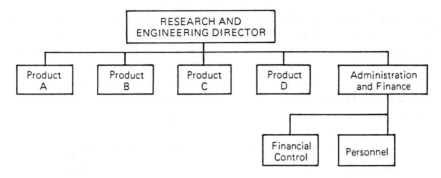

Figure 9-3.   Product-Oriented R&E Organization Utilizing a Financial Control Group.

- The name of the personnel, department, and salary number charged to each project.
- Other charges, such as materials, use of computers, and programmer time
- How much money has been spent and how much money remains for each program expressed as actual dollars and as a percentage of the initial amount of funds allocated

This type of financial report enables the R&D manager to remain well informed of the financial status of the various technical efforts. Close financial control can allow time for all possible options, such as reducing the number of employees, decreasing material costs, and eliminating unnecessary tasks or tests. In addition to collecting, organizing, and publishing cost data on expenditures, the financial control group can

- Issue work orders (Figure 3–5)
- Maintain cost records and files
- Keep track of time cards
- Maintain work flowcharts

Actual Versus Estimated Expenditure Charts

The comparison of programmed versus actual expenditures can be an important measure of what is happening financially to the technical effort (Figure 3-4). The graph of anticipated expenditures versus time, prepared during the planning stage, can be compared with actual expenditures as the work progresses. Milestones[2] can be indicated on the graph so that technical performance as well as costs can be

---

[2]Milestones mark the occurrence of a key event in a technical program or project; they are discussed more fully in Chapter 10.

evaluated. This is usually done for each project or program and can be integrated into an overall expenditure and performance chart for a particular group or segment of the organization (Figure 3-4). Additional versions of the chart can show the percentage of work done versus time (Figure 9-4) or the percentage of work done and the percentage of work programmed to be done versus time (Figure 9-5).

These charts are not always easy to develop but are worthy of the effort,

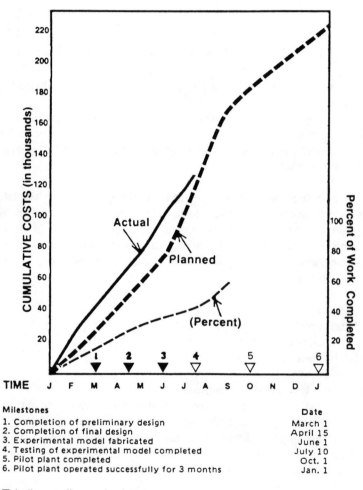

Milestones   Date
1. Completion of preliminary design   March 1
2. Completion of final design   April 15
3. Experimental model fabricated   June 1
4. Testing of experimental model completed   July 10
5. Pilot plant completed   Oct. 1
6. Pilot plant operated successfully for 3 months   Jan. 1

▼ Indicates milestone has been met.

Figure 9-4.   Expenditures Plotted Against Time and Milestones. Percentage of Work Completed also Shown.

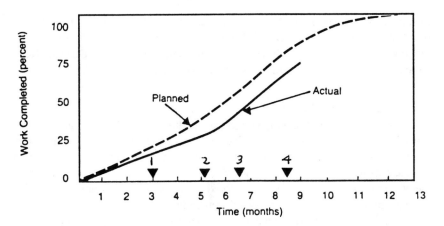

Figure 9-5.   Percentage of Work Completed and Percentage of Work Planned Versus Time.

particularly for large projects. In using the charts it should be kept in mind that the estimated expenditure rate and the programmed milestones are at best only estimates, made by the technical personnel who are going to do the work or by their supervisors, and therefore should be treated as estimates. Unfortunately, in real life, estimates are often considered to be firm by upper management and by company accountants or customers, so that when they are not fulfilled, the technical personnel are thought to have failed in their performance.

Accounting Procedures
Various companies use different accounting procedures for categorizing, monitoring, and reporting product development and research costs. The method of treatment has a direct bearing on tax statements and returns for federal and state governments. The currently acceptable method is to treat R&D as an overhead expense. A fixed amount, often a percentage of total sales, is allocated for the R&D budget, and this is treated as the R&D cost for tax purposes. This cost is further allocated to the various product lines to which the research programs relate, and these costs are subtracted from the profits derived from the particular product line. This is a straightforward approach from a tax standpoint since the product development costs are considered part of the costs of the goods sold.

In the past some firms have dealt with R&D costs differently. Because of the possibility of new products, patents, copyrights, leases, licenses, good will, and other benefits, the accountants considered the value of the assets being created by the R&D effort and then amortized or depreciated them from year to year. This was referred to as "capitalizing" the asset and was advantageous for taxes, particularly when revenues resulting from the R&D effort exceeded expenditures and could be

identified. Amortization or depreciation was usually carried out over the anticipated lifetime of the asset. This method of accounting is no longer used for tax
reporting since it has been disallowed by the Internal Revenue Service (IRS),
although it may still be used internally by the company.

Direct Versus Indirect Costs

Categorizing product development costs into direct and indirect costs is a useful
procedure for planning and monitoring technical effort. Indirect costs are often
referred to as overhead or burden. This classification has the advantage of spelling
out the expenses that are directly attributable to the technical effort, and which
therefore can be planned for and monitored by the principal engineer or scientist,
as contrasted with the fixed expenses the project or program must bear, which are
not under the control of the technical or research manager. Examples of direct costs
are the following:

- Technical personnel (scientists, engineers, technicians, and test personnel)
- Materials
- Shop labor
- Special instrumentation
- Travel
- Consultants
- Photo laboratory
- Computer and programming costs
- Documentation

In every case the direct cost represents an expenditure that can be directly
attributed to the technical effort needed to carry out the research. For example, the
travel cost chargeable to the project could be a trip to inspect a component or
perhaps to a general technical meeting where the principal subject matter of the
program will be discussed. Such a meeting might be sponsored by a technical
society, a university, or a government agency. It is extremely important that the
elements and subelements of these direct expenses be itemized, recorded, and
monitored so that appropriate financial control is maintained. Code numbers can
be assigned to each major category of expense item to facilitate monitoring.

Indirect costs have to do with the supporting services, benefits, and management that are necessary to keep the technology and product development operations continuous and viable. These costs extend over a long period of time and
represent continuing expenses that are incurred by the company year after year.
Technical personnel have little or no control of these expenditures, but nevertheless the services and facilities supported by them are needed to carry out the work.
Typical indirect, or overhead, costs are the following:

- Administrative salaries (usually middle and upper management)
- Secretarial help
- Marketing
- Vacation and sick-day costs
- Insurance
- Taxes (city, state, and federal)
- Utilities (electricity, heat, water, and phone)
- Library (books and librarians)
- Rent
- Stationery and office supplies
- Depreciation of buildings and equipment
- Legal staff
- Model shop
- Maintenance

In work done for other companies or a government agency, the technical manager, in pricing the cost of the proposed effort, will use labor dollars that are "burdened," that is, include not only the salary of the technical and other personnel directly involved but also an estimated amount for the overhead expense required. Such burdening of the labor dollar has varied between 50 percent to 150 percent of the unburdened rate. For example, a labor rate of $10 per hour without burden would be $15 at a burden rate of 50 percent. This overhead rate can also be expressed as 150 percent where 150 percent represents the ratio (times 100) of the burdened rate ($15/hour) to the unburdened rate ($10/hour). In bidding on government contracts, in which the overhead rate is an important factor, the percentage overhead rate is sometimes decreased by charging some overhead costs to direct costs. For example, if a building is to be used only for a particular project, it would not be unreasonable to charge the utilities and rent for that building directly to the project. In so doing, however, the total cost of the contract could increase, even though the overhead cost would decrease.

9.5   EVALUATION OF GROUP PERFORMANCE

The word *evaluation* implies measurement or comparison with a standard; this is difficult when the object of the evaluation is a group, an individual, or a technical effort. Attempts to quantify completely the performance of R&D groups, engineers, scientists, or technicians are challenging, if not impossible, endeavors. Of necessity, every evaluation consists of a combination of objective and subjective factors that depend on the judgment and personal preferences of the evaluator. Nevertheless, the process of evaluation, however inexact, must still be carried out to increase the probability that company and customer goals will be achieved.

Group performance can be evaluated by comparisons with other similar groups or by consideration of performance criteria that management has designated as being important to the healthy operation and growth of the company. Typical of such performance criteria are the following:

1. Is significant technical progress being made on the various programs or projects?
2. Are milestones being met for the various programs or projects?
3. What is the relationship between actual versus budgeted group expenditures?
4. How many new products, processes, systems, and components have been or are being developed?
5. How effectively is the department cooperating, communicating, and interacting with other departments and product groups? Often activities going on in one group can be beneficial to another group. Discussion among technical, marketing, and sales personnel can be helpful to new product development.
6. Is there a satisfactory number of publications such as company reports, articles in technical journals, patents, and papers presented at meetings? A technology group that shows a void in all of these areas could be suspect in its performance.
7. Is there an unsatisfactory rate of turnover? A turnover of 10 percent per year is considered high for an R&D organization. The cost of hiring and training new personnel is expensive.
8. How is the esprit de corps, or morale, of the group?[3] Groups with high esprit de corps are usually much more productive than groups in which the personnel seem highly dissatisfied.
9. In many organizations there are opportunities and requests for work to be done by technology groups. The amount of such work carried on by a particular unit can be an index of its activity and how valuable it is to the organization. A group that is constantly being asked to carry out tasks and programs would certainly rate higher than one that receives few if any requests for assistance. Sometimes this workload can be assessed from the backlog of work that has accumulated. However, the latter situation could

---

[3]Admittedly, this is difficult to measure, but the morale of a group can usually be guaged by the attitude of its members, the productivity of the group, in general and its rate of personnel turnover.

also indicate inefficient operation, and some groups are working in technical areas that are much more in demand than others.

9.6   EVALUATION OF INDIVIDUAL PERFORMANCE

Ultimately the element or basic component of the R&D effort that must be monitored, evaluated, and controlled is the individual research worker. If this performance is not up to par the technical effort will suffer. At the same time, if the individual is performing well, he or she should be recognized and encouraged by management and, if possible, rewarded. This policy can encourage continued good performance. Conversely, if the worker is doing poorly, he or she should be so informed and an attempt made to help improve performance.

Performance Review

It is customary in many research organizations to review an individual's performance once a year. Occasionally a company will review its personnel twice a year; some companies review personnel once every two years and some not at all. The last practice is deplorable, but we have seen some actual instances of it. The evaluation is usually carried out by having the supervisor or manager meet with the individual in the manager's office for discussion and frank interchange of information. The conference should have the dual objective of (1) telling the employee how he or she is doing with respect to standards the supervisor and the company have set and (2) allowing the employee the opportunity to ask questions, discuss his or her personal situation, and express any complaints.

The performance review may be coupled with a salary review, in which the individual's salary is discussed and a merit raise possibly given. If no raise is to be given, the reasons should be presented and explained. Ideally the performance review and the salary review should be combined, but in practice, because of accounting procedures and other reasons, it is not always possible. If not coupled with the salary, the results of the performance review should be documented and referred to in the salary review so that any action taken with respect to a raise or no raise is consistent. It could be quite disconcerting to a technical worker to receive excellent performance reviews and yet year after year receive no increase in salary; some explanation from management should be given. Conversely, it would be grossly inconsistent for a person to receive severe criticism and censure for poor performance and then shortly thereafter receive a merit raise. In this connection it is important for raises to be identified as either merit or cost-of-living raises. Employees who mistake a cost-of-living raise for a merit raise would mistakenly believe they are performing well when they are not.

There is little in the literature on the performance review of technical personnel;

procedures vary from company to company. We have identified the following general procedures based on our own experience and queries made to a number of companies performing R&D.

Method A: Research managers may call the employee into their office once a year or even more frequently, but not at a regularly scheduled time, and discuss job performance informally and with no documentation. Although this catch-as-catch-can type of performance review is better than none at all, its rather impromptu nature tends to downgrade its importance and effect. If there is no record kept of the key points brought up in the discussion, there will be nothing to refer to in later conferences or merit reviews. This method can work if the staff is small and the manager is conscientious and has a good memory.

Method B: On a regularly scheduled basis the supervisor makes out a special form that has been developed by the company specifically for the purpose of reviewing technical personnel (Figure 9-6). Such forms vary from company to company, but key questions relating to job performance, work output in terms of quality and quantity, ability to meet schedules, and management potential are usually included. Before the scheduled conference with the employee, the supervisor answers the specific questions asked in the form. Then the supervisor calls the employee into the office, allows him or her to read the evaluation, and discusses it. The employee can agree or disagree with the points raised and has the opportunity to express his or her views, air any complaints, and ask questions. The form may call for the signature of the employee as well as that of the supervisor. The signature corroborates the fact that the interview was held on the date specified and that the employee had the opportunity to read the review. Finally the supervisor signs the form, and it is filed in the individual's personnel folder, where it can be referred to at a later date. In the next performance review there can be follow up of any points, such as recommendations, that were made in the previous review. The results of the review are also available as a basis for the merit raise decision.

Method C: This method is based on the evaluation and opinions of the employees themselves about what their work performance is and should be. It is initiated by supervisors or research managers announcing to the personnel in their group that they must each fill out a performance review form (Figure 9-7) by a certain date. Typical questions from such forms are these:

1. Identify your work function for the next review period.
2. Define your strengths and weaknesses.
3. Establish your work objectives for the next 12-month period.
4. Identify your career plans (short and long term).

After each employee fills out the form, he or she submits it to the research manager, who reviews the form and makes comments and suggestions. Then the

Name	Employee No	Dept No. Hire Date	From Evaluation Period To
Classification		No. Months on Present Job	No. Months Supervised by Evaluator

1. What were his major job duties and assignments during the period being evaluated?

2. How well did he meet the performance requirements and objectives for his job?
   (Budgets, goals, targets, schedules, etc.)

3. What have we agreed will be accomplished by him prior to the next appraisal?
   (Job objectives for next period)

4. List his strong points and indicate areas where he needs to improve.

5. How does the employee feel about this appraisal or any other feelings related to his employment?
   What are his career goals?

Appraisal was discussed with employee on
Employee   Signature   Date

6. Complete performance and potential ratings *AFTER APPRAISAL INTERVIEW WITH EMPLOYEE*, using definitions shown on the reverse side of this form.

OVERALL PERFORMANCE	POTENTIAL
(Circle one) 5 4 3 2 1	(Circle one) Z P K H

Ranking   Rank in numerical order beginning with 1, each employee with others in his classification who perform essentially the same work under your supervision

Employee is ranked _____ of _____ in his classification

Evaluator
Signature   Title

Figure 9-6.   Performance Appraisal Form (Method B).

EMPLOYEE S NAME (LAST. FIRST. MIDDLE)	EMP NO	LOC/DEPT	REVIEW DATE
CLASSIFICATION	GROUP	SHIFT	START DATE

A   DESCRIBE YOUR JOB DUTIES AND RESPONSIBILITIES

SUPERVISOR S COMMENTS

B   WHAT ARE YOUR CAREER OBJECTIVES AND PLANS FOR PERSONAL GROWTH?

SUPERVISOR S COMMENTS

HOW HAVE YOU IMPROVED IN YOUR PERFORMANCE SINCE YOUR LAST REVIEW?

SUPERVISOR S COMMENTS

D   HOW CAN YOU IMPROVE YOUR WORK PERFORMANCE IN YOUR PRESENT JOB IN THE NEXT 12 MONTHS?

SUPERVISOR S COMMENTS

E   SUPERVISOR S EVALUATION

WHAT QUALITIES DOES EMPLOYEE NEED TO IMPROVE?

WHAT ARE EMPLOYEE S BEST QUALITIES AND OUTSTANDING ABILITIES?

THE EMPLOYEE HAS BEEN UNDER MY SUPERVISION FOR _____ MO	ACKNOWLEDGED
SUPERVISOR _____	EMPLOYEE _____

Figure 9-7.   Performance Appraisal Form (Method C).

employee is called into the manager's office, and the answers to the questions recorded by the employee and the comments and suggestions of the technology manager are discussed.

This method has the advantages of saving the valuable time of the research manager and encouraging self-analysis by the research worker. Unfortunately its effectiveness is very much dependent on the honesty of the individual; if employees so choose, they could answer the questions falsely to portray themselves as devoid of weaknesses. Although this format for performance reviews has been used by some major companies, its true value is debatable. It does bring the research worker and supervisor together to discuss the worker's problems, but methods A and B can accomplish the same thing.

All three methods show the technical personnel that management does care about their progress in the company, and what can be done to improve their situation. This in itself is a major step forward in employer-employee relationships and can bolster morale and improve performance of the individual worker.

Ladder Ranking of Technical Personnel

Some companies that employ a large number of engineers will order-rank them in capability, present value, and potential value to the company. This determination is carried out by the supervisors and managers at conferences, where individual technical personnel are discussed and compared. An example of such a rating chart is shown in Figure 9-8. The rank and name of the individual is plotted against salary, and the best median curve is drawn through the points.

A ladder-ranking chart, also known as a *totem pole*, is useful in determining whether or not a technical worker should receive a raise. Curves can be plus or minus 5 percent from the median curve. This percentage is arbitrary; 5 percent is utilized here because it is a typical value and exemplifies the procedure that can be used. If a candidate for a raise is to the left of the median range, he or she is eligible for favorable consideration; if to the right, he or she is not considered to be eligible. If the candidate is within the median range, he or she is still eligible for a raise, but the need is not great.

Although there are disadvantages to this method, it can be used as an indicator along with other evaluation factors. If a layoff is necessary, companies have been known to use ladder ranking as a basis for deciding who will be terminated. For example, if a 10 percent layoff is required by upper management because of belt tightening, loss of business, or both, and there are 50 people on the ladder, theoretically the bottom 5 people would be released. In real life other factors might be taken into account, but in times of economic stress the procedure may be as straightforward as presented here. The order ranking of technical personnel is information that is kept privy only to supervisors and managers.

Rating	R-P	Name	Monthly Salary
1	1	Jones	
2	2	Smith	
3	1	Brown	
4	1	Etc	
5	3		
6	1		
7	3		
8	3		
9	3		
10	2		
11	1		
12	2		
13	2		
14	3		
15	2		
16	3		
17	1		
18	2		
19	2		
20	3		
21	2		
22	3		
23	3		
24	2		
25	2		
26	3		
27	3		
28	3		
29	4		
30	3		
31	3		
32	3		
33	3		
34	1		
35	3		
36	1		
37	3		
38	2		
39	3		
40	3		
41	3		
42	3		
43	3		
44	3		
45	4		

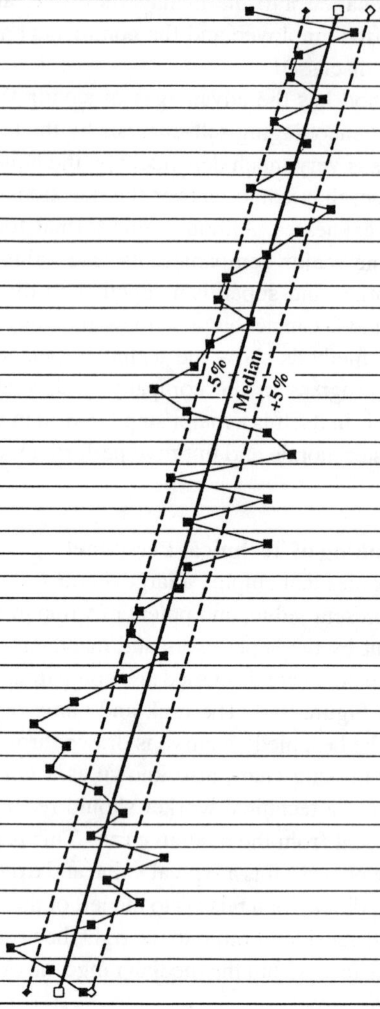

Rate of Progress (R-P)
1. Maximum potential
2. Above average
3. Normal
4. Below average

Figure 9-8.   Ladder Ranking of Technical Support.

9.7   LARGE PROJECTS

The monitoring and control techniques discussed in this chapter have been primarily directed toward work by functional technical groups and for relatively small projects. All of the procedures described are applicable to projects, but some additional planning and programming techniques are particularly suited to the monitoring and control of large projects. These techniques (e.g., work breakdown structure and work-flow charts) allow for systematic and timely review of complex systems development projects involving many components and subsystems and complex manufacturing process developments. They will be discussed in Chapter 10.

QUESTIONS AND TOPICS FOR DISCUSSION

9.1   Why is an effective minimum cost information system essential for successful technology management? What are the required elements of such a system?

9.2   What are the pros and cons of having a *separate* financial control group monitoring expenditures and reporting to technology managers rather than internal monitoring of expenditures by individual managers or technical personnel?

9.3   Why is it important in regularly scheduled planning or review meetings to have (a) closure of questions and problems to the maximum extent possible, (b) assignments of action items with names of responsible individuals and due dates, and (c) minutes?

9.4   Since the IRS no longer allows the capitalization of product and process development research costs, why would some companies still use such an accounting procedure for internal bookkeeping?

9.5   The evaluation of the effectiveness of the totality of R&D operations in a company has always been a difficult problem. Why?

9.6   In Figure 9-2 shows the effect of distance on the communication of technical personnel. Since there is no mention of telephone communication, it can be assumed that only face-to-face conversations are considered in the study. How would the inclusion of telephone conversations affect the results of this study?

9.7   Why is punctuality of financial reports important in technology monitoring, and what can be the consequences of a lag time of one month or more?

9.8   As a technology manager you are approached by a commercial vendor about purchasing a computer system that will provide automatic daily or weekly financial, cost, and schedule data, including summary charts for all your activities. The system could be adapted to the company's available computer capability. How would you decide whether or not to purchase the software and other accessories needed to use the system?

9.9   Compare methods A, B, and C for their effectiveness in evaluating technical personnel. Enumerate the advantages and disadvantages of each method.

9.10   What are some pros and cons of the ladder-ranking techniques?

References

Allen, T. J., and A. R. Fusfeld. 1976, May. Design for communication in the research and development lab. *Technology Review*, p. 66.

Szakonyi, R. 1990. *How to Successfully Keep R&D Projects on Track*. Mt. Airy, MD: Lomond Publications.

10

Project Management

10.1 THE PROJECT APPROACH

With the increased complexity of developing new products and manufacturing processes and the increasing use of many disciplines and technologies in such developments, the need for goal-oriented management techniques has surfaced. This need has been further accentuated by the increasing market, organizational, and economic pressures of completing a job within a specified time and with specified resources. Projects and project management have been developed to fill this need.

In the project approach a project leader (project manager) is designated by upper management and a specialized group of people is assigned to work under the project manager to carry out a sequence of activities dedicated to the attainment of a goal within the constraints of time, budget, and predetermined performance specifications (Stephanou & Obradovitch 1985). The position of project manager (P.M.) resembles that of the CEO of a company; project managers make all major decisions affecting the project and have all the responsibility for its success or failure.

The project approach in modern companies and organizations arose because of the difficulties encountered in trying to carry out the development of complex systems by working around and through the usual functional or discipline-oriented groupings of most organizations. Questions of priorities and control arose, and often a project had to wait in line for attention from a specialist doing other work. Subcontracting for various components was more difficult if various product groups were involved; access to expertise needed in purchasing, manufacturing, finance, quality control, and reliability had to be achieved through appropriate organizational channels. In conventional organizations, such conditions often proved unnecessarily difficult and inefficient from an accomplishment, cost, and control standpoint.

Advantages of the Project Approach

Advantages and reasons for the project approach can be summarized as follows:

- There is an urgent need for developing a complex product or system within a specified period of time and within a predetermined cost.
- The project can be operated as a financially independent unit from the rest of the company so that its formation, execution, and termination can bring about the least disturbance in other company operations.
- Numerous components, subsystems, and systems must be developed in parallel, involving various groups or entities within or outside the company.
- Performing technical work for another company or organization often requires closer control of cost, schedule, and performance than is customary within the company.
- The project concept allows cutting across organizational lines and technical disciplines so that technical and other required expertise can be drawn from different functional parts of the company and utilized 100 percent for the needs of the project. Experts can be released when their services are no longer needed.
- Outside vendors and suppliers are required to a greater extent than in usual company operations.
- Working toward definite goals, the charisma of an effective project leader, the technical challenge, and the potential benefits if the project succeeds can provide a high level of morale and camaraderie to the technical and other personnel. Personnel tend to identify themselves with the project and its success.

Projects Versus Programs

Projects are often confused with programs, and the two terms can be, and often are, used synonymously. Projects sometimes become programs. Projects usually have the following notable characteristics:

- They usually involve a one-shot technical effort.
- They are time- and cost-limited, often with a compressed schedule and a degree of urgency.
- They involve a relatively complex operation, product, or system development with clear-cut goals and objectives.

These characteristics can be contrasted with those of a program, in which the technical activity is ongoing, year after year, and can have an unlimited lifetime with continuous funding. For example, an appliance manufacturer has a product improvement research program that employs scientists and engineers in a continuing effort to improve the quality and durability of its line of appliances. Improvements in the operation, control features, materials of construction, and other features of the appliance are constantly being sought through the testing of new mechanisms, materials, and configurations. The objectives may be quite specific over the period of a year but may change from year to year. The overall objective remains the same, however—improve the salability and profitability of the appliances. The overall technical effort can continue year after year despite changes in the area of improvement and specifics of the technical effort. In the Department of Defense and other government agencies, programs often consist of a series of related, projects that can be sequential or concurrent.

10.2   THE NEED AND NEEDS ANALYSIS

Recognition of the Need

Before the actual start-up and execution of the project, certain activities or events occur that precipitate the technical effort. First, a need must be recognized by company personnel, another company or organization, or a government agency.

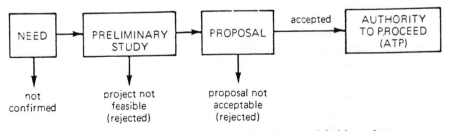

Note that the potential project can be rejected at several decision points.

Figure 10-1.

The need must be confirmed and funding obtained for a preliminary or feasibility study. The sequence of events is as follows:

Technology-Push Versus Technology-Pull

The need for an improved product, a new product, or improved process or operation can arise from within or outside the company. Within the company, the requirement may be identified by technical personnel or supervision. This is sometimes referred to as *technology-driven* or *technology-push,* the important feature being that the need for the work has originated with the technologists. In *market-driven* or *technology-pull,* a need for a new product or capability is observed by someone outside the technology organization and the technologists are asked to perform applied research to answer the need. An example of technology-push is the discovery of lasers in the research laboratory and their subsequent application to communications, weaponry, and medicine. However,it must be realized that what technical personnel consider desirable may not necessarily be what can sell. There have been many products that were technically attractive and professionally satisfying to the technical personnel who worked on their initiation and development, but the products were a failure in the marketplace.

An example of technology-pull is the recognition by consumer groups and the government of the need for improved driver and passenger safety in motor vehicles and the resulting applied research that has led to air bags, collapsible fenders and body parts, and other protective devices. Or a salesperson may, in the course of selling a product, hear from customers that there is a need for a certain additional capability that will make the product more salable. This information is reported through channels, and the R&D laboratory of the company can initiate a research study to investigate the feasibility of obtaining the required additional capability. However, before doing so, the need should be confirmed and established.

Confirmation of the Need

Many factors must be taken into account in the confirmation of a need, or needs analysis. Questions that must be answered and considerations that must be made include the following:

- Will the need still exist and will the customer be willing to pay the price for the product when it is developed and ready for sales? (This date can be as far away as three years or more.)
- Technical personnel may be enthused over the technical challenge rather than the economic payoff.

- Will some government action affect the need or sale of the product?
- What will the competitors offer in the way of a competitive system?
- What will the economic climate be when the system or product is mass produced and marketed?
- The observations and needs expressed by salespersons and marketing personnel are not always accurate and reliable.
- What are the safety, product liability, warranty, and environmental impact aspects of carrying out the project?

For commercial products, market research is often necessary to establish the need. Market research is a specialty in itself, requiring experts who have been trained in the art of consumer and customer sampling. What segment of the population would buy the item? Would it be sold to the public, industry, or the government? These and other questions would have to be answered by the market research specialist. It is important for the project to be revoked as quickly as possible if the need is not confirmed; otherwise unnecessary costs are incurred. The cumulative costs of developing a product or carrying out a project are shown in Figure 10-2. It is evident from the graph that costs are minimal at the early stages of the system development process but rise rapidly as the product development proceeds from applied research to the hardware, prototype, and pilot plant stage.

Needs analysis, or confirmation of the need, has been discussed here along with identification of the need. In practice, needs analysis is often included as part of a feasibility or preliminary study, which is normally carried out before embarking on a major product or system development.

10.3   THE FEASIBILITY OR PRELIMINARY STUDY

After the need for the project has been identified and confirmed, it is necessary to make a preliminary study to determine what will be necessary to satisfy the need. Depending on the nature of the new product or technical effort to be accomplished, the preliminary study can include several or all of the following factors:

- Concepts to fit the need
- Critical issues, technical and nontechnical
- Possible solutions to the critical issues
- Technical feasibility
- Economic feasibility
- Make-or-buy decisions (including subcontracting)
- Facility requirements
- Cost and schedule

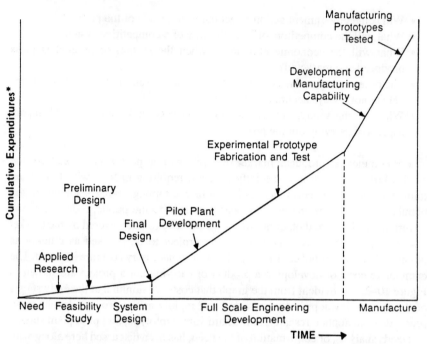

* Depending upon the particular product, this could be a logarithmic scale. Early steps in the development process are at least one order of magnitude less in cost than subsequent steps.

Figure 10-2.   Cumulative Expenditures in the Development of a New System.

- Personnel requirements and organization
- Enumeration of tasks and subtasks (WBS)[1]
- Development of preliminary specifications
- Environmental impact and other societal or public effects (technology assessment).

This can be a very short, preliminary type of effort, as mentioned in planning the annual R&D technical effort (Chapter 3), or it can be a complete and full-fledged evaluation of what will be involved in carrying out a major project. If the funding allows, the preliminary study can include detailed planning in the form of work flowcharts such as PERT or CPM and estimated expenditure versus time

---

[1]Work breakdown structure.

charts. The results of the feasibility study can be documented as a report, or they can be summarized as a proposal to the funding organization or customer.

In the case of technical effort or system development, the customer might request the preliminary study before funding the major development effort. In the past government agencies such as DOD have included the development of information of this type in a program definition phase (PDP) or a cost definition phase (CDP) for a system development. In industry the preliminary study is usually carried out by a special projects group, a new product development group, a technical and economic studies group, an advanced systems and technology group, or some other group that is particularly versed in making this type of study.

For larger projects that will involve many people and high costs, a study leader is designated by company management and is allowed to select or is given key personnel to help make the preliminary or feasibility study. It is advisable to bring the group making the study together into one physical location so that there can be frequent communication between the study leader and the personnel performing the study. If after the preliminary study the decision is made to proceed with the project, the study leader usually becomes the project manager and the key personnel who assisted become the deputies and key supervisors in the project.

10.4 THE PROPOSAL

If the feasibility or preliminary study shows the candidate project to be worthwhile, a proposal may be prepared to obtain funding for the full-fledged technical effort required. A proposal can be defined as an organized plan for carrying out a project or program. It can be used to propose technical work internally to company management or to another company or organization. In the case of government procurements it may be a solicited proposal in response to a request for proposal (RFP), or it may be an unsolicited proposal, which means that it is proposed by the organization that wishes to fill an apparent need of the customer. The unsolicited proposal is an example of technology-push, whereas the solicited proposal exemplifies the technology-pull, or market-driven, situation.

The contents of a technical proposal are commonly developed in two sections or volumes, a technical section and a management section. A typical format for a relatively small or medium sized project is shown in Figure 10-3. For a major product or system development involving large expenditures, a number of additional items could be added such as a PERT or CPM chart, work breakdown structure (WBS), estimated cost versus time graph, and percentage of work planned versus time graph. The work statement merits special attention if the proposal is to another company or organization since it involves commitments of work that have contractual implications. Care must be taken to ensure that the

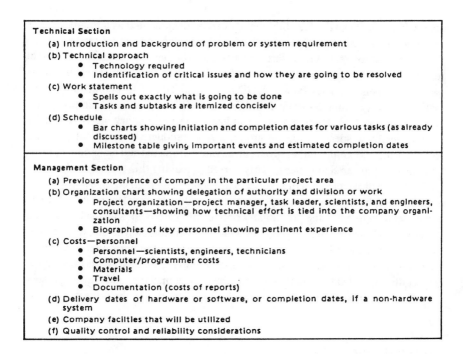

Technical Section

(a) Introduction and background of problem or system requirement

(b) Technical approach
- Technology required
- Indentification of critical issues and how they are going to be resolved

(c) Work statement
- Spells out exactly what is going to be done
- Tasks and subtasks are itemized concisely

(d) Schedule
- Bar charts showing initiation and completion dates for various tasks (as already discussed)
- Milestone table giving important events and estimated completion dates

Management Section

(a) Previous experience of company in the particular project area

(b) Organization chart showing delegation of authority and division or work
- Project organization—project manager, task leader, scientists, and engineers, consultants—showing how technical effort is tied into the company organization
- Biographies of key personnel showing pertinent experience

(c) Costs—personnel
- Personnel—scientists, engineers, technicians
- Computer/programmer costs
- Materials
- Travel
- Documentation (costs of reports)

(d) Delivery dates of hardware or software, or completion dates, if a non-hardware system

(e) Company facilties that will be utilized

(f) Quality control and reliability considerations

Figure 10-3.   Sample Proposal Format in a Small Project.

amount of work indicated is commensurate with the available funds. Structuring the tasks into subtasks is helpful in delineating the work and developing the costs (see Section 10.8).

10.5   THE PROJECT LIFE CYCLE

Following the feasibility or preliminary study and preparation and acceptance of the proposal, the project is initiated. The sequence or phases of activity and the number of personnel as a function of time in the execution of the project are shown in Figure 10-4.

Start-Up and Growth Phase

The start-up and growth phase involves staffing, ordering materials, making buy decisions, sending out requests for bids, selecting subcontractors and vendors, and arranging for the required technical support from within the company, to mention a few of the most important activities. The detailed planning for the project will be done in this phase; actually it may be the first order of business.

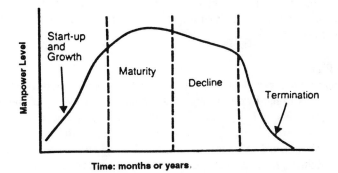

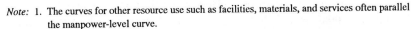

Note: 1. The curves for other resource use such as facilities, materials, and services often parallel the manpower-level curve.
2. The curve could also be applicable to a product life cycle. For some high-technology industries, the total lifetime of a product can be as little as 10 months or even less.

Figure 10-4.   Personnel Growth and Decline During the Execution of a Project.

It may have been done in outline form in the feasibility study, since there are usually insufficient funds available in a preliminary study to allow for the complete detailed planning and required programming. The term *programming* is used here in the sense of setting up the schedule of activities or planning the sequence or chronology of events and expenditures rather than in the sense of computer programming.

Maturity Phase
In the maturity phase major inroads have been made on the technical problems (critical technical issues), although there are still residual questions to be answered. Most of the components and subsystems are well underway, and deliveries are being received from the vendors. Subcontractors should have advanced in their technical work and already achieved a major degree of succcess, but tasks which still remain to be done may involve testing, systems integration, pilot plan operation, and a host of other developmental activities. During the maturity phase, levels of personnel and expenditures reach their maximum values. The critical technical issues have been attacked, and alternative solutions have been examined with selection and implementation of the most promising. Components and subsystems are being assembled and tested by the specific systems groups, and the subsystems are being integrated into the total system by the systems integration groups. There may also be some mockup and experimental prototypes set up. The nature and extent of these activities are functions of the specific project.

Morale of the engineers and scientists is high in this stage of the project since technical activity is still at a high level and there are still technical challenges and problems to be resolved.

Decline Phase

Following the maturity phase, the technical activity begins gradually to ebb and emphasis shifts to hardware or process development, including testing, building the pilot plant, and the identification and solution of production engineering problems. The project manager and staff must see to it that personnel are gradually relinquished to other projects, to other operations in the company, or to their original group. In the case of government-funded projects, technical personnel who can no longer be utilized within the company may be dismissed. In the past this practice has caused undue hardship to highly trained and professionally dedicated scientists and engineers, and it continues to be a problem. The problem becomes particularly acute in the termination phase of the project.

Termination Phase

The termination phase marks the conclusion of the dwindling technical effort. The total system has been fabricated or completed and is being delivered to the customer. A certain amount of continuing technical support is needed to solve minor problems in performance and provide technical consulting, but these problems are more of an operational rather than a design nature. Final documentation is required to provide the necessary information for future reference, modification, and product or manufacturing process improvement. This phase of the project can involve wholesale "destaffing," with all the attendant problems of relocating personnel. The project manager and staff usually remain to close out the project and make certain that customer or company requirements are fully met. If the project is a large one, resulting in operational systems, a cadre of technical personnel may be maintained specifically to service the systems and provide logistic support. If new or modified manufacturing processes are being developed, some personnel can be transferred to the new production facility.

10.6   PROJECT PLANNING AND PROGRAMMING

Because of the particular emphasis in carrying out a project on meeting stringent cost, schedule, and performance requirements, careful planning and programming of the work to be accomplished are crucial. As previously stated, *programming* refers to the scheduling or sequencing of the specific tasks, actions and key events. *Planning* refers to the identification of those tasks, actions, events, and expenditures that must be programmed. It can involve the same subjects that were considered in the feasibility study or proposal but in much more detail (see Section 10.3). In a preliminary study, funds and time are not usually adequate to allow for the in-depth analysis and planning needed for actually carrying out the project.

In the project planning process there are a number of tools that the project manager and team can employ: work flowcharts, task bar charts, milestone events and dates, and charts showing estimated expenditure rates or the percentage of work done versus time as well as similar charts. The overall objective of the planning and programming effort must include the identification of the elements of the job that must be fulfilled, how they are to be fulfilled, the appropriate allocation of resources, and their rate of use. Resources include money, personnel, materials, facilities, equipment, and so forth. Also included in the planning are make-or-buy decisions, project-control procedures, and the development of a project management information system (PMIS).

Task Bar Charts and Milestones
Task bar charts, setting up milestone events and dates, and estimated expenditure rates versus time have already been discussed as part of the planning of an annual research program (Section 3.7). In the case of a major project, these planning exercises would be documented for each particular component and subsystem to be developed and for each technical effort to be carried out. The project manager and staff would prepare overall charts spelling out the major milestone events and the estimated personnel and expenditure curves for the whole project. Although milestones usually mark the completion of an important activity or the occurrence of a key event in the program, they can also be set up as scheduled dates to review the project for fiscal and technical performance. The exact dates can be arbitrarily set by the project manager and staff or by the customer. An example of a milestone table is shown in Table 10.1.

Although task bar charts are useful in planning, since they set forth tasks and subtasks and the time span over which they are to be done, they have several disadvantages for complex projects with many systems, subsystems, and components. They do not show the interrelationship of tasks and events, and they may not be sufficiently detailed to permit early detection of slippages. These areas can be better portrayed by a network or work flowchart showing the sequential flow of work from one milestone to another or from one task to another.

10.7   WORK FLOWCHARTS (CPM, PERT, PDM)

Because of the complexity of most projects it is necessary to spell out the various technical efforts needed, the component and subsystem development that must be

TABLE 10-1.   Table of Milestones

Task	Completion Date
1. Develop preliminary design	February 1
2. Determine final design	April 15
3. Fabricate experimental model.	June 1
4. Test experimental model.	August 15
5. Develop manufacturing technique	November 1

performed, and the schedule for subcontractor and vendor performance. It is important for component and subsystem completion and system integration to be carried out in a timely manner so that the tight schedule that is usual in the execution of projects can be met. Work flowcharts can relate such a complex chain of activities in a manner that can be readily referred to, not only in planning and programming the project activities but also in monitoring and controlling them during their execution. The quickest possible time in which a project could be completed can be estimated, assuming there are no technical or other difficulties, and the potential bottlenecks identified. If there are several alternatives, the time to completion for each alternative can be determined and can help decide which alternative is best.

Three types of work flowcharts have been commonly used: critical path method (CPM), program evaluation and review technique (PERT) and precedence diagramming method (PDM). The basic technique for PERT and CPM is to draw a diagrammatic model showing the various activities (tasks) and key events and to assign estimated times for accomplishing each of the tasks. Although PDM is developed similarly, activities are considered to be modes or tally points rather than events or milestones (Obradovitch and Stephanou 1990); CPM and PERT are described below. Application of these techniques is called network analysis.

Critical Path Method (CPM).

The critical path method is the earliest of these techniques and illustrates the general procedure for both CPM and PERT. First, the events (milestones) and activities of the project are identified. Events are indicated by circles on the diagram and activities by arrows. The event is an anticipated or planned occurrence at a specified date, an activity is the work required to achieve that event, and activity time is the time required to proceed from one event to another. The activity time is estimated by individuals who have had experience with that particular type of activity; previous performance is generally used as a basis for the estimate. Events, activities, and activity times are tabulated for each path or sequence of activities. By adding the estimated times for the activities along various paths or sequences of events, the total time for each path can be arrived at. The path that requires the greatest length of time is referred to as the critical path, and the total length of time for that path is the critical time.

Thus in Figure 10-5, path B is the critical path and the project cannot be completed any sooner than that time. Any slippage of time in an activity along the critical path will mean a slippage in the final event or the total time to carry out the project. Since this is a planning and programming exercise, changes can be made to decrease the critical path time. In the example it might be possible to decrease the critical path time by purchasing more components rather than fabricating them in-house. The effect of this alternative on cost would have to be considered, and there would probably be a trade-off between the increased cost and the value of the time saved. It might be that revamping the manufacturing operation, including new or better equipment, might be the answer to reducing the critical path time for that activity. Another possible way might be to implement more quality control of the components being fabricated in-house during manufacture rather than waiting until all the components are fabricated. These are just a few possible ways that a manager might utilize the CPM chart for improving the planning and project operation. There can be many additional ramifications with full use of CPM. Only the basic elements have been described here.

Program Evaluation and Review Technique (PERT).

The program evaluation and review technique is similar to CPM, with the exception that the activity time is arrived at analytically and takes into account the fact that such times are variable, depending on the circumstances.

In PERT, as in CPM, the important ingredients are events, activities, and activity times. To determine the activity times the following formula is used:

$$T_{exp} = \frac{T_{opt} + 4T \text{ (most likely)} + T_{pess}}{6}$$

where T_{exp} = the expected time
        T_{opt} = the optimistic time
        T_{pess} = the pessimistic time

The formula provides a means of giving greatest weight to the most likely time and yet takes into account the optimistic and the pessimistic times. The optimum time is arrived at by looking at the previous history of such activities and observing what the shortest time for carrying out that or a similar activity has been in the past. The pessimistic time reflects the longest possible time that has been consumed by the activity in the past and takes into account major changes in approach or technical difficulties. To be truly realistic, the pessimistic time

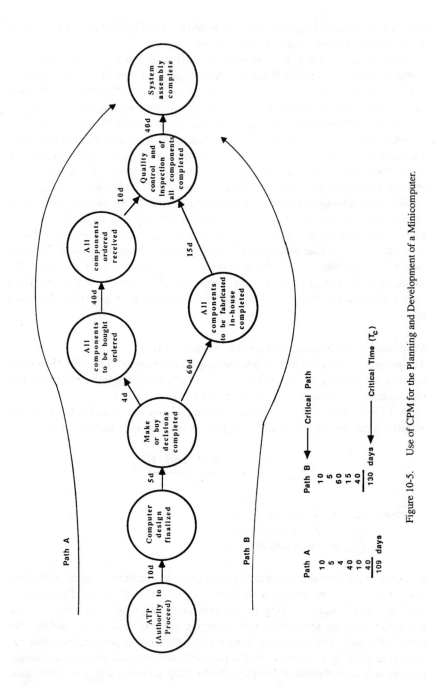

Figure 10-5.   Use of CPM for the Planning and Development of a Minicomputer.

should probably be given a weighting greater than 1, possibly 2 or 3, since the occurrence of difficulties is more common than the occurrence of no difficulties. If the activites are relatively new, with little repetitive experience to draw on, a formula such as

$$T_{exp} = \frac{T_{opt} + 4T\text{ (most likely)} + 2T_{pess}}{7}$$

is more realistic.

The steps in the development of a simple PERT chart are the following:

1. Decide on key events and activities.
2. Set up the network of events and activities in proper sequence of occurrence.
3. Determine and tabulate the optimistic, pessimistic, and most likely activity times.
4. Calculate the expected or mean activity time from the preceding formula.
5. Determine the total times for the various paths.

When the system to be developed is very complex—for example, there are hundreds of components and subsystems—the process can be computerized and the effect on completion time of various options and variations determined. The final PERT chart would have the same form as the CPM chart shown in Figure 10-5 except that calculated activity times would be utilized rather than estimated activity times.

An advantage of PERT over the CPM technique is that it allows for the calculation of the probability of meeting the schedule or potential schedule slippage. Assuming that the likelihood of predicting the activity time follows a beta type statistical distribution, the standard deviation for one activity time would be

$$\sigma_i\text{ (stand)} = \frac{T_{pess} - T_{opt}}{6}$$

For the critical path the total standard deviation $[*\sigma(\text{stand})]$ would be

$$*\sigma(\text{stand}) = \sqrt{\sum_{i-1}^{n} \sigma_i^2(\text{stand})}$$

where n is the number of activites in the critical path, and i refers to the particular activity and can have values equal to 1, 2, 3, 4 .... n.

$$\sum_{i-1}^{n} \sigma_i^2(\text{stand})$$

is the sum of the squares of all the standard deviations of the activity times in the critical path.

To calculate the probability of completing the project in a certain scheduled time, T_s, one can use the expression

$$Z = \frac{T_s - T_c}{*\sigma(\text{stand})}$$

where Z is a factor indicating the number of standard deviations expressed by the difference $T_s - T_c$, T_s is the scheduled or desired project time, and T_c is the critical path time.

From probability tables, a sample of which is shown in Table 10-2, the probability of meeting the schedule time, T_s, can be found. For the example of Figure 10-5 where T_c was 130 days, the probability of meeting a completion time of 140 days can be calculated. If a value of 5 days is assumed for the total standard deviation of the critical path ($*\sigma(\text{stand})$,

TABLE 10-2.   Probability for Various Values of the Z Factor

Z FACTOR		PROBABILITY
3.0	. . . .	0.9987
2.5	. . . .	0.9938
2.0	. . . .	0.9772
1.5	. . . .	0.9332
1.0	. . . .	0.8413
0.5	. . . .	0.6915
0.0	. . . .	0.5000
−0.5	. . . .	0.3085
−1.0	. . . .	0.1587
−1.5	. . . .	0.0668
−2.0	. . . .	0.0228
−2.5	. . . .	0.0062
−3.0	. . . .	0.0013

$$Z = \frac{140 - 130}{5} = +2$$

From the table a Z factor of +2 corresponds to a probability of 98 percent. If a schedule completion time of 120 days was desired, a Z factor of -2 would result, and the probability of meeting that curtailed schedule time would be 2 percent (not a very likely prospect).

PERT/COST

Thus far we have been using the term PERT for scheduling events and activities with respect to time. More accurately this usage of PERT is referred to as PERT/TIME. There is also PERT/COST, which can be used to determine the most expensive rather than the most time-consuming path. The costs for various activities are estimated, and the paths that are most expensive are identified. In the planning stage, resources, including personnel, materials, and facilities, may be adjusted to reduce the cost of the more expensive paths.

Calculation of Slack or Float Times

An additional feature of network analysis techniques is the ability to calculate the earliest possible time and the latest possible time that a milestone event will occur (Figure 10-6). This figure in turn allows for the calculation of the maximum time ("slack" or "float") that can be taken for completion of a given task without affecting the total time for completion of the project. All tasks on the critical path have a zero float time and therefore are critical to meeting the schedule.

To calculate float times, early start, early finish, late start, and late finish times for each activity within the network must be determined. These are defined in the following manner (Obradovitch and Stephanou 1990):

Early start (ES):   The earliest an activity can be initiated based on the completion of the preceding activities

Early finish (EF):   The earliest an activity can be completed assuming preceding activities are initiated at their earliest start times and do not slip

Late start (LS):   The latest an activity can be initiated without adversely affecting project duration

Late finish (LF):   The latest an activity can be completed without adversely affecting project duration

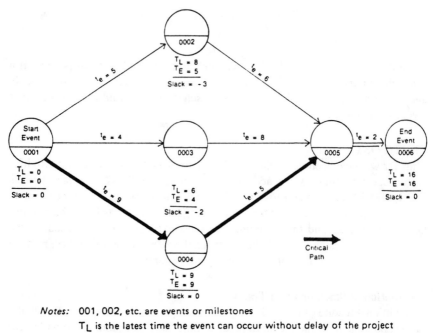

Notes: 001, 002, etc. are events or milestones

T_L is the latest time the event can occur without delay of the project

T_E is the earliest time the event can occur

Figure 10-6.   Use of CPM Showing Slack or Float Times.

First the earliest finish times are calculated for each activity by using the equation ES + duration of task = EF for all the activities along a particular path, starting with the first activity. This is referred to as the "forward pass." Then the latest starting time is calculated by using the equation LF - duration of task = LS for all the activities along a particular path, starting with the last activity and working backward. This is known as the "backward pass." The calculation of float time is quite valuable in that it can allow resources to be juggled from one activity to another and changing when and how a job will be done, in-house versus subcontracting performance of certain tasks, use of facilities, and so on. Increased automation of operational functions with linked Management Information Systems (MIS) make such planning and control systems less formidable to operate and potentially more effective.

10.8   WORK BREAKDOWN STRUCTURE (WBS)

For large projects a necessary activity that can be carried out in conjunction with setting up the task bar charts is the work breakdown structure (WBS). Actually the two exercises are so closely associated that they can be done concurrently. The WBS divides the total project work into major tasks and subtasks (Figure 10-7). The personnel and various other costs associated with each subtask can be estimated and listed. The work may be further subdivided, depending on the size of the project and the dollar volume, so that a final set of work packages can be arrived at for different hierarchical levels (see Figure 10-8). These levels may be based on a system, subsystem, component relationship, or an organizational relationship. The work package units should not be so small that they create an overly burdensome task for cost and performance monitoring and control.

The WBS can serve as a basis and reference document for planning, including estimating costs, issuing engineering work orders, controlling cost and technical performance, and reporting. A description of the work element (task and subtask) is needed and should be the same as the description used in the task bar charts.

Work Breakdown Structure		Costs		
Module Tester	Personnel	Facility	Material & Other	Total

1.0 Develop design concepts
    1.1 Select key design features
    1.2 Evaluate final design, including
           human factors criteria
	$8,000	$2,000	$3,000	$13,000

2.0 Develop work prints for build-up
    2.1 Review for any revisions
    2.2 Final prints
	5,000	500	1,000	6,500

3.0 Fabricate model of tester
    3.1 Develop final configuration
    3.2 Evaluate from user
           point of view
	2,000	—	150	2,150

4.0 Construct functional prototype
    of tester
    4.1 Complete check-out of design
    4.2 Test hardware on tester
           4.2.1 Evaluate test results
	6,000	500	1,000	7,500

5.0 Calibrate system
    5.1 Check out accuracy with
           established standards
	200	—	50	250

6.0 Release tester to inspection for production line use	20	—	—	20
Total costs	$21,220	$3,000	$5,200	$29,420

Figure 10-7.   Work Breakdown Structure Showing Associated Costs.

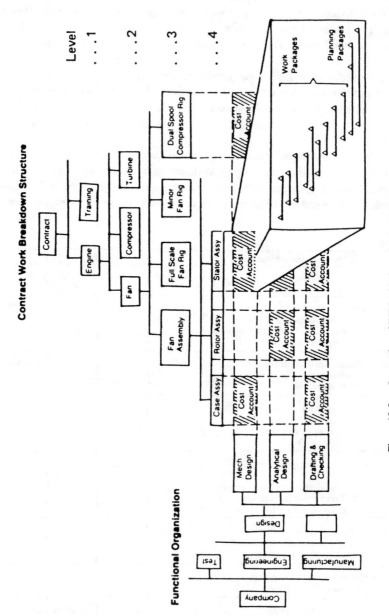

Figure 10-8. Integration of WBS with Organizational Structure.

Responsibility for a work package can be assigned to an engineer, scientist, or technology manager. Used in conjunction with task bar charts or work flowcharts, it is a powerful tool for project management.

10.9 MAKE-OR-BUY DECISIONS AND SUBCONTRACTING

Make-or-Buy Decisions

A necessary part of the project planning and start-up activities is making decisions about what technical work will be performed, which components and subsystems will be fabricated in-house, and what work should be subcontracted. The make-or-buy decisions and the selection of subcontractors may also be done during the proposal phase or even in the preliminary or feasibility study phase. The timing of the decisions would depend on the extent of the project commitment by the customer.

As technology development costs become increasingly higher, buying technical effort externally can be cost-effective. There are many pros and cons in going to an outside firm. The matter of secrecy, proprietary rights, and the desirability of building up in-house capability are important factors that mitigate against the purchase of technology. Nevertheless, because of the high cost of technology development, many companies utilize new technology in their products as it is developed by others. This use is accomplished by studying the pertinent technical, professional, and trade journals; attending trade and product meetings and symposia; acquiring personnel skilled in the new technology; studying government agency reports; and purchasing patents and know-how through licensing agreements with individual inventors or companies.

If hardware items are involved, a number of factors must be considered in arriving at the make-or-buy decision:

1. Can the item be made or the work be done within the company? That is, does the company have the necessary manufacturing capability, technical personnel, and available facilities?
2. What is the relative cost of making the item or doing the work in-house as opposed to having it made by an outside firm?
3. Would it be advantageous in the long run for the company to make the capital outlay and acquire or develop the capability for doing the work or making the particular component or subsystem?
4. If the company chooses to develop the capability for making the particular component or subsystem, would it have any undesirable effects on other units of the company or the sales of other company products? Would there

be any threat to products made by present customers? These factors might preclude making the item in-house.

These are just some of the factors that must be considered.

Subcontracting, Request for Proposal(RFP) and Proposals

If the decision is to have the work done by an outside vendor, it becomes immediately necessary to set up specifications or requirements. There are many types of specifications, but in system development and R&D work the most common deal with design and performance. Design specifications usually specify dimensions, materials, and configuration of the item; they may also specify weight, size, and other physical properties. Performance specifications describe the functions that the product must be able to perform to be acceptable. The ability of the product to meet these functions is usually determined by testing. After specifications and requirements are set, requests for information or proposals are solicited from bona fide producers of the item or engineering firms that can perform the technical work needed. This step usually means calling on specific vendors from a list of those with whom the company has had previous favorable experience. The request for proposal that is sent to the preferred vendors asks for such information as the following:

- Background discussion: problems and reasons why work is needed
- Task objectives: what is required in task accomplishments
- Performance of delivery schedule: which tasks should be done, when, and in what order; when hardware items are to be delivered
- Reporting requirements:[2]
     Written reports: weekly letters, monthly letters, quarterly reports, final reports
     Oral reports: results to date presented by project manager alone or with supporting personnel to contracting officer and other cognizant personnel and consultants
- Cost: number of engineering hours sometimes given to indicate level of effort and degree of design sophistication required.
- "Boilerplate" (material included in every RFP):
     Contract data requirements list
     Special facilities needed or furnished
     Format for reporting progress

---

[2]The frequency of reporting depends on the size and importance of the project and/or the requirements of the organization issuing the RFP.

How the proposal will be evaluated

Instructions regarding inventions and trade secrets

Special instructions

- For a project funded by a government agency: additional requirements in boilerplate section

Certification that facilities are nonsegregated

Statement of what government furnished equipment (GFE) and facilities will be provided

Penalties for false statements

Compliance with OSHA and other government regulations

Prospective subcontractors must be supplied with as much information as possible so that they can respond in the most complete and pertinent manner.

Evaluation of Proposals

Proposals from the prospective subcontractors must be evaluated and the winner selected. This step can be accomplished in a number of different ways:

1. The project manager singly makes the decision.
2. The project manager distributes copies of the proposals to key members of the staff and allows them to evaluate the proposals. At a joint meeting the project manager and staff decide who the winner or leading contenders should be.
3. The project manager appoints an evaluation committee made up of experts in the particular fields and allows them to make the evaluation and recommendations. The experts may make evaluations only in their specialties or they may evaluate all the criteria, depending on the capabilities of the evaluators and the nature of the work to be done.

For a major subcontracting effort, the third technique is particularly attractive and commonly used. It can be systemized and utilized to its full potential by having the committee first determine what criteria are most important for the fulfillment of the work required. These criteria are confirmed by the project manager, and a matrix is set up of the type shown in Figure 10-9. In this simple type of matrix evaluation the subcontractors are given a rating of 1 through whatever number of respondents there were to the RFP. In Figure 10-9 there would be ratings of 1 through 5 since there were five respondents. Each committee member would be given a blank form showing the criteria and would then evaluate the proposals and rate them. The results from all the evaluators would be totaled, and the companies with the lowest number ratings would be the leading contenders.

Key Criteria		Company				
		A	B	C	D	E
1. Responsiveness to system requirements		5	2	1	3	4
2. Knowledgeable technical personnel		4	3	1	2	5
3. Available facilities and manpower		3	1	2	4	5
4. Previous experience of company		3	2	1	5	4
5. Schedule		5	2	3	1	4
6. Cost		4	2	3	5	1
Totals*		24	12	11	20	23

*Companies B and C would be the leading contenders.

Figure 10-9.   Simple Matrix for Evaluating Subcontractors.

A more detailed matrix technique assigns maximum values or weights to each criterion (Figure 10-10). The maximum value or weight reflects the importance attached to the criterion by the committee and would be determined by the committee when making up the criteria list. The value of the weight should also reflect the importance of the criterion to the project manager and the company. (This decision-making technique has already been described in Section 6.6.) The value given a particular company for each criterion can be made up of components. For example, in the case of the criterion "previous experience of company in this area of work," there could be the following partitioning of points:

Contractor has no experience in this field	0 points
Contractor has limited experience	1 point
Contractor has built similar items for other companies	2 points
Contractor has built similar items for this company with satisfactory performance	3 points
Contractor has built similar items for this company with outstanding performance	4 points

The maximum value or weight in this case would be 4.

Key Criteria	Maximum Value	Company			
		A	B	C	D
1. Responsiveness to system requirements	10	7	9	7	8
2. Knowledgeable technical personnel	6	3	5	3	4
3. Available facilities	4	3	4	4	4
4. Previous experience of company	4	2	3	2	2
5. Schedule	6	4	4	3	5
6. Cost	10	9	6	7	8
Totals*	40	28	31	26	31

*Companies B and D would be the leading contenders.

Figure 10-10.   Weighted Matrix for Evaluating Subcontractors.

Final Selection of Subcontractor

Although a selection of the successful contractor could be based on the highest total score obtained, it is better to contact the two or three highest scorers and arrange for stand-up briefings during which they present the highlights of their proposal and how they plan to perform the work. At such meetings the project manager or the key personnel would be there to listen, evaluate, and ask pertinent questions to determine the true credibility and competence of the bidding firm. It sometimes happens that the company that scored highest on the proposal evaluation does not fare as well in the face-to-face briefing. Another company may have greater familiarity with the technical issues, have greater understanding of the developmental problems, and generally be more knowledgeable and experienced. These assets would not necessarily be reflected in a proposal, although they should be. Something may surface at the briefing that was not evident from the proposal. Thus the decision reached by the committee as a result of the decision matrix may be reversed. This latter possibility is more the exception than the rule, however.

Because of the importance of the cost criterion, the cost portion of the proposal is often considered separately. Representatives of the accounting or financial group of the company would evaluate the cost data, including the accounting methods to be used, and would decide which companies would be acceptable from a cost standpoint. A company that is rated first technically may be asked to reduce its costs in certain areas of work, and cost negotiations and trade-offs may be initiated between the contractor and the vendor or subcontractor. In the case of a government contract the lowest competent bidder is acceptable; this could be the firm that was rated third in the evaluation but was nevertheless acceptable technically. Government contracting is generally more rigid since it is regulated by public laws to protect taxpayers interests.

10.10   PROJECT MONITORING AND CONTROL

The monitoring and control of functional programs and small projects has already been discussed in Chapter 9. For large projects the same essential elements—namely, cost, performance, and schedule—must be carefully monitored. For projects being performed for another segment of the company or an outside organization, such as another company or the government, the monitoring must be even more stringent and painstaking. In such cases the reputation and credibility of the company is at stake as well as future business potential with the particular customer and other customers.

Technical Performance and Cost

The use of milestones is an excellent way to keep track of whether critical issues are being solved as planned or whether impasses have been reached that will delay the project. For this purpose curves showing anticipated cumulative expenditures plotted against time and milestones are valuable (Figure 3-4). The worst situation occurs when the money has been spent by an important milestone date and the milestone has not been met. Another technique is to compare the actual percentage of work accomplished at a given time with the planned percentage of work to be done at that time (Figure 9-5).

Regularly issued computer output sheets showing all expenditures charged to the project over a finite time are of inestimable value in cost control (see Section 9.4). Such computer output should be issued promptly so that false charging, errors in charging, and overcharging can be averted before an excessive drain on project funds occurs. Depending on the size of the project and the expenditure rate, computer accounting sheets may be issued daily, weekly, biweekly, or monthly. An inordinate time lag in issuing them diminishes control; for a large project a one-week lag can entail a sizable expenditure.

Where finances permit, the use of PERT, CPM, or PDM can be invaluable in keeping track of slippages in the schedule and consequent effects on completion time and cost. This use is usually not justifiable for small projects, but for large projects, in which there are many subsystems and components and considerable subcontracting, the expense is well justified. For large projects it can be advantageous to have a special PERT type group input slippages into the computer program to calculate the effect of delays on other components and subsystems and the new project completion date. This group would constantly update the control charts and provide information to the project manager and assistants on the status of the project in time, money, subcontractors, vendors, and project performance. In complex system developments, in which there are thousands of components and hundreds of subsystems, this is a necessary and valuable function.

Design Reviews

Another effective technique for monitoring and coordinating technical effort involving many groups is to have a design review, which for a hardware system, includes

- Examining and critiquing the system design at various stage of development to discern any flaws, omissions, or possible improvements
- Examining a model or prototype of the system to determine if components and subsystems are spatially and functionally compatible

Important events for design review would be the completion of the preliminary design and the completion of the final design. Design review meetings can be called by upper management, the project manager, the supervisor in charge of the design effort, or the customer. Attendees would include the project manager or a representative, the key design engineers, and other engineers whose expertise could contribute to the improvement of the design. It would be advantageous to include manufacturing and marketing personnel so that their input could be considered at this vital stage of the new development. Representatives of upper management and the customer can also be invited.

10.11   PROJECT MANAGEMENT INFORMATION SYSTEM (PMIS)

To keep management, the customer, and the involved supervision and personnel properly informed, an information system must be developed. A properly designed system informs in a timely manner those that should know what they should know about the progress of the project. Many project-oriented companies have developed their own computerized systems for integrating, printing and distributing the required information. Typically, the following items would be included:

- Task bar charts (showing slippages)
- Work flowcharts (PERT or CPM showing slippages)
- Performance, cost, and time charts (P/C/T charts)
- Computer output sheets showing details of expenditures to date and other financial data
- Itemization of problem areas and status
- Subcontractor performance status

A number of computer software companies market completely computerized systems that display project status on output sheets or on computer monitors as desired. The information is shown as tables, as graphs, or in printed word form. Such software packages are available to provide complete information systems for monitoring and controlling single projects or many projects with a variety of options concerning the format of the printout or display. Small packages for a single project can sell for as little as a few thousand dollars, whereas large packages for multiproject management may be $80,000 and over. An excellent discussion of the use of software for project management, including key features, classification, evaluation, and implementation problems, is given by Kerzner (1989).

For large projects there is a definite need for constant communication and information flow between the project manager, his or her staff, and the personnel performing the detailed work. In addition, the project manager must be in constant communication with management and the customer to implement any changes in direction or policy that are dictated by the decision makers. Since the project is usually goal-oriented with definite objectives, any policy or other change would not affect the ultimate goals of the project but might affect the method and ease of achievement.

Oral Communication and Meetings

Frequent oral communication is needed on both an informal and a formal basis so that problems can be quickly recognized and the full resources available to the project manager can be brought to bear on their solution. Formalized oral communication can consist of weekly reports or weekly staff meetings in which each supervisor reports on the status of his or her portion of the work and brings up any problems. An effective technique used by project managers is to assign "action items" to concerned and knowledgeable individuals to be carried out, or at least initiated, in the ensuing week. These action items are based on recommendations and conclusions arrived at during the open discussion at the staff meeting.

In addition to the staff meetings, there should be regularly scheduled meetings of the particular groups working on the subsystem and component developments or complex problem solutions. Staff meetings at the project manager's level could involve a number of subsystem and component development groups and cross disciplinary and organizational lines. There could also be special meetings called by the project manager or a member of the staff to solve problems that require immediate attention and involve several different groups and disciplines. Such meetings can result in assigning individuals to ad hoc committees or task forces, an effective means of attacking technical problems when time is important.

In addition to meetings of personnel within the project organization and company, there are meetings of the project management staff with vendors and subcontractors. These meetings must be held often enough so that subcontractor and vendor performance is commensurate with the achievement of project milestones and cost goals. Changes of direction, suggested improvements, and general evaluation of subcontractor efforts can be accomplished at such meetings, and in this regard coordination goes hand in hand with monitoring and controlling.

10.12   DOCUMENTATION

The remarks made in Section 9.3 concerning reports and documentation for programs and small projects are applicable to all projects. Adequate documentation for large projects is even more crucial because the work is often done for another company or a government agency. The frequency of the reporting may be weekly, monthly, bimonthly, or quarterly, depending on the size and complexity of the project. The format varies according to the type of project and is usually chosen by the project manager and staff, although it may be dictated by the customer or contracting organization. A typical progress report would include an introductory or background section, a section describing details of what had been accomplished during the reporting period, a summary of accomplishments, and finally a section stating what was planned for the ensuing period. There would also have to be a section or separate volume giving financial details of the expenditures during the reporting period. Because the project is frequently a one-time activity, the final report assumes particular significance. It usually describes what was accomplished during the last reporting period and summarizes the work of the whole project.

In technical efforts in which there is no hardware development, the reports are the end products of the project expenditures; sometimes a computer program is the final project output. Feasibility studies, testing programs, and product evaluations can fall into this category. For a company or organization that is primarily involved in project-type work, there is usually a publications group that finishes all project reports, ensuring that they are in the proper format; in good English; and suitably illustrated with diagrams, sketches, and the like. Such a group might also handle proposals, bulletins, handbooks, and other printed matter necessary for the functioning of a project-oriented organization.

QUESTIONS AND TOPICS FOR DISCUSSION

10.1   The term *project management* has semantic problems, particularly as it is used along with related terms. Distinguish *project management* from the following terms and indicate relationships, if any: (a) *systems engineering*, (b) *task force operation*, (c) *operations research*, (d) *systems management*, (e) *program management*, and (f) *systems integration*.

10.2   You are the manager of a functional group in a research or engineering organization and you are suddenly presented by your top management with a special technical effort. Under what conditions would you (a) lead and coordinate the effort yourself; (b) assign one of your staff people to handle it; (c) assign a supervisor in your department to head up the job; or (d) appoint a project manager, who reports directly to you, and a special group to carry out the work?

10.3   Market analysis to determine the need for a product or new system is a specialty field in itself. What are some of the evaluations that would have to be made in a market analysis? You select the product or system.

10.4   What important tools or techniques can be used by a project manager to plan a project? Explain how these tools can be effective in monitoring and controlling the project.

10.5   What basic items of information should be contained in a proposal?

10.6   Show by an example how a work breakdown structure (WBS) can be used in planning a project. You select the project. How can the WBS be integrated into the organizational structure?

10.7   Prepare a brief form RFP for a technology development that you feel is necessary in today's complex environment. It can involve hardware, software, or a problem in the public sector.

10.8   Assume the following scenario: (a) A company has a number of projects that are constantly being replenished by new projects coming in as old projects phase out; (b) a functional organization services the company's nonproject as well as project needs; (c) the company has approximately ten small projects being worked on simultaneously that each have dollar values of about $100,000 to $200,000. What would be the most advantageous way to integrate the projects into the technical organization, and how should the project managers be assigned?

References

Kerzner, N. 1989. *Project Management: A Systems Approach to Planning, Scheduling and Controlling*, 3rd ed., pp. 864–875. New York: Van Nostrand Reinhold.

Obradovitch, M. M., and S. E. Stephanou. 1990. *Project Management, Risk and Productivity*, p. 95. Bend, OR: Daniel Spencer.

Stephanou, S. E., and M. M. Obradovitch. 1985. *Project Management, System Development and Productivity*. p. 5. Bend, OR: Daniel Spencer.

11

Integrating Research and Development with Manufacturing

11.1 TRANSITION TO PRODUCTION

There are a number of methods for carrying out the physical transition from R&D to production (Figure 11-1).[1]

- Simultaneous engineering (see Section 12.1)
- Prototype development and manufacturing models
- Building and operating a separate pilot plant facility
- Building an initial or preliminary manufacturing facility that can be expanded to a full-fledged facility
- Modifying an existing production facility
- Building a new facility that easily permits changes of product and quantities of product (flexible manufacturing and group technology facility)
- CAD/CAE/CAM (Chapter 14)

---

[1]This assumes that a true manufacturing process is to be developed; that is, many copies of the item are to be made rather than a few isolated systems.

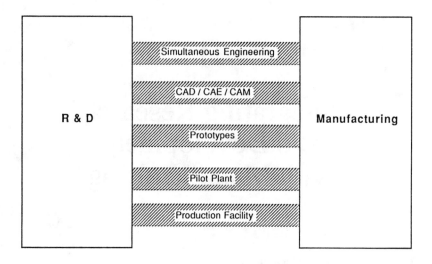

Figure 11-1.   Bridging the Gap.

There are obvious advantages and disadvantages to each of these methods, and the selection of one rather than another very much depends on the nature and specifics of the particular process. The degree of scaling up from laboratory processes is a major problem, as is the decision of whether or not to use batch or continuous flow processes, group manufacturing techniques, robots and automation, and so on. From a management aspect these are decisions that depend on such factors as cost, time to implement, degree of reliability, reproducibility, and available facilities. There are also marketing aspects in that the product must be produced in quantities and in a form that reflects the anticipated market demand; thus representatives from marketing must be involved in the decision-making process.

The question of scaling is an important consideration. If the product is a complex system of some size that has never been built before, should scaled-up models be built and at what size? The same is true of an initial production line. Is one pilot plant adequate before building the final full-scale production unit, or should there be two or more intermediate stages. What about prototyping? Should there be several prototypes including an experimental prototype, an initial manufacturing prototype, and then a final prototype, as in the case of new aircraft? These and other questions of a technical nature can best be answered by the combined inputs from experts in the relevant specific disciplines. Techniques for identifying and integrating the personnel who can provide the necessary information for making and implementing these decisions are described in the next two sections. Subsequent sections in this chapter discuss other management issues that are key to the successful bridging of the gap between R&D and production. The traditional sequence for introducing a product into production is shown in Figure 11-2.

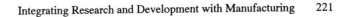

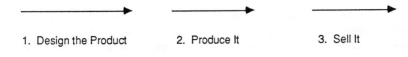

1. Design the Product   2. Produce It   3. Sell It

Figure 11-2.   Traditional Method of Production.

11.2   TECHNIQUES FOR INTEGRATING DIVERSE EFFORTS

For the critical transition step from R&D to production to be successful, the various groups, functions, and interests involved must be integrated. The quality, cost, and time needed to develop the new product will depend on how smoothly this transition and integration process is carried out. There are a number of ways in which it can be accomplished:

1. Personnel transfer
2. Multifunctional or cross-functional teams (teaming)
3. Special task forces and projects
4. Matrix organizations

In addition the use of computed-aided design/computer-aided manufacturing (CAM/CAM) and computer-integrated manufacturing (CIM) can facilitate the transition process in that considerable preliminary and final design and planning can be accomplished with these techniques.

Personnel Transfer
The transfer of personnel from one development stage to the other during a new product or process development can be an effective way of ensuring that important information and know-how are not lost during the transition to production. For example, in the case of a new chemical process developed in the laboratory, the key chemists or chemical engineers who initiated the process would be involved either directly or as consultants in the design and operation of the pilot plant facility and also in the design and operation of the manufacturing facility. This process could include development of the first manufacturing prototype as well as the final standardized product or process.

Multifunctional or Cross-Functional Teams
Another way to integrate personnel from different groups is to have cross-functional teams made up of personnel from the departments or divisions most intimately involved with the manufacturing process initiation and development. Such a team would include inventors of the process as well as development and manufacturing personnel; the team would be involved in the planning, design, and

operation of the manufacturing facility and could serve as consultants through manufacturing prototype production and finalization of the manufacturing operations. The *multifunctional team* concept is the cornerstone of several of the current techniques for improving manufacturing operations, including total quality management (TQM), simultaneous engineering (SE), and value engineering (VE).[2] In the broader scope of TQM, the early bringing together of personnel from various organizational entities such as R&D, engineering, quality control, and manufacturing can be effective in moving the laboratory process not only to production but also to successful marketing and use.

Special Task Forces and Projects

Special forces and projects are still another way for integrating diverse efforts. They can be identical to teaming or different, depending on how the project is structured (see Chapter 10). If the members are all more or less at the same organizational level, the group has the characteristics of a team of consultants, with perhaps a leader or coordinator for carrying out any administrative functions that are necessary. However, if a project manager heads up the team or task force and is given the full authority of a project manager, the group takes on the character of a true project. In the execution of a project a number of personnel with the needed discipline capabilities are assembled to work together toward a predetermined goal. The goal in this case would be the conversion of the R&D process to a pilot plant or full-fledged manufacturing process. A dramatic example of marshalling different capabilities in an organized fashion to achieve a common goal was the bringing together in one facility of 1,200 key people from various GM divisions into a project center for the express purpose of developing manufacturing processes for downsized automobiles (Peters and Waterman 1982).

Matrix Organizations

The matrix-type organization described in Section 7.7 is an excellent way of integrating research with manufacturing process development (Figure 7-9). In such an arrangement the necessary technical know-how is available to a project manager through the jurisdiction over personnel in various functional groups, including research, system design, manufacturing development, instrumentation, and so on. The P.M. can draw on the know-how of the experts to bring the process development to a final preproduction stage or even to initial production of a manufacturing prototype. This step could involve designing and building the manufacturing facility. Upon completion of this facility, the P.M. could move on to another project or be a part of the supervision of the new manufacturing operation.

---

[2]These subjects are discussed in Chapters 12 and 13.

11.3 TEAMING

A team can be defined as a group of individuals working together to achieve a common goal or objective. The use of teams is neither new nor novel; it is a proven method of conducting many types of operations. The military and paramilitary organizations such as police, which are involved in crisis management, have long ago recognized, emphasized, and perfected the use of teams in commando raids, "SWAT" operations, and emergency and rescue operations. In manufacturing development, as well as in R&D projects, the use of the team approach has proven quite effective in the development of new products and processes and the solution of operational problems. It combines the human relations aspect of people working together toward a common goal with the availability of all the required technical expertise needed for doing the job.

Use of Teams in Manufacturing Process Development
The effectiveness of teams in manufacturing process development depends on the utilization of the combined skills and effort of technical and other personnel in a number of situations in which R&D and/or manufacturing activities must be integrated.

- Concurrent/simultaneous engineering
- Value analysis/value engineering
- Total quality management
- Quality circles
- Cross-functional activities
- Special projects

The selection of the type of team is usually based on the particular need and reflects the organization's culture, resources, and management style. A special-purpose team may be set up to write a proposal, develop a new design, or perform any of the tasks needed to convert the laboratory process into a manufacturing process.

Team Formation
The selection of personnel for a particular team is critical to the team's success. It should be based on the experience, attitude, and willingness of a worker to contribute. The pertinent areas of knowledge and technology should be identified, and they should be adequately covered. Economy and poor selection in this aspect of team formation can doom the effort at the outset; there is a limit to the effective performance of even the most capable personnel if resources are inadequate, and if some of the personnel selected are not competent, the situation is worsened. The selection of individuals who are experienced and known to be capable will lend a

completely different cast to a team than will the selection of people who the contributing groups would like to be rid of. This is not to imply that teams cannot be used to train young personnel who may need to broaden their perspectives (on-the-job training).

It is important not to involve a manager and direct subordinates in the same team if the individuals cannot successfully deal with open personal exchanges. Some organizations have resorted to psychological testing and professional psychologists to find potentially negative personal characteristics. Also companies have used "sensitivity training" to strengthen individual abilities to interact successfully. Almost always, the synergism of good team efforts will show greater results than the sum of the individual efforts, especially when the personnel involved are properly chosen and have a common desire for the success of the team. In this regard, it is only proper that team members be fully advised of the true purpose of their efforts as well as any involved risks and rewards. Severe demoralizing consequences can result if employees do their utmost to reach a goal and then find out that it was never intended to be achieved.

Team Motivation

The motivation of the team participants is a critical element, not only in the team selection and formation but also throughout the implementation cycle. If possible, teams should be given tangible motivation based on defined and measurable objectives and goals. Motivation can take a variety of forms: monetary compensation (bonus), increased responsibility, formal recognition by upper management, and so on. Special care should be taken to avoid the perception that being the leader or member of a team could be career limiting. Care should also be taken, particularly in those organizations where team functions are relatively new, to keep the motivation of teams a continuing management concern until their functioning is a recognized and accepted operational phenomenon. Outstanding performance should be a proven path to rewards and career progression. Training should be offered to some or all of the selected individuals on the team, and in some cases it should be a requirement.

Importance of Location

Close physical location, ideally the same location, of the members of a team is important in developing a new product, new manufacturing process, or simultaneous engineering (SE) effort. According to studies at MIT, engineers develop about 80 percent of their ideas as a result of face-to-face contacts with others (*Mechanical Engineering* 1989). Beyond 30 to 50 meters (100 to 160 feet) effective communication decreases markedly. This conclusion has been verified by other studies, which clearly point out that physical proximity not only enhances the communication process but also improves cooperation as people get to know each other better. For this reason, some of the most difficult and challenging commercial ventures have been carried out by closely knit and closely located multifunctional teams, for example, the so-called Skunk Works[3] of the Lockheed Company and the project teams formed by American auto companies to develop downsized automobiles (discussed below).

Another example is the organizational arrangement used by Bavarian Motor Works (BMW) in building a new office complex (*Mechanical Engineering* 1989). This complex, which covers nearly 1.2 million square feet, was built to house the engineers who are to design the BMW cars of the future. All functions, which were previously scattered around ten locations near Munich, are now situated close to one another. The buildings are laid out to support the flow of information, from styling to pilot production, in much the same way the physical material flows in an automobile plant. The final Research and Development Center floor plan follows the components of a car, such as subassemblies, body chassis, and drive train. As a result, work flow and function, rather than the traditional organizational grouping, determine an employee's physical location. This arrangement allows the designer to follow his or her idea as it progresses through the various phases of development to the final production model (*Mechanical Engineering* 1989).

Ten Ingredients for a Successful Team
According to P. R. Scholtes (1988) ten ingredients must be present if a team is to be successful:

- Clarity in team goals
- An improvement plan
- Clearly defined roles
- Clear communications
- Beneficial team behavior
- Well-defined decision procedures
- Balanced participation
- Established ground rules
- Awareness of the group process
- Use of the scientific approach

Controlling Team Performance
The control of team performances requires the setting of objectives, defining tasks and schedules, and monitoring team performance. Although budgets and schedules

---

[3]The Skunk Works, located for many years in Burbank, California, consisted of a highly specialized team that developed a number of revolutionary aircraft designs, such as the U-2 and the SR-71, used for high-altitude military surveillance.

are the most common forms of control, they may not properly reflect and reward the contributions of individual team members, or the team as a whole for that matter. To ensure the meaningful recognition of achievements within a team, we have used individual mutual evaluations, which are then averaged (Figure 11-3). If these evaluations are divided into technical as well as interaction capabilities, they can also provide the basis for further training.

The achievement of teams is perhaps more sensitive to continuous management monitoring than most other, more formally controlled tasks. A desirable pattern is a well-publicized start with an announcement of study objectives. Implementation—unless closely monitored by the team leader, with definitive personal assignments to team members and responsible organization elements—is likely to fade. We ourselves have utilized relatively simple systems, which show numbered action items with assigned personnel and due dates that can be easily tracked and computerized. Weekly internal status and planning meetings, with monthly management reviews, should ensure effective implementation and success. An important feature of such efforts must be a systematic way to introduce new or changed concepts into the organization, a way that involves the needed authorization, responsibilities, and resources to make the team plans a reality. The engineering change procedure described in Section 12-9 provides such a system. Another way is the updating of company practice and procedure notices authorizing specific changes.

The most important element of control, as demonstrated repeatedly in diverse management situations, is personal verification and interest by the manager or executive. This type of monitoring and control has often been referred to as the "walking around" technique. An ancillary benefit of this technique, in addition to getting the "feel" of the situation, is to detect more readily misinformation that may be intentional or simply caused by communication problems. To control the

**Name	*Creativity	*Effort	*Expertise	Overall Average
1. John Smith	8	7	9	8
2. Jane Doe	9	8	4	7
3. George Jones	7	6	5	6
4. William Kane	6	5	6	6
5. Stanley Crane	10	8	8	9
6. Sue Starr	6	5	4	5

* Scale of 1 to 10.
** Each team member including rater.

Figure 11-3.   Team Evaluations.

outcome of a task successfully, one must stay in touch with events as they are occurring because later no changes are possible.

Generally, team and project operations will not work if management and participants are not willing to practice honest, two-way or up-down communications and commitments. The willingness at the outset, to equip teams and projects with the necessary responsibility, authority, and resources to accomplish their mission should be explicitly shown by management. We ourselves have participated in too many team efforts that seemed to go only as far as the recommendation and initiation stage and then merely withered away for lack of adequate management support. Evidence of support can entail the provision of adequate resources—including personnel, facilities, and funds—and organizational backing—by letting other members of the organization know how important the effort is to the company so that the necessary assistance from involved groups is readily provided.

11.4   PRODUCIBILITY AND PRODUCTIVITY

Producibility

In the past, producibility has implied the optimization of the design for ease of manufacturing and assembly at an optimum product cost. The same concept is now more directly referred to as *design for manufacture* (DFM). Producibility can also imply that the item can be readily reproduced again and again within certain tolerable limits.

A design that is to be eventually transformed into a product should be interrelated to manufacturing; that is, each part or component of a product must be designed so that it not only meets design requirements and specifications but also can be manufactured economically. Such a comprehensive approach to the production of goods and resultant services is needed so that the design process is integrated with material requirements, manufacturing methods, process planning, assembly, testing, and quality control.

Requirements of Designers

Effectively implementing the design for manufacture requires the designers to have a fundamental understanding of customer needs as well as the characteristics, capabilities, and limitations of materials; manufacturing processes; and related operations, machinery, and equipment. This knowledge should include such characteristics as variability in machine performance, surface finish and dimensional accuracy of the piece, processing times, and the effect of processing methods on quality. It is well known in the manufacturing industry that individuals possessing all such specialized knowledge in addition to ingenious design expertise are rare indeed. Even if one encounters such talented people who have spent the necessary time in such diverse functions as engineering and manufacturing, they are frequently promoted into management positions because of their specialized talent and experience. To cultivate and bring such talent to the forefront, a special type of engineer has been trained—the producibility or manufacturing engineer.

By making designs producible within the constraints of the equipment and facilities available, many potential production problems can be avoided. Unfortunately, in some engineering-dominated companies, the advice of assigned manufacturing engineers may be overridden for the sake of short-term economy or schedules. Such action works against the concept that producibility, or design for manufacture, has to be considered important enough from a management perspective to be part of the normal operation of an organization. After-the-fact producibility studies, usually triggered by a major crisis, seldom permit the type of cost-effective manufacturing designs that are possible at the outset.

Typically, a crisis can occur as a result of a manufacturing process failure or the failure of a product in use. For example, a leading appliance manufacturer marketed a refrigerator with an inadequate cooling system. Customer complaints necessitated the replacement of all but a few cooling systems in that particular model—a costly replacement operation. The recall of an automobile because of a poorly designed part or the redesign of an engine seal on the space shuttle after a tragic accident are hardly examples of optimum design, manufacturing, and problem solution.

Thus designers must assess the impact of design modifications on the manufacturing process, assembly, inspection, test, and product cost. Such assessment requires close coordination with personnel from the involved functional areas. The establishment of qualitative as well as quantitative criteria is essential to optimize the design for ease of manufacturing and assembly at minimum product cost. These types of efforts and requirements are needed to create products that have been designed for maximum manufacturing flexibility.

Team efforts with diverse disciplines, from marketing through design and manufacturing to field service, can substantially improve the process of design to manufacture with due regard of the customer's needs. The use of CAD, manufacturing and process planning, artificial intelligence, expert systems, and the Taguchi method can improve and expedite the traditional design process to optimize producibility. These and other techniques will be discussed in Chapters 12 through 14.

Productivity

Productivity can be considered to be a measure of the effective use of all the resources of an organization such as materials, machines, energy, capital, labor, and technology (Kalpakjian 1989). High productivity requires that the producibility of a product must be not only considered but constantly improved. In terms of the total system, productivity can also be measured by the ratio of output to input in terms of measurable resources (usually dollars):

$$\text{Productivity} = \frac{\text{Value of output}^4}{\text{Value of Input}}$$

This measure could be well applied to a group, an entire organization, or even to an individual.

With the intensification of global competition, productivity has become a major concern. How then can productivity be improved? Mechanization of machinery and operation generally reached its peak during the World War II production drives. Drilling holes manually or electrically still required some measure of operational control and therefore required hands-on types of operation. The next major advance in productivity was through *automation*; this word as popularized by the U.S. automobile industry in the postwar period, indicated the automatic handling and transfer of parts between production machines during processing and assembly. In subsequent decades major breakthroughs and advances have been possible through computers, improved electronics, and new control systems. The application of automation to manufacturing processes to achieve higher levels of efficiency has resulted in substantial increases in productivity (Chapter 15).

11.5   MANAGEMENT'S ROLE IN THE PRODUCT SERVICE CYCLE

It is a common conviction of most practioners and theorists that top management involvement and support are essential to the success of any activity for which it has overall responsibility. It is important and often essential for a particular new product development to have an "angel," or sponsor, in upper management who can exert continuous pressure on the organization to see that the innovation is carried through to completion. New products or developments that lack such sponsorship usually fail. Having a sponsor does not necessarily guarantee success in the marketplace, however. For example, Dr. Land, the founder and CEO of

---

[4]Productivity has also been defined as the output per hour of work. In 1990 productivity in the United States on this basis increased 1.6 percent, primarily because of layoffs, hiring freezes, and limits on overtime (Associated Press 1990).

Polaroid for many years, had the personal desire to develop and produce a Polaroid-type movie camera and projector. Unfortunately, the new product was a technical success but a financial failure. Such an instant moving picture and sound system has since been achieved more economically through a video camera and recorder (VCR) that can also easily be projected on a television screen.

If upper management is convinced that a new product or process development is indeed worthwhile and has approved the expenditure of resources, there should be not only subsequent continued management support but also management involvement. Herein looms a real dilemma for many organizations: How can upper management be effectively involved within the constraints of available time? The answer is that any amount of time allotted to such involvement is worthwhile.

Most upper-level managers believe that they are already quite busy with traditional responsibilities and feel that their contribution can be best made by conventional delegation—, establishing goals and urging their subordinates to meet them (Juran 1988). Conventional delegations of such efforts as the improvement of quality or increased safety, which are often difficult to define, quantify, and measure, have generally resulted in disappointment. The failure to achieve the desired results has often surprised upper management since delegation is generally considered to be the best way to get things done; however, that is not the case in the matter of quality. The achievement of quality cannot be delegated—all levels of management must be involved.

Some ways in which management can improve the situation are these:

1. *Focus on the basic processes rather than short-term results.* Even in conventional manufacturing, with high rework and scrap rates, management is frequently appeased by meeting "hot" delivery dates at the expense of deliveries with less visibility. These schedules are frequently achieved through costly breaks in production runs and overtime. Top management must focus on more efficient manufacturing through improved training, equipment, and production flow. Short-term goals, concentrating on product or immediate service while ignoring fundamental manufacturing problems, should be minimized.

2. *Concentrate on in-depth resolution of priority problems.* Through such techniques as the Pareto's principle of finding cost drivers, management must emphasize the real resolution of problems rather than the treatment of symptoms. Frequently managers have the tendency to deal with the familiar rather than the critical issues of a problem. For example, a manager who was formerly an engineer or accountant will tend to focus on technical or financial issues, thus operating in a relative comfort zone. By the use of

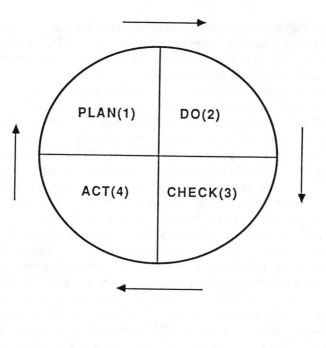

1. Plan   - Design the Product
2. Do   - Produce It
3. Check   - Sell It
4. Act   - Assess Consumer Satisfaction
   Repeat Cycle - Improve Continuously

Figure 11-4.   Plan-Do-Check-Act (PDCA Cycle).

value analysis teams and plan-do-check-act (PDCA) cycles, systematic problem resolution can be standardized (Figure 11-4).[5]

3. *Emphasize selective participation by top management*: Specific key decisions and critical actions have to be taken by management to substantiate statements of support and commitment. Such decisions and actions could involve allocation of necessary resources, attendance at key meetings,

---

[5]The PDCA cycle according to Suzaki (1987), consists of

1. Plan—developing a plan
2. Do—conducting the work as planned
3. Check—checking results for appropriateness
4. Analyze—analyzing and taking action where there is a need for further correction

Note the similarity of Suzaki's PDCA cycle to the systems approach for problem solving (Section 2.5).

approving teaming programs, and so on. It may be necessary to find out and understand what a new management concept such as TQM really requires. Deming (1982), in his treatise on management asks top managers not to preach quality, but to lead by actions.

4. *Institute walking around.* Staying in touch throughout the product cycle is a vital aspect of top management even though it does not really seem to lend itself to scientific quantification. Peters and Waterman (1982) mention "staying in touch" as a common denominator in leaders who strive for excellence and succeed. How believable are CEOs to their workers when they talk of the critical importance of a manufacturing operation but seldom set foot in the plant. Successful leaders in industry, the military, and government have understood the symbolic value of such visits, as well as the importance of staying in touch with untarnished reality.[6]

5. *Provide the resources.* A major failing of upper management has been and continues to be the failure to supply adequate resources for accomplishing the desired goals and objectives. This failure causes lower levels of management and ultimately the work force to doubt the real commitment of top management.

6. *Review progress.* The systematic review of progress is an essential part of making goals and objectives a reality. The fact that upper management is concerned about the progress of an effort sends a message concerning its priority. The most common ways are written and/or verbal reports and audits at reasonable frequencies. No required oversight over an extended period of time, will frequently be interpreted by lower levels of management and workers as a sign that the project is of little or no importance and ultimately will cause degradation of the effort.

7. *Provide recognition and reward systems.* The word *recognition* as used in the context of management practices refers to publicizing and rewarding employees for innovation and efficient conduct of operations (Figure 11-5). Rewards can include merit increases and sometimes bonuses. Reward systems should also be devised to encourage exceptional achievements in the special areas of quality improvement, better worker relations, and customer satisfaction. Such accomplishments should be recognized just as much as the development of a new product or the improvement of a manufacturing process. All recognition and reward systems should be

---

[6]Morris Asimow, a famous engineer, inventor, and scientific writer, in a joint venture with one of us convinced him that one should (1) never walk through a hallway or yard in a plant or organization when one can walk through a work area with just a few extra steps; (2) keep a mental score of how many people are working and how many are not; and (3) inquire about any unusual practices on the spot. The founder of the Douglas Aircraft Company, bearing his name, was known to appear almost anywhere and at anytime in the plant to verify for himself exactly what was going on, particularly when there was a problem.

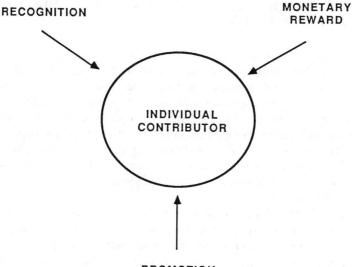

Figure 11-5.   Outstanding Effort should be Rewarded.

designed so that they can include the largest possible cross section of personnel, both vertically and horizontally, in an organization.[7]

It is important to note that the role of top management in the product service cycle should be continuous but not necessarily the same in character. Changing events require different strategies and policies. The current worldwide competition has forced alert organizations to engage in concerted efforts directed toward constant product and quality improvements, while simultaneously promoting innovation to widen the scope of perspective markets to international levels. These are primary management functions, which cannot be ignored because of preoccupation with the micro-management of daily operations.

---

[7]In U.S. companies, rewards have been excessively focused on the top levels of management. From the standpoint of worker morale, union relations, and public image, salaries at the higher levels should not be disproportionately high. For example, in the auto industry top executive reimbursement, not counting various extra "perks," such as a company car and stock benefits, may be 35 to 50 times that of the working-level employee. In Japan it is generally half that ratio. According to data from the Labor Department, the income and benefits gap between executives and workers has more than doubled in the past 15 years, and so has the spread between top executives in the United States and those in other industrial nations. Yet, the productivity of other industrial powers such as Germany and Japan has increased in relation to the United States during that the same period.

11.6   OVERCOMING PROBLEMS IN TRANSFERRING R&D TO PRODUCTION

The transition from the R&D stage to production is a critical step in bringing to fruition a new manufacturing process or product. It is a complex and difficult process not only in its technical and physical aspects but also in its human factor aspects. It requires the coordination of two general types of individuals with different perspectives concerning the relative importance of quality, time, and methods of achievement. For example, a research-oriented person stresses detail and quality over ease of production and time to produce. Cost to produce and ease of manufacture would not tend to be as important to the initiator or inventor of a new product or process as how closely the final product or manufacturing process duplicates the initial laboratory model.

This underlying problem continues to surface in many transitions of laboratory processes and products to production. The obvious solution is the constant getting together of key personnel from the involved functions to solve transition problems and management's awareness of such problems and its ability to compromise and resolve these conflicts. Marketing personnel can also present problems because they see the results of new product properties in terms of customer acceptance and marketability, and they can make demands on product characteristics and supply that are difficult, if not impossible, to meet.

In the physical transfer of R&D to production the best and simplest way to avoid and overcome potential production problems is to carry out process research at the desired production levels. This step means bringing people with the required manufacturing capability into the R&D effort when the innovation first appears to promise success. If such personnel are not available, it is best to develop a design suited for manufacturing (DFM) by having the R&D personnel work with designated production employees as a team at the outset of the project. This step frequently requires a prototype design different from that originally contemplated by the research personnel who first devised the item.

The learning process should be continuous in going from R&D to production (Figure 11-6). It is critical that the lessons of each phase be passed along to the next in a usable format. The application of computer-based expert systems (ES), as discussed in Section 14.7, enables organizations to operate consistently on the lower, more efficient end of the learning curve.

In the long term the capability of the organization to make the transition from R&D to effective production can be the overriding factor in product success. It can be argued that the primary reasons for Japan's dominance in the field of electronic products has been the ability to do so, as well as market a quality product. The VCR technology was originally developed by U.S. companies but went primarily to

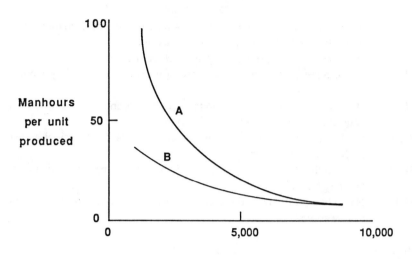

Number of Units Produced

A - **Without Concurrent Engineering and TQM**
B - **With Concurrent Engineering and TQM**

Figure 11-6.   The Learning Curve.

Japan in the production phase, mostly because mass production was more effectively achieved in Japan than in the United States.

QUESTIONS AND TOPICS FOR DISCUSSION

11.1   Name three methods for making the transition from R&D to product and compare them in (a) time to implement, (b) cost, and (c) organizational aspects.

11.2   Discuss the problem of scaling up a laboratory-developed process to a manufacturing facility.

11.3   How can computers facilitate the transition from R&D to manufacturing? What existing computer-based methods can be used?

11.4   What are the advantages of forming and using cross- functional teams? What are possible problems in their operation?

11.5   What are the differences between a project and a team?

11.6   What are the important guidelines for the selection of team members for going from R&D development to production?

11.7   How should management fully support team effort?

11.8   Name three ingredients for a successful team and how they would be implemented.

11.9   How can the location of functional departments and team members make concurrent engineering more effective?

11.10   Explain the role of design for manufacture (DFM) in transitions and how DFM can be implemented.

11.11   What is the difference between producibility and productivity and how are they related?

11.12   Name two problems in the transfer of R&D to production and how they can be solved.

References

Associated Press. November 7, 1980, *New York Times*.

Deming, E. W. 1982. *Quality, Productivity and Competitive Position*: Cambridge, Mass.: MIT Press.

Juran, J. M. 1988. *Juran's Quality Control Handbook*, pp.8.1-8.24. New York: McGraw-Hill.

Kalpakjian, Serope. 1989. *Manufacturing Engineering and Technology*. New York: Addison-Wesley.

Mechanical Engineering. 1989, October. p. 66.

Peters, T. J., and Waterman, R. H. Jr. 1982. *In Search of Excellence*. New York: Harper & Row

Scholtes, P. R. 1988. *The Team Handbook*. Joiner Associates.

Suzaki, K. 1987. *The New Manufacturing Challenge. Techniques for Continuous Improvement*. New York: Free Press.

12

Management Techniques for Improving Manufacturing Operations

12.1 SIMULTANEOUS ENGINEERING

Introduction

Simultaneous engineering (SE) can be defined as concurrently designing a product and designing a process to manufacture that product (Allen 1989). Concurrent engineering, as it is also called, is not a physical process or a set procedure; it is a way of conducting engineering operations so that all functional considerations from design to manufacturing are taken into account and solutions to potential problems are developed as early as possible. It does not require a large investment or massive new equipment.

In the past when basic product changes took place every ten years or more, manufacturing processes for a particular product were well understood so that there was ample time for process changes. For example, the manual typewriter was eventually offered in portable models, with a few improvements, until the electric typewriter came along. Even the change to the then revolutionary IBM letter "ball" did not even come close to the rate of personal computer development. The speed of development of lap-top computers, which are inherently much more complex than a portable typewriter, is typical of the present situation in which product design is based on the capability to manufacture, in this case, Intel 3865X computer chips.

When the supplier of standard parts was either in-house or not too far removed and engineers knew and trusted one another, critical engineering and manufacturing were carried out by relatively simple verbal and written methods. The current diversity and the differences of location and allegiance of specialists required for design and production make simultaneous engineering necessary for profitable production.

Current Status

The ever-increasing abundance of new and improved manufacturing processes, components, and materials presents challenges to even the most proficient manufacturing engineering specialists. Added to these complexities is the relatively quick turnover of qualified personnel in many U.S. companies—three to five years is an average period of employment. As a result, better methods of communicating technical and other data have been necessary to ensure the exchange of important information. The computerization of design operations through CAD/CAM has greatly accelerated such efforts and has also permitted the rapid transmission of results to remote parts of the world when necessary. More important, the ability to predict rapidly the probable outcome of market demands and production capabilities with computers has inherently increased the capability to perform "up-front" engineering. A vital part of up-front engineering activity is the early identification of possible manufacturing problems and the development of solutions. This factor can decrease or even eliminate the amount of reengineering and reworking required and result in fewer delays and less cost in making items producible.

Simultaneous engineering requires teams of key representatives from every function in a project. Such multifunctional teams start from the customers' needs and proceed from engineering through production in a cooperative effort that can ensure continuous communication and attention to important details through every step of the transfer process, resulting in a high probability of success (Curtindale 1989).

How to Implement Simultaneous Engineering

According to R. W. Garrett (1990), senior systems engineer for Litton Industrial Automation, a clear-cut documented plan must be developed for launching the program and providing ongoing support. The plan, like all plans, must state objectives and how they are to be accomplished; it should call out the key players and identify the resources to be used. Garrett recommends eight ways for a manufacturing-oriented business to achieve SE goals:[1]

1. Involve manufacturing with design, marketing, and the customer from the beginning of the design cycle.
2. Utilize employee participation to the maximum extent possible. SE teams can be formed to hold meetings with involved departments.
3. Emphasize cost awareness by using both shop and office workers in the cost-reduction program. Pareto analysis, pie charts, and bar graphs can be used to illustrate key issues.
4. Arrange workers for optimum communication. Face-to-face communication is preferred to phone communication. SE groups working on the same project should be in the same location.
5. Recruit engineering specialists so that each essential function, such as design, manufacturing, human resources, management, and marketing, is represented in the SE teams.
6. Offer training when necessary in SE and other areas pertaining to problem solving, value analysis, Taguchi methods, and the like.
7. Utilize CAD to the maximum extent possible within the financial constraints imposed; CAD solid modeling is particularly useful in the design phase.
8. Apply analytical tools including statistical methods, Taguchi methods, and the development of a data base of critical design and manufacturing factors.

Integration with Outside Suppliers
If outside suppliers are extensively used, the concept of SE dictates that they should also be part of the SE teams. It is not unusual for complex products to be assembled predominantly from suppliers' parts. Traditionally manufacturers prepare detailed designs with specifications, which are then sent to competitive suppliers to bid on. Suppliers and subcontractors were not usually given an opportunity to submit their own ideas about products they supplied or work they were to perform and were hesistant to propose their own versions. In the cooperative process of simultaneous engineering, however, suppliers are frequently given functional specifications from which they can develop their own design; in this way, the prime contractor is assured of receiving that which fits into the total requirement. The concurrent engineering approach can, in fact, be successfully applied by cooperative efforts of the company with its suppliers and also its system

---

[1]The eight ways presented here are a condensation of the more detailed steps given by R. W. Garrett in his article "Eight Steps to Simultaneous Engineering," *Manufacturing Engineering*, November 1990. Used with permission.

integrators. As stated by Frank J. Riley (1990), president of the Society of Mechanical Engineers, "The challenge is for senior management of global manufacturing organizations to forge genuine partnerships with their machine tool, production equipment, and systems integrator partners."

This approach of up-front cooperation between the supplier and customer frequently requires different contractual arrangements than have hitherto been used. The past practice of remaining aloof during the bidding phase may have to be altered by making prior selections of team members (suppliers) based on criteria other than price alone. For example, one of the earlier experiments in SE in the Pontiac Division of GM proved that the selection of suppliers based on their quality record and their ability to integrate their equipment into the system was ultimately more cost-effective, even if the initial acquisition cost was higher for the same item.

Achieving Needed Changes

To achieve the desired results of SE, companies and individuals must change the way they do things. It is a fact of life that most people, including engineers, are reluctant to change. A change requires learning new ways and a greater expenditure of energy and often more time and resources. Management must be realistically aware at the outset of simultaneous engineering efforts that extra human and physical resources will be required to reach desired goals. Total commitment must be demonstrated not only by words but also by meaningful actions, including personal participation whenever appropriate in evaluations and reviews.

All involved in the SE effort must clearly understand its goals and be motivated to achieve them from their own perspectives of personal gain. This means that they must become part of the change effort. It is management's responsibility to instil the proper motivation including job assurance. It must be made abundantly clear to all the participants that they are working on some mutual goals, such as greater profitability, survival of their organization, or personal growth.

As mentioned in Section 11-3, it is essential for team participants to be mutually compatible and preferably at the same organizational level. This selection is particularly critical at the start of concurrent engineering efforts within an organization since first impressions of SE are likely to become lasting ones and may easily influence subsequent efforts by engineers and managers in their use of SE.

Video Teleconferencing

When SE team members are located at far-removed facilities, video teleconferencing can be used. At Bendix/King, a division of Allied Signal Inc., in Olathe, Kansas, aviation engineers used video communication to work on an air collision avoidance system with the company's main aviation branch in Fort Lauderdale, Florida. As a result of its video network, Bendix/King designed and produced the system a year ahead of schedule and doubled its 30 percent share of this $1 billion aviation equipment market.

Examples of SE Success

There are many examples of the successful application of SE in various industries, but the most striking and most publicized have been those in the automobile industry. It has been claimed by some that the greater use of up-front engineering (SE) by foreign competition has given them a considerable edge over manufacturers in the United States. Japanese automakers normally take significantly less time (43 months) to introduce a new vehicle than U.S. and European automakers (about 5 years) (Dertouzas, M.L., R.K. Lester and R.M. Solow 1989). This decreased development-to-production time has been attributed in major part to SE. Consequently American car makers are now using up-front engineering to shorten the production process and quicken the introduction of a new automobile to the marketplace.

Although Ford's first attempt to apply concurrent engineering to the introduction of the Taurus and Sable models took five years, it was done with original parts and new equipment. The company is reaping the benefit from the SE team effort that resulted in the 1985 Taurus plant as seen by the fact that the Taurus/Sable line was still recommended in 1990 as well above average by *Consumer Reports*. Ford currently assigns project engineers to each model line along with other key team members, including vendors, who stay with the project from beginning to completion.

Equally notable successes have been reported by General Motors, Chrysler, and BMW. In the case of GM, SE was incorporated in a massive way with the opening of the Saturn facility in Tennessee (Szczesny 1990). There equipment operators have been involved in design and manufacturing process decisions that had traditionally been the strict prerogative of engineers and managers. In another example, "Honeywell developed a new thermostat in 12 months that previously would have taken four years. A change that not only reduced product development costs, but provided a competitive product much earlier" (Allen 1989).

12.2 MATERIALS REQUIREMENTS PLANNING (MRP-I)

Managing raw materials, tools and inventories to meet delivery schedules for products is referred to as materials requirement planning (MRP-I). Through MRP-I the exact quantity, need date, and order release date for each of the subassemblies, components, and materials required to manufacture the product can be calculated (Fogarty, Hoffman, and Stonebraker 1989). This generally computer-based system can control inventories of materials and supplies needed for various stages of production, including time-phased orders for purchasing. An extension and elaboration of MRP–I is manufacturing resource planning (MRP–II), which is designed to control all aspects of manufacturing planning.

These two systems, similar as acronyms, are actually quite different, as can be realized from their graphic visualization (Figure 12–1). MRP–I is only one phase of MRP–II. Since these computerized systems can be quite complex and difficult to implement, they are considered here in relation to each other by first describing the essence of MRP-I. Before MRP-I, most manufacturing organizations controlled components and subassemblies at specifically designated order points by

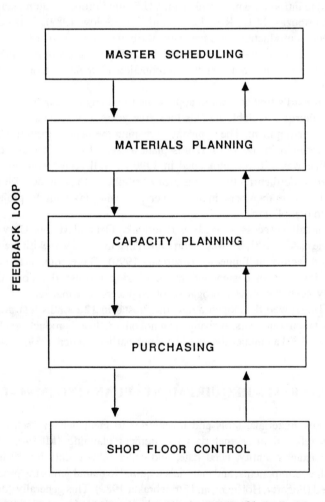

Figure 12-1.   Material Requirements Planning (MRPI) with Feedback Loop.

traditional methods. With the advent of affordable computerization, more complex interrelated systems have become possible.

Importance of a Master Production Schedule (MPS)

If a master production schedule (MPS) based on actual or anticipated customer demands and manufacturing capacity can be developed, a comparable MPS can also be developed as the basis of MRP-I (Figure 12-1). From the design and manufacturing engineering phases, the product breakdown must be transformed into a specific bill of materials (BOM) that then converts into requirements for MRP-I (Figure 12-2). It is necessary to have an accurate, ongoing account of the usable inventory from which MRP-I can generate the purchasing and production plans in time-sequenced requirements. The logic of this arrangement is not assailable in theory, but in practice, some data, such as customer requirements and

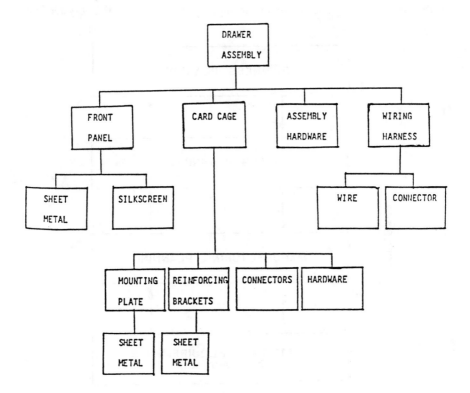

Figure 12-2.   Product Structure.
Source: C. S. Snead, *Group Technology* (New York: Van Nostrand Reinhold, 1989), p. 111.

schedules, may be difficult to obtain. As a result, marketing is often hesitant to make firm predictions.

Without a verifiable MPS, MRP-I may be based on unrealistic assumptions, which are subject to frequent and usually expensive changes. This customary state makes it essential for management to arrive at optimum MRPs based on the best available information of customer requirements and projected manufacturing capacity. In turn, effective materials requirements planning must be based on ongoing input from such diverse functions as marketing and quality. Lack of timely transmission of actual and anticipated quantity and schedule changes from marketing can be critical to economical MRP-I operation. Similarly, the failure of quality or production to transmit the actual availability of acceptable parts or assemblies can easily invalidate the best MRP efforts since MRP-I is a dependent system and no independent stock level of parts is usually maintained.

The control of materials, parts, and necessary purchases to supply production that meets customers requirements is the essence of a closed-loop system (Figure 12-3). In the past many companies attempting to implement an effective MRP-I system did

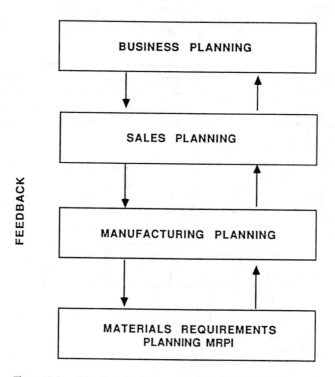

Figure 12-3.   Manufacturing Resource Planning (MRP-II) with Feedback Loop.

not succeed, even with the help of sophisticated computers and software. The reason for such failures, substantiated by our personal experiences, was usually the lack of compatible control systems with timely and accurate inputs for the computer. The more insidious reason for such open loops is that sometimes the personnel involved did not want the real truth to surface. For example, a high scrap and rework rate can be partially hidden by simply using more materials—thus the term hidden factory (Section 12-5). Lack of discipline in reporting changes or events can have a devasting effect on the validity of a complete MRP-I system. To restate an often-stated principle, "The validity of the computer output can only be as good as the accuracy of the required inputs," or more succinctly, "Garbage in, garbage out."

12.3   MANUFACTURING RESOURCES PLANNING (MRP–II)

Manufacturing resource planning (MRP–II) systems provide the information flow needed to manage a factory (Meridith 1987). They include not only the MRP-I information previously discussed but also information from other functions that interact with manufacturing, such as marketing, engineering, maintenance, and accounting. Figure 12-3 shows the relationship of MRP-II with MRP-I and closed-loop MRP, which is part of MRP-II. MRP-II, also called business resources planning (BRC), converts resource requirements such as facilities, personnel, and materials into financial requirements and production output into monetary value (Fogarty, Hoffman, and Stonebraker 1989). MRP-I uses a product breakdown structure such as that shown in Figure 12-2 to determine the quantity of components needed for each product item, and it calculates the number of components needed based on the total number of assemblies (systems) to be produced. The time to produce each of these components is utilized to determine the lead times required for establishing a start date for each assembly.

If properly used, MRP-II can be a very powerful tool in planning for all the resources needed to manufacture a product. The necessary personnel needed to support the desired production level provides the basis of projections for any needed overtime or new personnel. Conversely, a certain number of production adjustments may be required to maintain uniform personnel loading. Thus, in the use of MRP-II, the human resource or personnel function must also be involved to determine adjustments in hiring, transfers, or layoffs. Similarly, an astute marketing function can negotiate either early or delayed deliveries based on customers' needs.

Selection of Suitable Software
A variety of MRP-II software packages are available for all sizes of computers and types of operations. These packages offer MRP programs with a variety of formats

suitable for mainframes, and mini- and microcomputers and with consulting and training services, if desired. In deciding on and using a particular software package, the following should be considered:

1. Select software not for name recognition but for its applicability to your particular operation.
2. Get a list of previous users and discuss their experiences and level of satisfaction with the particular software.
3. Consider the probable overall cost of implementation rather than just software and hardware cost. Training and operational changes required by the software package can be expensive and can diminish the value of the MRP-II system.
4. Evaluate the MRP-II status as a system and consider the status of each element, including needed improvements. Implementation must eventually be total since partial implementation only can be very expensive.

Unfortunately, there have been more failures than successes in implementing MRP-II systems in the United States, mostly because of the lack of management commitment and application of necessary resources to carry it through.

Computerized Systems

In MRP-II systems electronic data processing may be real time, batch, or combinations of the two. For many applications, current up-to-date files of events as they occur in the factory are needed. Since inventory status in a moving production sequence may be critical, real-time processing is needed. This may require conveniently accessible input terminals in various locations in a factory including the shop floor. Input should be direct and immediate by operating personnel rather than delayed or through forms issued by supervisory or management information system (MIS) personnel. Too much may be lost, forgotten, transposed, or delayed in indirect transmission of data. If properly organized such data can yield other critical information, such as labor and material expended, as well as the percentage of completion.

In previous nonintegrated control systems, resources spent were frequently used to determine completion status based on previously established open-loop plans. Thus it was not unusual to "discover" that a project may have spent 80 percent of the funds but be only 40 percent complete. A good MRP system will prevent such surprises in time to institute corrective actions. However, most financial data used for monthly reports and weekly status checks are suitable for batch processing that does not require constantly updated information. Care should be taken in accepting even current cost figures, which are usually collected on a directly involved department basis as true total costs. Work is now being done on activity-based costing (ABC), that gives more realistic assessments of indirect costs such as computer systems.

During the 1980s there was a strong trend toward smaller and cheaper computers as minicomputers replaced mainframes for plant operations. Although inventory and production control systems require high-speed computers, MRP systems cannot always depend on mainframes because they are usually not cost-effective for small organizations. Since even large organizations may find their mainframe overloaded or even down for brief periods, minicomputers are now commonly used for offices and factory operations and are connected to the mainframe for up or down loading. This can be done on a "time-available" basis so that the mainframe enjoys optimum use while still ensuring no interruption in time-sensitive local operations, which can be controlled by independent but linked minicomputers.

12.4   CONTINUOUS PRODUCTION FLOW (KANBAN)

Continuous production flow, or Kanban, is a uniquely simple production control tool developed in Japan that should be considered in comparison to and in conjunction with MRP-I and MRP-II. *Kanban* in Japanese means "display" or "instruction card" (Suzaki 1987). Its principal concept is to authorize materials for production only if there is a need for them. Through the use of Kanban authorization cards, production is pulled through the system instead of pushed out before it is needed and then stored (Meridith 1987). Thus, the Kanban concept works very well with just-in-time (JIT) systems.

Taiichi Ohno, founder of the just-in-time production system at Toyota, wished to confirm the effectiveness of Kanban by studying the operation of American supermarkets during his first visit to the United States in 1956.[2] Ohno (1978) saw the downstream process, the customer, go to the upstream process, the supermarket, to obtain the required parts, the commodities, at the required amount and desired time. The upstream process replenishes the required goods for the next process, which was receipt by the customer, just as is commonly done in department stores to reorder and replenish merchandise. Although Ohno had already begun to introduce a supermarket type of operation at Toyota as early as 1953, his 1956 visit confirmed that the combination of continuous production flow and JIT was practical.

Supermarket operations in the United States have been significantly improved since then and much more widely applied in other material transfer fields. The bar

---

[2]This is an excellent example of the cross-fertilization of technology in which a technical development in one commercial field is modified and adapted to a different field with comparable operations, namely, material transfer and handling.

coding of almost all items with scanning and computerized transmittal and manipulation of significant data have made stock, financial, and sales control possible at speeds and efficiencies that were previously impossible (Figure 12-4a). Even the further upstream of stock at central supermarket chain warehouses is now controlled through a computerized, bar-coded stock card system on standard pallets (Figure 12-4b). Perhaps the most innovative application is at Ralphs, a Western

(a)   Bar-Coding for Printed Circuit Board (PC) Identification

and Control.

FEED THIS WAY

⚠ CAUTION ⚡
STATIC SENSITIVE

LAT-9-572

Example Label for
Special Controls

Example Bar Code
on PC Board

(b)   Bar-Coding for Identification and Control of Grocery Items.

401-0666290
RALPHS PINEAPPLE JUICE
401-073694   0001/0012   46 OZ
08 X 05   LARGE
UPC: 73694   02-13-91   10:07
DOOR: 001
PICK: 401-77162
UNITS=   40   CASES=   40

Figure 12-4.   Use of Bar Coding

food market chain, which now controls its entire distribution through a ten story warehouse (Figure 12-5) that handles stock with vehicles moving in three dimensions and transferring items in and out of 50,000 storage spaces. This system requires a fraction of the floorspace and cost that would have been previously needed. The accuracy and speed of this system by far exceeds conventional approaches (Figure 12-6). This complex operation is automated and computerized so that the movement of all pallets in and out of the facility is controlled by only three operators in a centralized control center (Figure 12-7).

The adoption and improvement of the Kanban type system in U.S. factories has not been widespread, but there are strong movements to use bar coding in the production control of many manufacturing systems. For example, it is already being used for printed circuit board identification as well as for many other components during manufacturing (Figures 12-4a and 12-4b). Although, bar coding using electronically scannable display labels has many advantages, the simplicity of visual display labels makes them more cost-effective for some operations. For example, in some simple operations it can be advantageous simply to use boxes with the right spaces for the right number of parts (Figure 12-8). Color coding of boxes, parts and wires can prove to be an effective way of handling and then assembling components, but all workers must be tested for color blindness if it has not already been done as part of a preemployment review.

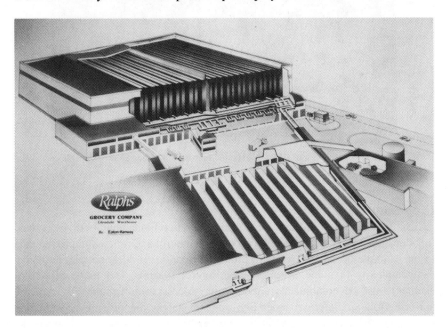

Figure 12-5.   Overview of Distribution Center Including 10-Story ASRS Warehouse.

Figure 12-6.   Interior of ASRS Warehouse Showing Automatic Storage Capability (50,000) Bin).

Implementation of Kanban

To implement the Kanban system effectively, two fundamental but dependent functions must be utilized, namely, production control and process improvement. In the example of the supermarket, production control is fairly simple, avoiding the complexity of some inventory and control systems. But to be effective, Kanban must be combined with constant process improvement. To achieve uniform flow in the final assembly, adjustments in the feeding process are frequently considered at the outset. For example, if a specialized upstream process has limited capacity, it may be expedient to produce to stock to avoid any

Figure 12-7.   Two-Person Control Center for ASRS 10-Story Bin Warehouse.

Manufacturing Area   **Assembly Area**

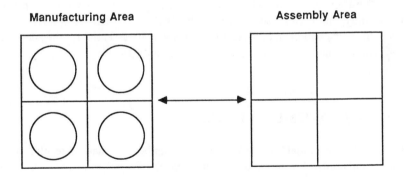

   ๏ **Case filled with parts at manufacturing area**

   ๏ **Case emptied of parts for use in assembly area**

   ๏ **Box is returned for refill**

   ๏ **Control is visual**

Figure 12-8.   Kanaban use.

line stoppages. However, inexpensive items like fasteners or washers cannot usually be bought or delivered in small lots. Again some extra stock may be desirable, but discretion must be used to control it. Glass jars or small bins can be used to control this type of inventory. An empty jar or bin can be used as a signal to reorder. Even a "withdrawal" card may be more economical than an on-line, real-time computer system. Preparation should also consist of determining a leveled production schedule with marketing and manufacturing, which may by necessity have some mixed production.

Basic rules that should be considered in applying a Kanban system are these:

1. Workers from the downstream process should obtain components from the upstream process.
2. The movement and processes should be in accordance with Kanban cards.
3. The production process is based on 100 percent quality of parts before they are introduced them into the Kamban containers.
4. The Kanban cards and the processes they control should be subject to constant improvement (Kaizen) to reduce any waste or rework.

In solving problems the systems approach (Section 2.5) or value analysis (Section 12.8) should be utilized to arrive at fundamentally sound solutions rather than superficial fixes. For example, repeated errors in a manufacturing process may require a basic change in the process rather than just more specific instructions. The Kanban system, when properly used, can reduce the work in process significantly, and it can also be used with MRP-I and MRP-II to arrive at JIT production. Innovation and constant improvement are essential for the successful application of these tools for improving operational efficiency.

12.5   JUST-IN-TIME METHODS

Because of the potential for cost savings and other benefits that can result from the timely availability of materials and manufacturing facilities, there has been a great deal of interest in just-in-time methods. The concept of just-in-time means that the exact number of required units is brought to each successive stage of production at the appropriate time. This is a variation from normal procedures, in which material and parts are stockpiled and units are sent to the next production stage, regardless of the quantity needed.

Since JIT can have a major impact on manufacturing planning and control as well as other manufacturing functions, it is necessary to consider it when developing and using MRP-I systems. Effective JIT systems can simplify transactions in both purchasing and shop floor operation, and can also improve efficiency, quality, worker attitudes, and vendor relations.

However, poorly conceived and fragmented JIT programs can create operational and financial havoc. For the lack of availability of such relatively inexpensive parts as bolts or washers purchased and delivered through the JIT philosophy, a whole production line could be stopped; for example, one minute of downtime in a medium-sized GM plant that produces about one car per minute can cost about $15,000. The superficial concept of receiving all materials just in time for the manufacturing process has to be reviewed in the context of the operational economies of the entire system, including nonrepetitive manufacturing environments and the degree of perfection that operation of the production line can reasonably achieve.

The global adoption of JIT has resulted in many interpretations of it, including several that focus on reducing waste in manufacturing. In the application of JIT it is important to subdivide waste into time, energy, materials, and mistakes. Then the goal of JIT is to pursue zero inventory and zero disturbances to the execution of schedules, day in and day out; this in turn sets conditions for striving for what is commonly called zero operational slack.

JIT Applications
The best known applications of JIT occur in organizations with high-volume repetitive manufacturing processes such as Toyota. Toyota developed a technique for continuous production with almost a zero inventory of parts. This was made possible by the timely delivery of all needed components of usable quality exactly in time to sustain continuous flow. Perfection in delivery schedules, quality, and assembly was required; otherwise expensive stoppage costs could result. An important feature of such an operation is the elimination of discreet batches in favor of continuous production rates, which result in the reduction of work-in-process inventories and in production schedules that maintain level capacity.

For effective JIT application, processes can be designed to permit mixed operations, with master production schedules, so that all common products can be made more or less at the same time instead of changing lines from one mode to another. In such an operation, JIT can be implemented through simple visual control systems, in which the workers can easily see and remember how to build products to schedule without extensive paperwork and other overhead support. These visual control systems can be relatively inexpensive, for example, color coding or delivering work in progress on discreet, clearly marked containers and simplifying assembly flow so that overages or shortages are immediately evident. Such procedures can be used by vendors to deliver high-quality products when needed and must be made part of manufacturing plans and controls.

Attainment of JIT Objectives

The objectives of JIT can be achieved only through physical changes in the relevant systems. Typically, setup time is reduced as well as lot sizes. This system is consistent with making a large number of models with smaller inventory levels and utilizing the input of personnel directly involved with these processes on a daily basis. Meaningful involvement of personnel must occur from the bottom up as well as from the top down. Job security may be a less obvious but significant factor in the success of JIT programs, but who would realistically expect workers to pursue enthusiastically improvements that they may perceive to be endangering their jobs? Would one expect executives knowingly to make career-limiting decisions? These questions must be continually answered by management through effective motivational programs for all participants; otherwise, JIT can be a potentially very profitable concept that actually fails in practice.

Another critical aspect of JIT is the pursuit of improved quality through process improvement no matter where the part is made. Thus all vendors and subcontractors must have the required capability for supplying components of acceptable quality and in the required quantity precisely when needed. To this end most companies using JIT have engaged in quality awareness programs and statistical process controls (SPC). Since quality problems can result in line stoppages that are usually masked by undesired buffer inventories, the lowering of inventory levels will tend to reveal problems that previously had not been fully recognized or resolved (Figure 12-9).

Transfer Processes

The formalization of the concept of fixing problems as opposed to simply passing them downstream is accredited to Kaoru Ishikawa over 30 years ago. At that time he coined the now-famous phrase "The next process is the customer" (Imai 1986), which was later formalized and referred to as the Kanban system (Figure 12-10). This challenge has required management and workers to acknowledge manufacturing, operational, delivery and product performance problems and to do everything within their power to resolve them. Today this concept has also been applied to other transfer processes; for example, the design engineer's customers are the manufacturing personnel, and they must address such questions as this: Is the design too difficult to produce? This concept of constantly solving in-process problems is the key to effective quality assurance as opposed to inspecting shoddy products and then trying to improve them.

Without quality materials and an efficient plant layout, which are fundamental to the Kanban process, lowering inventory levels could become a devastating and expensive experience. Accordingly many firms that utilize JIT group their machines into cells that manufacture a family of parts (Section 12.6). The layout of the equipment is designed to minimize both travel distances and inventories

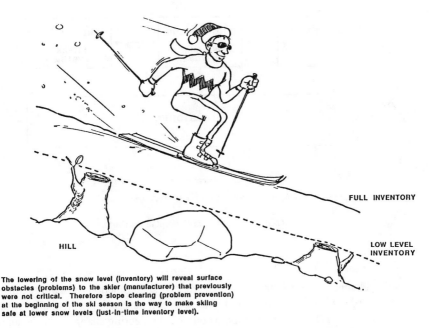

The lowering of the snow level (inventory) will reveal surface obstacles (problems) to the skier (manufacturer) that previously were not critical. Therefore slope clearing (problem prevention) at the beginning of the ski season is the way to make skiing safe at lower snow levels (just-in-time inventory level).

Figure 12-9.   Effect of Lowered Inventory.

between machines; workers are cross-trained so that they can operate several machines. The capacity can also be made flexible in cellular manufacturing so that surges and mix changes can be readily accommodated.

An important aspect of successfully applying JIT is significant worker participation, which can include suggestions and comments to improve the manufacturing process. Such participation could be stimulated by a company culture that makes workers feel that they are an integral and respected part of the organization rather than "hired hands." In the words of a union official at the GM/Toyota plant in Freemont, California, "This is the way work ought to be. With JIT this plant employs our hearts and minds, not just our backs" (Curtindale 1989).

The Hidden Factory

A manufacturing firm can be viewed as the factory that makes products, while the hidden factory processes papers, traces transactions with and without computers, repairs and chases defective parts, and expedites unforeseen delays caused by poor quality and lack of customer focus. These corrective support actions, along with subsequent solution of unresolved problems (usually at higher cost), have almost become an accepted part of conventional manufacturing management.

Any changes in the manufacturing process, usually triggered by needed engi-

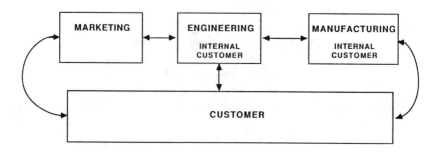

* Engineering is the internal customer of marketing for customer requirements.
* Manufacturing is the internal customer for engineering.

Figure 12-10.   The Modern Concept of the Customer.

neering changes, may require additional work by such functions as manufacturing engineering, line management, production control, purchasing, and quality assurance. By using JIT and studying the pattern of engineering changes, the Japanese manage their changes so that they can accomplish planned block improvements on a quarterly and annual basis to the greatest extent possible. The U.S. plants operated by conventional push management concepts respond to unanticipated problems as they occur on a daily basis. It is not surprising, then, that hidden factory activity accounts for about 30 percent of the total manufacturing costs for many U.S. companies.

The fact that Japanese labor costs have generally exceeded those in the United States speaks against the argument of proponents of conventional, crisis-oriented management that lower Japanese labor costs have provided the competitive edge. Another rationalization has been that the greater dedication of Japanese workers vis-à-vis their U.S. counterparts has been the main cause of higher U.S. costs. This allegation has been disproved by the fact that a few Japanese-owned companies manufacturing in the United States with American workers are operating at about the same or even lower costs than in Japan. More integrated JIT-oriented systems are resulting in a significant return of investment on the initial improvement costs. The stabilization of manufacturing processes must be the focus for continuous improvements before attempting to automate. Efforts to automate before implementing simple JIT concepts, such as quality assurance through process control; timely problem solving; lowered inventories; and well-conceived simple, process-oriented layouts, are comparable to building expensive houses on quicksand. The JIT system is clearly a key to eliminating the costs of the hidden factory.

The Impact of JIT on Manufacturing Planning and Control

The implementation of JIT can eliminate a significant number of the traditionally required manufacturing and control systems as demonstrated by the continuous production flow system (Section 12.4). This in itself can constitute a considerable savings in manufacturing operations, particularly if one considers the cost of personnel for control and expediting, along with the more difficult to quantify expenses of disrupted parallel operations. By reducing lead times and improving vendor scheduling and delivery performance, JIT can be greatly enhanced by the purchasing function.

An important advantage of JIT centers on the prospect that orders will move through the factory so rapidly that it will not be necessary to track their status through complex, conventional shop and inventory control systems. Extensive work-in-process inventories and stockrooms can be eliminated with substantial shop floor savings. Simple systems can be routinely used by shop personnel without detailed records or extensive overhead staff support. For example, colored storage boxes with specific spaces for a certain number of parts needed for assembly provide a means for storage, moving, and requisitioning.

In summary, JIT concepts require several multiple-integrated action programs. These range from improved plant layout to reduced setup times and lot sizes based on high quality and significant worker involvement, with a constant focus on continuous improvement. There has been more than sufficient evidence to show that firms utilizing JIT achieve significant improvements relative to organizations that do not.

12.6   GROUP TECHNOLOGY (GT)

Benefits of Group Technology

The challenges of international competition combined with fast-changing markets for new products demand greater flexibility in rapidly and profitably producing in smaller lots. In the past custom manufacturing or special models permitted higher costs to simply to be passed to the consumer. Now, the possibility of making changes while still maintaining competitive price structures makes the application of group technology (GT) highly desirable. By simply grouping similar parts of various products into families that require similar manufacturing functions, simple design changes are facilitated and common tooling and processing functions can be used (Figure 12-11).

El Wakil (1989) defines GT as "a manufacturing philosophy that involves grouping of components having similar attributes to take advantage of their similarities in the design and/or manufacturing phases of the production cycle." Although computers are not required to implement this technology, they greatly

Group technology in shaft production

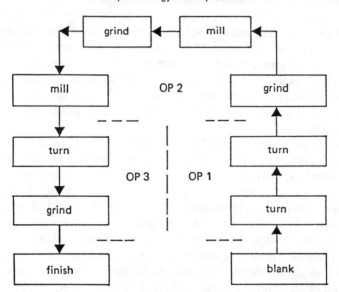

In this cell several dissimilar machines are grouped together to produce shafts. The machines are dedicated as in an assembly line so that operations on different machines are conducted in quick succession and so the lead time to produce a completed shaft is measured in hours rather than weeks. The movement of work from one machine to the next is facilitated by the proximity of the machines. There are three operators in the above cell and their areas of responsibility are indicated.

Figure 12-11.   A Group Technology Cell.   Source: Anthony Dear, *Working Towards Just-In-Time* (New York: Van Nostrand Reinhold, 1988), p. 39.

enhance the effectiveness of the process, particularly as the product groups become more complex. Additional benefits of using GT include standardization of designs such as materials and transfers and the development and use of flexible tools and holding devices. According to Gunn (1982),

> In many companies only 20% of the parts initially thought to require new designs actually need them; of the remaining new parts 40% could be built from an existing design and the other 40% could be created by modifying an existing design.

The memory and rapid recall of computers can also be utilized to check quickly through available old tooling, jigs, and fixtures, which can frequently be used as is or with minor modifications. In fact, astute contract and forging houses have long understood this concept by retaining old dies and utilizing them for later customers, who are still billed a tool and setup charge. Most major automotive and electronic manufacturers learned this lesson a long time ago and have been profitably practicing it for many years. General Motors, Ford, and Chrysler have utilized common or extremely similar parts for several of their lines such as Chevrolet, Buick, Pontiac, Oldsmobile, and Cadillac. The use of common parts in the chassis of upgraded models of television or computers is widespread and economical since the upgrade can be performed by simply adding extra modules to a standard chassis.

If complete standardization is not feasible for technical or visual reasons, similarity in handling and processing can be optimized by rearranging the plant from a purely functional job shop layout to a group layout for part families (Figure 12-12). The reduction of inventory lead times can be well in excess of 50 percent if the layout of the plant is changed, and with modern equipment such as flexible machining systems (FMS) and robotic manufacturing cells, improvements approaching 90 percent are feasible (Meridith 1987). With so much to gain, the question can be asked, "Why are not more organizations implementing GT?" The saving of valuable production flow time is graphically illustrated in Figure 12-13.

Problems with Group Technology
Fundamental problems in implementing GT are these:

1. Major commitment of resources for new more automated equipment
2. Relocation and potential redesign of existing equipment and facilities and personnel
3. Changes required in the duties of the key participants from engineering, manufacturing, and management

Group technology, similar to simultaneous engineering (which could include GT as an inherent factor), is a highly leveraged up-front effort. Even though $1 spent in the beginning may save $70 at the end, it may not seem that attractive when a $100,000 initial commitment may be required up front, without any guarantee of return at the end of the transformation. The only guarantees in making a changeover to a GT setup are carefully prepared plans and unwavering commitment by the participants.

12.7   TAGUCHI METHODS

The contributions of Taguchi to improved quality and decreased development time and cost have had a major impact on product manufacturing. In the context of statistical process controls and management techniques, introduced by Deming (1982) and Juran (1988) in post-World War II Japan, Taguchi techniques have

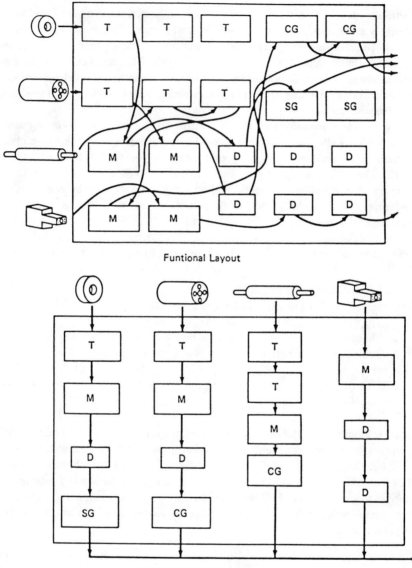

Funtional Layout

Process Flow or Cell Layout

Figure 12-12.   Functional Versus Process Flow Layout.
Source: C. S. Snead, *Group Technology* (New York: Van Nostrand Reinhold, 1989), p. 10.

Time In The Shop

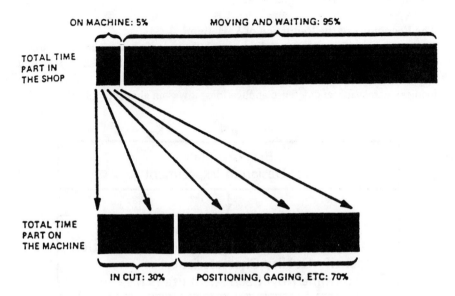

Figure 12-13.   Factory Que Time Versus Fabrication Time.
Source: C. S. Snead, *Group Technology* (New York: Van Nostrand Reinhold, 1989), p. 11.

proven to be powerful additions. Obradovitch and Stephanou (1990) describe Taguchi methods as

> ...techniques for optimizing and integrating product design and manufacturing processes on the basis of a combination of engineering and statistical methods. The Quality Loss Function is a by product of Taguchi's efforts in this area. It is a mathematical theory that relates loss to customer and society based on product variation from target value. Loss is viewed in very broad terms including both tangible (performance) as well as intangible considerations (dissatisfaction). Taguchi's Parameter Design is an optimization procedure to determine product design or process levels such as to minimize sensitivity of output to input variations.

Taguchi methods achieve high quality at a low cost by combining engineering and statistical methods to optimize product design and manufacturing processes. The loss of quality is usually defined in financial terms (Kalpakjian 1989). This quality loss is considered not only in internal terms, like costs for extra rework, servicing and repairs, but also in external consequences, like customer dissatisfaction and consequent loss of market share. Thus the loss of quality is viewed as a financial loss to society that should be lowered by utilizing cost-effective means. Brainstorming is used as an integral part of the Taguchi philosophy in a manner similar to value analysis (Figure 12-14).

The Economics of the Reduction of Variation

The economics of improving quality through the reduction of variations in toler-ances and processes were, from traditional perspectives, simply those of increased costs, for which, it was hoped, the customer was willing to pay. Particularly in medical, aerospace, and defense applications, it was an almost predictable reality

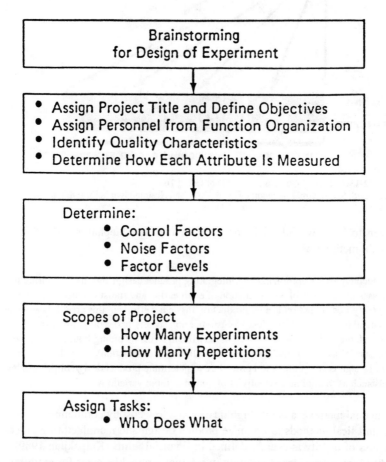

Figure 12-14.   Brainstorming—an Integral Part of the Taguchi Philosophy.
Source: Ranjit K. Roy, *A primer on the Taguchi Method* (New York: Van Nostrand Reinhold, 1990), p. 177.

for many years that the customer would be willing to pay a premium for a high probability (99 percent plus) of success. Thus the concepts of improving quality that Deming and Juran tried for many years to introduce to post-World War II U.S. industry were not readily accepted as ways to increase profitability. Crosby (1979) put it into more simple terms by coining the phrase "quality is free." Taguchi uses a different cost model for product characteristics than is typically applied, one that places more emphasis on reducing variation.

In fact Taguchi also addresses the loss of function of product within the specification limits (Ross 1988) and the fact that traditional "go or no go" philosophy of inspection does not necessarily represent the true economics of the system. Considering the acceptance of a simple shaft, the accept or reject concept is quite clear (Figure 12-15). A shaft that falls below or above the acceptable limits may be reworked by plating or further machining or grinding. Yet as long as it actually was, or was statistically assumed to be, within the acceptable limits, it was good enough.

This "goalpost" philosophy would be valid if the results of the product system were simply measured in terms of goal points. The experience of Ford and Mazda in manufacturing transmissions illustrate the case for the loss of quality function even within acceptable tolerances. Ford contracted with Mazda to make some of their front-wheel-drive transmissions in Japan, and the balance were to be produced in their Batavia, Ohio, plant. Both sites were making transmissions to the same blueprints and specifications for American cars. Yet based on warranty records, Mazda's version showed significantly fewer claims than the U.S.-made transmissions. Upon closer examination of Mazda's methods (Ford is reported to own about 30 percent of Mazda) it was found that Mazda made most of its parts much closer to the target value. By using much less of the allowable tolerance range, parts were made more alike (Figure 12-16).

In the example of the shaft, it is easy to recognize that random, even allowable, variations of mating parts may ultimately cause more wear through fits that are looser or tighter than the optimum design. Mazda was using slightly more expensive and complex grinders to finish the parts. Using the traditional approach, that improved quality costs more, we are not considering the loss of function costs of more warranty work. Thus, without even trying to quantify increased customer satisfaction, the cost of the higher-quality Mazda transmission was less. By using this information, the U.S. Ford plant was able to improve its quality significantly and surpass Mazda's in 1987.

There is, however, a limit to striving for perfect quality (Figure 12-17). Although the quest for target value may be advantageous for the consumer, for the producer expenses for the last bit of perfection can rise dramatically. Thus, an optimum value must be found that will be a compromise between what the consumer really wants and what the manufacturer can economically produce. This value must still be balanced against the true loss of quality function. In some

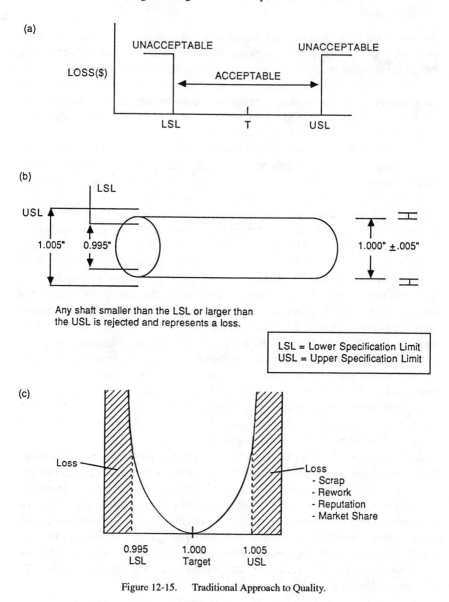

(a)

LOSS($)

UNACCEPTABLE   UNACCEPTABLE

ACCEPTABLE

LSL   T   USL

(b)

LSL

USL

1.005"   0.995"

1.000" ±.005"

Any shaft smaller than the LSL or larger than
the USL is rejected and represents a loss.

LSL = Lower Specification Limit
USL = Upper Specification Limit

(c)

Loss

Loss
- Scrap
- Rework
- Reputation
- Market Share

0.995   1.000   1.005
LSL   Target   USL

Figure 12-15.   Traditional Approach to Quality.

Average value off target.
Too much variation around average value.

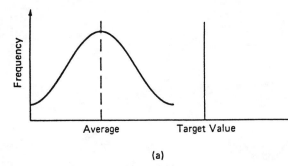

(a)

Average value on target.
Too much variation around target value.

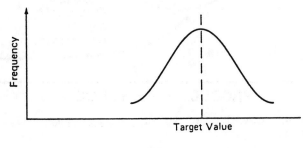

(b)

Average value on target.
Little variation around target value.

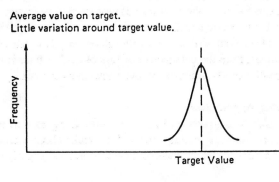

(c)

Figure 12-16.   Typical Quality Distributions   Source: Ranjit   K.
Roy, *A primer on the Taguchi Method* (New York: Van Nostrand Reinhold, 1990), p. 21.

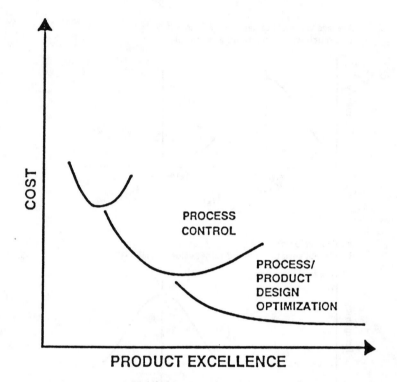

Figure 12-17.   Cost Reductions from New Quality Assurance Methods.   Source: USAF/LE-RD.

extremely critical applications such as medicine or space we may intentionally shift the improvements further in the customer's favor, despite increased costs. The significant issue is that there are usually important economic considerations to the achievement of quality, even within allowable tolerances. Through continuous reductions of variances, from the perspective of loss of quality functions, significant increases of quality can be achieved at lower total system costs.

Quality Engineering Approaches
Although Taguchi addresses quality on-line, in manufacturing, as well as off-line, in engineering, we are focusing mainly on the front end.[3] Conventional on-line quality control techniques are better understood but do not have nearly the poten-

---

[3] Off-line quality control and improvement are carried out during the product and process development stages, whereas on-line quality control occurs when manufacturing processes are monitored for desired levels of quality.

tial cost and benefit impact of improvements early in the product life cycle. To implement these early changes the Taguchi method generally requires the interaction of cross-functional teams, leading to quantifications between design requirements and manufacturing processes (Figure 12–18).

The *analysis of variance (ANOVA)*, particularly of existing processes and products, is also required to provide direction for potential improvements and new experimental designs. This statistical method was developed by Sir Ronald Fischer in the 1930s as a way to interpret results from agricultural experiments. It can also be utilized in orthogonal arrays.

Orthogonal arrays are ways of searching for advantageous methods of resolving two generally divergent goals in the development process:

1. To optimize the performance characteristics
2. To find the least expensive alternative design or material that will accomplish the same results

When searching for improved or new designs the traditional approach was to run some tests that could be used as a basis for change, usually by changing one

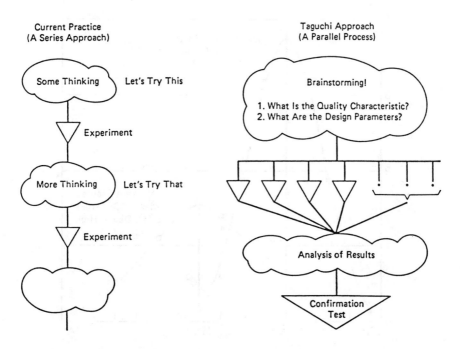

Figure 12-18.   Comparison of Current Practice and the Taguchi Approach.   Source: Ranjit   K. Roy, *A primer on the Taguchi Method* (New York: Van Nostrand Reinhold, 1990), p. 30.

variable at a time and keeping the others constant. This can be an extremely expensive and time-consuming process, arriving at haphazard test points with best guesses. Taguchi developed a family of matrices in which factors and the level of factors may be considered and chosen to minimize the costly effect of interactions in a design (Figure 12-19). Thus the number of tests needed to produce a robust design is reduced significantly since only the main effects are examined. Undesirable interaction effects are revealed by the extent to which the predicted performance matches verification testing. The important contribution that Taguchi made to the earlier statistical design of experiments is also to include parameters and tolerances in the design of experiments. The parameters are separated into those factors that can be controlled (control factors) and those that constitute uncontrolled variables (noise factors).

Although this process is mathematically complex, it still involves statistical approximations, which allow rapid identification of controlling variables and the determination of the best approaches to control the processes. Some of these variables can be controlled, once they are identified, frequently without the need of costly new equipment and tooling. For example, in machining, changes in

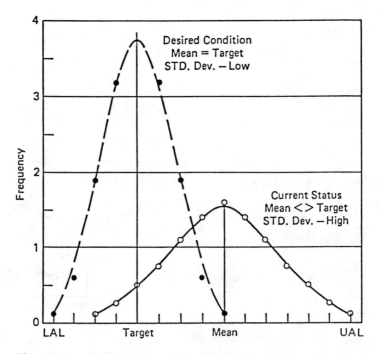

Figure 12-19.   Quality measure.   Source: Ranjit K. Roy, *A primer on the Taguchi Method* (New York: Van Nostrand Reinhold, 1990), p. 30.

cutting speeds, feed rates, tools, and coolants can have a significant impact on resultant variations in tolerances and finishes, without major changes in machines or equipment. However, the experimental design may reveal that noise factors common to the environment in which the product is used are not changeable but significant. Thus the choice of a different material that is more resistant to temperatures and corrosion may be advisable.

Even a high initial cost could be cost-effective in view of the loss of quality function of the product system. Through experimental models it may be shown that a more robust design can be created, one that is not as sensitive to temperature and moisture changes. The gradual substitutions of higher-strength steels, which are dipped in corrosion-resistant paint, constitute attempts to create more robust designs for automobiles. The current substitution of composites into structural and body components of automobiles are further examples of robust designs, which have higher initial costs but are intended to create greater consumer value and satisfaction. Based on the Taguchi approach, the customary tightening of toler-ances is suggested only after the adjustment of controllable factors has been accomplished. Subsequently the tightening of tolerances in critical areas may be cost-effective. The application of the Taguchi methods should be considered in engineering for quality, particularly in the design, testing, and improvement of processes and products.

12.8 VALUE ENGINEERING

Origin
Value engineering (VE) or value analysis (VA), was started by the General Electric Company in 1947, when some strategic materials and components were difficult to obtain. Larry Miles, then a GE purchasing agent, developed the concept of examining the basic functions of materials and components rather than simply accepting requirements at face value. General Electric continued these efforts to reduce the cost of its appliances and other consumer products. Company engineers were directed to examine the components and functioning of the various product lines and determine whether these same functions could be performed with less expensive components and manufacturing processes. The company found that it could, in fact, significantly improve the functioning and quality of its products at lower costs. The positive results of its concerted efforts were rewarding to both GE and its customers.

Paralleling the effort of GE and the civilian sector in initiating and applying VE, the Department of Defense included VE as a necessary part of its contractual arrangements. This was an effort to decrease and contain the spiraling costs of government procurements and provide incentives for better cost performance.

Definitions and Quantifying Functions

Value engineering is the systematic analysis of the functioning and physical makeup of a product to provide at least as good a product (or even better) at a decreased cost. *Value* is the worth or utility of the items or function. *Functions* refers to the purpose or operation of the item. It is the basis of VE and requires a systems approach to consider all possible ways of performing the function and ultimately determining which way is most cost-effective.

In many processes, functions can be quantified by multiplying their value by their cost:

$$\text{Function} = (\text{value})(\text{cost})$$

$$\text{Value} = \frac{\text{function}}{\text{cost}} \quad \text{or cost} = \frac{\text{function}}{\text{value}}$$

If we compare the cost of a trip by airplane and by automobile between Los Angeles and New York, taking into account the cost of meals, lodging, and time, it is evident why air travel is a better value today for longer distances than automobile or train travel.

for 3,000 air miles $\text{Cost} = \dfrac{3{,}000 \text{ air miles}}{7 \text{ miles}} (\text{less}) = \$430[4]$

for 300 car miles   Cost = \$1,000 (this includes gas, oil, meals, lodging, depreciation, and extra time)

The same concept can be used in other determinations of value in which output or performance is compared to cost. In the past, some practitioners have broken down value into various categories of worth such as use value, cost value, esteem value and exchange value. In this definition, value is the ratio between the worth of an item in dollars and the actual cost of the item. Defining value in this way, however makes it difficult to determine worth since value, like beauty, is in the eyes of the beholder.

Cost and Pareto's Principle

Because cost is the key consideration in VE, the various elements making up the cost of the item must be identified—labor, materials, special equipment, and so on. Value engineering tries to eliminate or mitigate those elements that are excessive

---

[4]This is a "ball-park" figure; it varies with the time of the year, rate wars, price of fuel, and so on, as does the cost of gasoline for autos.

TABLE 12-1.   Pareto Analysis—"Broke" Losses in a Paper Mill
Source: J.M. Juran and F.M. Gryna, 1980, *Quality Planning & Analysis* (New York: McGraw-Hill), p. 21.
Reproduced with permission of McGraw-Hill, Inc.

Product type	Annual "broke" loss, $000	Cumulative "broke" loss, $000	Percent of broke loss	Cumulative percent of broke loss
A	132	132	24	24
B	96	228	17	41
C	72	300	13	54
D	68	368	12	66
E	47	415	8	74
F	33	448	6	80
47 other types	108	556	20	100
Total 53 types	556		100	

or unnecessary and improve the value of the product by decreasing the cost—all this without decreasing performance and reliability.

Pareto's principle can be advantageously used to determine the major cost elements involved in the development of a new product or manufacturing process. As applied to manufacturing, Pareto's principle states that a few contributors are responsible for most of the cost. Typically, 10 to 30 percent of the items may account for 70 to 90 percent of the cost or problems, so the question arises, "Why waste resources working on improvements whose benefits may, at best, not exceed the cost of their analysis?"

Mathematical estimates, considering the probability and cost of pertinent factors, can be utilized (Table 12-1). Such attempts to quantify potential gains, at worst, force consideration of diverse aspects of problems that otherwise might be ignored. An all too common example is the prevailing practice to teach time-and-motion studies to industrial engineers as a primary cost-savings tool with subsequent reinforcement by management's focus on cutting direct labor costs. Yet with ever-increasing automation, direct labor costs have shrunk to less than 10 percent in many companies that use computer-integrated manufacturing (CIM). This is a significantly different situation than when direct labor costs were often a major cost factor. Still, many organizations fail to analyze critically the productivity of their big-ticket expenses like management, engineering and other ever-increasing indirect costs. Activity based costing (ABC) will give more realistic readings of the actual costs of functions and products than customary direct and indirect classifications.

How to Carry Out VE
In carrying out VE it is essential to follow a definite job plan. This plan has been enumerated in different ways by different authors and proponents of VE, but

basically the scientific problem-solving approach is utilized with the following sequential phases:

1. Project selection/definition
2. Information gathering
3. Functional analysis
4. Creating alternatives
5. Evaluation and selection
6. Proposal and presentation
7. Implementation

During the implementation of this procedure there may be a need to return to some previously completed phase such as phase 2, the information phase; that is, more information is needed, or there may be need for further analysis, phase 3. A reasonable amount of iteration should be allowed for and expected since it can improve the final outcome.

In the *project selection* phase the specific project and scope for the VE study must be determined. If there is a fixed level of resources for VE projects, the selection of projects should attempt to optimize the use of available funds. Candidate projects can be ranked according to their potential for savings, ease of implementation, length of time required for modifications or changes and probability of success. Some or all of these factors may be of critical importance, depending on the particular product or process to be improved.

In the *information-gathering* phase, all available information concerning the item being studied should be assembled and organized. The specific information required will depend on the item and its function and can include customer requirements, blueprints, product performance, test data, material costs, reliability data, and manufacturing process data, etc.

The *analysis* phase involves the determination of the specific functions of the item being studied. The word *function*, the cornerstone of VE, is directly linked to the desired performance by the customer. L. Miles (1972) recognized this fundamental fact while developing VE, as did Deming and Juran when they set forth the customers' requirements as the basic tenet of total quality management (TQM). Contrary to some opinions VE and TQM are *not* mutually exclusive but complimentary as discussed in Chapter 13.

In VE, much effort is initially spent on keeping the definition of the function as simple as possible by utilizing only an active verb and a measurable noun, for example,

Automobile	Move people
Lawn mower	Cut grass
Satellite	Transmit information

It is evident that "cutting grass" may not adequately describe all the characteristics and functions of a lawn mower, and one or more of these functions may be classed as primary and the others as secondary (Fallon 1980). To generate torque may be a secondary function for a power mower, and to collect cuttings may be evaluated as an even lower-degree function (Figure 12-20). In the practice of VE all functions can be evaluated in terms of their importance and cost. Customers for many products may place a value on esteem, as evidenced by the purchasers of expensive cars like Cadillacs, whose functions could be duplicated by less expensive models, such as Oldsmobiles or Buicks, and whose subsystems have a surprising number of the same components. Thus primary, secondary, and lower-degree functions may have to be defined as well as different types of value.

The *creative* phase involves the generation of ideas, usually in free-wheeling brainstorming sections. To tap available brainpower fully the techniques discussed in Section 4.7 can be used. In addition, checklists of possible ideas can be developed, similar items can be compared and evaluated concerning how they could be modified to do the job, ideas can be combined, and so on. Creativity can be stimulated by an animated discussion in an atmosphere of economic safety and

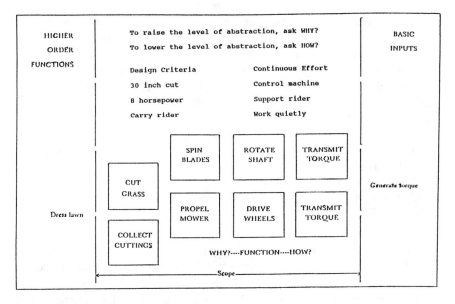

Figure 12-20.   A riding lawn mower.
Source: C. Fallon, *Value Analysis* (New York: Triangle Press, 1980), p. 200. Reprinted with permission of Value Foundation.

intellectual freedom. A wide diversity of skills provides the fuel. But there are ingrained barriers to innovation and the exercise of creativity, such as

1. Undue dependence on custom, tradition, and procedure
2. Undue caution
3. Lethargy and inertia
4. Fixed ideas (inflexibility)

These roadblocks are usually verbalized in team discussions by a variety of "killer" phrases, ranging from "this is not the right time" and "this is not our problem" to outright ridicule. Such barriers must not be allowed to inhibit or hold back the work of the VE team.

In the *selection and evaluation* phase the various alternatives developed in the creative phase are examined and compared from the standpoints of cost and fulfillment of the essential functions. The costs and risks involved in not taking chances or making changes must also be appraised. In the decision process, the discussion should focus on the selected objectives and their relative importance.

Typically, the selected method will provide the required functions and will lead to a net reduction in overall cost, without degradation of any other essential characteristics of the item. There are numerous methods available for making choices (see Chapter 6), which frequently involves the difficult process of quantifying the customer's needs. There is a danger, since many utility functions coincide with well-known mathematical curves, to assume that other functions behave in similar, neatly predictable mathematical ways. Because many do not, prudent scientific caution, as sometimes can be planned into a decision tree, is advisable (Figure 6-5).

The *proposal and presentation* phase involves the preparation of a plan to describe the value improvement problem and its recommended solution. Relevant information must be presented, including

Analysis results
Technical adequacy
Advantages over previous parts or procedures
Cost estimates and potential savings
Procedure for implementing

During the *implementation* of improvements resulting from the VE effort, the importance of time must not be overlooked (Figure 12-21). Unnecessary delays may reduce or even eliminate the profitability of the best of ideas. Implementation calls for an achievable schedule and follow-up and control by management to ensure that it is carried out within the established budget. The involvement of the original team members is desirable since the choice of team members should have

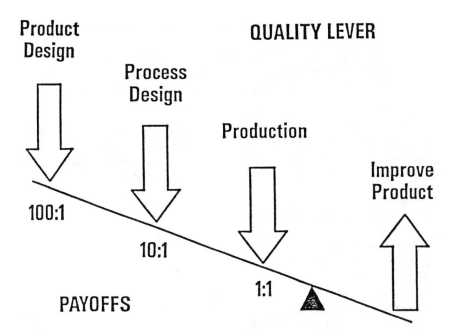

Figure 12-21.   The value of early product improvement. The earlier improvements are introduced in the product development cycle, the greater the payoff.

been based, at least in part, on their ability to implement potential solutions. Contributions to a successful VE effort should be recognized and rewarded to make participation in future VE teams attractive (Figure 11–5).

12.9   CONFIGURATION MANAGEMENT

When numerous components, subsystems, and systems are involved in making a product, there is a need for keeping track of all the parts that make up the total system. This is particularly important when the product becomes operational and replacement parts are needed or when parts of the product are improved or changed in subsequent models. This need is prevalent in a myriad of products (systems) such as home appliances, automobiles, construction equipment, communication systems, electronic control systems, engineering equipment, and so on. Configuration management (CM) is a management technique that has been developed for the express purpose of parts and total system accounting. It accomplishes this task by:

1. Accurately identifying and describing each part, subassembly, and assembly used in the product
2. Keeping close track of all changes to the product, including changes to product description as well as to the product itself
3. Keeping track of all blueprints, software programs, test data, operating instructions, and other documents related to the product

The term *configuration* refers to the key characteristics of the product or system, subsystems and components, including size, weight, spatial arrangement, materials of construction, and interfaces. In addition to the physical characteristics, CM also identifies and maintains original requirements and changes in

Design
Power and operational requirements
Test procedures
Repair procedures
Components and subsystems
Documentation
Software programs
Inventory and storage locations
Other data pertinent to the system

Configuration management starts in the planning phase by setting up initial baseline requirements for the product and then continues through the various phases of R&D and production according to the sequential phases shown in Figure 12-22.

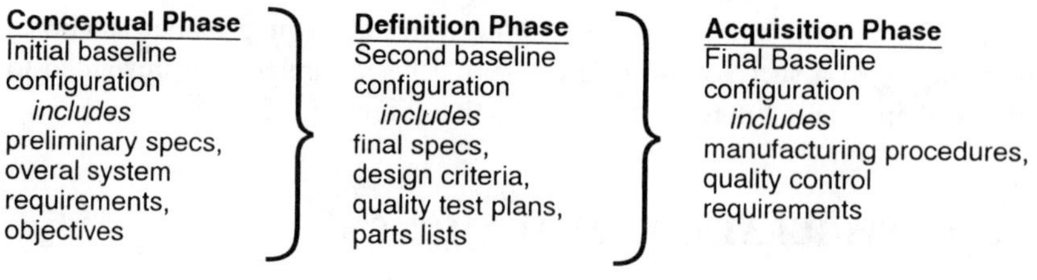

Conceptual Phase
Initial baseline configuration
includes
preliminary specs, overal system requirements, objectives

Definition Phase
Second baseline configuration
includes
final specs, design criteria, quality test plans, parts lists

Acquisition Phase
Final Baseline configuration
includes
manufacturing procedures, quality control requirements

Figure 12-22.   Sequential Phases of Configuration Management. (Stephanou and Obradovitch, 1985)

During the development and transition to production of the product, CM monitors whether the actual configuration is conforming to the original baseline requirements (baseline Management). In carrying out this objective, CM must maintain the following activities:

1. Setting up and monitoring baseline requirements during the system development
2. Identification of parts, subsystems, and systems

TABLE 12-2.   Hardware Item Identification

Configured Item	Configured Item Description	Specification	C.I. Number	Responsibility
	Stabilization and Control Subsystem (con't)			M. Nelson
236880	Sensor and Drive Electronics Assembly		AK100 (Ref.)	
236884	Chassis Assy, SSE-1020A1	EQ4-432	AK116	L. M. Lewis
236883	Chassis Assy, SIE-1010	EQ4-431	AK118	L. M. Lewis
236885	Chassis Assy, DAE-1030A1	EQ4-430	AK127	L. M. Lewis
236886	Chassis Assy, DAE-1030A2	EQ4-430	AK128	L. M. Lewis
236830	Chassis Assy, ESE-710A1	EQ4-419	AK129	L. M. Lewis
236834	Chassis Assy, ESE-710A2	EQ4-419	AK130	L. M. Lewis
236744	Chassis Assy, SRE-810A1	EQ4-426	AK131	L. M. Lewis
236743	Chassis Assy, SRE-810A2	EQ4-426	AK132	L. M. Lewis
	Electrical Power Subsystem	SS14-03	AK200	H. Kelly
237034	Battery	EQ3-168	AK201	R. Weber
237032	Converter No. 1	EQ3-161	AK202	M. Monaco
241198	Solar Paddle	EQ3-167	AK203	C. Lindley
235118	Shunt Element Assembly	EQ3-162	AK204	R. Rubin
235119	Power Control Unit	EQ3-163	AK205	R. Rubin
237033	Converter No. 2A	EQ3-164	AK206	M. Monaco
237031	Converter No. 2B	EQ3-164	AK207	M. Monaco
	Telemetry Subsystem	SS6-17	AK300	A. Anderson
236408	PCM Encoder	EQ4-437	AK301	E. B. Smith
238763	"S" Band Transmitter	EQ4-438	AK302	J. Olsen
237028	Antenna Assy, "S" Band	EQ4-439	AK303	B. Ash
235800	Command Decoder	EQ4-440	AK304	S. Cobb
H244904	Transport Case		AK305	F. White
F240632	Antenna Hat Assy		AK306	F. White
EG238047	Telemetry Demodulator	EQ4-442	AK350	B. March
EG238048	Command Demodulator	EQ4-443	AK360	B. March
	Electrical Integration Subsystem	SS4-07	AK400	C. R. Bennett
237955	Electrical Integration Assy	EQ3-158	AK401	M. Harris
240369	Cabling	EQ3-160	AK402	L. DeSilva
237956	Auxiliary Electrical Integration Assy	EQ3-159	AK403	M. Hoffman

3. Accounting—keeping records of parts, tests, and so on
4. Change control—keeping track of changes in the system

As indicated above, the initial baseline configuration is established from the product requirements, which in turn are the basis of the preliminary product or system specification. The second baseline configuration is developed after modeling and testing of the final product from engineering drawings and other information pertaining to product operation and use. The last baseline configuration provides the final design from which the product will be manufactured. It includes detailed engineering drawings, quality assurance data, list procedures, operational data, and so on.

Principal Activities of Configuration Management

Configuration identification, based on the product requirements, indicates what the system will "look" like and what it will consist of in terms of specific subsystems and components. Part of the identification process involves setting up a system for monitoring and controlling the items to be used in making up the system, including their identification numbers (inventory), location, description, specifications, and so on. In addition, documentation and software requirements must be identified. An accounting system for keeping track of hardware items must be developed. Such numbering systems relate components to subsystems as shown in Table 12-2.

Configuration accounting carries out the continued tracking of the component parts and subsystems as product development continues from design to the final manufacturing stages. It keeps track of the configuration in the form of reports and documentation during the lifetime of the system, including all changes to

Software programs
Engineering drawings
Product specifications
Procedures
Shipping specifications
Operating manuals

Configuration change control personnel are concerned with the procedures for making changes to the baseline-configured items (components, subsystems, and systems) so that proposed changes are appropriately made, evaluated, and acted on. Changes can be suggested to improve performance and quality of service, reduce complexity of manufacture, and decrease costs or any coordination of attributes. Changes in design can be integrated by design reviews, held during various decision points in the development of the product. Formal design reviews usually involve the designers and key personnel involved in the development of the product as well as representatives of the participating functions such as manufacturing, marketing, sales and management. In such reviews all pertinent aspects of the product design should be carefully examined. Where possible mock-ups, breadboards, or prototypes should be used to detect design flaws and determine any problem with interacting components or subsystems.

A select group of knowledgeable engineers can be used as a Configuration Control Board (CCB) to evaluate recommended changes and make decisions about their suitability. Depending on the nature of the product, the composition of the board can be varied to include production, purchasing, quality assurance, and marketing personnel. The CCB must verify that the change is necessary, is physically and technically feasible, and makes economic sense. The use of bar coding on components, along with computerized control systems like MRP-II, can make the configuration change control process much easier, providing it is integrated into the other systems.

QUESTIONS AND TOPICS FOR DISCUSSION

12.1   How can teams be used in concurrent engineering?

12.2   How can concurrent engineering shorten the product development cycle?

12.3   When using outside suppliers, why is it important to involve them in a concurrent engineering effort?

12.4   What are the essential features of material requirements planning (MRP-1) and how do they relate?

12.5   What is manufacturing resource planning (MRP-II) and how does it relate to MRP-I?

12.6   What are the advantages and disadvantages of using computers systems with MRP-I and MRP-II as compared with manual and visual systems such as Kanban?

12.7   What relationship does a Kanban system have to plant layout?

12.8   List three advantages and three disadvantages of just-in-time (JIT).

12.9   How does quality affect JIT planning?

12.10   Explain the significance of the term *hidden factory*.

12.11   How can the hidden factory be exposed?

12.12   How can group technology be used in enhancing the manufacturing process?

12.13   Describe the important features of the Taguchi methods.

12.14   Describe how value analysis (VA) can be used in improving the manufacturing process.

12.15   Why is configuration management necessary in the manufacturing of complex systems?

References

Allen, C. W. 1989. "Simultaneous Engineering: What? Why? How?" Technical paper no. MM89-495. Dearborn, MI: Society of Manufacturing Engineers.

Crosby, P.S. 1979 *Quality is Free: The Art of Making Quality Certain*: New York: McGraw Hill.

Curtindale, F. 1989, July. Simultaneous engineering: Culture shock for the auto industry. *Careers*.

Dear, Anthony. 1988. *Working Towards Just-in-Time*. New York: Van Nostrand Reinhold.

Deming, E.W. 1982 *Quality, Productivity and Competitive Position*. Cambridge, Mass: MIT Press.

Dertouzas, M. L., R. K. Lester, and R. M. Solow. 1988. *Made in the U.S.A.* Cambridge, MA: MIT Press.

El Wakil, S. D. 1989. *Process and Design for Manufacturing*. Englewood Cliffs, NJ: Prentice Hall.

Fallon, C. 1980 *Value Analysis*.:Chicago Triangle Press

Fogarty, D. W., Hoffman, Thomas R., and Stonebraker, PW. 1989 *Production and Operation Management*. Cincinnati: South-Western.

Garrett, R. W. 1990. Eight steps to simultaneous engineering. *Manufacturing Engineering* 105(5), 41-47.

Gunn, T. G. 1982, September. The mechanization of design and manu- facturing. *Scientific American*, p. 121.

Imai, Masaaki. 1986. *Kaizen—The Key to Japan's Competitive Success*. New York: McGraw-Hill.

Juran, J. M. 1988. *Juran's Quality Control Handbook, Upper Management and Quality*. New York: McGraw-Hill.

Kalpakjian, Serope. 1989. *Manufacturing Engineering and Technology*. New York: Addison-Wesley.

Lipkin, Richard. 1990. Callers look each other in the eye. *Insight* 6(38), 42-43.

Manufacturing Engineering. 1989, October. p. 66.

Meredith, J. R. 1987. *Management of Operations*. New York: Wiley.

Miles, L. D. 1972. *Techniques of Value Analysis and Engineering*. New York: McGraw-Hill.

Obradovitch, M. M., and S. E. Stephanou. 1990. *Project Management Risks and Productivity*, p. 443. Bend, OR: Daniel Spencer.

Ohno, T. 1978. *Toyoto Production System*: Columbus, OH. Diamond Publishing.

Riley, F. J., Jr. 1990. Simultaneous engineering: Blessing or boondoggle? *Manufacturing Engineering* 104(4), 7.

Ross, Phillip J. 1988. *Taguchi Techniques for Quality Engineering*. New York: McGraw-Hill.

Roy, Ranjt. 1990. *A Primer on the Taguchi Method*. New York: Van Nostrand Reinhold.

Snead, Charles S. 1989. *Group Technology Foundation for Competitive Manufacturing*. New York: Van Nostrand Reinhold.

Stephanou, S. E., and Obradovitch, M. M. 1985. *Project Management, Systems Development and Productivity*. Bend, OR: Daniel Spencer.

Suzaki, K. 1987. *The New Manufacturing Challenge*. New York: Free Press.

Szczesny, J. 1990, October 29. The right stuff. Detroit. *Time Magazine*.

13

Total Quality Management

13.1 INTRODUCTION

An important part of proceeding from R&D to successful production is planning for quality and for meeting the requirements of the customer. This customer-oriented planning may be accomplished at the time of initial concept or by reverse engineering. In the latter case the manufacturing process is designed to give customers what they want and with the quality they want. Successful companies have realized that the ability to provide its customers with quality products at the right price and time is essential for survival in today's competitive, international environment. The quality of products has assumed an importance not hitherto appreciated by manufacturers, partly because monopolies in any given product area have diminished to a very small number and partly because there is now a plethora of competing products on the market, with quality and performance as well as price being the criteria for selection by the customer.

This abundance of goods and choices available to consumers all over the world means that mere slogans of quality products do not suffice. Being the "Cadillac" of an industry is no longer a guarantee for the manufacturer, who may have earned that reputation many years ago.[1] Indeed, the Cadillac Division of General Motors has been and still is being challenged by such established lines as Mercedes-Benz, BMW, and now Japanese luxury cars as well. Zenith appears to be the only maker of television receivers still manufacturing in the United States, and such names as Sony, Toshiba, and JVC have established a reputation as quality producers of many types of electronic devices and other products.

The Japanese Story

As a result of the Japanese success in the manufacturing and sale of such products, a success that can be linked to their commitment to producing quality products at competitive prices, the concepts of total quality management (TQM) and total quality control (TQC) have become popular subjects for management and techni-cal courses, seminars, books, and articles. The works of such pioneers as Deming, Juran, and Feigenbaum on quality, as well as Peter Drucker on management, that had long been ignored by American management, were implemented in Japan after World War II (Figure 13-1).

Before that period, the Japanese had established a reputation for producing low-quality, cheap products, which were usually poor copies of items developed in other countries. Recognizing the need to rebuild their war-torn economy, the Japanese were determined to make whatever changes were required to improve. They had neither abundant natural resources nor a large land mass with a favorable climate to produce food and had failed to gain such wealth by force through war. With the help of a generous and constructive peace treaty, other methods were chosen to gain adequate subsistence, more abundant goods, and greater recognition and wealth, In about one and a half generations (fewer than 40 years) the Japanese have learned to produce quality goods and services that have found a receptive worldwide market.

This success has been attributed, at least in part, to the practice of TQM along with a national culture that promotes commitment to the success of the organiza-tion. This is not to say that similar commitment cannot be realized in our country. Other Pacific Rim countries, as well as Germany, France, and developed countries in general, have adopted quality procedures and production philosophies similar, if not identical to, TQM. Such emphasis on quality has made these countries formidable competitors on the international market.

---

[1]The Cadillac Division of General Motors won the 1990 Malcolm Baldridge National Quality Award, the country's highest honor for quality in business. This represents a rebirth of the repututation that Cadillac had for quality for many years.

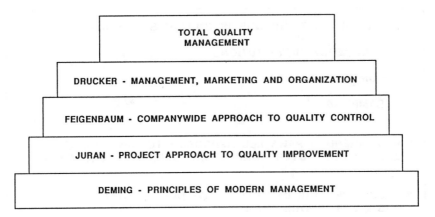

Figure 13-1.   Total quality management originating concepts.

Importance of Quality

Product quality has always been one of the most important elements in manufacturing operations; in today's market conditions, quality has become even more important. As emphasized by Deming, Juran, and Feigenbaum, the prevention of defects in products and on-line inspection are now major objectives in manufacturing. After many years of working with traditional quality controls, they recognized, perhaps even more clearly through the application of statistical controls, that quality must be built into the product, not merely checked after the product is made. They stressed the importance of close cooperation and communication among development, design, and manufacturing engineers and the need for improvements of the overall manufacturing process. An important part of the TQM philosophy is that the customer determines quality in products or services and that techniques must be developed to give customers what they want (Figure 13-2).

13.2   PRODUCT QUALITY AND QUALITY ASSURANCE

Product quality has often been evaluated by such terms as *poor quality* or *high quality*, yet quality is a broad-based characteristic that may consist of several well-defined technical requirements as well as other subjective considerations.

The more traditional definition of quality has been a product's fitness for use and the totality of features and characteristics that ensure the product's ability to satisfy a given need. More recent definitions include other dimensions of quality, such as performance, durability, reliability, maintainability, aesthetics, and per-

• **PRINCIPAL QC TECHNIQUE IS ON-LINE STATISTICAL ANALYSIS**

  - **FREQUENCY DISTRIBUTIONS**

  - **CONTROL CHARTS**

  - **SAMPLING**

• **RECOMMENDED PARALLEL APPROACH TO NEW PRODUCT DEVELOPMENT OVER TRADITIONAL SERIES DEVELOPMENT**

• **RECOGNIZED THE IMPORTANCE OF DESIGN, STARTING WITH CUSTOMER REQUIREMENTS**

• **STRONG EMPHASIS ON WORK FORCE EDUCATION, COST OF QUALITY, VENDOR RELATIONS, AND SAFETY**

Figure 13-2.   A.V. Feigenbaum's total quality control techniques.

ceived quality. These concepts can be fairly well evaluated in products such as automobiles, televisions, and computers. In fact, many rating services like *Consumer Reports* provide evaluations of products and services that reflect the broader definition of quality. Such rating services, as well as manufacturers, realistically recognize that most products that have better-quality properties are more expensive to process. For example, steel bicycles are being surpassed in performance by bicycles made from aluminum alloys, carbon fibers, and high-strength titanium alloys. At about $2,500, the Merlin titanium bicycle provides the lightest frame with the smoothest and best road-holding ride (Design 1990). However, improvement in quality does not necessarily involve an increase in cost.

Customers Determine Quality
Even in such standard products as light bulbs and automobile tires, manufacturers are required to describe quality in specific terms such as hours of expected life, heat resistance, and traction. In general, for higher prices, we can get longer-life light bulbs and better-quality tires. However, with advanced technology, automated processes, and constant efforts for improvement on the part of workers and supervisors, better products can be and have been produced at lower costs. Therein lies the true essence of the current definition of quality, namely, that customers

constitute the market that ultimately determines the desired quality. Enlightened manufacturers constantly strive to meet the customer's needs by translating desired characteristics into quality requirements, which are achieved through trade-offs. As a result, total product cost will depend on numerous interrelated variables, which may range from the level of commitment of personnel to the level of automation. In the past higher quality was obtained by adding more inspection and correcting problems as they appeared (Figure 13-3).

Cost and Quality

Contrary to general perceptions, quality products do not necessarily cost more. Higher quality usually means lower overall cost; poor quality usually has inherent costs that may be difficult to quantify but are significantly greater in the final analysis for both the manufacturer and the customer. For example, difficulties in processing and assembling products cause rework and scrap; undetected problems cause field repairs, customer dissatisfaction, and ultimately loss of market share. The term *hidden factory* (Section 12.5) was coined to account for the fact that as much as 30 percent of many factory efforts are spent in repairing and reworking designs and hardware without realistically identifying wasteful practices. Most labor tracking and accounting procedures are not structured to assess such costs accurately, even though companies devote considerable effort in isolating and eliminating these hidden expenses. Thus the actual costs of high quality may indeed be "free" if the true costs resulting from poor quality are realistically documented and analyzed.

In recognition of the large potential cost savings of this far-reaching concept, Crosby (1979), one of the modern purveyors of quality training, has emphasized the slogan that quality is indeed free. To understand the concepts of quality implied by TQM, its various components must be examined. As will become apparent, most of these components are not new, but their timely use in effective combination and the strong underlying emphasis on quality *is* new—and therein lie the value and contribution of TQM.

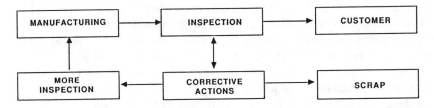

Figure 13-3.   Quality control: the traditional inspection cycle.

Quality Assurance

The most direct approach to acceptable quality is to make certain that a product is correctly made in the first place. To make sure that every product is perfect, we could inspect everything completely, but in most instances, 100 percent inspection would be too expensive to maintain. The other extreme is not to inspect the products at all and depend on user feedback to control the quality of the manufacturing process and the final product. In some inexpensive products, for example, give-away key rings, this latter procedure might be acceptable. In the past the method of letting the customer do the final inspection was considered economically advantageous by some manufacturers, but class-action lawsuits and customer rejection of questionable products have reduced this practice. Fortunately, methods of checking smaller, statistically relevant samples have been devised and used for many years. These methods use statistics to determine the probability of success or failure (Section 13.3). Several steps may be involved, depending on the nature of the product (Kalpakjian 1989):

1. Control and inspection of incoming materials to ascertain whether they meet the properties, dimensions, and finishes required
2. Inspection of any made or bought components for the required specifications
3. Verification of the satisfactory assembly of the product
4. Testing of the completed product to make sure that it meets the designed and intended functions

Variations in most materials and processes necessitate the continued verification of the accurate repeatability of manufacturing processes and final product quality. For example, variability can occur as tools, dies, and machines wear out. In addition to machine errors, human limitations and mistakes can play a continuous role in causing variations, so that no two products are ever precisely alike. Therefore, a critical aspect of quality control is to establish the acceptable limits or tolerances for the manufacturing process and the product. Another critical aspect is to document failure trends, determine the causes of defects, and reduce them to acceptable levels. In a broader and more critical sense, examination of the design of the product, including its manufacturability or producibility, should be ongoing to make certain that it meets the customer's need. The sum of such activities have been referred to as total quality control or quality assurance.

Many organizations, in addition to the customary inspectors, employ quality engineers, who work with manufacturing engineers to ensure that products can be manufactured and inspected to meet specific quality requirements. Test engineers must devise and implement tests to ensure the satisfactory performance of the product. As indicated, economics plays an important factor in the degree to which these functions are applied. For example, the cost of inspecting nails or screws could easily exceed their worth. However, the devising and implementing of the most cost-effective process to make an acceptable product may be a difficult problem.

13.3   STATISTICAL PROCESS AND QUALITY CONTROL

Statistics deals with the collection, analysis, interpretation, and presentation of large amounts of numerical data. Statistical techniques in modern manufacturing and testing operations are required because of the increasing variety of materials and procedures used and the large potential for variations in the manufacturing process. For example,

Tools, dies, and molds wear, causing dimensions to vary with use.

Equipment and machinery perform differently depending on the model, age, condition, and degree of maintenance.

Cutting, lubricating, and cleaning fluids degrade with use, thus causing changes in dimensions and processes.

Different lots of materials may have different properties, dimensions, and surface finishes.

Environmental conditions such as temperature, humidity, and air quality may change from hour to hour, affecting machines, equipment, and employees. Strict environmental control is expensive but often necessary.

Operator skill and attention may vary from machine to machine and among the operators.

If such conditions or events occur randomly without any particular pattern, they are called *chance variations*. Those that can be traced to specific causes are called *assignable variations*. The existence of *variability* in manufacturing has been recognized for centuries, but Eli Whitney (1765–1825) first grasped its full importance when he determined that interchangeable parts were vital to the mass production of firearms. With the help of automated equipment, computers, and controlled environmental conditions, we can now control many variables that were previously much more difficult to maintain within acceptable standards. All sophisticated automated machinery, with built-in inspection equipment, computerized controls, and record-keeping capability, are investments that ultimately must be justified by the type and quantity of production. Indeed, these are the types of decisions that enlightened management, must deal with as technology continues to generate a variety of options.

Definitions and Equations
To discuss and understand the fundamental concepts of *statistical quality control*, some commonly used terms must first be defined:

Population—the totality of individual parts of the same design from which samples are to be taken

Sample Size—the number of parts to be checked to gain information about the whole population

Random Sampling—taking a sample from a population or lot in which each item has an equal chance of being selected

Samples are usually inspected for certain features, such as tolerances and surface finishes. These characteristics can be measured quantitatively by the *method of variables* or observed qualitatively by the *method of attributes*.

During the inspection process measurements will vary. A commonly used example that is easily understood is the measurement of the diameters of shafts turned on a lathe. After these diameters are measured with a micrometer or some more sophisticated instrument, it becomes evident that they vary within a certain spread. In Figure 13-4 the distribution of the values of the diameter show the effect of improving process capability and process control. If these measurements are plotted in bar graph form in groups representing each size, they will show a distribution over the dispersion of values. The resulting bell-shaped curve is referred to as a frequency distribution (Figure 13-5). Data from manufacturing processes often fit such bell-shaped distribution curves, which are referred to as normal or Gaussian distribution curves. Figure 13-4 shows the product distribution between upper and lower limits and the product loss if relatively narrow allowable upper and lower limits are targeted.

Most parts' diameters tend to cluster around the *average* value or *arithmetic mean*. This average, usually designated as $\bar{x}$ is calculated from the following ratio, in which the numerator is the sum of all the measured values, and the denominator is the number of measurements:

$$\bar{x} = \frac{x_1 + x_2 + x_3 + - - - x_n}{n}$$

The second feature of the curve is its width, indicating the dispersion of the sizes of diameters measured. The difference between the largest and smallest values is designated as the range R, and

$$R = x_{max} - x_{min}$$

The dispersion, which is referred to as the *standard deviation* (σ), is obtained by the following expression, in which x is the measured value for each part:

$$\sigma = \frac{(x_1 - \bar{x})^2 + (x_2 - \bar{x})^2 + (x_3 - \bar{x})^2 + - - - (x_n - \bar{x})^2}{n - 1}$$

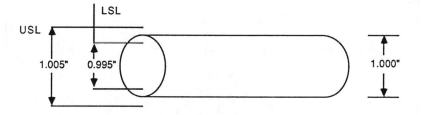

Any shaft smaller than the LSL or larger than
the USL is rejected and represents a loss.

LSL = Lower Specification Limit
USL = Upper Specification Limit

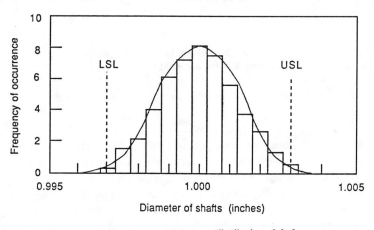

Diameter of shafts (inches)

Figure 13-4.   Frequency distribution of shafts.

Since we know the number of machined parts that fall within each group, we
can calculate the percentage of the total population represented by each group.
Thus, Figure 13-5 shows that diameters of 99.73 percent fall within ± 3 sigma,
95.46 percent with ± 2 sigma, and 68.26 percent within ± 1 sigma of all the values.

In complex systems in which human safety is involved, for example, spacecraft,
4 sigma may not yield a satisfactory reliability for astronauts. A 98 percent or 99
percent systems reliability may simply not be acceptable, considering the magnitude of the financial and human investment. Even in complex, relatively risk-free

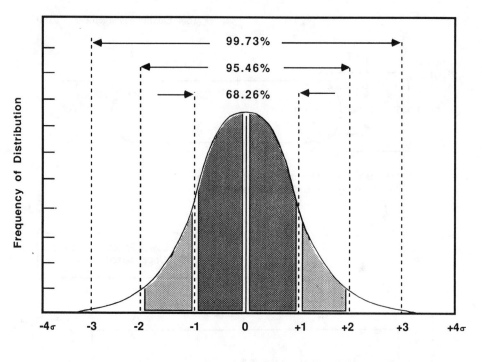

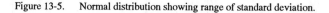

* **Note that the greater the allowed deviation the greater
the number of parts that will be acceptable.**

Figure 13-5.   Normal distribution showing range of standard deviation.

commercial communication equipment, companies like Motorola have adopted a
6 sigma standard (99.999998%) for their critical components (Harry 1990).

Manufacturing according to the concepts of TQM, in which the customer's
desire for reliability and quality is honored from the start of product development,
has shown long-term returns, despite initially expensive start-up and operating
costs. For example, based on its emphasis on quality and at considerable cost,
Motorola, with an apparently more reliable product, has succeeded in capturing a
substantial share of the cellular telephone market even though Japanese electronic
manufacturers initially dominated.

Self-Inspection
One of the most direct ways of improving quality is to motivate, train, and equip
personnel to perform self-inspection as they work. The advantages, in addition to saving
extra inspection labor, are significant. Most important, expensive rework is reduced and
better workmanship is promulgated. Inspectors can be relieved from unproductive,
repetitive work so that they can analyze trends and solve inherent problems that may not

be apparent to workers or even under their purview. With such obvious advantages one might wonder why more self-inspection is not practiced. Self-inspection has indeed been the trademark of master craftspeople and outstanding professionals in their fields. With the advent of more production lines and automation, the trend toward less costly unskilled or semiskilled labor became more prevalent. To monitor their output, inspectors and statistical process control (SPC) have been utilized, but these methods are no substitute for trained and motivated workers.

The common practice of equipping workers with less accurate inspection tools than the inspectors is self-defeating. For example, in the electronics industry inspectors are equipped with glasses of greater magnification capability than those of the workers. Therefore, it is not surprising that the inspectors see more variations than do the workers. This is not to negate the importance and usefulness of impartial inspection. It is not unusual for workers to be unable at times to discover their own error in a process, despite repeated and honest self-checks. This human weakness is a valid justification of inspection and SPC.

Control Charts

One of the common tools of SPC is the control chart, which graphically represents variations of processes over a period of time. The charts consist of data plotted during manufacturing and other processes. After allowable variations from a sufficient sample size are established, upper-control and lower-control limits that will maintain the processes in acceptable ranges can be determined. Techniques for such determinations are described in considerable detail in books on statistics (e.g., Kalpakjian 1989). An example of the production of shafts that may initially fall beyond the predetermined design tolerance range has already been illustrated in the bell-shaped curve of Figure 13-4, which includes the specified tolerances for the diameter of turned shafts.

In control charts the quantity x is the average of samples taken and inspected. The frequency of sampling depends on the nature of the process. Since such measurements are made consecutively, the horizontal axis of the control charts represents time (Figure 13-6) and the solid line $\bar{x}$ represents the average of the averages, and thus the population mean. The upper and lower horizontal broken lines of these control charts represent the control limits of the process.

The control limits are set according to statistical control formulas designed to keep the actual production within a usually acceptable range. In the past, control limits of ± 3 sigma have been used for many processes; in present practice ± 6 sigma is used as the target for many complex products when the reliability of the final system has to be 99 percent or more. Medical devices such as pacemakers, electronic controls and nuclear control devices are examples of systems in which the high cost of failure make the striving for 6 sigma quality not only necessary from the standpoint of safety and performance but also cost-effective. Thus, for x

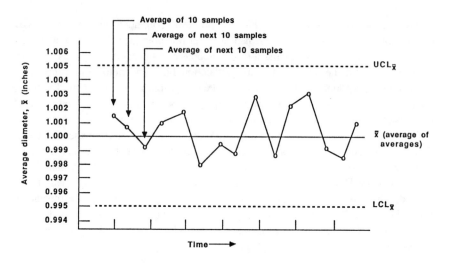

Figure 13-6.   Average diameter of shafts produced versus time.

$$\text{Upper control limit (UCL)} = \overline{x} + 3 \text{ sigma}$$
$$\text{Lower control limit (LCL)} = \overline{x} - 3 \text{ sigma}$$

These limits are calculated on the historical capability of the equipment itself as well as workers' capabilities and should be within the allowable design tolerances and specifications. The major goal of SPC is to improve the manufacturing process and to remove assignable causes with the aid of the control charts. In addition the control charts continually record the progress of improvements. Often limitations of the equipment used in the process may require substantial investments to improve their accuracy and repeatability. This improvement can ultimately achieve handsome returns on that investment, and although "quality is free" may be true in the long run, it may not be true initially.

Quality Function Deployment

The lowering of the variability of processes, as seen by increased sigma values in statistical analysis, can frequently result in measurable savings, even if the processes are within acceptable limits. As we deviate from the target value there are ever increasing probabilities of wear until we finally get to the lower and upper specification limits, where actually increasing repair costs are experienced (Figure 13-7). This phenomena was encountered when the Ford transmissions manufactured by Mazda demonstrated a longer life even though they were made to the same specifications.

The same concept was somewhat differently but dramatically demonstrated by the famous Deming red ball experiment. In this experiment a large number (3,200) of

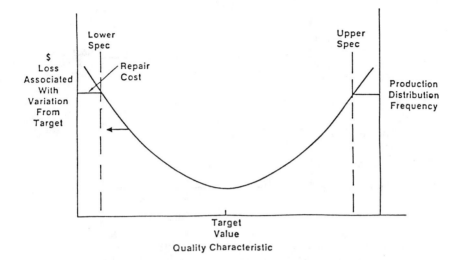

Figure 13-7.   Quality function deployment.

white balls were intermixed with a much smaller number (800) of red balls. Worker, inspector and supervisor teams were to withdraw continuously, with an indentured scoop, a set number of samples that preferably contained no red balls. Each scoopful had different numbers of red balls interspersed with the white, and only occasional scoops were free of red balls. The quality of red versus white balls in arbitrary samples could not be fundamentally improved until the actual number of red balls in the total aggregate of white balls was decreased. The experiment shows that quality cannot basically be improved until the variability of the process is decreased.

Other Methods

If organizations do not have the capability to document and analyze the effectiveness of their processes, the maintenance of control charts may initially seem expensive. Therefore, care should be taken first to control those processes that are most costly. Tools such as Pareto's law (Figure 13-8) should be considered in making the selection of those processes that are to be controlled. The subsequent application of value analysis (see Section 12.8) can be used to ensure the most cost-effective way to accomplish a truly needed function. Although such methods can be used at any stage of the improvement process, they are particularly effective in the beginning since the psychological attitudes of the members of improvement teams and management are generally sensitive to false starts, setbacks, and no immediately discernible returns on investments of time and money. Success tends to breed success (Figure 13-9).

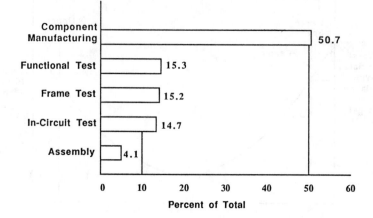

Figure 13-8.   Pareto analysis of percent total annualized failure costs.
Source: J.M. Juran, *Juran's Quality Control Handbook*, 4th Ed. (New York: McGraw-Hill, 1988) section 22.21. Reproduced with permission of McGraw-Hill, Inc.

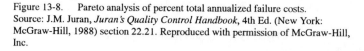

Figure 13-9.   The ladder of success.

Failure mode effects analysis (FMEA) of the system and/or the determination of the criticality of an item in relation to the functioning of a product must be considered in deciding which statistical process control will be most cost -effective. Failure is commonly defined as the cessation of the ability of a system, subassembly, or component to meet any of the specified performance requirements.

13.4   PRODUCT ACCEPTANCE

As has already been mentioned, there are basically three ways of ensuring acceptable products:

1. 100 percent inspection and test
2. Statistical sampling
3. No inspection—consumer feedback

The first method is economically feasible in only a relatively few instances, such as custom precision products for critical use in medicine, science, space, and military and special commercial applications. Even if the customer is willing to pay for such extensive product verification, it may not always be technically feasible. Many parts may have to be destructively tested or carefully examined to determine the true failure rate or actual structures. Some electronic parts, which have to be examined by burn-in tests to determine their characteristics, can lose part of their operating life through the very tests that are supposed to verify them.

Acceptance Sampling

As a result of these consideration, it becomes necessary to rely on a sampling technique that is sufficiently controlled to yield the required quality. Acceptance sampling is such a technique; it consists of taking a few random samples from a lot and inspecting them to determine if the entire lot is acceptable, should be reworked, or should be rejected. It was developed in the 1920s and is still widely used, particularly for high-rate production, where 100 percent verification may not be economical or feasible. In the use of such a random sampling technique the probability that a particular lot is within certain specified limits can also be determined (see below). Automation of processes has had a marked positive effect on the technical feasibility of 100 percent verification; for example, techniques such as optical and laser inspection systems can allow for 100 percent verification of some automatic processes. However, such systems are expensive and must be economically justified.

A variety of acceptance sampling plans[2] have been prepared for determining standards, based on an acceptable, predetermined, and limiting percentage of nonconforming parts in the sample. If this percentage is exceeded, the lot is rejected or reworked if reworking is economically feasible and permissible. The greater the number of samples taken from a lot, the greater will be the percentage of nonconforming parts and the lower the probability of acceptance of the lot. Probability is defined as the likelihood that an event will occur. It can be expressed as a fraction or percentage and can vary from 0.0 to 0.1 or from 0 to 100 percent. The probability of acceptance is obtained from various operating characteristic curves, as shown in Figure 13–10.

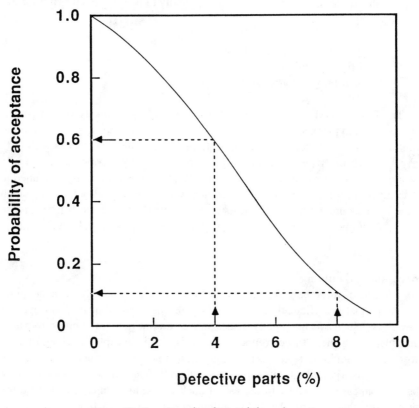

Figure 13-10.   Operating characteristics and acceptance curve.

---

[2]Sampling plans vary according to the type of product, required degree of conformance, variability of the process, and cost of verification.

Acceptance Quality Level

The acceptance quality level (AQL) is commonly defined as the level at which there is 95 percent probability of acceptance of the lot. This percentage would indicate to the manufacturer that 5 percent of the parts in the lot may be rejected by the consumer (called the producer's risk). Similarly, the consumer knows that 95 percent of the parts are acceptable (called the consumer's risk). Lots that do not meet the desired quality standards can be salvaged by the manufacturer through a secondary rectifying inspection. In this method, 100 percent inspection is made of the rejected lot, and the defective parts are removed. This time-consuming and costly process is an incentive for the manufacturer to improve and control the production process. If products are being made that require almost 100 percent acceptance, 6-sigma quality, the process must be sufficiently controlled to reduce the need for such sampling techniques. Acceptance sampling, however, requires less time than do more extensive sampling methods. Consequently, inspection and analysis of the parts can be more detailed, leading to gradual improvements. Automated process controls, including verification of critical characteristics, will make acceptance controls feasible to ensure high reliability at acceptable costs.

Models and Prototypes

To preclude the modification of expensive manufacturing processes and plant layouts, when changes in the product are to be made test models of the product system can be fabricated to evaluate the suitability of the design and performance under actual service conditions. Changes in design and product performance are much more economically made at the modeling stage rather than after the manufacturing process has been finalized and the plant facility completed.

When possible, *preproduction models* or *prototypes* should be fabricated to evaluate the design for suitability for production. There should be assurance of the producibility of the design before committing to full-scale production. The concepts of design for manufacturing (DFM) and concurrent engineering dictate the use of multidiscipline considerations to arrive at a design that is suitable for manufacturing with a minimum of expensive production changes. Thus, prototypes can be fabricated that test some or all of the design changes and can be used to verify production tooling and test equipment.

If *production models* are used to check out the production jigs, fixtures, and tools, care must be exercised to avoid major (class 1) and minor (class 2) changes during production.[3] Automated systems, such as computer-aided design (CAD) linked to computer-aided manufacturing (CAM), do not necessarily eliminate

---

[3]Class 1 changes represent major damages that affect form, fit, and function; class 2 changes are necessary but do not affect critical parameters.

tedious testing sequences. In fact, without "expert systems" in the form of human or computerized guidance for producibility, automation may merely accelerate the production of junk.

Many industries make what are called *service test models* to subject such replicas of the final product to evaluations for suitability and performance under service conditions. Such items must closely approximate or equal the final design and utilize approved parts or interchangeable equivalents. In some cases, the service test models may have to meet total customer requirements, with the workmanship and appearance of the final product.

Performance Testing

Although acceptance criteria and inspections are helpful in controlling quality during the production process, the ultimate evaluation of quality must be determined by performance testing, that is, how closely the final product meets customer requirements. Performance testing has become a sine qua non for most manufactured products, for example, light bulbs, electric motors, and washing machines. When only a few systems are being built, such as large electrical power generators, tailored to specifications for a specific electric utility plant, the system (product) may be operated for a limited number of hours to ensure its operational capability. A striking example in which lack of performance testing before use had serious negative results was the failure of NASA to test properly the Hubbell telescope before it was launched into space. This omission resulted in a major loss of capability and a substantial financial loss to U.S. taxpayers.

Environmental Testing

Environmental tests under conditions simulating actual service are frequently used to verify the reliability that has been designed into various components, subassemblies, and systems. Establishing and operating such test facilities is usually quite expensive, but the results are invaluable in providing information about the performance characteristics of a product. The expense involved, particularly for small firms, has fostered the use and growth of a number of independent test laboratories. A relatively complete environmental test laboratory would handle tests involving temperature, humidity, pressure, rain, solar radiation, sand or dust, salt spray, fungus resistance, vibration, shock, explosion, acoustics, and acceleration.

In addition to environmental testing, current technology has provided manufacturers with the capability to perform sophisticated tests yielding endurance and fatigue information on an accelerated basis, and products which can be tested to destruction for increased reliability and safety. Automobile as well as airplane crash-and-burn tests with instrumented human dummies are examples of environmental testing that, indeed, could be life saving. Product liability laws and class-action lawsuits by people injured in accidents, which may not even have been directly caused by the malfunctioning of the product, are commonplace. As a result, environmental testing has become a part of the acceptance process for many products.

13.5   CONTINUOUS IMPROVEMENT—KAIZEN

Origin of Kaizen

Technology-breakthrough inventions, such as the steam engine, telephone, light bulb, and transistor, are impressive accomplishments of R&D, but such discoveries cannot be scheduled or counted on. Another aspect of the R&D process must be fully recognized and supported if quality products are to be developed— the continuous improvement process that inventions must undergo to be commercially viable. The extent to which this process is continuous and pervasive marks the difference between the gradual degradation of quality (as new developments and requirements occur) and the attainment of excellence. In fact, looking at the history of many current electronic products and other products with high technical content, one finds numerous examples of innovations in which the United States first predominated, only later to lose the competitive edge to others in production.

This concept of continuous improvement in production and product quality (called *Kaizen*), which has been basic to Japanese management, has great potential for successful application in the Western world. Kaizen requires the involvement of *everyone*, from top management, including the board of directors, down through middle management to staff and the lowest level of workers. The Kaizen concept is crucial to understanding the differences between Japanese and Western approaches to management (Imai 1986).

In the first two decades following World War II, the world economy enjoyed substantial growth with continued breakthroughs in manufacturing techniques and a host of resulting new products. According to Imai (1986) it was a period when innovative strategies paid off handsomely and it flourished in a climate of fast growth and high profit, featuring

- A rapidly expanding market for all types of products
- Consumer orientation focusing more on availability than on quality
- Abundant and low-cost resources
- Success based on innovative products
- Continued use of outdated equipment and facilities
- Management more concerned with increasing sales than with reducing costs

Imai further states that the oil crises of the 1970s radically and irrevocably changed the international business environment, so that the new situation is now represented by[4]

- Sharp increases in the cost of energy, materials and labor
- Increasing industrialization of all nations, with resulting overcapacity of production facilities
- Increasing awareness and concern with the environment and dwindling natural resources, which tend to increase production costs
- Changing consumer values that focus more on quality and safety
- Increased worldwide competition in saturated or shrinking markets
- The need to introduce new products more rapidly to meet rapidly expanding technology fueled by increased competiton
- A need to lower the break-even point for more profitable production prior to needed product changes

Ignoring these changes in the market environment, many companies continue to focus on the innovation strategy and have failed to develop a strategy for these new conditions. Delays in adopting the latest technology and management techniques are costly and in some cases fatal. Such delays almost turned the U.S. industrial heartland, around the Great Lakes area, into a rust belt. Despite the emergence of Japanese companies (using the Kaizen philosophy) as formidable competitors, most Western managers are not aware of the applicability of the Kaizen strategy, and others have been slow to evaluate and adopt it. Although numerous cultural, social, and political factors have been set forth as reasons for the Japanese success, few have identified and appreciated the importance of continuous improvement and the fact that it can be carried out in any country.

Not an essential part of the Kaizen strategy but closely related is the practice of many large companies to carry on R&D programs of constant product improvement. One of us participated in such a program for a number of years with the DuPont Company. The incremental product improvements during a one-year period, did not seem impressive, but taken over a period of five to ten years, the product improvements were equivalent to a technical breakthrough. This constancy of effort on fixed objectives for product improvement over a continued period of time is invaluable, but one subtle different between this approach and Kaizen is that it does not aggressively solicit and receive the support of the workers involved, and this can make a significant difference in the quality of the final product.

---

[4]The Gulf crisis in 1990–1991 further accentuated the dependence of the world community and the international business enviroment on oil.

Important Features of Kaizen

According to Imai (1986) and Suzaki (1987), who have written books exclusively devoted to this subject, Kaizen is the basic philosophical concept for the best of Japanese management and is the key to Japan's success in the international marketplace. In Japanese the word Kaizen means improvement. The various subjects that fall under its umbrella are shown in Figure 13-11. It starts with the recognition that any organization has problems and then proceeds to solve these problems by establishing an organizational environment in which anyone can freely address them. Since developing new products and processes usually can involve different groups and functions of the company as well as the originating research group, the involved groups (e.g., engineering, manufacturing, and marketing) should be brought into the development as early as possible. In this respect Kaizen utilizes concurrent engineering. Western companies generally carry out such developments in a sequential manner or in a conflict resolution mode because of the organizational separation of functions like engineering and manufacturing (Imai 1986). However, multifunctional approaches like value analysis and simultaneous engineering have successfully resolved many such problems in the United States as well as in Japan.

* Customer orientation
* TQC (total quality control)
* Robotics
* QC circles
* Suggestion system
* Automation
* Discipline in the workplace
* TPM
  (total productive maintenance)

* *Kamban*
* Quality improvement
* Just–in–time
* Zero defects
* Small–group activities
* Cooperative labor–
  management relations
* Productivity improvement
* New–product development

Figure 13-11.   The Kaizen umbrella.   Source: M. Imai, *KAIZEN* (New York: McGraw-Hill, 1986) p.4. Reproduced with permission of McGraw-Hill.

In addition, Kaizen, like total quality management, realizes that management must satisfy the customer and continue to serve the customer's needs if the company is to stay in business and make a profit. The Kaizen strategy uses the systems approach and all the problem-solving techniques that can be effectively used to deliver better products at a lower cost. Both the continuous improvement approach and statistical process control (SPC) (also a Kaizen technique) emphasize the process rather than just results as seen by the fact that the Kaizen approach acknowledges and rewards workers' *efforts* for improvements in both product- and process-oriented activities. This is in sharp contrast to Western management practices of evaluating workers' performance strictly on the basis of *results* and not recognizing the effort made. Such focus on immediately apparent results frequently precludes more significant achievements that can occur later as a result of persistent efforts to improve. In like fashion, many U.S. companies are simply evaluated on the short-term bottom line, without evaluating the process that may actually be destroying the company by reducing capital investments, improvements, and R&D. The basic principles underlying Kaizen are shown in Figure 13-12.

KAIZEN FUNDAMENTAL PRINCIPLES
(THINKING BEHIND CONCEPTS AND TOOLS)

● YOU CANNOT IMPROVE RESULTS -
ONLY THING THAT CAN BE IMPROVED
IS PROCESS

● FOCUS ON TOTAL SYSTEMS -
DON'T TAKE FRAGMENTED APPROACH

● LOOK AT THINGS IN NON-BLAMING OR
NON-JUDGMENTAL WAY

Figure 13-12.   Kaizen fundamental principles. These principles were presented by Imai (1986).

13.6   QUALITY CIRCLES

The beginning of the quality circle (QC) concept has been attributed to activities of the Union of Japanese Scientists and Engineers in 1962. At that time and continuing to this day QC circles have concentrated on applying quality control primarily to the manufacturing process, although other business entities have used and continue to use the concept successfully.[5] As a byproduct of the activity, ideas for decreasing costs and increasing safety may surface as well as improvement of processes and products. The emphasis has been on the continued involvement of manufacturing and hourly personnel on process and product improvements. The quality circle concept is an important part of both the TQM and Kaizen philosophy.

The principal purposes of quality circles are to

1. Develop a genuine interest on the part of the workers in the work that they are doing
2. Obtain the benefit of workers' knowledge of the processes and products in which they are involved
3. Improve relations of management with workers
4. Improve relations among workers

Key Features

Quality circle groups can consist of anywhere from 5 to 15 members who meet on a regular basis to discuss work-related problems. This is a convenient size since a larger group is more difficult to organize and coordinate and a smaller group does not involve sufficient input to the activity. Membership is voluntary and the typical circle leader is usually the natural supervisor of the work unit, although this person can be a facilitator or one of the workers. In the study of work-related problems a variety of techniques are used, including checklists, flow diagrams, cause-effect diagrams, histograms, Pareto diagrams, control charts, and graphs. Brainstorming is commonly used as an effective technique for generating ideas and synergistic thinking (Section 4.7). Needless to say, training is required to develop and apply the capability of the circle members.

To initiate and facilitate the work of the circle, a facilitator or coordinator, usually a specialist already versed in the operation of quality circles, is utilized at the outset and may continue to monitor and report on the proceedings to upper management. The role of the facilitator is to coordinate the mechanics of the

---

[5]The Security Pacific National Bank of California is an example of a nonmanufacturing organization that has utilized quality circles with considerable success.

quality circle operation; this person should be a neutral servant of the group and should not evaluate ideas. The steps of the quality circle process are as follows:

- A quality circle identifies problems and proposes solutions.
- Management reviews the proposed solutions and makes the decision about whether to implement them.
- The organization implements the solution.
- The organization and quality circle evaluate the effectiveness of the solution.
- The quality circle views the results and recommends improvement, if necessary.

Examples of Quality Circle Successes

There have been many claims about the effectiveness of quality circles first in Japan and subsequently in the United States. There have also been reports of failure, although they have been much less frequent and much less publicized. Examples of successes are these (Tortovich et al 1981):

- Honeywell: In a nonunion electronics assembly shop, 10 circles with 120 members reduced costs by 46 percent over a two-year period.
- Martin Marietta Corp.: In a facility dedicated to mechanical and weld assemblies and to the application of various thermal protection materials, 142 circle members decreased their rate of defects per person from 0.49 to 0.20 over a six-month period.

Officials of Toyota Auto Body Division list the following to illustrate the successes and benefits of quality circles over a five-year period (Shimata 1983):

- New techniques and machinery suggested by quality circles brought about significant savings in costs and time.
- Defect rates declined from 0.95 defects to 0.60 defects per car completed.
- Worker-hours per car were reduced from ten to eight.
- Accidents were reduced from 53 per million worker-hours to zero.
- Employee turnover declined from 18.2 percent in 1968 to 8.5 percent.
- The proportion of workers who feel their work is worth doing rose from 29 percent to 45 percent as shown by annual attitude surveys.

Causes for Failure of Quality Circles

Quality circles can fail for a variety of reasons such as:

- Lack of sustained management interest and support
- Incapable or noninterested leadership

- Inadequate training of participants
- Not appropriately started by a person versed in quality circle techniques and operation
- No reward or recognition system

Quality circles have been a short-lived fad for some organizations but a way of life for others. For the latter, it has more than paid for itself by the motivating influence it has had on workers as well as the actual process and product improvements that have resulted.

How a quality circle is implemented is as important, if not more important, than the fact that it is implemented. As mentioned, management should be intimately involved in setting up the quality circle program including monitoring its progress, evaluating its recommendations, and providing the necessary recognition and reward system.

13.7 COMPREHENSIVE QUALITY PLANNING AND CONTROL

For long-life products, and to a degree for all products, the quality reputation of the manufacturer depends extensively on the quality of field performance—not just conformance to specifications. Fitness for use is the basic satisfaction of the user, but this cannot be determined unless field performance is monitored and there is feedback. Although product acceptance activities are frequently regarded as the final act of the formal manufacturing phase, there remains a number of preuse phases such as packing, shipping, receiving, and storage, that affect the quality of the product. Finally, there are the usage phases involving delivery, installation, checkout, operation, maintenance, and ultimately disposal. The number of field problems increases with the product's complexity, and the extent of the problems depends on the quality planning and management that was used in the entire product cycle from concept to delivery, service, and disposal.

There is clearly a limit to quality control through inspection no matter how many levels of inspection are used. If the processes used for transforming materials into products are carefully controlled, repetitive quality at a more moderate cost is more likely to be achieved. If quality is emphasized as a critical factor from the time of the initial design of the product and the processes used to manufacture it, high quality can be achieved at a much lower cost.

The trend toward comprehensive quality planning has made significant progress in the last 20 years, and international competition will undoubtedly ensure continued progress. The sum of such efforts has been included under the umbrella term of *total quality control* and *total quality management*, depending on the number of activities or functions involved. Total quality control is a vital aspect of total quality management. However, quality planning for the final operations such as packaging, transport, and storage has not received the same level of attention and formalization as design and manufacturing activities.

Packaging, Transportation, and Storage

Since many customer complaints have been received when otherwise acceptable products are degraded in the final phases before formal user acceptance, corrective activities must be considered. For example, sealed sea containers, which can be readily transferred to rail and truck carriers, have improved not only delivery quality but also security. Air containers, which make rapid transport of time-sensitive and critically needed products an economic reality, are another example of improved postmanufacturing maintenance of quality and service. Increased international manufacturing and distribution have forced improvement of packaging and storage capabilities. It is necessary to use the system concept not only in package design but also in planning for potential hazards in transport and storage so that product quality is not impaired. Although these precautions may seem obvious, the frequency of damaged goods sent to customers, with all the ensuing paper work for obtaining credit and/or redemption, is all too high—not to mention impairment of product performance that is not realized until after use.

To minimize the deterioration and degradation that might occur in the total manufacturing and delivery process, actions such as the following should be taken:

1. Obtain shelf-life and recommended storage conditions from material producers.
2. Establish the shelf life of the resultant product from laboratory and field data.
3. Identify and date materials to facilitate material and stock control throughout the process.
4. Design the storage and package and control the environment during the entire processing and delivery cycle to minimize expected and unexpected degradation.

A common error is the failure to date conspicuously the material and product. Bar-coding, serializing, and special marking techniques can make the identification process easier. However, tracking time-sensitive materials is frequently relegated to checking the date when materials are needed or using a manual tracking system. This can lead to the disruption of production and delivery schedules since the time required for replacing time-sensitive materials may be excessive. The availability of computerized stock and production control can greatly enhance the control process if the identification and tracking of time-sensitive materials are part of the process. Time-dating of time-sensitive pharmaceuticals has been required for a long time and, more recently, of certain food products. Care should be used by both the consumer and user to implement some system, such as last-in first-out (LIFO), to prevent needless waste or delays.

Audit

Operations such as in-process and final storage, packaging, and transport may be widely dispersed and may involve several departments and companies. Nevertheless, the manufacturer, whose brand name or identity is identified with the product, is inevitably regarded by the user and the legal system as responsible for any failures, no matter how they were caused. Thus, manufacturers are faced with the need to audit supplier systems just like any other department directly under their control. The general approach to quality verification may be more complex in packaging, transport, and storage since independent carriers and merchants may be used over geographically dispersed areas. Quality verification can be made even more difficult by the lack of familiarity of some of these organizations with the specific requirements for handling and storing a particular product. If such a product is very critical but represents only a minor portion of that organization's work in providing storage, handling, and delivery services, even preliminary audits may be cost-effective.

Installation, Use, and Maintenance

Before the packaged product is put into use, it may have to be assembled, installed, and checked. These processes are just as much a part of the progression of the product cycle as is manufacturing. In fact, they might be even more critical because they directly affect the customers' use and their perception of the product quality. As a part of planning, these operations must provide specific instructions to those involved in the final preparation of the product before use, be they service personnel or customers. It may be necessary to include special instructions to offset poor technological skills or differences in language and culture. Such problems may be at their worst when such preparatory operations are to be performed by the ultimate user.

If possible, the need for extensive installation by the user should be eliminated or at least minimized. When assembly is required, the product should be designed for simple, foolproof installation with clear, illustrated, step-by-step instructions. Quality-conscious manufacturers sometimes supplement these instructions with free information lines to assist the user during installation and use.

Instructions for appropriate use and maintenance of industrial and consumer products are almost always provided by the manufacturer in some form of operating or owner's manual, instruction sheet, or pamphlet. For major systems and difficult installations, companies will provide specialists with factory training.

These specialists are also available for servicing products to assure continued customer satisfaction; this type of comprehensive service is valued by users. The worldwide acceptance of IBM equipment, such as computers, has been built in large part on the reliance of IBM service, whenever or wherever needed.

The maintenance of customer satisfaction during the actual use and maintenance of products is a much more complex problem. Frequently, customers may carelessly throw out operating instructions and precautions with the packaging or just ignore them. This practice was recognized in a slide projector package that included a separate insert with the owner's manual that said in bold print, "If all else fails, read the instructions." The use of the product in environments never contemplated by the designers, like extreme heat or subzero temperatures, and the application of sustained stresses not originally expected can cause premature failures. That is why some hand tools are clearly marked "Not for professional use."[6] Lack of scheduled maintenance and neglect are other common consumer problems. Some manufacturers have created profit centers by offering maintenance or repair service, discounts, and various types of warranties. Sears and Roebuck, General Electric, and other companies have successfully used such approaches for many years. The best policy is to expect the worst possible abuse from the users and design and plan the product accordingly. The recent trend in the interpretations of consumer lawsuits on manufacturers' liability tends to reinforce the thesis that all possible care must be taken to assure safe and continued use.

13.8   FIELD USE AND INTELLIGENCE

Even after all these aspects of quality have been considered by the manufacturer, the question can be asked, "How do we really know that the product in its final delivered form and use is meeting customers' needs?" To develop and market its products, an organization requires information about quality during actual use. An obvious source of information is customer feedback, but unfortunately, it may represent only a small percentage of user dissatisfaction. Field intelligence and market research as discussed by Juran and Gryna (1980) try to discover user reaction and to learn the basic elements of quality problems during customer use.

The loss of customers because of poor quality generally represents varying aspects of real and perceived problems. Minor problems that are inadequately serviced may well be the cause of the silent switch to another product. Ultimately, such unresolved service and possible manufacturing problems may only become evident in a loss of sales and market share. The same problem when immediately resolved by

---

[6]Some inexpensive hammers made from castings rather than steel forgings, typical of professional models, carry such warnings.

responsive field service and accompanied by any needed product changes can be turned into an opportunity for customer loyalty that tends to be contagious.

To avoid problems before they occur at the customer level, extensive field tests of products by especially selected consumers, testing laboratories and facilities for more complex items, and other methods focusing on the prevention of problems before production release are used. Since only extended use of some products, for example, automobiles, can reveal potential areas for improvements, formal and informal contacts with the users have to be pursued in a systematic fashion. Common formal data sources are

- Natural field contacts and customer service centers
- Controlled use—by executives and employers
- Purchase of data from contracted sources
- Special surveys and studies including sampling
- Continuing measurements of customers' perception of quality

Some other ways of gathering field intelligence are relatively simple and straightforward and often give surprisingly informative results:

- Telephone calls to customers
- Warranty card information
- Visits to individual customers
- Mail surveys
- Focus groups discussing current and potential product problems

Ultimately, all such data should be quantified and analyzed in a systematic fashion with appropriate corrective action being taken in terms of short and long range production goals. However, this data collection should be carried out as a continuous feedback cycle that is part of an organization's strategic planning for product quality and survival in a rapidly changing and competitive environment.

QUESTION AND TOPICS FOR DISCUSSION

13.1   Define total quality management.

13.2   Define total quality control. How does it relate to TQM?

13.3   How can the application of TQM increase quality while reducing total costs? Give an example.

13.4   Who in the final analysis determines the quality of a product?

13.5   What functions does quality assurance perform in manufacturing operations?

13.6   What are the advantages and limitations of statistical process and quality control?

13.7   What are the limitations of product inspection in improving quality?

13.8   How can a manufacturing process be improved to give a higher-quality product?

13.9   What are some of the additional costs and negative effects of poor quality?

13.10   Explain acceptance sampling and how it can be used to improve product quality.

13.11   Name four key features of continuous improvement (Kaizen)

13.12   How would you organize and implement a quality circle in an organization?

13.13   How can quality of the product be maintained during the phases after manufacture, such as packaging, transportation, and storage?

13.14   How can it be determined if a product really meets the customers' needs?

References

Crosby, P. B. 1979. *Quality Is Free: The Art of Making Quality Certain.* New York: McGraw-Hill.

Design, zeal on wheels. 1990, March 19 *Insight on the News* 6, (12).

Harry, M. J. 1990. *The Nature of Six Sigma Quality:* Motorola. Scottsdale, AZ.

Hayes, G. E. 1990. *Quality Assurance: Management Technology*, 9th ed. Capistrano Beach, CA: Charger Productions.

Imai, M. 1986. *KAIZEN. The Key to Japan's Competitive Success.* New York: McGraw-Hill.

Juran, J. M., and Gryna, F. 1980. *Quality Planning and Analysis.* New York: McGraw-Hill

Kalpakjian, S. 1989. *Manufacturing Engineering and Technology*, p. 1046. New York: Addison-Wesley.

Shimata, Haruo. 1983, May–June. Japan's success story. *Technolgoy Review*, pp. 51–58.

Suzaki, K. 1987. *The New Manufacturing Challenge: Techniques for Continuous Improvement.* New York: McGraw-Hill.

14

World-Class Manufacturing

14.1 THE FRAMEWORK FOR COMPETITIVE MANUFACTURING

World-class manufacturing has global business and technological perspectives, that is, looking at manufacturing from the total organizational and marketing viewpoint rather than just the factory viewpoint. It also means dealing with competition from a worldwide, strategic perspective rather than a short-term, profit view.

The need for a company to engage in global competition has in many cases been thrust on companies regardless of their innate interest or desire to do so. Faced with the problem of competing with products from companies all over the world, American manufacturers have been forced to obtain components, subsystems, and

311

supplies and to solicit customers and clients from overseas and even to set up manufacturing facilities outside of the country.

According to William T. Archey, international vice president of the U.S. Chamber of Commerce, the reasons for reaching out beyond our borders are both offensive and defensive:

- In certain industries, the high cost of research and development and the heavy capital investment require a larger risk participation than is available in the United States. (The next generation of supersonic transport aircraft may fall into the category of a joint European and American venture.)
- Companies involved in the international marketplace can observe their competitors' technologies and strategies overseas to prepare for them better at home. (Some American companies are doing so now with Japanese business strategies.)
- Knowledge of competitors' technologies and strategies abroad can be used to improve one's own products and services.
- Direct private investment is no longer being motivated solely by low labor costs but also by access to new markets. Expanded markets, as well as lowered transportation expenses and the access to low-cost skilled labor, can contribute considerably to the value of final products. (Eastern Europe is presenting such opportunities in the 1990s.)

It is not necessary to be a large, multinational corporation to succeed in the global marketplace. The ability to be successful, Archey states, may be more of a function of knowledge of industry and the international marketplace rather than specific trade expertise. It is possible to be a niche player all around the world. In regard to manufacturing for worldwide consumption, there are numerous other possibilities such as joint ventures and licensing. Just as in servicing national markets, the integration of manufacturing from inception to actual service and support to the international customer is of the utmost importance.

Many U.S. companies have adopted a wait-and-see attitude concerning business around the world. The surprising political developments in eastern Europe have opened up potential opportunities there and in the Soviet Union itself. Success in capitalizing on such opportunities will require a thorough understanding of the available technical tools and how to apply them, as well as the ability to operate and market products in an unfamiliar and relatively unstable environment.

The Malcolm Baldridge National Quality Award

The degree of urgency in competing internationally is generally recognized by most American companies. The virtual demise of the U.S. manufacturing base is exemplified by the growing list of products and components that are no longer manufactured in our country, ranging from sewing machines, VCRs and television sets to motorcycles, automobiles, and heavy construction equipment. Many of these products are still sold under an American brand name but are manufactured elsewhere. The textile, clothing, shoe, and even machine toolmakers have followed such patterns (Figure 1-4). From a major steel exporter, the United States has become increasingly dependent on foreign steel production. According to many surveys and observations of manufacturing operations around the globe (Gunn 1987), United States manufacturing companies have continued to be mediocre performers.

In an effort to reverse this trend, the U.S. government instituted an award for high quality, namely, the Malcolm Baldrige National Quality Award.[1] In the words of President George Bush, "The improvement of quality in products and the improvement of quality in service are national priorities as never before." The Malcolm Baldrige is an annual award to recognize U.S. companies that excel in achievement and quality management. The award promotes

- Awareness of quality as an increasingly important element in competitiveness
- Understanding the requirements for excellence
- Sharing information on successful quality strategies and on the benefits derived from their implementation

It is similar to the Deming Quality Award, which was established in Japan several years ago. The 1988 Malcolm Baldrige award recipients were Globe Metallurgical, Motorola, and the Commercial Nuclear Fuel Divison of Westinghouse Electric. In 1989 Milliken & Company and Xerox Business Products and Systems won the award. In 1990 Cadillac, a division of General Motors and Federal Express, used its winner status extensively in advertising. Thus public knowledge of these achievements should not only encourage the recipients to make continued improvements but also enhance their efforts through customer recognition.

14.2 COMPUTERS—THE SECOND INDUSTRIAL REVOLUTION

The Industrial Revolution in England during the 1900s brought about significant changes by using steam power and machines to manufacture new products. Yet the rates of change that occurred during this period cannot compare with those that have been brought about by computers and information systems. Information

---

[1]This award was formalized in the form of the Malcolm Baldrige National Quality Act, which was made Public Law 100–107 on August 20, 1987.

technology has existed since the early 1950s but was generally used only in business systems until the 1970s.

The widespread adoption of computers in schools, businesses, and government is well known. Their use in manufacturing operations has been particularly advantageous since it allows accurate accounting of parts, components, subsystems, and systems and the movement of materials and products through the production, warehousing, and marketing cycle. Computers are useful from the inception of a new product to its final acceptance and use, as evidenced by the following techniques:

Computer-aided design (CAD)
Computer-aided engineering (CAE)
Computer-aided manufacturing (CAM)
Computer-integrated manufacturing (CIM)
Computer-aided planning (CAPP
Group technology (GT)
Artificial intelligence (AI)
Flexible manufacturing systems (FMS)
Computer-aided inspection (CAI)
Automated storage and retrieval systems (AS/RS)
Automated guided vehicle systems (AGVS)

Desktop computers can now be readily integrated with other desktop computers or mainframes in the same or other facilities worldwide. High-level software languages have been developed so that design, manufacturing, and management data can be linked into comprehensively formatted information. More important, data can be manipulated to simulate various design, manufacturing, and business alternatives with such rapidity that optimum choices can be determined at the outset. Even material procurement and handling before, during, and after the production cycle have been merged into total material handling systems, which can form the basis of just-in-time (JIT) manufacturing systems.

14.3 COMPUTER-AIDED ENGINEERING (CAE)

Computer-aided engineering (CAE) is now a reality in most engineering schools and engineering-oriented companies worldwide. It has become common practice for many engineering students and engineers to master the operation of computers before they really understand the mathematical basis of many technical relationships expressed in formulas and operations. This reliance on rapid data manipulations, without grasping the significance of the underlying principles, can be one of the few potential disadvantages of CAE.

The big advantage of current and developing CAE operations is the ability to handle complexity, speed, memory, and integration of computer systems. The increasing capacity of computers, while becoming smaller in size and price, now enables engineers to perform calculations with speed and accuracy that were not heretofore possible. The advent of supercomputers has opened new vistas for the rapid processing of previously overwhelming amounts of engineering and manufacturing data. In addition, CAE can utilize analytical software to verify part of the design.

14.4   COMPUTER-AIDED DESIGN (CAD)

Computer-aided design makes use of computers to translate physical dimensions and configuration into a diagram, shown on the monitor. Changes can be made to meet specific product requirements, and alternative designs can be considered until the optimum is achieved. In CAD the traditional drawing board is replaced by electronic devices. The electronic input is generated from a graphics workstation (Figure 14-1), where the designer can enter the information on a keyboard by selecting the desired geometric information with an electronic stylus or trackball

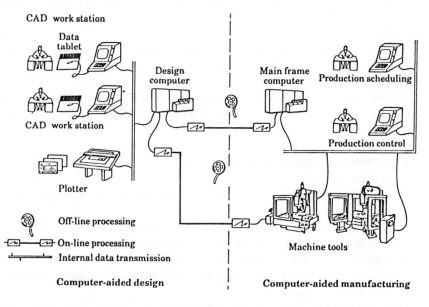

Figure 14-1.   Information flow chart in CAD/CAM application.   Source: S. Kalpakjian, *Manufacturing Engineering and Technology*, (Boston: Addison-Wesley, 1989), p. 1129. From *Flexible Automation*, 87/88, The International CNC Reference Book. © 1989 Addison Wesley Publication Co. Reprinted with permission.

commonly referred to as a *mouse*. The resulting design can be manipulated, modified, and evaluated much more rapidly than by traditional manual means, and it can be continuously displayed and compared with the current design on the cathode-ray tube (CRT). Once finalized it can, like a drawing, be printed on the plotter that is usually part of the computer output. Afterward the design can still be readily altered if necessary.

As in any manual system, the appropriate configuration management control has to be maintained over any released designs, regardless of the method of the physical release to the factory. Since releases ultimately should be on a central data base, current data can be almost instanteously released to all parts of the organization; pertinent information relating to that particular design can readily be retrieved at a later date with accuracy and rapidity. Some examples best illustrate the achievements of CAD by U.S. companies (Gunn 1987):

- Electronics—circuit board design drawings reduced from three to one
- Mechanical—drafting and design efforts typically reduced from three or more to one; revisions of detail design from ten to one
- Drawings—retrieval in minutes instead of days; storage space from significant to minimal; transferability from days to seconds by computer and satellite links; accuracy from questionable to precise with configuration controlled design drawings
- Illustrations—reduced from 70 to 1.
- Prototypes—building prototypes completely eliminated because of the ability to manipulate designs three-dimensionally.

In making a decision to install CAD systems, particularly in smaller organizations with limited budgets, a few potentially inhibiting factors should be considered:

- The initial acquisition and training costs must be made part of a funded installation plan.
- Workable provisions for the transition period from the old to new drawing system must be made.
- Provisions for the conversion or storage of older drawings must be realistically made, particularly when old products are still in service.
- Potential compatibility and linkage costs of the CAD with such systems as CAE and CAM should be considered before acquiring any system, regardless of initial sales claims.

Visits to organizations who installed similar systems may be invaluable and are highly recommended. Most sellers of CAD equipment are willing to provide a list of previous customers. Offices of professional organizations such as the Society of Manufacturing Engineers (SME) or the American Production and Inventory Control Society (APICS) and local chapter members of such societies or qualified impartial consultants can be good sources of information.

In considering acquisition, installation, operating, and maintenance costs, potential CAD users should realize that the return on investment (ROI) is usually less than that claimed by those selling the equipment and longer in rising to the full potential than originally anticipated. Acceptance by users as well as their required training must be considered. Job assurance because of expected reduced labor demands and at least some period of maintaining of dual systems are potential problems. Experienced workers might point out that drafting boards are less likely to crash than computer systems and a quickly drawn sketch may still be quicker as a shop aid when a computer specialist is not available. It may be prudent to retain limited manual backup capability. Considering the specific capabilities of CAD systems, it is apparent that they can become part of an information system that ultimately leads to computer-integrated manufacturing (CIM) (Figure 3-8). Like manual systems, CAD is generally conducted in sequential phases.

Geometric Modeling

The designer starts by creating a geometric model, giving the computer commands to generate or modify lines, surfaces, solids, and dimensions and putting in the text necessary to create a two- or three-dimensional drawing (Figure 14-2). The capability to change such images rapidly and even to rotate them two and one-half and three dimensions in space provides a tremendous advantage of visualization that previously could be achieved only by actual models. Moreover, the ability to describe complex exterior as well as interior surfaces in various colors is an advantage over solid models. The fact that all data are digitized permits numerous useful manipulations. Perhaps the most powerful and cost-effective use of CAD is to translate the final configuration into operational instructions for numerically

(a)	(b)	(c)	(d)	(e)	(f)
2D lateral model	2½D profile body	2½D rotating body	3D wireframe model	3D surface model	3D volume model

Figure 14-2.   Types of modeling for CAD.
Source: S. Kalpakjian, *Manufacturing Engineering and Technology* (Boston: Addison-Wesley, 1989), p. 1131. From *Flexible Automation*, 87/88, The International CNC Reference Book. ©1989 by Addison Wesley Publishing Co. Reprinted with permission.

controlled machines. In this way there is a direct link from CAD to computer-aided manufacturing (CAM), which in turn is one of the key elements of CIM. As is the case with most such systems, there are risks involved—these will be considered in the section on CIM. For example, when CAD is linked to CIM, a poor design will generate scrap faster in an automated mode.

Design Analysis
Any CAD should be subjected to the same analysis for product requirements as manually generated designs. Thermal expansion, stresses, strains, heat transfer, deflections, vibrations, dimensional stability, and other properties may have to be mathematically or physically analyzed. Frequently processes have to be optimized during this phase. For example, the stronger one makes a structure, the heavier it will be. If, however, it is decided to optimize properties such as strength and weight at elevated temperatures, materials such as titanium alloys or composites may be required. Because these selections affect manufacturing processes and costs as well as other aspects of the product cycle, experiments and field tests may be required to substantiate their selection. Unfortunately, even the most extensive tests may not reveal flaws, which may become evident only after years of service under special operating conditions.

The peeling away of the fuselage section of a Boeing 737 airliner used in Hawaiian interisland service demonstrated the adverse effect of the moist and corrosive environment combined with the fatigue caused by repeated flexures of the skin under pressurization and depressurization from frequent landings. This startling failure, after years of worldwide service of seemingly proven materials and fabrication methods, triggered more stringent overhaul techniques for older, similar aircraft and design changes for newer aircraft. Such incidents typify the sometimes difficult-to-predict interaction of multiple variables, like temperature, pressure, vibration, and corrosion. These complex interactions can explain the seeming reluctance of the design community to accept rapidly advantageous, newer materials, like titanium alloys and composites. The increasingly litigious nature of U.S. society has made the introduction of new products, materials, and processes even riskier.

Increased competitive pressures for product improvements and inherent risks have made design analysis more critical than before. However, through the appropriate use of computerization in the CIM process and improved test techniques like the Taguchi methods, the time required for design analysis can be greatly reduced.

Design Reviews
Many previously difficult and laborious evaluations, such as possible interference between mating surfaces, can now be more rapidly determined with available or specially developed software programs. However, with the advent of compressed

cycles to production, design reviews have to encompass more far-reaching aspects, such as the producibility, quality, and reliability of the product. Producibility in the more formal sense is called design for manufacturing (DFM). The need for designs that can be readily manufactured to meet the user's requirements has always existed. To survive in the world of CIM (see below) such considerations have to be evaluated realistically during design reviews. It may be necessary, depending on the complexity of items, to subdivide such reviews into sections like DFM, quality, reliability, and human engineering and then to fit the pieces together. Although such a process may seem tedious and difficult, it is significantly more cost-effective than making hardware that has to be redesigned and rebuilt in the development or production cycles. Early teamwork among various functions through the utilization of such techniques as value analysis and simultaneous engineering can greatly enhance design analysis.

Documentation and Communication

After the previous stages, including the design review, have been completed, the drawings can be released for use and implementation. The release process in most organizations is a formalized procedure requiring the approval of the various functions, from engineering to quality. The design review can and should be broadened from the primarily technical perspective to the other consequent functions, like cost schedule and customer approval.

Many large contracts, including those sponsored by such government agencies as DOD and NASA, require participation if not approval by the customer of design reviews. Although customer approvals can cloud the legal responsibility of the performing contractor, the advantages of the active participation of the customer usually far outweigh potential contractual conflicts. The approval and release of a design means that it is ready for implementation. Particularly with multiple production sites, which may be located in several countries, production and changes can be rapidly activated. Although the documentation needed is usually clearly marked to identify different releases, care must be taken that older drawings and instructions are purged from the operations.

14.5 COMPUTER-AIDED PROCESS PLANNING (CAPP)

Process planning selects, specifies, directs, and documents methods of manufacturing, tooling, fixtures, machinery, sequence of operations, and assembly (Kalpakjian 1989). It can be compared to the role of the drawing and is frequently referred to as the *blueprints* in the design process. Process planning is the blueprint of the manufacturing and assembly operations and may consist of written and pictorial sequences, which can be manually and also subsequently computer-generated (Figure 14-3). Computer-aided process planning (CAPP) can contain other important information like interim dimensions, equipment settings, target times, and quality checkpoints. The generation of such instructions in larger organizations is usually the task of experienced personnel, who may be process or manufacturing planners or engineers. These efforts are usually labor-intensive and critical to the effectiveness of manufacturing operations. Based on our experience when managing such groups, their successful efforts were seldom recognized with the same appreciation as brilliant designs. In fact, it seemed that manufacturing planning and engineering were generally taken for granted by top management until something major went wrong.

Advantages and Disadvantages

The computerization of process planning efforts can greatly reduce the tediousness while simultaneously standardizing similar operations. At the same time, lead periods for generating process plans can be significantly shortened. Yet managers often encounter seemingly irrational resistance from planners in implementing such obvious labor-saving techniques. The resistance to change, along with job insurance, a frequently hidden motivator or detractor, depending on one's vantage point, frequently sets in. Constructive management actions and skills are needed to convince process and manufacturing planners that the time saved from manually generating or revising detailed instructions can be much more effectively utilized by preventing future problems with the designers and solving potential or actual difficulties on the shop floor.

ADVANCED MANUFACTURING COMPANY OPERATION SHEET			
Customer: Ford Motor Company Quantity: 100		Part Name: Shaft Part Number: 133-101 Drawing Number: 133-100	
Operation Number	Description of Operation	Machine	Operator/ Inspector ID
101-1	Inspect bar stock, check hardness	Rockwell tester	
101-2	Machine bar stock and chamfer	Automatic Lathe #12	
101-3	Cut off and chamfer	Automatic Lathe #12	
101-4	Inspect and move to assembly area	Test fixture #3	

Figure 14-3.   Example of a simplified operation sheet.

Also the quality of CAPP is usually an improvement, as are the acceptance and uniformity of the process plans by shop personnel. In terms of total quality management (TQM), the users of CAPP are the customers. Therefore, particular attention should be given to the format, clarity, and consistency of CAPP. The return on investment (ROI) on the inclusion of pertinent information, rather than referring to the quoted specifications or including simple sketches, can be significant. By the inclusion of operation time, work standards and work status can also be derived from CAPP. Such information can be valuable for future estimates of similar work.

Elements of CAPP
If group technology (GT) is used, parts can be grouped into part families according to how they are to be manufactured (DeGarmo, Black, and Kahser 1988). Process plans for similar parts can then be retrieved and used with only the minimum amount of changes. To prevent any possible confusion between process plans for different products, the same type of identification or configuration control system as developed for drawings has to be used for CAPP. It can be readily programmed into most computer systems. The CAPP should be cross-referenced to the CAD to ensure the consistency of manufacture of a product for extended periods of time. The process plan may even include detailed information about machine and tool setting, thereby providing the basis for computer-aided manufacturing. Such information can subsequently be directly programmed into numerically controlled (NC) equipment, leading to computer-integrated manufacturing (CIM) and ultimately to a "paperless" factory. The essence of successful implementation is an incremental process for most organizations. For example, in short-run, complex, custom electronics, CAPP may be quite effective without the installation of expensive, automated equipment, which may be more expensive to set up then to complete the entire run with an experienced technician.

The use of expert systems (ES) or artificial intelligence (AI) can become an integral part of a good CAPP, and the knowledge of an expert manufacturing engineer can be captured and retained. Recall and modifications can be accomplished, even on late or weekend shifts. Accessibility and the ability to manipulate information extend the use of CAPP systems to such other functions as capacity planning, inventory control, purchasing requirements, and production scheduling in a real-time mode. For example, computer terminals on the shop floor can be used to receive instructions and to relay pertinent input as the work is completed. Even difficult-to-quantity questions such as the value of work in process and the related budget status can then be accurately assessed by the financial staff and management. The productivity of groups, down to the individual operator, can be determined through relatively simple inputs and commercially available software. Quality assessments can also be made by self-, audit, or automated inspection points that are programmed downstream. Elements of a good CAPP system can provide the basis for significant CIM improvements.

El Wakil (1989) considers CAPP to be an application or subset of CAM (discussed below) and states that it "involves employing the computer to determine the optimal sequence of operations that should be employed to manufacture a desired part and meanwhile bring the production cost and the production time to a minimum."

14.6   COMPUTER-AIDED MANUFACTURING (CAM)

Computer-aided manufacturing (CAM) involves the use of computers and computer technology in all phases of manufacturing (Kalpakjian 1989), including MRP-I, MRP-II and CAPP to cover the scheduling, processing, and quality aspects of the product. As already mentioned, it may be possible to establish a direct link between the design phase and manufacturing, from the dimensions of parts to their manufacture on specific machines. The CAD and CAM interaction has to be based on proven CAPP to ensure the production of acceptable parts. It is not unusual to have to adjust the initial CAM setup several times before perfect parts are produced on NC and computer numerical control (CNC) systems. Industrial robots, as well as other computer-controlled process equipment, provide significant savings in labor between design and production. Since many of such concepts may have been acquired as separate systems, their integration requires expert help, which is frequently available on a consulting basis if it is not integral to the organization.

Personal computers (PC), which are also independently operable, can be tied into the mainframe or other nets within the organization and used for retrieval and use of design data. The purchase of seeming bargains in computer hardware and software may prove to be uneconomical if they are not compatible with newer systems. APT and COMPACT II are commonly used language-based computer-assisted programming systems in industry (DeGarmo, Black, and Kahser 1988) that are particularly useful in the application of CAM. The ROI is generally a function of the technical synergy of such systems as well as the determination and skill used in their introduction into a plant. An example of the synergism that can result in using the team approach to develop new technology was experienced by one of us in the development of computer-actuated surface-mount technology (SMT) for making circuit boards. Under his direction, a cross-functional team representing design engineering, production engineering, and manufacturing was formed to implement this process successfully in a timely manner (Figure 14-4).

There have been numerous cases, even with major companies like General Motors and John Deere, in which management decided that it was more cost-ef-

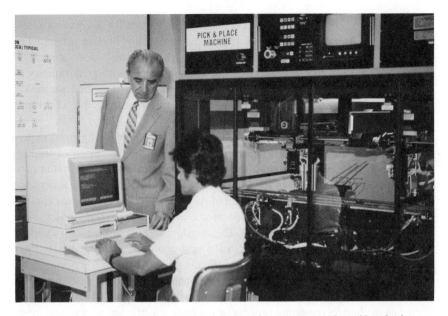

Figure 14-4.   Control station for computer-actuated surface-mount system for making circuit boards.

fective to close older plants with outdated equipment and to start fresh with better plant layout and equipment than may have been economically feasible at the old location. The real message here is not necessarily to start from scratch if the goal is to implement CAD/CAM, leading into CIM, but to plan the whole process with the best available information. The evaluation and conscious choice of long-range alternatives are preferable to rushing into subsystems like MRP-I or MRP-II, CAD, and CAM, which may seem attractive as they are usually portrayed by enthusiastic sellers. However, implementation problems of computer-based techniques should not dissuade management from using such techniques to achieve the ultimate goal of becoming a world-class manufacturing organization.

14.7   ARTIFICIAL INTELLIGENCE (AI) AND EXPERT SYSTEMS (ES)

By capturing the knowledge of experts on software on a permanent but changeable basis, a knowledge base can be created that will greatly expedite the design for manufacturing (DFM) cycle that was discussed previously. In this way, even if experienced design and manufacturing engineers ultimately leave an organization (as many do), their know-how is not necessarily lost. Ordinarily larger companies, or even small specialty houses, try to train replacements and backup personnel to ensure the transition of expert knowledge. Through computer-based AI systems such knowledge can routinely be passed to many locations with great rapidity to enhance design and manufacturing processes. This is not to imply that we should rely soley on past knowledge, but it can eliminate reinventing the wheel and repeating past mistakes.

Other areas, like the medical profession, are already benefiting from expert systems. For example, a young local doctor can have the assistance of leading specialists in methodically making the correct diagnosis. Special computer programs can also form the basis for and record of the diagnosis and treatment for others to follow. Through the application of AI techniques, expert systems capture basic knowledge that allows someone to act as an expert when dealing with complicated problems (Rolston 1988). These systems are used to perform a variety of extremely complicated tasks that in the past could be performed only by a limited number of highly trained experts (Figure 14-5).

Artificial intelligence is a computer application that solves complicated problems that would otherwise require extensive human expertise (Figure 14-6). To do so it simulates the human reasoning process by applying specific knowledge and inferences. Perhaps the most powerful characteristics of AI and ES, in contrast to traditional computer applications, are their capabilities to deal with challenging problems through the application of the processes that reflect human judgment and intuition.

The analysis of knowledge generally can be viewed as having three components:

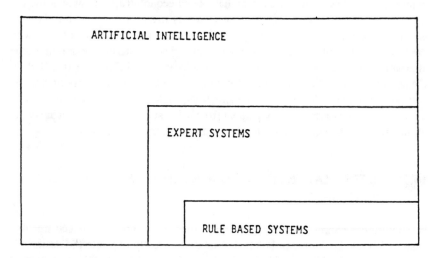

Figure 14-5.   AI applied sets.
Source: C.S. Snead, *Group Technology* (New York: Van Nostrand Reinhold, 1989), p. 225.

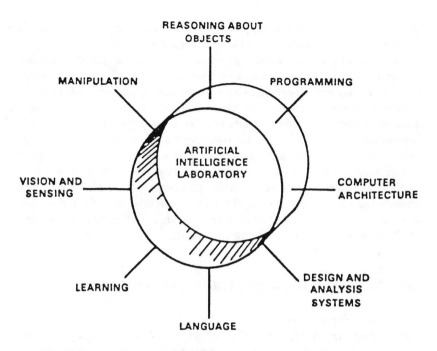

Figure 14-6.   Subfields of artificial intelligence.
Source: C.S. Snead, *Group Technology* (New York: Van Nostrand Reinhold, 1989), p. 225.

- Facts—some element of truth relating to the subject
- Procedural rules—well-defined, invariant rules that describe fundamental sequences of events
- Heuristic rules—general rules of thumb or hunches when specific invariant rules are not available

The selection of the knowledge representation scheme is one of the most critical decisions in ES design. This process of acquiring specific domain knowledge and building it into a knowledge base is called knowledge engineering. The knowledge engineer (KE) is the person who acquires a fundamental understanding of the key concepts and then distills succinct knowledge from the information provided by the expert.

The definitions of AI and ES used here have avoided the fascinating but controversial questions of "What is true intelligence?" and "Can computers ever be made to think?" We are simply dealing with the complex but factual reality of developing software programs to simulate reasoning processes on specific problems. The mechanics and strategy of creating ES are described in considerable detail in a number of textbooks and articles (e.g., Rolston 1988).

From the perspective of world-class manufacturing, AI should be considered as an important tool for many organizations that for a variety of reasons that inevitably occur are losing their experts. We have seen many examples of what happened to design, estimating, engineering, and manufacturing activities, as well as the businesses themselves, when experts left. For critical operations, ES should be implemented while the expert is still available; related costs can usually be repaid more quickly than anticipated. While in the process of applying a needed ES system, improvements can be added and complex problems brought on line with available help in multiple locations. Although an entire AI-based industry is yet to come, using ES in appropriate applications is essential to achieve the goal of world-class manufacturing. Other concepts of competitive manufacturing (Figure 14-7) will be examined in the following sections.

14.8   FLEXIBLE MANUFACTURING SYSTEMS (FMS)

A Historical Perspective

Flexible manufacturing systems (FMS) offer some of the most significant advantages in productivity gains since fixed assembly lines were instituted for mass production. The Industrial Revolution introduced the benefits of powered machines vis-à-vis the limitations of human and water power in England, and automation expanded on the mechanization of efforts. When automation technology was applied to the assembly line, the productivity of workers increased and the United States grew to lead all nations, both in productivity and prosperity (El Wakil 1989). However, the gains of the fixed assembly and transfer lines are limited to large production volumes, which provide a good return on high initial investments. Their inherent inflexibility makes major design or product changes time-consuming and expensive. Typically only the color of an automobile, its accessories, engine size, and so on can be varied in a fixed assembly line. In contrast, FMS offer exciting potential physical changes in the type of product as well as in the quantities and times required to make significant changes economically feasible. That is, FMS integrate major elements of manufacturing into a highly automated, flexible system (Kalpakjian 1989).

A Technical Perspective—Manufacturing Cells

The evolvement from flexible manufacturing cells (FMC) to FMS is a logical progression to consider when wishing to implement FMS. Cellular manufacturing involves the organization of a small group of workers and/or machines in a repetitive production flow layout (Figure 14-8) to produce a group of similar items

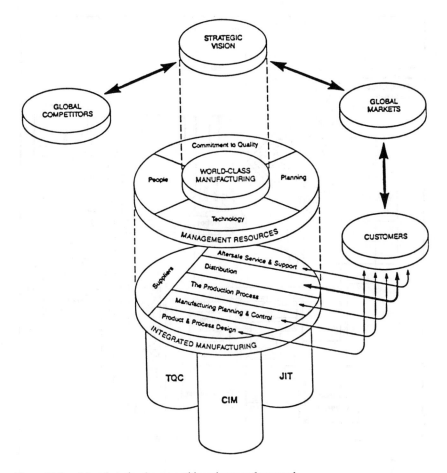

Figure 14-7.   Manufacturing for competitive advantage framework.
Source: T.G. Gunn, *Manufacturing for Competitive Advantage—Becoming a World Class Manufacturer* (New York: Harper Business, 1987), p. 24. Reprinted with permission of T.G. Gunn.

(Fogarty, Hoffman, and Stonebraker 1989). The similarity of such items, if not readily apparent through being the same function for different models of the same product, can be determined through group technology (Section 12.6). Then FMC can be developed to accomplish manufacturing and service functions for a product or group of products (Figure 14–9). Computer numerical controlled (CNC) machines can be the building blocks of a manufacturing cell with some manual operations and setups. When CNC equipment is augmented with computer-controlled variable setups and automated transfer of work, it is called FMS.

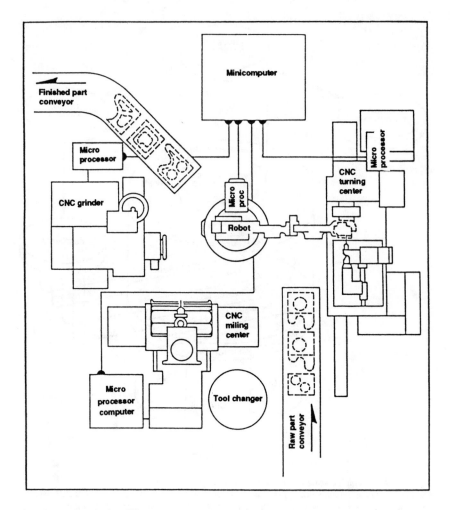

Figure 14-8.   Robotic cell layout.
Source: C.S. Snead, *Group Technology* (New York: Van Nostrand Reinhold, 1987), p. 180.

Programmable material-handling machines, commonly referred to as RO-BOTS, can also be utilized in physically converting manual into automated material-handling systems (Figure 14-10). Automated storage and retrieval systems (ASRS) and automated guided vehicle systems (AGVS) are also used for handling materials, tools, work in process (WIP), and finished products. Therefore, ROBOTS, ASRS, and AGVS should be considered in the design and operation of FMS (Figures 14-11 and 14-12). Typical FMS are automated cells used to produce

Figure 14-9.   Flexible manufacturing cell with a single operator.   Source: Cincinnati Milacron.

a group of parts or assemblies. If these systems are linked into applications that fully utilize computer technology, with hardware and software developments as well as appropriate management practices, we have the essence of CIM.

Elements of FMS

Human beings, from the designer to the operator of automated equipment, have definitive roles, which are critical to the selection, operation, maintenance, and ultimately the effectiveness of FMS:

- Select, develop, and install a workable hard and software system.
- Develop and enter new and revised software programs.
- Enter necessary data for and during operations.
- Perform routine and emergency maintenance.
- Remove or add tools to tool magazines.
- Load materials into the system.
- Monitor and trouble-shoot as needed.

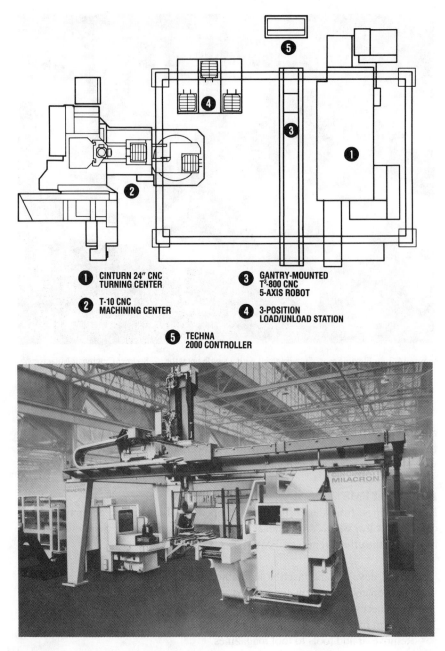

Figure 14-10.   Robotic material-handling system.   Source: Cincinnati Milacron.

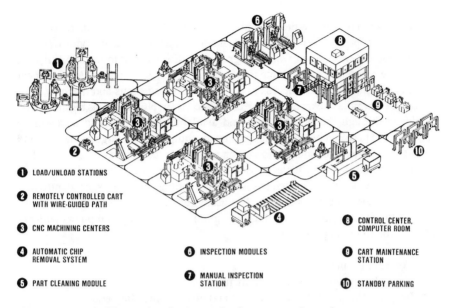

① LOAD/UNLOAD STATIONS

② REMOTELY CONTROLLED CART
WITH WIRE-GUIDED PATH

③ CNC MACHINING CENTERS

④ AUTOMATIC CHIP
REMOVAL SYSTEM

⑤ PART CLEANING MODULE

⑥ INSPECTION MODULES

⑦ MANUAL INSPECTION
STATION

⑧ CONTROL CENTER,
COMPUTER ROOM

⑨ CART MAINTENANCE
STATION

⑩ STANDBY PARKING

Figure 14-11.   Flexible manufacturing system showing sequence of operations.
Source: Cincinnati Milacron

Figure 14-12.   Portion of flexible manufacturing system   Source: Cincinnati Milacron.

Computers provide the programmed brainpower to control the operations in a continuous, repetitive, and accurate manner. Direct numerical control (DNC) systems were developed in which programs are directly sent to machines from a mainframe computer, with remote terminals for access to operators. Management could simultaneously have access to current production status and machine utilization (DeGarmo, Black, and Kahser 1988). However, NC machines became CNC machines through the development and availability of small and inexpensive computers. These can be readily programmed, equipped with large memories, and linked with other minicomputers and/or mainframe computers (Figure 14-13). Such technical advances have provided alert management with building block approaches, which offer financial as well as psychological advantages in introducing new systems into an operation. The usual but frequently unpredictable problems of the change process can thus be minimized. Typically computers perform some of the following functions:

- Control machine tools.
- Control material-handling equipment.
- Integrate the work of machine tools and material-handling equipment.
- Plan, schedule, and control the production flow through FMS.

Figure 14-13.   Flexible machining cell.   Source: Cincinnati Milacron.

Economics of FMS

The economic aspects of FMS are critical since they can affect not only the practicality and usefulness of FMS itself but also the financial health and stability of the entire operation. The competitive advantages of organizations using FMS are so significant that it may force companies using conventional operations out of business. However, the start-up costs and potential risks are so substantial that they may threaten the survival of organizations with faulty implementation plans. The following are some of the economic considerations that should be evaluated when implementing FMS:

- Reduced costs from improved technology and management techniques (+)
- Increased revenues from the capability to vary rapidly the manufacture of different models and products (+)
- Less dependency on the skills of experienced operators, who frequently are critical to the job-shop type of operation (+)
- Increased dependency on the skills of specialists who can design, program, and trouble-shoot FMS equipment (-)
- Significant capital requirements for the facility equipment including computer hardware and software (-)
- Retraining of personnel and subsequent start-up costs, which can range from unexpected modifications to production delays (-)
- Higher consistent quality, reduction of lead times, and reduced inventory needs (+)
- The ability to respond more rapidly to customer demands, ranging from product improvements to model changes and reorders of older models (+)

It is difficult to quantify economic factors for implementing FMS with any degree of accuracy. However, sufficient actual experience in implementing available systems provides ranges of costs for comparable operations, and some results can be cited from past FMS applications (Gunn 1987):

- Mitsubishi Shipyards in Japan reduced the process time for making turbine blades as well as the number of people required by over one-sixth.
- Renault Industries in France reduced the work-in-process (WIP) time for truck transmission housings from two months to one day.
- Dresser Industries, International Hough Division, reduced the number of machines from 27 to 4 through FMS with a reduction of process time from 30 to 6 days.

Sufficient hard data have also been accumulated to provide some guidelines for the type of system that should be considered, based on the variety of parts on projected volume.

There are many examples of verified success data, including initial investments and ROI. Yamazaki Machinery, a Japanese international builder of machine tools, has been a successful innovator of FMS and CIM concepts since about 1980. The results to date indicate significant reductions in direct labor, floor space, lead time, and number of machines required to turn out products of higher quality in a shorter period of time. The passage of time has only resulted in positive learning curves on FMS operations. Unlike other cost-savings operations, such as cutting preventative maintenance, R&D, or essential personnel—which may show temporary profit gains, only to trigger subsequent disasters—FMS savings tend to increase as their applications become more effective and pervasive in the plant operations. Yet for every impressive success story there are also tales of failure for a variety of reasons (seldom publicized). Most failures can be avoided by a thorough cost-benefit analysis, backed by realistically phased implementation.

Economic justification should be a prerequisite to any planned installation since FMS installations are generally very expensive; the starting range of over $1 million per system may account for the relatively slow FMS start-up in small and medium-sized U.S. companies. Generally such systems take two to five years to install. Once in place it usually takes half a year or more to debug the system and get smooth production. In our experience, about the same amount of money is required to install and get a system into production as to acquire it.

For a variety of parts of similar or the same configuration, a total volume of at least 100,000 may be needed to justify completely automated FMS. Low-volume, high-variety production may still be more economically accomplished with conventional NC or CNC equipment. Even in such operations, expert systems can be successfully applied to reduce labor costs. As ominous as these figures may appear, the ROI of FMS, particularly over an extended period of time, make the start-up cost insignificant. However, the economic health of a company has to be sufficiently robust so that the FMS does not die in childbirth. Therefore, the phased introduction of an FMS, while providing cost-saving learning experiences, may also generate sufficient cost savings to help in the introduction of other automated systems. This process requires management conviction to reinvest in significant improvement of the manufacturing operation rather than merely looking for short-term profits.

The competitive advantage of CIM operations of which FMS are a part is so great that the demise of the numerous U.S. manufacturing companies that were unwilling to commit the necessary resources is now a matter of public record. This factor is related to another critical element of making FMS work, namely, management. Management must provide the necessary leadership to do the right things, as well as the concern that things are done right (Bennis & Nanus 1985).

14.9   COMPUTER-INTEGRATED MANUFACTURING (CIM)

Definitions and Concepts

Computer-integrated manufacturing (CIM) is a combination of systems linked by computer technology to achieve greater efficiency and effectiveness in the transformation processes of materials and/or services into products that serve customer needs. The term *transformation,* according to *Webster's New Dictionary*, means "To change form or appearance of and to change the condition, character, or function of," a more general way of describing manufacturing. The transformation process can be used in conjunction with the systems concept in converting input into the desired output (Figure 14-14). It provides the basis for operations management, in which a value-added process is used to provide goods and services (Meridith 1987). If we accept this more expansive concept of operations in implementing CIM, we are less likely to view manufacturing from the limited traditional perspective of just the factory. All the outside and inside influences must be considered to develop a really effective CIM system, which integrates most of the computer-based technologies related to manufacturing (Fogarty, Hoffman, and Stonebraker 1989).

Elements of CIM

Note that CAE, CAD, CAPP, GT, CAM, ES/AI, and ROBOTS are all elements of CIM (Figure 3-8). Flexible manufacturing systems (FMS), as discussed in the previous section, can incorporate the other computer-linked tools in one system and can be part of a phased development of CIM operations. These have been

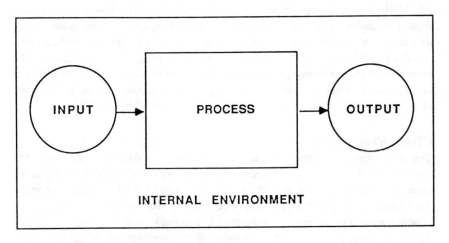

Figure 14-14.   The systems approach to operations.

perfected to the degree that complicated items such as printers for computers can be produced in a manufacturing facility that is virtually unattended during the second or third shift. However, much experience and training are required in many different but related areas to have CIM operate effectively within a company. Particularly for new plants, strategic planning covering all phases of the operation is a prerequisite for taking full advantage of CIM and avoiding costly failures. Such plans must include resources for all elements, not just the technical ones. The organizational goals and business plans must provide for everything, from marketing to service support for the new product.

CIM Advantages

The effectiveness of CIM is to a large degree dependent on integrated communication systems involving computers, machines with their controls, and people who create and maintain the system. The development of such an integrated system, from what are frequently different or incompatible information subsystems, is one of the most valuable benefits. A common data base will usually have to be created to accommodate technical and nontechnical data, from customer demands to production schedules, operations, quality, and delivery information.

The resultant physical integration of all these critical elements enables a greater responsiveness to customer demands, with shortened production cycles. Improved quality and uniformity through the controlled processes in CIM can contribute to an increase in market share. The reduction of costs through better use of materials, machinery, and people, with less inventory, can give CIM significant economic advantages.

The fact that CIM is still more of a methodology to reach goals than just an off-the-shelf collection of proven equipment and computers should make it more logical to implement in stages. If installed all at once, CIM, can be prohibitively expensive for large companies and fatal for smaller ones. Management commitment, as previously mentioned, should be unwavering but supportive in the resolution of the problems that are inherent in the introduction of new or different concepts and processes. Management support and encouragement to facilitate changes successfully are critical in implementing such efforts as CIM.

CIM Implementation

The development, integration, and use of a computer data base are really the essence of CIM. A data base consists of a vast array of information stored in the computer memory that can be added to, changed, and recalled as needed to control the transformation, delivery, and service process. The potential complexity of creating, maintaining, and accessing such a data bank (as it is sometimes called) frequently requires the expert knowledge of management information systems (MIS) specialists. The data may come from many sources, such as CAE, CAD, AI, and CAM. Most current automated machines have various types of built-in sensors that automatically collect and transmit data through a data-acqusition system (DAS). Since much of the data regarding production, quality, schedules, status, and changes have to be accessed and/or inserted by users, it is essential that MIS be readily accessible; accurate; timely; and most of all, user friendly. Most practioners, including us, have found that the success of such a system starts with a design (arrived at by a team effort) that incorporates the needs of the actual users rather than relying solely on the MIS specialist's perceptions.

We previously defined CIM as being a concept to increase productivity and profitability. Physically, CIM is the computerization of design, manufacturing, distribution, and financial functions into one coherent system (DeGarmo, Black, and Kahser 1988). It makes use of the computer, whenever possible, and is advantageous in a carefully planned manner throughout the design, manufacturing, and shipping phases of the product. To have an effective CIM system, all the necessary elements (including people) must function as an entity with a common goal. Such closely integrated functioning must be stimulated and maintained by management interest, encouragement, and support.

14.10   IMPLEMENTING TECHNICAL AND ORGANIZATIONAL CHANGES

The management of transformation processes fundamentally involves implementing technical and organizational changes. The reluctance of organizations to make needed internal changes may mean even more drastic, unavoidable changes at a later date because of economic pressures from the outside environment. The nature and results of positive preventive changes vary significantly from those taken in reaction to negative events. For example, it is much easier to make organizational changes and technical improvements to maintain market share than to recover it after its loss because of poor quality and excessive costs. To avoid the painful pitfalls of reactionary defensive actions, which are typical of many organizations, there must be vision and leadership from management (Bennis and Nanus 1985).

Varying Approaches to Technical Changes
Gradual implementation of technical changes by motivated and trained people is a major step toward success. Various and pertinent factors have been described in a number of books. We will discuss briefly some of the most cogent of these approaches.

The *leap-frog approach* is best exemplified by government-funded programs, for which funding is relatively generous. The development of the atomic bomb, manned space vehicles (Apollo), and the nuclear submarine (Polaris) are good examples. These developments required solutions of previously unsolved major technical problems, while simultaneously trying to meet production deadlines. In the industrial sector the discovery and development of laser fiber optics, nylon, and transistors are comparable examples of the leap-frog, or technical breakthrough, approach. There have been expensive failures with this type of approach, for example, the economic development of electrical power from nuclear fusion and the nuclear-manned aircraft. Large sums have been expended in these attempted developments but with no success to date.

Stepped or continuous improvements (Section 13.5) can achieve equally significant changes, but generally in more efficient and less risky fashion. The gradual operational improvement of the original Volkswagen and the modernization of refrigerators, freezers, and other appliances to include the latest technology are examples of successful applications of continuous improvements. The steady, gradual improvement approach tends to yield more rewards with less risk than the constant attempt for technical breakthroughs.

One should minimize the number of variables involved in a particular improvement effort. In many developments it can be shown mathematically that the more unknowns that are varied at one time, the less likelihood of quick success. Fortunately, computer simulations can help to reduce the time and effort required. However, reliance on computer simulation without tests under realistic operational conditions can be very risky, as recognized by many manufacturers of consumer goods faced with expensive recalls of products already in service.

Taguchi methods (see Section 12.7) take cognizance of the problem of interacting variables by considering the actual function of the product and then changing only those elements that are likely to affect the results. Similarily, it may not be prudent to introduce changes in devices that have demonstrated superior performance for long periods of time.[2] The fact is that often we do not sufficiently understand the numerous interactions of all the variables in a process to risk change. The Taguchi method can indicate what changes need to be made and what changes will have questionable benefits.

Psychological factors play a role. For smaller tasks, people are generally more confident of their abilities than facts may warrant (Peters & Waterman 1982). This quality of optimism and confidence is particularly true of innovative people who have the drive needed to sustain the trials and tribulations of implementing change. There is a tendency for most people to accept credit for success readily and to blame failure on factors other than themselves. It is therefore important to create an

---

[2]This fact was forcefully brought home when one of us wanted, in typical engineering fashion, to improve further a very satisfactory, working complex titanium alloy welding process. At that time Dr. M. Asimow (a friend and a consultant), in what appeared to be a very unscientific mode, asked, "Is it working well?" After having to reply "yes" to that question, he simply cautioned, "Leave it alone."

atmosphere of "let us solve the problem" rather than "who is at fault?" The impetus of solving problems one at a time creates confidence in continued progress.

For seemingly immense tasks people have a greater apprehension of failure and less confidence of success than may be warranted. Finding a cure for AIDS, becoming a millionaire, making dramatic changes in life-styles all appear as such insurmountable obstacles to most individuals that they may have difficulty even getting started. This is certainly understandable and human. Only a relatively few individuals have the inherent drive to start and sustain an effort for extended periods of time to reach difficult goals. By breaking difficult technical challenges into manageable chunks, however, success is more likely for technical and budgetary as well as psychological reasons.

Varying Approaches to Organizational Changes
It is evident to most people who have been involved in implementing CAD/CAM and CIM that the organization has to make numerous changes to integrate such systems effectively. These changes include the type of workers, their supervisors, and their training and motivation. Usually significant changes in the organizational structure, makeup, and operation are also required. Reduction of supervisory levels from ten to three and employing supervisors who are more comfortable with computer operations and participative management are examples of the more significant organizational shifts that may be necessary. The more conventional, cosmetic shift of reporting responsibilities usually does not suffice.

Conventional and Scientific Management
To understand the importance of needed organizational changes it is helpful to consider the relevant forms of organization that have been and are still being used. The bureaucratic form, as defined by Max Weber, was improved by Fredrick Taylor, who applied scientific concepts to management. In the late 1930s Elton Mayo proved on the shop floor of Western Electric's Hawthorne plant that attention to employees can increase productivity, even if working conditions are worsened. The structured organization, primarily governed by rule-driven impersonal relationships, also began to reflect the importance of personal relationships. Subsequently, Charles Barnard asserted that the chief function of an executive officer is to harness the social values of the organization and to shape and guide its values. The groundwork for modern management was laid earlier but not readily accepted in the very structured environment that had grown rapidly in the period of traditional organizations and mass production. The matrix organization (Figure 7-9) has been a relatively successful attempt to handle multiple projects within the framework of an existing line organization.

Leadership and Entrepreneurship

The increasing complexity of products, the rapidly advancing technology, and increased international competition have required improvements in managerial theories and practices. The concepts of systems management and total quality management previously described are ways to meet the new challenges. Thomas Peters and Robert H. Waterman Jr. in their studies on management noted that customer focus and people orientation were key ingredients for U.S. companies successful in this competitive environment. Attributes previously mentioned, such as action-oriented, hands-on, value-driven approaches, were vital to the success of IBM, Hewlett Packard, MacDonald's, Marriott Hotels and other companies that were started by leaders with visions and the persistence to make it a reality.

Action-driven operating units even within large organizations are necessary to keep autonomy and entrepreneurship alive and well. The advent of computerized information and control systems enable centralized and decentralized operations to function simultaneously. For example, stores within the Sears and Roebuck organization are run as independent business units by their managers. Yet ordering, pricing, quality standards, and customer relations are tightly controlled to maintain organizational goals. The rapidity, accuracy, and capability of current and developing communication and transportation systems permit the implementation of changes at rates that would not have been possible a generation ago.

Team Concept

According to Group Vice President James Warren, the ASRS facility of Ralphs Grocery chain (previously described) has been successful because of the close cooperation of its builders and users. Ralphs used its own Management Information Systems (MIS) Department to ensure practical functioning. The ASRS design and construction were based on proven industrial models from experienced fabricators who actively worked with Ralphs. The *team concept* was implemented from concept to use.

Compensation Incentives

As impressive as Ralphs high-rise ASRS facility is for its high-tech efficiency, so is the selection distribution center, across the bridge from the ASRS building, for its combination of equipment, system, and worker efficiency. The selection center buzzes with activity as order selectors operating conventional material-handling equipment work at a vigorous clip to meet or exceed the standards established for the operation. Forklift drivers receive credit for each pallet putaway based on engineered labor standards. If the actual time is less than the standard, the operator receives extra compensation or paid time off. According to Vice President Larry Cooper this incentive program has worked so well that only half as many forklift operators are required as before for about the same workload. As a result, less supervision is needed.

Direct meaningful compensation can be a vital factor in bringing about and maintaining organizational changes. Despite the claims of many motivational theories that money is not a strong incentive, the fact is that compensation does provide practical, psychological, and symbolic rewards for effort. The critical factor when structuring incentive compensation plans is to integrate individual objectives with those of the company. This relationship can be easily grasped if visualized in the form of vectors (Figure 14-15). If employees were rewarded despite poor work, such as moving merchandise without putting it into the bin for the correct market, the system would be counterproductive. If unclear instructions and/or faulty equipment is provided, the system would lose effectiveness. If the threshold requirements for rewards are raised to impractical and unachievable levels, the incentives for maintaining organizational changes would ultimately be considered a sham and would fail. *Technically feasible standards with incentives*

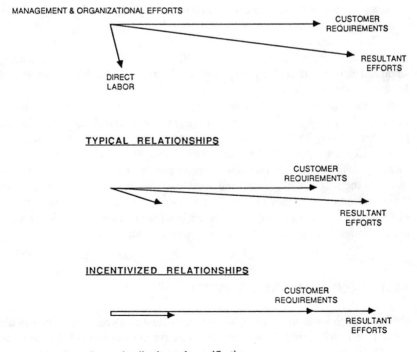

Figure 14-15.   Incentives—visualization and quantification.

that are sound and are also perceived as reasonable and fair make incentive programs successful.

Other incentives in the form of stock ownership and profit-sharing plans have been successfully used in many organizations for a long time. These are also powerful tools for implementing technical and organizational changes by ensuring the support and ultimate success of the changes. The continued growth and profitability of Lincoln Electric, a manufacturer of a very competitive type of welding equipment, has become a common textbook example of the effectiveness of a well-structured system of individual and organizational incentives.

These principles have been effectively used in other very competitive transformation processes such as the fast-food industry. To enhance many technical and organizational changes, the Pepsi Company has instituted stock options not only for executives but also for over 100,000 employees who average at least 30 hours a week. Pepsi hopes that its "Share Power" program, along with its other efforts to spread decision making and build team spirit, will make employees identify more with the company and their work, encourage them to stay longer, and increase their productivity. Considering that the food service business not only is highly competitive but also has a high labor turnover, Pepsi's success shows that organizational incentives can be effectively implemented even under difficult circumstances. By focusing on more efficient techniques and technologies in the manufacturing side of its business, namely, food preparation, service is being improved while crew size is being reduced. Meanwhile Pepsi's Taco Bell chain has steadily cut the size of its kitchens from 70 percent to only 40 percent of the new units. Through advanced designs in cooking technologies, President John Martin expects the kitchens to shrink to 30 percent.

The powerful human desire to be part of a major, meaningful endeavor has been recognized for a long time as an effective motivator. Nietzsche, a classic German philosopher, stated that "he who has a why to live for can bear almost any how." John Gardner, a noted management author, stated, "Man is a stubborn seeker of meaning." This ability to harness the efforts of people to a higher, common purpose has been the secret of successful religious, political, military, business and other diverse efforts throughout history. The resultant feeling of self-realization and fulfillment is what people have been known to work and even die for. But it usually takes a leader with vision to focus on and harness such efforts.

14.11   SURVIVAL AND GROWTH

Vibrant international competition has generated new challenges and opportunities, but as noted earlier, there is built-in reluctance for most of us to change the status quo. Unfortunately, not to act may be a more detrimental decision than to take preventative measures. Wanting to avoid the effects of rain, hurricane, or increased competition will not change the reality of these events. There is one general admonition that must be internalized: Risk is inherent to change. To avoid all risk usually results in inadvertently incurring greater expenses than taking timely actions. It is therefore necessary to manage change so as to minimize risks in the short term and assure survival with long-term gains.

Strategic Planning, Policies, and Subsequent Actions

Strategic planning, on a company, industry, and national level, is critical to ensure survival in the world of international competition. That former or still remaining manufacturers of slide rules, electromechanical calculators, records, record players and U.S. owned and manufactured television sets should have engaged in meaningful strategic planning would hardly be disputed by most executives. Yet many leaders of successful, money-making companies might well consider preoccupation with things far away or a long time from their current maximization of profits a waste of their valuable time. The more enlightened of such "realistic" executives at least delegate such functions to professional planners, who may get some attention when strategic plans are desired by the board of directors or other governing bodies. Most frequently their advice is sought when it is too late for effective actions.

Improved Performance and Production Efficiency

Improved performance and production efficiency resulting from continued research and improvements can bring about a significant synergistic effect. A case in point is the increasing commercial use of solar cells. Solar energy is "clean" energy; it does not have the real or perceived problems of nuclear energy and is a proven method of generating power.

Photovoltaic cells have been a primary source of power for space vehicles for many years because exposure to the sun is only a problem of rotation and unit power-generating cost is not a significant factor. Nuclear energy does not have any such time, climatic, or geographic limitations. However, the flexibility of photovoltaic cells have made them advantageous for pocket calculators, remote emergency telephones, or lighting in areas where the running of electric wires would present problems. Improved efficiency of laboratory cells can gradually make photovoltaics for utility scale applications (Figure 14-16) a more economic and common alternative to conventional power generation. Yet the economic production of photovoltaic power is the typical chicken-and-egg start-up problem of most technical developments. The development of low-cost production methods can not be justified until there is a sufficiently large market (Figure 14-17), but there will not be a significant demand till the price becomes more competitive. Direct and indirect government support in the form of research grants and tax advantages for

Price in 1987 Dollars — left axis
Percentage or years — right axis

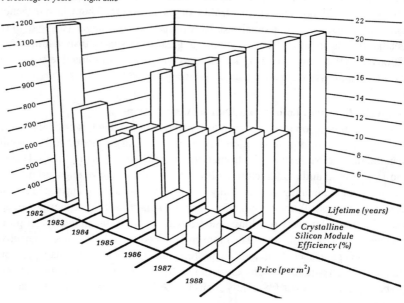

Figure 14-16.   PV module efficiencies and lifetimes have increased as prices have declined.
Source: Solar Energy Research Institute. 1989. *Photovoltaics Entering the 1990s*. Golden, Colorado. p.8.

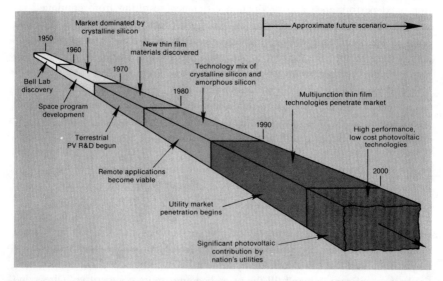

Figure 14-17.   Photovoltaic history.   Source: U.S. Department of Energy. National Photovoltaics
Program. 1987. Five Year Research Plan 1987–1991. p. 6

energy consumers and users can greatly enhance commercial flexibility through production breakthroughs. Utlimately the organizations that can survive the risks of the R&D process and capitalize on the commercial aspects of large-scale production will enjoy technical success and profits. The increased use of composites in the aviation, automobile, and recreation industries is a current illustration of decreasing production costs through increased use.

The Imperative of R&D for Growth

In all fairness to enterprising and farsighted management, many factors are beyond their control. Top scientists in the United States are appalled at the low priority for research in government and industry. According to a prominent Yale University chemist, "The funding situation is the worst that I have seen in 25 years as a successful researcher" (Lipkin 1991). Additionally, the decline in the quantity and quality of science and technical education may impede the United States in meeting increased foreign competition. There is really no room for complacency for companies that wish to retain a position of leadership. Motorola, after selling its failing television business to Matsushita, rebounded with improved quality and technology. It is now successfully competing in cellular tephones with Japanese companies in Japan. Xerox, whose name became almost synonymous with copiers, is now trying to recover some market share in a field in which it pioneered and once dominated.

International Aspects

The high cost of R&D and the tremendously great stakes of being first and best in the international market may have changed the popular perceptions of "free enterprise." It should come as little surprise that the major U.S. car manufacturers have finally joined in a consortium to develop improved batteries for the new generation of electrically powered automobiles. The interpretation of U.S. antitrust laws as well as some laws themselves had to be changed to counter the nature of international competition, which for years has been played by different, much more internally cooperative rules.

A further complication is that many companies are increasingly international in operations and ownership. Magnovax, a household name in commercial and defense electronics, along with formerly Westinghouse Electric light bulbs, is now owned by North American Phillips, a Dutch-owned company. Arco Solar is now Siemens Solar a German-owned company. The list could go on. American-owned companies like GM, Ford, IBM, and John Deere have also established themselves internationally for many years. It is hoped that multinational operations may to some degree alleviate the potential problems of trade barriers triggered by uneven playing fields. The formation of a "United Europe" will have an obvious economic effect in the future. There have been serious and difficult attempts to more closely unite the economies of Mexico, the United States, and Canada into a similar economic union. The pervasive message is to be cognizant of the changes in the world marketplace since they certainly can affect us, even if we cannot always influence these conditions by our actions.

It is appropriate to reemphasize that R&D risky and expensive as it inherently may be, is the key to long-range profitability. Consequently most organizations wisely want to protect the results of their R&D efforts in any way possible to recover the expenses for their groundwork and reap benefits in the form of profits. Other organizations may want to obtain such benefits without incurring the full expenditure of the required resources. These efforts may range from industrial espionage to more direct means, that is, simply buying the company or sharing technology by subsidizing research organizations like MIT and other universities. Recent articles have complained of the relative ease with which vital research information can be obtained for minimal fees from U.S. public sources and government- and industry-funded research organizations. More important, the originating organizations should not only protect their developments but also plan for the retention of sufficient resources to be able to capitalize on them.

This brings us to another imperative of modern business, namely, the need for continuous refinement of the planning, management, and manufacturing process. Initially, the foreign automobile manufacturers, starting with the German Volkswagen, focused on the small-car U.S. market. The Japanese manufacturers were so successful in meeting U.S. customer requirements that they have been able to charge more for some of their small and medium-sized vehicles than for comparable U.S. models. Yet the entry of even more price-competitive Korean manufacturers into the small-car market caused the major Japanese automobile producers to rethink their long-term strategy. Honda, Nissan, Toyota, and Mazda have now all entered the larger luxury-car market because of its greater profitability. To enhance the perception of uniqueness, new names and dealerships have been created.

Growth and the Customer
If we accept the fundamental customer orientation advocated by proponents of modern management from Deming and Drucker to Peters, we should not have any difficulty altering our paths to increased profitability. The rapid expansion of technology is a two-edged sword. It offers tools and techniques with capabilities, speeds, and accuracies that were previously extremely difficult to obtain, and at the same time it can increase profits. Accurate multifunctional watches and calculators, at very reasonable prices, are common examples of the benefits of modern technology and manufacturing. The operational, organizational, and management techniques described above apply equally well to a variety of transformation processes. In some instances, like bar coding, the food industry and retailers seem to have been more agressive in implementing computer-based techniques and increasing their competitiveness than manufacturers of hard goods.

The subject of what it takes to become and remain a world-class manufacturer is a complex one that has many facets and involves many factors. Technology transfer and cross-fertilization from other industries as well as the flexibility to incorporate change have to be included as key ingredients of success. Other equally important factors are summarized in Chapter 15.

QUESTIONS AND TOPICS FOR DISCUSSION

14.1   What is meant by world-class manufacturing?

14.2   What are some of the aspects of international competitiveness that make world class manufacturing necessary?

14.3   How do national awards like the Deming Award in Japan and the Malcolm Baldridge Award enhance the competitiveness of participating organizations?

14.4   How can computers be used to automate manufacturing processes? Give four examples.

14.5   Name four key areas that should be addressed in a design review.

14.6   What are some advantages and disadvantages of artificial intelligence and expert systems?

14.7   How can FMS enhance the profitability of manufacturing small quantities of changing product lines?

14.8   What are the important factors that must be considered in determining whether to proceed with the installation of a FMS?

14.9   Define computer-integrated manufacturing. Name four essential elements.

14.10   What are four considerations that make the gradual implementation of CIM necessary?

14.11   Why is continuous improvement in a product line necessary in addition to efforts for innovation and leap-frog approaches?

14.12   How can labor standards be used to provide incentives for transformation processes?

14.13   How can functional analysis be used to transfer technology from one industry to another? Explain with an example other than an automated storage and retrieval system.

14.14   What are some incentives (name four) that can motivate workers for greater productivity?

14.15   How does demand for a material or product influence efficient manufacturing methods and vice-versa?

14.16   What is the correlation of competitiveness with world-class manufacturing?

References

Bennis, W., and B. Nanus. 1985. *Leaders*. New York: Harper & Row.

Deal, T., and A. Kennedy. 1982. *Corporate Cultures*. New York: Addison-Wesley.

DeGarmo, Paul E., Temple J. Black, and Ronald A. Kahser. 1988. *Materials and Processes in Manufacturing*. New York: Macmillan.

El Wakil, S. D. 1989. *Processes and Design for Manufacturing*, p. 411. Englewood Cliffs, NJ: Prentice Hall.

Emery, Glenn. 1990. "*Close Encounters of a Virtual Kind.*" *Insight*. (52).

Fogarty, D. W., T. R. Hoffmann, and P. W. Stonebraker. 1989. *Production and Operation Management*, p. 154. Cincinnati, OH: Southwestern Publishing.

Gerber, M. E. 1986. *The E-Myth*. New York: Ballinger.

Gunn, Thomas G. 1987. *Manufacturing for Competitive Advantage—Becoming a World Class Manufacturer*. Cambridge, MA: Ballinger.

Kalpakjian, Serope. 1989. *Manufacturing Engineering and Technology*. New York: Addison-Wesley.

Kerzner, H. 1989. *Project Management*, p. 923. New York: Van Nostrand Reinhold.

Lipkin, Richard. 1991. "Dismal Funding Alarms Scientists." *Insight*.(6).

Meridith, Jack R. 1987. *The Management of Operations*. New York: Wiley.

Obradovitch, M. M., and S. E. Stephanou. 1990. *Project Management: Risks and Productivity*. Bend, OR: Daniel Spencer.

Pearce, John A., II, and Richard B. Robinson, Jr. 1988. *Strategic Management—Strategy Forumulations and Implementation*. Homewood, IL: Irwin.

Peters, T. J. 1987. *Thriving on Chaos*. New York: Harper & Row.

Peters, T. J., and N. Austin. 1985. *A Passion for Excellence*. New York: Random House.

Peters, T. J., and R. H. Waterman, Jr. 1982. *In Search of Excellence*. New York: Harper & Row.

Rolston, David W. 1988. *Principles of Artificial Intelligence and Expert Systems*. New York: McGraw-Hill.

Snead, Charles S. 1989. *Group Technology—Foundation for Competitive Manufacturing*. New York: Van Nostrand Reinhold.

15

The Future

15.1 TRANSFORMATION PROCESSES AND CROSS-FERTILIZATION

In the discussions of previous chapters we have referred primarily to manufacturing processes, but in a broader sense the term *transformation processes* could have been used in all cases. This interpretation recognizes that the manufacturing process transforms inputs into outputs by adding value (Meredith 1987). According to this concept transformation processes include not only manufacturing per se but also many other, related processes, such as food preparation and sales, supermarkets, utilities, and any other processes in which incoming materials and/or services are transformed into an improved or salable item.[1] With this thought in mind, the future improvement of transformation processes (which include manufacturing) takes on an even greater significance. From the standpoint of managing the new transformation processes that are coming to the fore as a result of rapidly

---

[1] With an even broader interpretation, the offering of a service could be interpreted as a transformation process, but this aspect will not be considered here.

advancing technology and worldwide competition, many organizations must adjust to cope with the ever-changing and challenging situation.

One aspect of world-class manufacturing that will play a key role in the success of any organization is the extent of cross-fertilization, or technology transfer. Some of the major breakthroughs and improvements in a particular industry or field have been a result of the introduction and application of technology from a different discipline. An outstanding example of such technology transfer is the application of electronics, mechanical, chemical and electrical engineering to medicine and health, resulting in spectacular advances in heart surgery, orthopedics, disease treatment, and many other medical fields. In similar fashion, improvements in other related transformation processes can benefit manufacturing.

15.2   ORGANIZATIONAL SURVIVAL

A number of tangible and intangible factors must be considered to compete successfully in today's complex international market. Some of these are relatively obvious. Certainly the available financial, physical, and human resources are necessary bases, but the important factor that will separate success from failure is the ability of management to cope with the challenges of innovation, R&D, manufacturing, marketing, logistics, and the whole spectrum of bringing a product to worldwide acceptance. The effective integration of these efforts is the key to success rather than specific capability in one or two aspects of the total process.

There is no magic recipe for success, but in manufacturing some factors and capabilities that must be present include the following:

- The organization must be able to adjust and make changes both organizationally and technically as required by changing technology and market situations. This includes the identification of new technology and its inclusion in the manufacturing process where suitable and possible.
- The most current measures of automation and computerization must be used where economically viable. Trade-off studies comparing present with automated and computerized techniques can confirm cost effectiveness and viability. In the long run initial capital outlay may well be worth the conversion.[2]
- The use of modern management and operational techniques such as the team concept, project management, concurrent engineering, just-in-time, group

---

[2]Recent studies by the Society of Manufacturing Engineers have borne out the fact that the manufacturing organization of the future must "innovate, automate or evaporate." (Koska and Romano 1988)

technology and others described in this text are necessary in today's competitive environment.

- Top management must be willing to invest in long-term gains through adequate R&D expenditures, improved and up-to-date manufacturing equipment and facilities, and competent personnel to ensure the future of the organization. This must be done even at the expense of short-term losses when such losses are necessary.
- The management methods and technology chosen to improve existing capabilities and operational practices must be compatible with the value system and culture of this organization.

In the final analysis, human aspects are the most important part of successful R&D and manufacturing operations. If the physical and financial resources are present, how the personnel are treated and what the motivational aspects are will make the difference between a vibrant, successful company and a less successful competitor. The company must have a personality (culture) and positive outlook that fosters growth and success. How such a personality can be developed and maintained is a problem that until recent years has not been fully recognized or discussed. This and related management problems have been the focus of recent writers such as Austin (Peters and Austin 1985), Bennis and Nanus (1985), Drucker (1973), Peters (1987), and many others. The solution continues to be a somewhat elusive elixir, whose exact formulation is difficult to describe. However, certain general truths have been brought forth with convincing evidence of their utility.

- The value of each person at whatever level in the organization must be recognized by management with a relationship that is more of a family member than that of a hired-hand.
- Organizational practices of the company should be such that the potential contribution of each member is realized, nurtured, and fulfilled so that maximum improvement of the manufacturing and other operations can occur.
- All levels of management must act in a manner that leads rather than directs by edict alone. Such leadership must actively support innovation as well as have credibility and the ability to delegate and yet not lose control.[3]
- Uppermost in all company activities must be the recognition and satisfaction of customer needs (TQM).

---

[3]The qualities and strategies for effective leadership are eloquently enumerated and described by W. Bennis and B. Nanus in "Leaders, The Strategies for Taking Charge." 1985. New York: Random House.

15.3   THE 1990S AND BEYOND

Some obvious developments in R&D and manufacturing will occur in the 1990s and early years of the next century, most of which are extensions of what is already current:

- The use of computers and their inclusion in R&D and manufacturing operations will continue to proliferate. The use of expert systems and artificial intelligence will be a key element (Figure 14-6). More persavive user-friendly computer-based information systems will become common-place.
- The number of partially or fully automated manufacturing facilities will increase with more use of robotics, group technology, FMS, and the other advanced manufacturing and management techniques described in Chapters 12 through 14.
- The emphasis on automation will result in fewer personnel in actual plant operations and more personnel in the design, maintenance, and repair of the complex equipment involved. The labor mix will tilt toward the more skilled workers, but the overall effect may not be as negative as many fear. More extensive in-house training of personnel by companies will become a common activity,.
- Product development and product cycle times will continue to shorten with increased monetary rewards and a competitive edge to those companies that can make product changes and develop new products quickly.

15.4   TECHNOLOGY AND MANUFACTURING MANAGEMENT

The Use of Computers

Changes in technology and manufacturing management will more or less parallel changes in other types of management. The number and scope of computerized data bases that can be used for extracting valuable background information needed for planning and carrying out advanced R&D and manufacturing improvements will increase markedly. Improved programming techniques for indexing and selecting information will accelerate the search and utilization process and result in the creation of additional data banks even more encompassing than those presently available. Managers using computer terminals that are connected to large mainframes will be able to draw on the extensive data supplied by company information systems. The decision-making process will be aided by prospective, present, and past sales; profit; capital investment; labor; and manufacturing costs for various product areas. Television conference capability will be increasingly used for rapid, direct questioning of and discussions with key individuals of the company to reinforce or modify technical efforts and manufacturing decisions. The impact of the computer not only on manufacturing but also on all aspects of a company's activities will be substantial. As expressed by Allen Puckett, former chairman of the board and CEO of Hughes Aircraft Company,

> Rather than a role as a tool, the digital data-processing system is becoming the backbone or framework around which we will plan, organize, and operate in most of our business and industrial functions. The organization of the data-processing system and in particular of its software—the hierarchy in the system of information handling—will determine the organization of our people and the way they work together. (Obradovitch and Stephanou 1990)

Use of Teams

There will be increased emphasis on the use of teams in a variety of company activities as well as in new product and process development. The organizations of the future will have interdisciplinary teams that can relate rapidly to social, economic, government, and technological change. Such teams will require versatility in knowledge and capability that is not available in most companies today. They will have direct communication links with top management; constantly monitor the economic, social, and political environment; and make analyses and recommendations that are responsive to changes in the environment. They will be well versed in the development and use of large data banks as part of a company information system that will be essential to company operation.

Project Management

The use of projects in organizing and executing technical, product and process development activities will increase markedly. Kerzner (1989), an international expert on project management, predicts,

> By the year 2000, product lines that cannot justify continuous full-time utilization of resources will be controlled by product managers using project management. The terms "project management" and "product management" may even become synonymous. Companies of the future will be structured by market segment, with each market segment run by a product manager. These product managers will constitute a project team one level below the functional vice presidents. The project team will be responsible for the complete operation of existing products, and will also be part of the planning function project, which will also include vice-presidents and the CEO. Product managers will report to the vice-president of operations, whereas full-time project managers will report to the vice-president of marketing.

15.5   OTHER TRENDS AND CHANGES

Other trends and changes that can be expected in the near future include the following:

- There will be a trend toward streamlining organizational structures so that there are fewer levels between the bottom-line worker and top management. Present levels of 10 to 16 for many large U.S. companies create serious communication and other problems. Many middle-management and administrative positions are being replaced by quicker and more accurate computerized and expert systems.
- There will be a modification of company culture toward the goal of providing a more people-oriented environment.
- There is a continued and increasing trend toward telecommuting and flex time by many employers, although both these variations from customary working arrangements have obvious limitations.[4]
- There will be an increase in industrial research on minimizing product liability and more emphasis on product safety.
- There will be continued major expenditures on defense and space-oriented R&D based on changing threat scenarios and customer needs. In addition, major efforts will continue in programs directed toward the mitigation of social and medical problems such as crime, drugs, AIDS, common diseases, and the like. Cross-fertilization will play an important role in all such programs.

In the 1990s and thereafter a number of new technologies will appear that can cause major advances in engineering design and manufacturing. Some of these technologies are already evident, for example cyberspace. *Cyberspace* is a term coined by William Gibson to denote a vast region beyond the edge of perceived reality that can include three-dimensional visualization by computers (Emery 1991). For example, movement in cyberspace can be simulated by shifting the optics in the field of vision of certain body parts like the head or hand. The importance of this virtual reality (VR) has not been well understood outside of the fledgling industry. In its simplest forms it can be compared to elaborate three-dimensional engineering, architectural, or video game technology. The potential of cyberspace is illustrated by the fact that surgeons can use VR applications to rehearse operations before carrying out actual surgery. Extension to product design

---

[4]In telecommuting, workers remain at home to perform desk-type duties and communicate with their supervisors and other workers by computer or telephone. Flex time allows the worker to come to work at prearranged and agreed-to hours, most of which, but not all, occur during the normal work day.

and manufacturing application would not be a difficult step. Current practical applications and future remote applications of VR are still limited by the current high cost and relative clumsiness of the required equipment. However, there have been ample demonstrations in the past that during the rapid growth of a particular technology, lowering of equipment cost and improvement of its use soon follow as knowledge and applications of the technique increase.

The exploration and utilization of outer space provide a challenging opportunity to expand further the benefits of technology to manufacturing processes. The weightlessness and lack of atmosphere in outer space have unlimited possibilities for manufacturing when vacuum conditions and the lack of gravity are desirable. For example, elaborate and expensive means have to be taken when melting and casting certain metallic alloy ingots to avoid potentially harmful contaminants. Such precautions would not be necessary in space. Outer space stations with manufacturing laboratories offer a germ-free, weightless environment for biological research and the manufacture of medicines. In addition to these obvious possibilities there are other, not yet conceived applications in space whose value may be significant. Here on earth there are even more challenging and potentially rewarding developments that can occur in automation, equipment improvement, material handling, and many other facets of transformation processes and manufacturing.

World-class manufacturing can have a tremendous impact on the subsistence and well-being of many third-world countries. The challenge remains in the vision, leadership, and management of the vast physical and mental resources available. Effectively managing manufacturing from concept to use in an integrated manner is of far-reaching importance, is deserving of concerted efforts, and has the prospects of substantial economic and social rewards.

QUESTIONS AND TOPICS FOR DISCUSSION

15.1   How do transformation processes relate to manufacturing? Name three transformation processes that do not involve conventional manufacturing.

15.2   How is cross-fertilization of technology and management enhanced by companies that operate internationally?

15.3   Explain what is meant by the term *organizational culture*. and how can it affect organizational operation and success?

15.4   How does cross-fertilization of technology improve the profitability and survivability of an organization?

15.5   What is the difference between leading and managing?

References

Bennis, W., and Burt Nanus. 1985. *Leaders*. New York: Random House.

Drucker, P. F. 1973. *Management: Tasks, Responsibilities, Practices*. New York: Harper & Row.

Emery, G. 1991. *Insight*. May 6. pp. 20–24.

Kerzner, H. 1989 *Project Management: A System Approach to Planning, Scheduling and Controlling*. 3rd Edition. New York: Van Nostrand Rheinhold. p. 923.

Koska, D. K., and J. D. Romano. 1988. *Coundown to the Future: The Manufacturing Engineer in the 21st Century*. Profile 21, Executive Summary. Society of Manufacturing Engineers. Dearborn, Michigan.

Meredith, J. R. 1987. *The Management of Operations*, 3rd ed. p. 5. New York: John Wiley.

Obradovitch, M. M., and S. E. Stephanou. 1990. *Project Management Risks & Productivity*. Bend, OR: Daniel Spencer.

Peters, T. 1987. *Thriving on Chaos*. New York: Harper & Row.

Peters, T., and N. Austin. 1985. *A Passion for Excellence*. New York: Random House.

APPENDIX

List Of Acronyms

AGVS	Automated guided vehicle system
AI	Artificial intelligence
ANOVA	Analysis of variance
APT	Automatic programming of tools
AQL	Acceptance quality level
AS/RS	Automatic storage/revival system
ATE	Automatic test equipment
BASIC	Beginner's all-purpose symbolic instruction code
BMW	Bavarian Motor Works
CAD	Computer-aided design
CAD/CAM	Computer-aided design/computer-aided manufacturing
CAD/D	Computer-aided drafting and design
CAE	Computer-aided engineering
CAI	Computer-aided inspection
CAM	Computer-aided manufacturing
CAPP	Computer-aided production planning
CATI	Computer-aided testing and inspection
CCB	Configuration control board
CDP	Cost definition phase
CE	Concurrent engineering
CHM	Chemical machining
CIM	Computer-integrated manufacturing
CL	Center line
CM	Configuration management
CMS	Cellular manufacturing system
CNC	Computer numerical control

COBOL	Common business-oriented language
CPM	Critical path method
CPR	Capacity resources planning
CPU	Central processing unit (computer)
CRT	Cathode ray tube
DBM	Data-base management
DDAS	Direct data acquisition system
DDC	Direct digital control
DFM	Design for manufacture
DNC	Digital (or direct or distributed) numerical control
DOD	Department of Defense
DOS	Disk operating system
DRO	Digital readout
EBM	Electron beam machining
ECM	Electrochemical machining
EDM	Electrodischarge maching
EDP	Electronic data processing
EF	Early finish
EMI	Electromagnetic interface
EOP	End of program
EOT	End of tape
EPC	European Patent Council
EPO	European Patent Office
EROM	Erasable read-only memory
ES	Early start
ES	Expert System
FMC	Flexible manufacturing cell
FMEA	Failure mode effects analysis
FMS	Flexible manufacturing system
FORTRAN	Formula translation
GT	Group technology
HGVS	Human-guided vehicle system
IBM	International Business Machines
IMPS	Integrated manufacturing production systems
I/O	Input/Output
IOCS	Input/output control system
IQR	Intraquartile range
JIT	Just-in-time
KAIZEN	Continuous improvement (translation)
LAN	Local area network
LASER	Light amplification by stimulated emission of radiation

LBM	Laser beam machining
LBO	Leveraged buy-out
LCL	Lower control limit
LED	Light-emitting diode
LF	Late finish
LS	Late start
LSI	Large-scale integration
MAP	Manufacturing automation protocol
MAPIM	Materials and processes in manufacturing
MBO	Management by objective
MCU	Machine control unit
MDI	Manual data input
MIS	Management information systems
MITI	Ministry of International Trade and Industry (Japan)
MPS	Manufacturing production system
MPS	Master production scheduling
MRP-I	Materials requirement planning
MRP-II	Manufacturing resource planning
MS	Manufacturing system
NASA	National Aeronautics and Space Agency
NC	Numerically controlled
NDT	Nondestructive testing
OR	Operations research
OS	Operating system
OST	Objectives strategies and tactics
PC	Personal computer
PCB	Printed circuit board
PDCA	Plan-do-check-analyze
PDES	Product design exchange specification
PDM	Precedence diagramming method
PDP	Program definition phase
PERT	Program evaluation and review technique
PLC	Programmable logic controller
PM	Project manager
P/M	Powder metallurgy
PMIS	Project management information system
PR	Public relations
PROM	Programmable read-only memory
PS	Production system
QC	Quality control
QMS	Quality management system

RAM	Random access memory
R&D	Research and development
R&E	Research and engineering
RFP	Request for proposal
ROI	Return on investment
ROM	Read-only memory
SE	Simultaneous engineering
SMT	Surface mount technology
SOA	State of the art
SPC	Statistical process control
SQC	Statistical quality control
TOP	Technical office protocol
TQC	Total quality control
TQM	Total quality management
UCL	Upper control limit
VA	Value analysis
VCR	Videocassette recorder
VE	Value engineering
VR	Virtual reality
WAN	Wide area network
WBS	Work breakdown structure
WIMS	Work-in-manufacturing system
WIP	Work in Progress
ZBB	Zero-base budgeting
ZD	Zero defects

Index

Index

WITHDRAWN